Also by Alan Palmer

The Gardeners of Salonika
A Dictionary of Modern History, 1789–1945
Napoleon in Russia
The Lands Between
Metternich: Councillor of Europe
The Life and Times of George IV
Russia in War and Peace
Kings and Queens of England
Frederick the Great
Alexander I: Tsar of War and Peace
Bismarck
The Kaiser: Warlord of the Second Reich
The Princes of Wales
Who's Who in Modern History, 1860–1980
The Chancelleries of Europe
A Dictionary of Twentieth-Century History
An Encyclopaedia of Napoleon's Europe

with Veronica Palmer

Quotations in History
Who's Who in Shakespeare's England
Royal England: A Historical Gazetteer

Crowned Cousins

Crowned Cousins

The Anglo-German Royal Connection

Alan Palmer

Weidenfeld and Nicolson · London

First published in Great Britain by
George Weidenfeld & Nicolson Limited
91 Clapham High Street
London SW4 7TA

ISBN 0 297 78711 X

Printed in Great Britain by
Butler and Tanner Ltd, Frome and London

Contents

❧ Illustrations ❧

Elizabeth of Bohemia, painted by Gerard Honthorst (National Gallery, on loan to the National Portrait Gallery)

The Electress Sophia (by kind permission of the Duke of Brunswick and the Herrenhausen Museum, Hanover)

Sophia Dorothea, with her son and daughter (Bomann Museum, Celle)

George I's coronation procession (British Library)

George II on the field of Dettingen (National Army Museum)

Frederick the Great returning from manoeuvres (Mansell Collection)

Princess Charlotte and Prince Leopold, by William Thomas after George Dawe (National Portrait Gallery)

Cartoon of April 1819 depicting a fictitious visit of the royal dukes to the Duke and Duchess of Cambridge (British Library)

The Duchess of Kent and her daughter, the future Queen Victoria (by gracious permission of Her Majesty The Queen)

Schloss Rheinhardtsbrunn (by gracious permission of Her Majesty The Queen)

The royal family in 1846, painted by Winterhalter (BBC Hulton Picture Library)

William I, King of Prussia and first German Emperor (Mary Evans Picture Library)

'Vicky', Princess Royal and Empress Frederick (by gracious permission of Her Majesty The Queen)

The wedding of Prince Henry of Battenberg and Princess Beatrice (by gracious permission of Her Majesty The Queen)

Prince Louis of Hesse, Princess Alice and their children (by gracious permission of Her Majesty The Queen

Grand Duchess Augusta of Mecklenburg-Strelitz (by gracious permission of Her Majesty The Queen)

King George V and Kaiser William II (Popperfoto)

Hitler greeting the Duke and Duchess of Windsor at Berchtesgaden (Press Association)

Map: Royal Germany   p. xi

❧ Preface ❧

When, during the First World War, H.G. Wells castigated the English Court
for being 'alien and uninspiring', King George v is said by Sir Harold Nicolson
to have remarked, 'I may be uninspiring, but I'll be damned if I'm an alien.'
His indignation is readily understandable: he was as proud to 'remain an
Englishman' as Gilbert's Ralph Rackstraw, while his disenchantment with
'abroad' matched the splenetic insularity of Nancy Mitford's Uncle Matthew.
Yet, although George v and his consort, Queen Mary, were born in London,
there remained a strong Germanic influence at court. Of his seven predecessors on the British throne two were German by birth and upbringing
and the remaining five had at least one parent who was German. Since the
First World War the influence has, of course, been much less marked; but the
German connection is not entirely a matter of past history. In 1915 ten of King
George v's first cousins were members of German royal dynasties. Seventy
years later the Prince of Wales has sixteen first cousins born into the old
princely families of Germany.

In the 1980s such connections carry no political significance. A century ago
it was otherwise. Personal links between Britain and the German states in the
last years of Queen Victoria were as marked as the contact between the great
families in Churchill's or Macmillan's Britain and the America of the
Roosevelts and Kennedys. The royal special relationship could, in theory,
mellow Great Power antagonism by introducing into diplomatic exchanges
the informalities of a shared supra-national social life. It is true that there was
a dangerous tendency for one monarch to misunderstand the constitutional
limits of another monarch's influence; and occasionally personal quarrels
were magnified until they distorted the political actions of rival governments;
but in general it was thought, at least until the first decade of the present
century, that the Anglo-German royal connection contributed to peace and
understanding between two fundamentally Teutonic nations who shared
religious and cultural links stretching back to the Reformation and beyond.

This book provides, for the first time, a survey of that close Anglo-German
dynastic relationship from its beginnings in the marriage of James I's only
daughter to the Elector Palatine down through three and a half centuries to the
Second World War and the unique situation created by a severed Germany.
The book has been written at a time of growing friendship between the British
and German peoples, a reconciliation on which Queen Elizabeth II felicitously

commented in her Christmas Day Broadcast of 1984. If *Crowned Cousins* in any way promotes a sympathetic interest in the common heritage of the two nations I shall be well satisfied.

I wish to acknowledge the gracious permission of Her Majesty The Queen to make use of material from the Royal Archives at Windsor Castle; and I would like to thank Miss J. Langton, M.V.O., Registrar of The Queen's Archives, for her friendly counsel during my visits to the Round Tower.

The debt which I owe to the authors and editors of the works cited in the reference notes – especially the *Letters of Queen Victoria* series (published by John Murray), and Roger Fulford's collection of exchanges between the Queen and Vicky (published by Evans Brothers) – will be clear to all readers of this book. My publishers have been of particular assistance to me in the preparation of *Crowned Cousins*: Lord Weidenfeld suggested the title; Mr John Curtis showed ready interest in the subject matter when first I discussed the possibility of a study on the German Connection with him; and Miss Linden Lawson has edited the book for publication with care and enthusiasm. To all of them I am grateful, as I am also to Mr John McLaughlin for once again giving me sound advice. Above all I am indebted to Veronica, my wife, who has discussed each chapter with me as it was written, accompanied me to Hanover, Potsdam and Coburg, and patiently prepared the Index.

Woodstock,   *Alan Palmer*
Oxford
July 1985

NORTH SEA

BALTIC SEA

SCHLESWIG

Kiel

HOLSTEIN

MECKLENBURG

• Neu Strelitz

HOLLAND

Weser

Osnabrück

• Hanover

BRUNSWICK

Elbe

• Berlin

Potsdam

ANHALT

Oder

The Hague

• Doorn

P R U S S I A

• Cassel

Brussels

WEIMAR

SAXONY

Dresden

BELGIUM

NASSAU

HESSE

Rheinhardtsbrunn

Prague •

Kronberg

Frankfurt

• Dettingen

• Coburg

Main

• Darmstadt

PALATINATE

Heidelberg

BAVARIA

AUSTRIA

FRANCE

• Stuttgart

WÜRTTEMBERG

BADEN

Danube

Vienna •

• Munich

Rhine

• Gmunden

Royal Germany

Rhine

•••••• indicates international borders

•••••• indicates state borders

The Hanoverian Succession

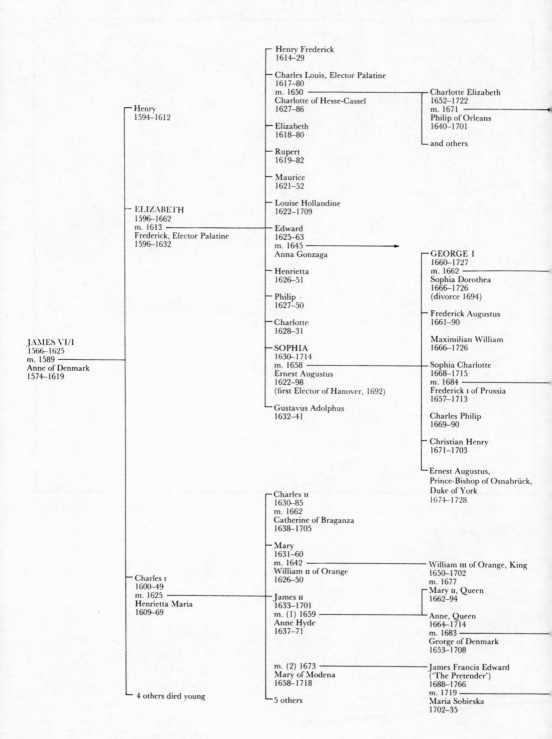

JAMES VI/I
1566–1625
m. 1589
Anne of Denmark
1574–1619

Henry
1594–1612

ELIZABETH
1596–1662
m. 1613
Frederick, Elector Palatine
1596–1632

Henry Frederick
1614–29

Charles Louis, Elector Palatine
1617–80
m. 1650
Charlotte of Hesse-Cassel
1627–86

Elizabeth
1618–80

Rupert
1619–82

Maurice
1621–52

Louise Hollandine
1622–1709

Edward
1625–63
m. 1645
Anna Gonzaga

Henrietta
1626–51

Philip
1627–50

Charlotte
1628–31

SOPHIA
1630–1714
m. 1658
Ernest Augustus
1622–98
(first Elector of Hanover, 1692)

Gustavus Adolphus
1632–41

Charlotte Elizabeth
1652–1722
m. 1671
Philip of Orleans
1640–1701

and others

GEORGE I
1660–1727
m. 1662
Sophia Dorothea
1666–1726
(divorce 1694)

Frederick Augustus
1661–90

Maximilian William
1666–1726

Sophia Charlotte
1668–1715
m. 1684
Frederick I of Prussia
1657–1713

Charles Philip
1669–90

Christian Henry
1671–1703

Ernest Augustus,
Prince-Bishop of Osnabrück,
Duke of York
1674–1728

Charles I
1600–49
m. 1625
Henrietta Maria
1609–69

4 others died young

Charles II
1630–85
m. 1662
Catherine of Braganza
1638–1705

Mary
1631–60
m. 1642
William II of Orange
1626–50

James II
1633–1701
m. (1) 1659
Anne Hyde
1637–71

m. (2) 1673
Mary of Modena
1658–1718

5 others

William III of Orange, King
1650–1702
m. 1677
Mary II, Queen
1662–94

Anne, Queen
1664–1714
m. 1683
George of Denmark
1653–1708

James Francis Edward
('The Pretender')
1688–1766
m. 1719
Maria Sobieska
1702–35

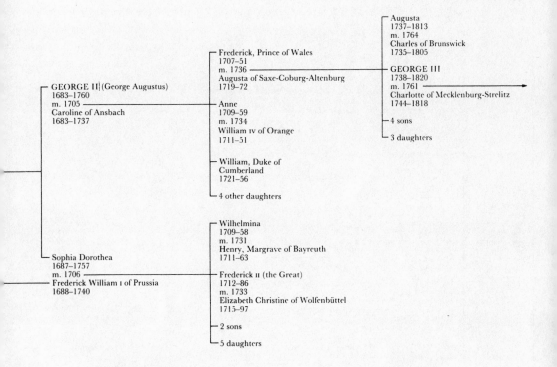

Augusta
1737–1813
m. 1764
Charles of Brunswick
1735–1805

GEORGE III
1738–1820
m. 1761
Charlotte of Mecklenburg-Strelitz
1744–1818

4 sons

3 daughters

Frederick, Prince of Wales
1707–51
m. 1736
Augusta of Saxe-Coburg-Altenburg
1719–72

Anne
1709–59
m. 1734
William IV of Orange
1711–51

William, Duke of
Cumberland
1721–56

4 other daughters

GEORGE II (George Augustus)
1683–1760
m. 1705
Caroline of Ansbach
1683–1737

Wilhelmina
1709–58
m. 1731
Henry, Margrave of Bayreuth
1711–63

Frederick II (the Great)
1712–86
m. 1733
Elizabeth Christine of Wolfenbüttel
1715–97

2 sons

5 daughters

Sophia Dorothea
1687–1757
m. 1706
Frederick William I of Prussia
1688–1740

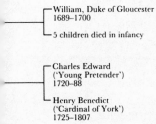

William, Duke of Gloucester
1689–1700

5 children died in infancy

Charles Edward
('Young Pretender')
1720–88

Henry Benedict
('Cardinal of York')
1725–1807

George III and his Descendants

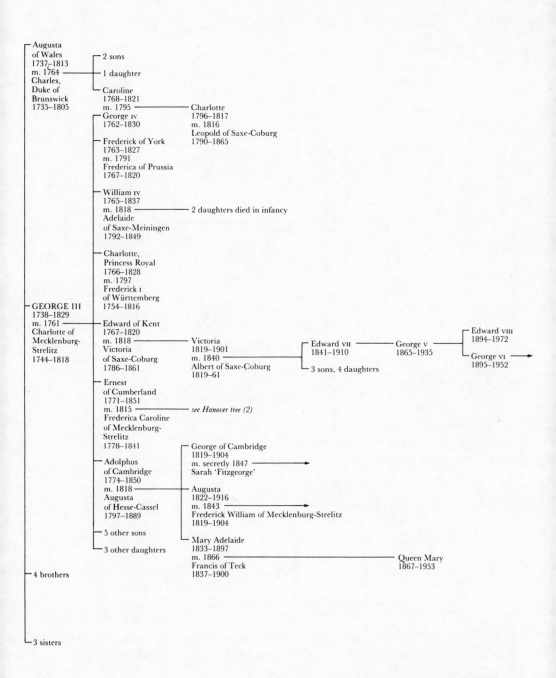

Augusta
of Wales
1737–1813
m. 1764
Charles,
Duke of
Brunswick
1735–1805

┌ 2 sons
├ 1 daughter
└ Caroline
  1768–1821
  m. 1795 ─────────── Charlotte
                       1796–1817
                       m. 1816
                       Leopold of Saxe-Coburg
                       1790–1865

GEORGE III
1738–1829
m. 1761
Charlotte of
Mecklenburg-
Strelitz
1744–1818

George IV
1762–1830

Frederick of York
1763–1827
m. 1791
Frederica of Prussia
1767–1820

William IV
1765–1837
m. 1818 ─────────── 2 daughters died in infancy
Adelaide
of Saxe-Meiningen
1792–1849

Charlotte,
Princess Royal
1766–1828
m. 1797
Frederick I
of Württemberg
1754–1816

Edward of Kent
1767–1820
m. 1818 ─────────── Victoria
Victoria   1819–1901
of Saxe-Coburg   m. 1840
1786–1861   Albert of Saxe-Coburg
                     1819–61

┌ Edward VII ─── George V ─┬ Edward VIII
│ 1841–1910   1865–1935 │ 1894–1972
└ 3 sons, 4 daughters   └ George VI
                             1895–1952 →

Ernest
of Cumberland
1771–1851
m. 1815 ─────────── *see Hanover tree (2)*
Frederica Caroline
of Mecklenburg-
Strelitz
1778–1841

Adolphus
of Cambridge
1774–1850
m. 1818
Augusta
of Hesse-Cassel
1797–1889

┌ George of Cambridge
│ 1819–1904
│ m. secretly 1847 →
│ Sarah 'Fitzgeorge'
│
├ Augusta
│ 1822–1916
│ m. 1843 →
│ Frederick William of Mecklenburg-Strelitz
│ 1819–1904
│
└ Mary Adelaide
  1833–1897
  m. 1866 ─────────────────────── Queen Mary
  Francis of Teck   1867–1953
  1837–1900

5 other sons

3 other daughters

4 brothers

3 sisters

CHAPTER ONE

↬ Fair Phoenix Bride ↫

St Valentine's Day in 1613 fell on the last Sunday before Lent. In London and Westminster there was a rare mood of festive excitement. For the first time in over a century court and capital were about to share the delights of a royal wedding. Not since Henry VII's son, Prince Arthur, married the young Catherine of Aragon in November 1501 had the public revelled in such a spectacle, for later Tudor nuptials, when celebrated at all, became private affairs, clouded by an ominously discreet introspection. But in this matter, at least, James I appears a natural extrovert. His only daughter, Princess Elizabeth, was to wed Frederick; the Elector Palatine; and he had every intention of basking in the reflected popularity of the match.

Marriage to a German electoral prince was an innovation in English dynastic diplomacy. In the past, French and Spanish families traditionally provided consorts in the absence of a suitable choice within the English or Scottish peerage; links with Germany were few, the most recent – Henry VIII's unconsummated marriage to Anne of Cleves – proving politically abortive and, for its leading advocate, personally disastrous. But in 1613 the prospect of union with the youthful Prince of Germany's Calvinists pleased the zealous Protestants of London. As soon as Elizabeth's betrothal was announced, two days after Christmas, James's subjects began to welcome the proposed marriage. The Elector Frederick V, who by then had already been in England for two months, possessed all the gifts to win an easy popularity.[1] He was good-looking, unusually dark for a Rhinelander, easy-tempered and gracious; opponents of the marriage, who included the bride's Roman Catholic mother, Queen Anne, searched in vain for vices in the 'Palsgrave's' character. Critics might suggest he was weak and ineffectual, but nobody gave much credence to their complaints. When he arrived in England with a suite of over 400, Frederick seemed socially embarrassed by the loss in a North Sea storm of the richly elegant clothes with which he had hoped to dazzle James's foppish court. But, whatever the gibes at Whitehall and Greenwich, the absence of an expensive wardrobe lost him no standing with the people of London. To them he seemed hardly more of a foreigner than the Scotsmen who had come south with their sovereign in 1603. Now, a decade later, the Puritan Opposition could at last find a royal cause to champion. The most eligible princess in Europe was about to marry, not the Catholic heir of Spain or the Catholic heir of France, but the pledged upholder of German religious liberty, a prince who was also the grandson of that martyr-hero of the Dutch struggle for independence, William the Silent. Small wonder that prayers of gratitude for the Palsgrave were offered by his Calvinist brethren in London that February.

The St Valentine's Day marriage stirred more than bible-reading consciences in the capital. Elizabeth and Frederick were both sixteen, born in 1596, within three days of each other. Their youthfulness, together with the happy chance that a politic betrothal visibly quickened into love, fired the creative imagination of poets and dramatists. Thomas Campion's *Lords' Masque* apostrophized the auburn-haired bride, wishing her the joys of 'fair nymphs and princely boys'. Francis Bacon was 'chief contriver' of the Inner Temple masque, which Beaumont wrote especially for presentation in the week after the wedding, and during the protracted celebrations Shakespeare's company of actors presented no less than fourteen plays at court. But it was John Donne who, in his *Epithalamium* for Elizabeth perpetuated the hope of his generation that the wedding marked a new beginning:

> Up then fair Phoenix Bride, frustrate the sun,
> Thy self from thine affection
> Takest warmth enough, and from thine eyes
> All lesser birds will take their Jollity.
> Up, up, fair Bride, and call,
> Thy stars, from out their several boxes, take
> Thy rubies, pearls and diamonds forth, and make
> Thy self a constellation of them all, And by their blazing signify,
> That a great Princess falls, but doth not die;
> Be thou a new star, that to us portends
> Ends of much wonder; and be thou those ends.
> Since thou dost this day in new glory shine,
> May all men date records, from this thy Valentine.

Inevitably the reality of the wedding momentarily dimmed such poetic allegories. The marriage was celebrated in the Chapel Royal of the Palace of Whitehall. The King devised a circuitous processional route from Inigo Jones's improvised Banqueting House to the steps of the chapel so that as many as possible of his subjects might enjoy the pageantry of the day. It was as well he had done so. For so cramped was the chapel that few witnessed the marriage itself: sixteen bridesmaids waited on the Princess, but there was room for only one person to escort her down the aisle. Sixteen bachelor members of the nobility similarly attended the Elector Palatine; but there was not even a chair for the heir-apparent, the future Charles I. The Queen, like the bride herself, was 'attired all in white'; the dresses of both mother and daughter were adorned with pearls and diamonds, the bride's magnificent mane of hair plaited down over the shoulders to her waist. King James, a critical onlooker in Whitehall noted, 'methought somewhat straungely attired in a cap and a feather, with a Spanish cape and a long stocking';[2] the young

Elector bridegroom wore white satin and, not surprisingly, looked ill-at-ease; he could barely master enough English for the responses. As dynastic theatre, the marriage ceremonies seem poorly stage-managed. But, once the wedding itself was over, revelry again relieved the February gloom. There was entertainment on land and on the water, torchlit processions and tilting. Yet even James I's enthusiasm had begun to wane. Three days after the wedding he roundly declared that if he had to sit through another masque it would kill him. The festivities dragged on well into the following month; the King survived another twelve years.

Frederick and Elizabeth left Whitehall for Greenwich on 10 April. They said farewell to the King and Queen at Rochester four days later, lingered with Charles at Canterbury, and on 21 April at last embarked in the new warship *Prince Royal* at Margate. There followed a further delay of four days before a favourable wind allowed them to cross to Flushing, where they went ashore on 29 April.[3] Never again did Elizabeth see her father, her mother or her brother; nor was she to return to England for forty-eight more years. Over the following three centuries other princesses crossed the North Sea to settle in the principalities and kingdoms of Germany; but for none was the break so final as for Donne's Phoenix Bride.

Frederick, leaving Elizabeth to make a slow journey down the Rhine, went ahead to Heidelberg, the capital of the Palatinate. He was determined to welcome his bride in her new home with sufficient pageantry to impress her old guardian, Lord Harrington, and the courtiers who escorted her to the Neckar. For more than half a century his branch of the Wittelsbach dynasty had accepted the Calvinist faith, but Frederick himself was no conventicle killjoy. A week of hunting, jousting and other revelry followed the ceremonial entry into Heidelberg, with its procession through flower-strewn streets; there was even a mock battle in the hills around the city. Elizabeth astonished the Rhinelanders by her skill as a huntress, making dexterous use of a crossbow. Harrington's first reports back to the King in London were favourable enough: the Rhinelanders treated Elizabeth with the respect due to a princess second in succession to the English and Scottish throne. He might have added that her greatest problem was the greed and insular arrogance of the Englishmen who had attached themselves to her suite; but, as an experienced counsellor, he preferred to remain judiciously discreet about such matters.[4]

In the German lands Frederick's English marriage was seen as a major diplomatic victory for the Palatinate. It confirmed the dynastic status of the Wittelsbachs as second only to the Habsburgs, who had provided the ruling emperors since 1438; for the political map of Germany in 1613 remained as fragmented as ever. The conflicts of the Reformation and the religious compromise which brought an uneasy peace in 1555 hardened, rather than changed, the centuries-old mosaic of a 'Holy Roman Empire of the German

Nation'. The pattern was familiar enough: seven ruling princes elected a
German king who was in due course crowned emperor and to whom thereafter
every duchy, county and ecclesiastical principality owed feudal allegiance.
The seven Electors were headed by the Archbishop of Mainz, while the
Archbishops of Cologne and Trier were senior in precedence to the four lay
Electoral Princes, the King of Bohemia, the Duke of Saxony, the Margrave of
Brandenburg and the Count Palatine of the Rhine (*Pfalzgraf* – 'Palsgrave' – *bei
Rhein*), the young Frederick v. The throne of Bohemia had belonged to the
Habsburgs for almost a century, but the remaining three temporal Princes
were all Protestants: the Duke of Saxony was a Lutheran and the ruler of
Brandenburg a Calvinist, although his subjects were mainly Lutherans. The
Palsgrave, a third-generation Calvinist, was the recognized head of the
'Evangelical Union', a Protestant alliance of nine Princes and seventeen
German cities who had come together in 1608 under the leadership of
Frederick's father to safeguard Germany's liberties against the insidious forces
of the Counter Reformation. Frederick's journey to England by way of
Holland had doubly strengthened the Union, for he was able to conclude
treaties both with James I and with Maurice of Nassau, the dominant
statesman of the Dutch Republic, who was Frederick's uncle. To have brought
back an English bride as well seemed a guarantee of greater triumphs ahead.
Signatories of alliance treaties possessed notoriously short memories, but it
was hard to believe that distance would blunt the indulgence of a royal father
towards his only surviving daughter.

If the English marriage bore testimony to Frederick's tact, good looks and
charm of manner, the political successes owed more to his Chancellor, Prince
Christian of Anhalt, the forty-five-year-old soldier and statesman responsible
for negotiating the Evangelical Union. Anhalt, who had assigned his own
principality to administrative deputies in order to serve Frederick's father, was
an inveterate opponent of Habsburg political designs, whether they originated
in Madrid or Vienna. More than most contemporaries he saw how the
Palatinate's curious territorial configuration gave strategic advantages to
whoever ruled in Heidelberg: the Lower Palatinate, straddling the central
Rhine, probed the wealthy possessions of the princely bishops in Mainz,
Worms, Speyer and Trier; and the distant Upper Palatinate stretched
northwards through the forests to the frontier of Bohemia, above the head-
waters of the Danube. Alliances with the English, the Dutch and the lesser
German princes ensured that, should internal strife return to Germany,
Anhalt would have the commanding voice in Protestant affairs, even were he
to speak ventriloquially through the compliant Elector Palatine. To humble
the Habsburgs, assert princely independence and safeguard Protestantism
made a programme of action on which Anhalt and Frederick could work
closely together, particularly if, in pursuing it, the Palsgrave acquired a
throne.

It is harder to see what James I gained by his new German connection. The best known of his diplomats, Sir Henry Wotton, thought that this policy of 'knitting knots' was sufficient in itself, a way of binding together all the enemies of Spain and the Emperor.[5] But the King lacked his envoy's singleness of purpose. Momentarily James seems to have believed that astute marriage diplomacy could make him arbiter of Europe: a German Calvinist son-in-law in Heidelberg; and a Spanish Infanta to be wooed in Madrid for – and some years later by – his surviving son, Charles. But there were at least three serious flaws in James's calculated policy: he did not appreciate how far Frederick's visit to London involved English ministers in German affairs; he did not sense the mounting interest of the Commons in the shaping of foreign policy; and he failed to understand his children, ignoring both the backwardness of Charles and the ambitions of Elizabeth, for herself and for her husband. By 1621, with a vigorously Protestant parliament sitting at Westminster, he had come to regret the St Valentine's Day marriage.

Doubt troubled him as early as the summer of 1613; Elizabeth, he grumbled, was extravagant and the Palatine court slow to accept the precedence she should by right enjoy as daughter of a King of England and Scotland. But by the following January he had recovered much of that old, testily hearty benevolence which he affected in genial mood. He was delighted to hear he was now a grandfather. Elizabeth was promised an extra £2,000 a year from his privy purse; the King ordered a partial amnesty of London's gaols in honour of his grandson, while in one of the few measures passed in its nine-week session, the 'Addled Parliament' declared the infant Prince 'true and lawful successor to the crown after his mother, the Princess Elizabeth'.[6] With the thirteen-year-old Prince Charles puny and delicate, family news from Heidelberg continued to make anxious reading in London. But when a second son, Charles Louis, was born in 1617 and a daughter, Elizabeth, a year later, the succession looked secure in Britain and the Palatinate.

At this moment, early in the spring of 1618, Elizabeth and Frederick began to contemplate an extended visit to England. But a dramatic incident far away in Bohemia on 26 May threw all plans for the future into disarray. About nine o'clock that Wednesday morning a deputation of Czech Protestants burst into the chancery of the royal palace at Prague and, after an exchange of unpleasantries, ejected three Catholic members of the governing council of regency from a convenient window into the castle moat, sixty feet below. Accumulated piles of rubbish in the dried-up moat broke the councillors' fall, saving their lives, if not their dignity. They escaped into the city, dodging ragged shots from the chancery windows.[7]

The 'Defenestration of Prague' brought latent unrest in the German–Czech provinces to the surface. Most cities in Bohemia were predominantly Protestant, Hussite nationalism antedating Luther and Calvin by more than a century. But the 'Electoral Kingdom of Bohemia' had been in Habsburg hands since 1526 and, although successive emperors gave lip-service to the kingdom's national identity and constitutional rights, recognition in 1617 of the bigoted Archduke Ferdinand as heir to the Habsburg titles provoked uneasiness throughout the Czech lands. Moreover, as Christian of Anhalt had long argued, if the ancient crown of Bohemia could be wrested from the Habsburgs and bestowed on a Lutheran or a Calvinist, then the whole character of the Empire might be changed: all four lay Electors would be Protestants; they could outvote the three ecclesiastical Electors and thus choose, for the first time, a non-Catholic emperor. The Defenestration served notice to the reigning Emperor, Matthias, not merely that Bohemia was in revolt, but that Habsburg primacy in central Europe was under challenge.

For Elizabeth and Frederick there followed sixteen months of anguish, uncertainty and irresolution. Anhalt had spent many years promoting Frederick among the Czech notables as a possible candidate for the Bohemian throne, but it seemed doubtful if the rebels would offer it to him. Their first choice was the Lutheran Duke of Saxony, John George. He, however, was too cautious to accept. So, indeed, by nature was the Elector Palatine. Nothing therefore was resolved by March 1619, when Matthias died, and five months later the Electors, Catholic and Protestant alike, voted unanimously for Archduke Ferdinand to succeed him. But at the end of September, only four weeks after the imperial election, Frederick secretly informed the Czech rebels he was prepared to become their King in defiance of the Emperor he had helped to choose. It was a remarkable change of front.

Frederick personally was content with the pleasures, and occasional tantrums, of married life at Heidelberg. His mother, his councillors and even his allies in the Evangelical Union urged him to remain in the Palatinate. An emissary from London, unsure how his king would take this latest shift of fortune, advised Frederick to weigh in his mind 'the number and qualities of his enemies' and 'the affection and power of his friends'.[8] Nor did only foreign diplomats urge caution. On the day Ferdinand was chosen as Emperor Count Solms, Frederick's envoy in Frankfurt, had written to his master predicting that 'if Bohemia elects another king, everyone should make ready at once for a war lasting twenty, thirty or forty years'. Solms added, 'The Spanish would rather cast away the Netherlands than see their House lose control of Bohemia so shamefully and so outrageously.' When despite these prophetic warnings Frederick accepted the Bohemian crown, popular prejudice blamed pressure from within his private apartments. Elizabeth, it was said, craved for the title of queen. 'I would rather eat sauerkraut with a king than roast beef with an elector,' she is alleged to have remarked.[9]

The phrase, though sometimes held apocryphal, carries the authentic ring of Stuart aphorism. Her letters to her husband leave little doubt she was inclined towards acceptance, even though she acknowledged that Frederick could resolve his hesitancy only through prayer and meditation. 'Since you are persuaded that the throne to which you are invited is a vocation from God by whose Providence are all things ordained and directed,' she wrote, 'then assuredly you ought not to shrink from the duty imposed; nor, if such be your persuasion, shall I repine whatever consequences may ensue, not even though I should be forced to part from my last jewel, and to suffer actual hardship, shall I ever repent the election.'[10] A supine husband bowed to the iron will of his consort; she was contemplating a winter journey of over 350 miles in the seventh month of her fourth pregnancy.

They left Heidelberg on 7 October 1619, drizzling rain and mist soon blotting out the rust-red castle, which Elizabeth was never to see again. More than 150 baggage wagons trundled eastwards behind the royal couple on the two-week journey. Soon after crossing into Bohemia, they were greeted at Waldsassen Abbey by a deputation of Czech notables and by Anhalt, who remained Frederick's chief counsellor. A coronation in the cathedral of St Vitus at Prague followed speedily, on 3 November; it was accompanied by all the customary pageantry. So, too, were the christening ceremonies of Elizabeth's third son, Rupert, born on 18 December. Court life showed a happily illusory permanence, with little concern for the armies gathering around Bohemia's frontiers, intent on fulfilling the Habsburg prophecy that Frederick would be only a 'Winter King'. Among the earnest Czechs Elizabeth gained a reputation for frivolity, much as had her grandmother in Knox's Edinburgh. Her dresses, they complained, were immodestly cut; she enjoyed hunting in the spring and bathing parties in the Moldau when the summer came. King and Queen, it was said, entertained far too many foreigners, especially visitors from England.[11]

Two envoys from James were indeed dining with Frederick and Elizabeth on that momentous afternoon in November 1620 when a joint Habsburg-Bavarian force surprised and defeated Anhalt's army amid the chalk-pits of the 'White Mountain', little more than four miles from the centre of Prague. The King, who had been told the night before that an attack was unlikely, rode out westwards after he had finished his meal to find that his Czechs had suffered the most disastrous defeat in Bohemia's history. The rout led to panic in Prague, feelings turning rapidly against the 'foreign' King and Queen. Their reign was as good as over. Next morning, as Frederick and Elizabeth fled for their lives, eight wagons of personal treasures were seized at the gates. Proudly a Belgian pillager handed to his commander a heraldic decoration found among them. It was the insignia of the Garter, given by James to Frederick a week before his betrothal to Elizabeth.

The changing fortunes of the Phoenix Bride continued to arouse interest in the British Isles long after the tearful farewells at Rochester. One imaginative printer put an account of Frederick and Elizabeth's arrival at Heidelberg on sale in London while their vessel was still delayed by contrary winds off

Margate; and, though later anticipatory journalism rarely scooped such high fiction, the presses regularly kept an avid public informed of events in Germany over the following seven years. There were accounts of the 'ceremonies professed in the Palatinate', printed letters of 'occurrences in the Palatinate', and optimistic bulletins: *Good News for the King of Bohemia*, and *Victory of King of Bohemia's Forces 1620*. Public sympathy was almost entirely behind Frederick and Elizabeth. Popular ballads linked support for the Protestant cause in Germany with renewed war against Habsburg Spain, holding out a prospect of 'gold prizes' taken at sea. But the mood was not simply a relapse into traditional Hispanophobia. It was said that for every loyal toast to King James in the London taverns, ten were drunk to the Palsgrave and his wife.[12]

Yet though such instinctive sympathies could be expressed easily enough, there seemed at first little chance they might influence political behaviour. For, apart from nine querulous weeks in the spring of 1614, parliament did not sit for ten years, from February 1611 to January 1621. James himself strongly disapproved of Frederick's acceptance of a crown from rebels against their legitimate sovereign; and, despite the support of Archbishop Abbot, no prayers were offered for 'King Frederick of Bohemia' in the churches of England. In the autumn of 1619 James told Baron Dhona, Frederick's envoy to London, that he would not support his son-in-law in 'an unjust and needless quarrel'. 'Can you', he asked Dhona, 'show me a good ground for the Palatine's invasion of the property of another?'[13] He was, however, prepared to protect the integrity of the Palatinate by diplomatic means. Moreover when troops from the Spanish Netherlands invaded the Palatinate, James permitted Sir Horace Vere to raise a force of volunteers who would cross to Holland and make their way to the Palatinate to fight for his son-in-law's electoral title and possessions.

The disastrous news that Prague had fallen was confirmed for James by a letter from his daughter, writing from Silesia in the last week of November 1620. 'Send us good aid to resist our foes,' she begged him. 'Otherwise I know not what will become of us.'[14] James, still anxiously pursuing his plan of a Spanish marriage for Charles, convinced himself that Madrid would call off the assault on the Palatinate in return for the hand of the next King of England. Meanwhile he sent Sir John Digby to Vienna in a vain attempt to persuade the Emperor to allow Frederick to retain the Palatinate. This was not the type of aid his daughter had sought; nor did it prove in the least effective.

Elizabeth had higher hopes of parliament; for it was largely concern over foreign affairs that had prompted James at last to summon parliament again. Elizabeth knew she could count on the Earls of Pembroke, Southampton, Essex and Warwick in the Lords. In the Commons many members wished to ease 'the afflicted estate' of their sovereign's 'children abroad'; they spoke of their willingness to give their lives and their money for the Protestant cause.

They certainly favoured some form of intervention in the war. So, with reluctance, did the King. Yet James remained uneasy: when he opened the session he stressed that it was wrong to 'make religion a cause of deposing kings'.[15] His mind conjured up expeditions to Germany which would relieve his son-in-law while, at the same time, he genuinely believed that the King of Spain could induce his cousin in Vienna to accept a truce as a preliminary to solving the whole problem of the Palatinate. To the radicals in the Commons this was appeasement; they favoured a strategy of diversion, striking at Habsburg primacy by renewing the naval war with Spain. But in Vienna, in the very week that James opened his parliament, Emperor Ferdinand placed Frederick 'under the Ban', effectively depriving him of his possessions. At this nadir of misfortune it was hard to see what practical aid King or Commons could give.

Meanwhile Elizabeth and Frederick found safety some fifty miles east of Berlin at Kustrin Castle, which belonged to Frederick's brother-in-law, the Margrave of Brandenburg. There, on 16 January 1621, in a grim keep above the confluence of the Oder and Warthe, Elizabeth gave birth to a fourth son, named Maurice, to emphasize the family link with the Protestant House of Orange-Nassau. But once Elizabeth was well enough to travel, the Margrave hurried the fugitives out of his lands; he had no wish to incur the displeasure of the victorious Emperor. At last, in mid-April, 'the King and Queen of Bohemia' were given welcome sanctuary by the republican burghers of The Hague.[16] Elizabeth resigned herself to a short exile in the United Provinces. In fact, the great European crisis dragged on for so long that Elizabeth spent almost all the remaining forty years of her life in Holland.

Her friends in London continued to support the cause of the Palatinate, at least until 1630, when the birth of the future Charles II made the possibility of Elizabeth's accession to the English throne more remote. Both Southampton and Sir Edwin Sandys were briefly imprisoned for their intemperate language in favour of war; and, conversely, Parliament – with doubtful legality – imposed savage penalties on Edward Floyd, an elderly Roman Catholic rash enough to criticize Elizabeth and her husband. But, by the autumn of 1621 the Commons had come to realize that an all-out war implied heavier taxation; now, with two subsidies already granted that year, there was a general reluctance to approve a third unless the King was prepared to recognize the right of the Commons to advise him on foreign policy. This constitutional development James rejected; it was, he said, 'far beyond their reach and capacity'. In the end the third subsidy was grudgingly voted; but it was significant that the intensifying conflict over political principles at home had begun to distract attention from the war on the Continent.[17]

Sentimental sympathy for 'the Princess' – few people thought of her as Queen of Bohemia any more – remained close to the surface in London for several years. When Frederick's least unsuccessful mercenary leader, Count

Mansfeld, came to England in April 1624 his call for a new volunteer
Protestant expeditionary force evoked a ready response: 12,000 men were
gathered at Dover. Uncertainty over where and how to employ them left this
wretched force without pay and short of food throughout the following winter.
When the campaigning season of 1625 began, only 3,000 of 'Mansfeld's
Englishmen' were fit to fight. Many deserted, and the efforts of those who
survived were sadly ineffectual.[18] The whole miserable episode was characteristic of a war remembered, not for occasional feats of arms, but for a cumu-
lative burden of human suffering spread over three decades of strategically
confused campaigning.

From her sanctuary in the Dutch Republic, Elizabeth watched as Spanish
Habsburg troops occupied the Lower Palatinate and the German Habsburg
Emperor in Vienna assigned the Upper Palatinate, and Frederick's electoral
dignity, to Duke Maximilian of Bavaria, head of the Catholic branch of the
Wittelsbach dynasty. Soon the original causes of the war were lost in a general
conflict fought to curb or confirm Habsburg imperial authority, and the
fighting spread northwards to Denmark and the shores of the Baltic. Life for
the exiles in Holland began to follow a regular pattern, with Frederick
departing on fruitless campaigns and Elizabeth maintaining the semblance of
a court at The Hague. Her brood increased steadily, the almost annual
choosing of names echoing hopes of political backers, Dutch, English, French
or Swedish: thus Louise Hollandine was born in 1622, Louis in 1624, Edward
1625, Henrietta Marie 1626, Philip 1627, Charlotte 1628, Sophia 1630, and
Gustavus Adolphus 1632. The children were educated at Leiden but Elizabeth
made the principal family home at Rhenen, a small town west of Arnhem and
on the right bank of the great river which flowed down from the Palatinate and
beyond. Two children, Louis and Charlotte, died in infancy, and the eldest
son, Frederick Henry, was drowned when a coastal vessel in which he was
travelling with his father was rammed by a larger ship off Haarlem in 1629;
but ten children survived, to strain the limited resources of the exiled Palatine
court.

With the coming of winter in 1631–2 the tide of war seemed at last to be
turning in Frederick's favour. Gustavus Adolphus of Sweden – 'Lion of the
North' – freed the Rhineland, his army cutting like a deep scythe across
northern Germany. In February 1632 Frederick was received with royal
honours by the victorious Swedish King in Frankfurt; he was even able to visit
the Lower Palatinate once again. But Gustavus soon made it clear he regarded
Frederick as a vassal, and relations between the two men became strained in
the course of the summer. These newest tensions mattered little, however:
Gustavus was killed in the battle of Lützen on 16 November 1632; the Swedes,
robbed of his leadership, faltered and the Palatinate passed once more into
Habsburg hands. And, within a fortnight of Lützen, Frederick himself
succumbed to the plague at Bacharach, a riparian town on the borders of his

old Palatinate. Suddenly Elizabeth was left alone to seek the recovery of the German lands for their dispossessed children. It was a formidable task.

The news of Frederick's death revived sentimental sympathies for Elizabeth in England. Woodcuts of the young widow sold cheaply and well in London at a time when feelings were hardening against her brother, Charles 1, for the ingenious devices by which his ministers sought to raise the royal revenue. Charles personally wished Elizabeth and her family to settle in England but she preferred to remain in The Hague and at Rhenen.[19] She was more certain of Dutch support than of effective assistance from England, where policies were increasingly shaped by two men whom she regarded as her enemies: Archbishop Laud and Thomas Wentworth, later Lord Strafford. Parliamentarian traditionalists, smarting under the policy of 'Thorough', idealized the King's sister in exile. Some crossed to Holland and, though puzzled by Elizabeth's delight in frivolous entertainment, returned home impressed by the sincerity of her Protestant zeal.

Her two eldest surviving sons, Charles Louis and Rupert, began campaigning in the army of the Prince of Orange as soon as the exiled court recovered from the shock of Frederick's death. But Elizabeth, hoping to arouse greater sympathy in London, sent both boys to England. The Princes were fêted and honoured when Charles and his court came in grand progress to Laud's Oxford, but on the King's advice they returned to Germany to build up a military reputation more gratifying to family pride.[20]

Unfortunately, when the fighting began again in Germany, the army that they raised was decisively defeated at Vlotho (October 1638). Rupert was taken prisoner by the imperialists. Charles Louis, having successfully escaped from the battlefield, had his customary bad luck: he trespassed on French soil and was seized at Moulins by order of Cardinal Richelieu, on whose sympathies he had rashly counted. Both Princes were released, with somewhat contemptuous disdain, when their captors had no further use for them. They were mere pawns in a contest which, by 1640, was no more than a power struggle between France and Spain, disputed in a German arena.

This last phase of the Thirty Years War held little interest for England. What was to become the 'Long Parliament' met at Westminster in November 1640, and the attempt to impose the will of the more radical members of the Commons on church and state led to civil war by the summer of 1642. Charles Louis, returning to London in March 1641, cultivated the parliamentarians, for he believed they, rather than his uncle, would actively champion German liberties. His brothers, Rupert and Maurice, were less politically devious; they held high rank in their uncle's army from the first raising of the royal standard at Nottingham. Charles Louis, who was with the King at Hull, soon afterwards chose neutrality and denounced his brothers' activities. More remarkably, he induced his mother to back him.[21]

Neither Rupert nor Maurice was likely to be inhibited by the disapproval of

Charles Louis or Elizabeth. Prince Rupert soon showed he was something more than a fearless cavalry commander, with largely intuitive military gifts: he personified the Cavalier spirit, capturing the public imagination as his father had done thirty years before. Yet, unfortunately for the peace of England, he remained at heart a dispossessed firebrand. Although his strategic vision was sound, he tended to indulge himself in military adventures with the ruthless caprice his mother had once shown on the hunting field. Inevitably he became the staunch adversary of those parliamentarians who had so recently supported his mother's cause. 'She fareth the worse for the impetuousness of her son who is quite out of her governance,' complained one of Elizabeth's ladies at court, writing from The Hague in January 1643.[22]

Elizabeth's dilemma defied easy solution. Family sentiment united her to Charles I and to the two sons who were fighting for him; but she was desperately short of money. Before the breach between King and parliament she had been able to count on receiving a regular monthly pension from Charles, which reached £18,000 a year after Frederick's death. Only parliament could authorize a new pension once the Civil War had broken out. In February 1643 the interception of letters between Elizabeth and her family nearly damned her chances of getting money from the Long Parliament, for she seemed to be encouraging the royalists. But two months later she sent an apology to the Speaker of the House of Commons and, at the same time, asked for a parliamentary grant. Her request was treated with sympathy, but the parliamentarians were themselves short of funds, and no sum was settled on her. She economized as best she could at The Hague and Rhenen, surviving for the most part on the generosity of Lord Craven, her Master of the Horse. Craven, twelve years younger than Elizabeth, had long been infatuated with her and, so long as he had the money, delighted in meeting her needs. But Craven never hid his royalist sympathies; and, once his estates in England were forfeited, this source too began to run dry.[23]

In the spring of 1644 Elizabeth again asked parliament for money. The Commons, however, declined to make any offer unless she dismissed a court chaplain of whom they disapproved. Reluctantly Elizabeth gave way, but it was not until the first week of March 1645 that she was granted a pension of £2,000 a year. When the Civil War was over and the King held prisoner by the Scots, Charles Louis in London negotiated a better settlement and, in the spring of 1646, Elizabeth's pension was raised to £12,000 each year. Little of it was received by her.

When, in the second week of January 1649, news reached The Hague that the King was to stand trial in London, Elizabeth contemplated crossing over to England and making an appeal to the Cromwellian Council of War for her brother's release. She hesitated: how would she be received at Westminster? It was almost thirty-six years since she had left the country and the residue of sentimental loyalty to the Winter Queen might have run low in London. She had little following among the new generation of Cromwellians; most of her old champions were dead by now. Moreover she had no wish to impede efforts by the Prince of Wales to secure French mediation. Not until 23 January did either Elizabeth or her nephew realize Charles's life was in danger. By then it was too late to influence events in London. Time outpaced their hesitant efforts. Grim rumours reached the exiled court on 3 February. Two days later it was confirmed in The Hague that Charles I had perished on the scaffold.

Elizabeth denounced the execution and the subsequent establishment of the Commonwealth. In May she was in consequence deprived of her pension, but since it was by then two years in arrears the decision of the Council of State made little difference to her way of life. She disbanded her stables, turned again to Lord Craven and sought help from the States General of the Netherlands. Momentarily her prospects in Germany looked brighter. With the Thirty Years War over and Charles Louis restored as ruler of the Rhenish Palatinate, Elizabeth counted on receiving funds from her husband's lost lands. She even hoped she might return to the palace assigned to her, Frankenthal. But she was out of touch with popular feeling in the Palatinate. There it was still widely believed that her ambition to be accepted as a queen had brought war and ruin to western Germany. Charles Louis judged it impolitic to invite his mother to a region still devastated by the recent campaigns. 'Your Majesty has surely forgotten what condition Frankenthal is in,' he wrote icily to Elizabeth from Heidelberg.[24] She remained at The Hague, her debts mounting year after year. There was no political role for Elizabeth in the Germany created by the Peace of Westphalia.

Her children afforded her little comfort. Edward settled in France, accepted Roman Catholicism and married a Princess of Mantua-Nevers. Philip was forced to flee from Holland after stabbing to death a French nobleman with whom he had quarrelled; he took service under Louis XIV and was killed fighting against the Spanish in 1650. Maurice's health had given way during the siege of Oxford; he died in 1652. Both elder daughters fell out with their mother over the harsh way in which they believed she treated their brother Philip. They left Holland for Brandenburg: the thirty-year-old Princess Elizabeth entered a German Protestant community but Louise Hollandine joined her brother Edward in France, converted to Catholicism and became a nun at Maupuisson, where she survived well into the next century. The most vivacious daughter, Sophia, was five months younger than her cousin, Charles II, and for a few months in the winter of 1648–9 Elizabeth played the role of matchmaker. However, when it became clear that Charles's romantic intentions lay elsewhere in The Hague, Sophia induced her eldest brother to invite her to join him in Heidelberg. Thereafter she accepted Charles Louis, rather than her mother, as head of the family. She had no doubt that her future lay in Germany.

Elizabeth lived on, pleasantly enough, in The Hague and at Rhenen. She enjoyed the company of her niece, Charles II's sister, Mary, the widowed Princess of Orange; she was amused at the precocious gravity of Mary's son, the future William III of England; she welcomed visits from her own children and from her favourite grandchild, Charlotte Elizabeth ('Liselotte'), Charles Louis's daughter. It was the seven-year-old Liselotte who, in November 1659, amused the whole court by mimicking every gesture of her grandmother as she swept out of a reception at the Binnenhof with all the regal dignity of a long, proud exile; for Elizabeth never allowed the Dutch to forget she was a crowned queen. When, in May 1660, the States-General of the Netherlands gave a banquet to Charles II on the eve of his departure for Dover they took care to seat the Winter Queen in the place of honour, on her nephew's right. Next day she watched from the shore at Scheveningen as the *Royal Charles* sailed out into the North Sea, a king coming into his own again.

It was, she felt, time to leave the Netherlands. If Charles Louis did not want her in Heidelberg then she, too, would return to England. 'Now I hear that the coronation is so happily passed', she wrote to an English friend the following spring, 'I have no more patience to stay here but am resolved to go myself to congratulate that happy action.'[25] The French ambassador provided a coach, the States-General two vessels, Lord Craven offered lodgings at his house in Drury Lane. A plea from the King to delay her journey as London was not yet ready to receive her fittingly was brushed aside. On 16 May 1661 she sailed for Gravesend.

The Phoenix Bride was a few weeks short of her sixty-fifth birthday when she returned to England. In Restoration London the cause of 'German Protestant Liberties' was hidden in mists of oblivion, a puzzling enthusiasm from a distant past. The Queen of Bohemia became an object of curiosity, someone who was interesting, not in her own right, but as the mother of Prince Rupert. She was eyed quizzically from a respectful distance when she accompanied her royal nephew to the new theatre in Lincoln's Inn Fields or was escorted by the Earl of Craven in a borrowed carriage. With resilient vitality she fought off the melancholy attendant on old age; little vanities of deceit concealed from strangers at court her dimming eyes and the ravages of time on the oval face which had bewitched two earlier generations. Inevitably it was a lost battle. At the time of Elizabeth's Prague coronation Sir Henry Wotton was moved to praise in verse an animated spirit which compared favourably with the beauty of the flowers, birds and stars. Pepys, first meeting the Winter Queen at The Hague in 1660, was candid in his assessment: 'very debonair, but a plain lady', he had noted in his diary.[26]

Early in the New Year she decided to ease the burden on Lord Craven, vacating his Drury Lane mansion and leasing Leicester House. But already she was suffering from bronchitis, which developed into pneumonia soon after she moved in. With her nephew Charles at her bedside, life silently slipped away on the eve of the forty-ninth anniversary of her wedding. Ten days later a cortège of candle-lit barges brought her body at midnight up the Thames to Westminster from Somerset House where – like Cromwell – she had lain in state. Neither of her English royal nephews attended the interment in Henry VII's Chapel and of her six surviving children, only Rupert was there to mourn his mother. An unseasonable thunderstorm broke over the Abbey as the service began, lightning flashes adding-supernatural theatre to her burial. For some it seemed a portent.[27]

But a portent of what? Elizabeth's German marriage, which in 1613 gave a new twist to the wheel of dynastic fortune, counted little in English diplomacy half a century later. The strongest royal connections were once again French, not German; and it seemed unlikely that the Princess buried as 'Queen of Bohemia' over 600 miles from a Prague she barely knew would leave any lasting mark on Europe's history. She had reigned as consort in the Palatinate for six years and in Bohemia for thirteen months; thereafter courtly life became a shadow pretence in exile, with Elizabeth a phoenix in borrowed plumage. Yet Donne's *Epithalamium* contained substance in prediction and not mere hyperbole. 'May all men date records, from this thy Valentine,' Donne had written: today all the reigning monarchs in Europe, and the claimants to every dispossessed European throne except the Albanian, are descended from the marriage of Frederick and Elizabeth. Small wonder if it thundered that midnight in Westminster Abbey.

CHAPTER TWO

∽ The Purple Ermine Cap ∾

In the spring of 1653 two young German Princes passed through the Palatinate on their way back to Hanover from Venice, where they had been enjoying the annual pre-Lenten carnival. The elder, George William of Brunswick-Lüneburg, was ruling Prince of the Duchy of Callenberg-Göttingen, a bachelor and notorious womanizer. As his companion and younger brother, Ernest Augustus, was also unmarried, it was assumed in Heidelberg that the brothers were suitors for the hand of Sophia, the Elector Palatine's sister, who had lived at Heidelberg for the past three years.

Sophia, young, proud and high-spirited, showed little interest in the rakish George William. She did, however, admire Ernest Augustus, whom she first met at The Hague in 1648, when she was seventeen and he nineteen. He was a gifted guitar player, with elegant hands; Sophia enjoyed playing duets with him. Many years later she wrote, 'He was considered so handsome that everyone liked him.' [1] Yet, despite his physical attractions, the Prince's social ranking made him a poor marital prospect for a granddaughter of King James I. He was a Guelph and descended from Henry II of England but, as youngest son of a junior branch of the ducal House of Brunswick, he languished in the lower reaches of the German princely league. Elizabeth of Bohemia and Charles Louis felt that Sophia could do better for herself; and she dutifully agreed with her mother and brother. The Princes resumed the journey northwards, their bachelor status unimpaired. Ernest Augustus sent Sophia music for her guitar; but they did not regularly exchange letters.

More than three years later, in the closing weeks of 1656, the Princes returned to Heidelberg, on their way to Venice for the carnival season or, as Sophia's mother sourly termed it, the 'whoring festival'. [2] By now, the notables of Hanover (as most people called the Duchy of Callenberg-Göttingen) were petitioning their ruler to marry, settle down and raise a family. Sophia, too, was looking for a husband and saw fewer faults in George William than on his previous visit. A marriage contract was sealed before the two Princes left for Venice, but for the moment it was kept secret. George William, however, had second thoughts as soon as he reached Venice: marriage was not for him. He accordingly persuaded Ernest Augustus to come forward as a substitute bridegroom. George William pledged himself never to marry, thus ensuring that Ernest Augustus or his heir would in time become a ruling prince. Sophia raised no objection. She gathered that, while in Venice, George William had contracted a disease which 'rendered him unfit to take a bride';[3] and Ernest Augustus duly married Sophia at Heidelberg on 18 October 1658, four days after her twenty-eighth birthday.

In her fiftieth year Sophia, a woman of sharp intelligence, became one of the earliest royal autobiographers. About her mother, brothers and sisters she is frequently astringent, and her surviving letters are shot through with irrational prejudice against those she believed had let her down. But the memoirs treat her husband indulgently. She did not particularly love him at the time of her marriage, but she soon found they were well suited to each other. They enjoyed music, creating elegant princely residences, landscape gardening and all the intellectual delights of late seventeenth-century culture. Husband and wife were ambitious for themselves and for the future of their dynasty within Germany. The Peace of Westphalia in 1648 had changed the constitution of the Empire to accommodate eight Electors, instead of the seven decreed by the Golden Bull of 1356. The ruler of Bavaria was now a lay Elector, along with the Duke of Saxony, the Margrave of Brandenburg, the King of Bohemia and the Count Palatine. If there could be a Bavarian Elector, then Ernest Augustus saw no reason why there could not be a Brunswick Elector, too. To secure for his family the purple ermine cap of an elector became his overriding ambition. As he was not yet even a reigning prince, it seemed an unattainable objective.

Sophia gave birth to a son at the Leine Palace, Hanover, on 28 May 1660.[4] It was the day before Sophia's first cousin, Charles II, entered London at the Restoration. But, though the boy was destined eventually to reign in England, the names chosen for him were traditionally German, 'Georg Ludwig' (George Louis); and hopes held out for him by his father were centred on narrowly German affairs. Nevertheless, the link with the House of Stuart was re-affirmed a year later. In April 1661, accompanied by her eight-year-old niece Liselotte, Sophia travelled with her baby son down the Rhine to visit her mother. And at Rotterdam that spring the future George I was duly fondled by the daughter of James I before she returned to England.[5]

Much of the boy's childhood was spent at the castle of Iburg, south-west of Osnabrück; for in December 1661 Ernest Augustus became Prince-Bishop of Osnabrück. This elevation was a curious consequence of the peace settlement of 1648, which stipulated that the Prince-Bishopric should alternate between a Roman Catholic, who would be in holy orders, and a Protestant, normally a lay member of the House of Brunswick. As Prince-Bishop Ernest Augustus gained independence and status within Germany. Characteristically, husband and wife gave priority to building a new *Residenz* in Osnabrück itself. It was an impressive Italian palace, similar in design to the Luxembourg in Paris, but they continued to prefer the quiet of Schloss Iburg. Sophia's second son, Frederick Augustus, was born while she was visiting Heidelberg in 1661;

but her remaining four sons and her daughter, Sophia Charlotte, were all born at Iburg.

At last, in 1665, Ernest Augustus received the first territorial possession which he could pass on to his family. It was the small county of Diepholz, south-west of Bremen, and George William ceded it to his brother as a double reward: for accepting his morganatic marriage to an attractive French Huguenot; and for raising troops to enforce a re-shuffling of duchies by which George William became ruler of Celle and their middle brother, John Frederick, ruled in Hanover. Although Sophia was pleased with the acquisition of Diepholz – 'Not bad, merely for raising a regiment,' she wrote to Charles Louis[6] – the dynastic arrangement was not entirely to her liking. The obese John Frederick was a Roman Catholic and a bachelor; if he married and had an heir, his branch of the family might obtain from the Catholic Emperor the electoral cap which Ernest Augustus sought for himself and for their son. John Frederick's marriage to her brother Edward's daughter, Benedicte Henriette, in 1668, further alarmed Sophia; but Benedicte Henriette only gave birth to three girls. By 1674 Sophia was confident there would be no offspring of John Frederick to block George Louis's advancement.

'Goergen', as Sophia's eldest son was called in the family circle, remained his mother's favourite, at least until he was fourteen; and her husband referred to the boy in letters to his wife as 'your Benjamin'.[7] A less partisan onlooker might have found George dull. He was a conscientious student, eager to please his mother and father, willingly accepting responsibility for shepherding his younger brothers and sister. As he grew to adolescence he became emotionally cold, affirming a maturity which he strove hard to possess. For George saw himself, first and foremost, as a soldier. At the age of six he paraded a company of sixty boys before his father and mother; at fifteen he accompanied Ernest Augustus to the wars and, on 11 August 1675, was in the thick of the fighting when Crequy's French invaders were defeated at Conzbrücke, where the Saar flows into the Moselle. By 1679, when Ernest Augustus became ruler of Hanover on John Frederick's death, George was already a veteran of four campaigns. He spoke and wrote French well, could understand Italian and Dutch, and was reckoned a sound Latinist. No one troubled to interrupt the education of a good German princeling by teaching him English. Why should they? At his birth he had stood twelfth in line of succession to Charles II; by 1679 he was nineteenth, and likely to fall lower with each new marriage contracted by his kinsmen in London, Holland and the Palatinate.

Not that the Stuart royal connection was forgotten. Although Sophia had never crossed the sea, both she and Charles Louis used occasional English words and phrases in their letters (written normally in French rather than in German). Moreover George's uncle, Prince Rupert, settled in England after the Restoration and was Governor and Constable of Windsor Castle from 1668 until his death fourteen years later. It was on Rupert's initiative that George came over to England in December 1680, travelling by way of Holland, where he was entertained by his second cousin, William of Orange. Two months before George's departure Sophia wrote to Liselotte (by now married to the Duke of Orleans) and told her to take no notice of rumours that George would propose to Princess Anne of York; Sophia, who was a snob over such matters, could never forget that the mother of the York Princesses had been a commoner.[8] London society, however, gossiped about George's Christmas visit. 'There was some discourse that he came on purpose to see the Lady Anne but that, not liking her person, he left the Kingdom without making any motion to the King or the Duke of York for their consent to marry her,' wrote Bishop Burnet some years later;[9] and historians have long maintained that Anne, resenting George's indifference, was thereafter bitterly prejudiced against her second cousin from Hanover. Recent evidence suggests that Anne and George were indeed attracted to each other, but that the marriage was unacceptable to Charles II and to the Duke of York. It is significant that George stayed on in London for three months after his first meeting with the Lady Anne; and as late as September 1682 Uncle Rupert was still persevering as a matchmaker.[10]

Ernest Augustus, however, had other plans for his eldest son. Briefly he considered a Hohenzollern marriage, and in the early spring of 1682 both George and his sister accompanied their parents to the court of the Great Elector, in Berlin. Nothing came of the visit: the Hohenzollern Princess paraded for inspection was 'unhealthy', and there were rumours that her brother was incapable of fatherhood. When the suitors returned to Hanover Ernest Augustus reverted to an earlier marriage project which would bind his own family closer together and prepare the way for the union of Hanover and Celle. In the evening of 21 November 1682 George married his cousin, Sophia Dorothea (George William's daughter) in the private apartments of Schloss Celle. Ten days later bride and bridegroom, preceded by heralds and trumpeters, were escorted by cavalry in triumphant progress from the village of Celle to the heart of Hanover, twenty-eight miles to the south. Sophia Dorothea, a few weeks beyond her sixteenth birthday at the time of her marriage, was petted by her mother-in-law and spoilt by the more spirited of George's brothers, her younger cousins.[11] Her relationship with her husband was congenial enough, too, in those early years: a son, George Augustus – the future King George II – was born at Hanover twelve months after the marriage; a daughter, named after her mother, followed two and a half years later.

The marriage was, of course, an act of state. It complemented Ernest Augustus' grand dynastic design for unifying the two Brunswick Duchies, Hanover and Celle, and advancing their status within Germany. There was good reason for assuming that this union would come about naturally, on George William's death, as the brothers had intended for many years; but had

Sophia Dorothea married another German prince – a Hohenzollern, for example – he might well have disputed the Brunswick family compact. Only by building up his territorial possessions in north-western Germany could Ernest Augustus hope to persuade the Habsburg Emperor that his House was of sufficient influence and standing to merit the coveted electoral cap. By 1683 it was clear that the Emperor Leopold I was looking favourably on Brunswick pretensions. For in July of that year Leopold made an important concession: he secretly agreed to support the introduction in Ernest Augustus' will of the principle of primogeniture, thus making it possible for George to inherit all his father's lands rather than share them with his five brothers. In return for Leopold's support, Ernest Augustus had to send his eldest sons, George and Frederick Augustus, with Hanoverian troops to help save Vienna from the Turks. Both fought with distinction in the campaigns of 1683 and 1684.

So far all had gone well for Ernest Augustus; in October 1684 he even succeeded in having his daughter accepted as second wife to the recently bereaved eldest son of the Great Elector, thus securing the valuable link with the Hohenzollerns which had eluded him two years before. But that Christmas saw the end of family harmony at Hanover. Ernest Augustus informed his sons of his primogeniture plans and was surprised that they found his proposed monetary compensation inadequate. So deep was the family rift that the second son, Frederick Augustus, and the fourth son, Charles Philip, enlisted in the Emperor's army rather than continue to serve their father; and both were killed fighting against the Turks in 1690. The third and fifth sons (Maximilian and William) also subsequently opposed primogeniture as unconstitutional; their contacts with other German princes came close to treason. It was, too, in that same disastrous year, 1690, that Sophia Dorothea, bored both with Hanover and with her husband, began a secret correspondence with the Swedish soldier, Count von Königsmarck, to whom she had been introduced by her favourite brother-in-law, Charles Philip, the previous summer.[12]

Yet, despite the rift in the family, by the beginning of the year 1692 Ernest Augustus and Sophia could see the purple ermine cap at last within their reach. The Hanoverians were good soldiers and the Empire needed them now against France as well as in the perpetual struggle to clear the Turks from the Danubian plains. Ernest Augustus made participation in these campaigns dependent on the creation of a new Electorate for Hanover. On 19 December 1692 Leopold I formally approved the constitution of a ninth Electorate, at a ceremony in the Vienna Hofburg. The new Elector would provide troops to fight in Hungary and Flanders, a special auxiliary force of 2,000 men to be employed by the Emperor wherever he wished, and money for the imperial treasury. News of the creation of the Electorate reached Hanover three days after Christmas, but the principal celebration was delayed until March 1693. Ernest Augustus' wife, surviving sons, daughter-in-law and two grandchildren were present at a magnificent ceremony in the Rittersaal of the

Leine Palace when he placed the electoral cap on his head. Hanover, he believed that day, would henceforth rank beside Saxony, Brandenburg, Bavaria and the Palatinate within the Empire. Fittingly, it was carnival time along the banks of the Leine, an occasion of happy make-believe; for, though Emperor Leopold might sanction the ninth Electorate, the German princes were slow to accord Ernest Augustus the dignity he had so long cherished.[13] Despite the long history of the House of Guelph, the other Electors looked on the Brunswicks as mere interlopers on the make.

The ceremony in the Leine Palace Rittersaal was the climax of Ernest Augustus's reign. He did not live to see Hanover absorb Celle, a peaceful union which followed his brother's death in 1705. Ernest Augustus's health gave way in the spring of 1695 and, although he lingered on until the end of January 1698, almost every decision thereafter was taken by Sophia or by his eldest son. But he was still active, and politically alert, in the summer of 1694 when the Königsmarck affair came to a head. It was Ernest Augustus and his brother George William who resolved this dynastic scandal in their House, agreeing on the divorce and banishment of Sophia Dorothea; and it was Ernest Augustus, rather than his son, who connived at the covert removal of Königsmarck by courtiers who mistakenly believed they were preserving the new electoral dignity from dishonour.[14]

Sophia Dorothea holds a high place among downtrodden heroines in historical romance. To Thackeray she became that 'beautiful and innocent wife' shut away by George I because 'he preferred two hideous mistresses'. But her surviving letters – almost all of them subsequently read by her husband – make Sophia Dorothea seem silly, vindictive, disloyal and deceitful, even expressing a hope that George would perish in the wars so that she might marry her Swedish lover.[15] Nor are Königsmarck's replies any nobler. Both made light of the hints and warnings they received as the melodrama of their love turned inexorably towards tragedy. Suspicions that they planned an elopement at midsummer 1694, when Königsmarck resigned his Hanoverian commission to take command of a Saxon regiment, forced Ernest Augustus to act. George was sent on a political mission to Berlin, the Elector broke precedent by moving into the Leine Palace in the city despite the heat of summer, Sophia Dorothea was confined to her apartments in the palace, and on the night of 11 July Königsmarck disappeared. Almost certainly he was murdered by an Italian hit-man, Nicolo Montalbano, and his body hidden in a sack which, weighted with stones, was dumped in the River Leine. Sophia Dorothea's father agreed with his brother, Ernest Augustus, that the marriage should be dissolved on the grounds that she had declined to cohabit with her husband. She was kept under virtual house arrest in her father's castle at Ahlden; and there she remained for almost all the last thirty-two years of her life. Never again did she see her divorced husband, her son or her daughter.

The divorce and banishment of Sophia Dorothea left an enduring wound on the Brunswick family. George himself, a shy man of limited intelligence and coarse sexual appetite, increasingly assumed the peremptory manners and style of a regimental officer; it is as though he were asserting the soldierly masculinity called in question by Sophia Dorothea in the intercepted letters she had written to her lover. His son, forbidden at the age of ten even to mention his mother's name in his father's presence, passed his formative years in an atmosphere of bullying tempered by neglect which seemed to his sister a natural form of family life. Thus began the conflict between generations characteristic of the Hanoverian dynasty and their Hohenzollern kinsmen in Berlin. Only the Electress Sophia remained little affected by the Königsmarck affair: she had despaired of her daughter-in-law's good sense several years before; and she wastes no words of sympathy for her in such letters as have survived from this period. Inevitably Sophia Dorothea's incarceration at Ahlden guaranteed the Electress her continued precedence at the Hanoverian court; and Sophia remained First Lady of the Electorate throughout her sixteen-year widowhood. This arrangement suited the new Elector's subjects. For, though Ernest Augustus had raised the status of the old Duchy by his statecraft, he was always too sour-tempered to win popular regard; and it was to Sophia, châtelaine of Herrenhausen and patron of the finest opera house in northern Europe, that the burghers of Hanover attributed the prosperous embellishment of their city.[16]

During the last ten years of her husband's life, Sophia had come to give more and more attention to news from London. The Glorious Revolution of 1688 had ousted her first cousin, the Roman Catholic James II, in favour of the joint Protestant rule of James's elder daughter, Mary, and her husband, his nephew William of Orange. Sophia, who was twenty years older than William and twenty-two years older than Mary, had known the Prince of Orange all his life: he spent much of his boyhood at her mother's exiled court at The Hague; and in October 1680, as *Stadholder* of the Netherlands, he was extravagantly entertained for five days at the Hanoverian court, an occasion when he vigorously supported Prince Rupert's project of marrying off Anne of York to Sophia's eldest son. She knew Mary less well, but from 1688 onwards there was a regular correspondence between the new Queen in London and her kinswoman at Herrenhausen: 'I cannot forget my father and I grieve for his misfortune,' the embarrassed Mary wrote soon after her coronation. At times Sophia's conscience, too, strayed towards the exiles at St Germain.[17]

Nor were the letters she received from Mary her sole source of information from London. Ernest Augustus, recognizing William of Orange as principal architect of the coalition against France, sent to England two of his best agents, Johann von der Reck and Ludwig von Schutz; and the English envoy to Celle and Hanover, Sir William Croft, was a shrewd commentator on events as well. The Hanoverian court were kept well informed on the depth of feeling in Britain over the religious issue, but they also knew that parliamentary government posed unfamiliar problems: 'Dealing with a parliament is a never ending business,' Reck warned Ernest Augustus from London as early as March 1689; and eighteen months later Queen Mary II wrote candidly to Sophia, 'The personal animosities people have for each other are very unpleasant, and the different parties are too difficult for me to manage . . . I am tired of it.'[18]

At first, in the winter of 1688–9, Ernest Augustus sought formal recognition of the claims of his wife and son in the constitutional settlement, since they were now the closest Protestant heirs after Mary's sister, Anne. But he soon abandoned the idea: William and Mary disliked the proposal; Anne – who had already lost six children – gave birth in July 1689 to a boy who survived infancy; and there was, too, the possibility that one or more of the fifty-two Catholics with better claims to the succession than Sophia might think London worth renouncing a Mass. At the same time, the incorrigible evasiveness perfected by the English politicians as they welcomed their Dutch Protestant liberators dampened enthusiasm for the British connection at the Hanoverian court; and George, for one, never overcame his conviction that 'the kingkillers' were not to be trusted.

But resistance to Louis XIV's France inevitably drew Britain and Hanover closer together. Heavily subsidized troops, who owed allegiance to the rulers of Brunswick and Hanover, participated in the campaigns of the Grand Alliance from 1689 to 1697 and again from 1702 to 1714. Along the Rhine, George enhanced his reputation as a military commander, winning some-what grudging respect from the two greatest soldiers of his generation, Marlborough and Prince Eugene, both of whom visited Hanover in April 1708. Hanoverian troops fought with distinction at Blenheim and at Oudenarde, where the Elector's son – the future King George II – had his horse shot under him in a cavalry charge on the French rearguard. Although the Elector frequently complained that Marlborough, as Captain-General, did not take him into his confidence over questions of grand strategy, British and German soldiers and ministers came to know each other, establishing closer contact than had existed with the Dutch before the accession of William of Orange. But, significantly, the Englishmen who visited Hanover itself found the Dowager Electress, serenely detached among the lime trees and fountains of the Herrenhausen, more cordial than either her son or grandson. These years saw the creation of the Sophia legend, a sentimental cult of the wisest queen Britain never had.[19]

The legend is not entirely fabricated. Sophia was always brighter than her husband; she possessed more wit and intelligence than either of the Georges, and certainly more than those ill-starred daughters of James II, Mary and

Anne. Just as Elizabeth of Bohemia had given her patronage to Descartes, so her daughter would enjoy the company and good talk of the polymath philosopher Gottfried von Leibniz, who was court librarian and ducal historiographer for the last forty years of his life. There are allusions to the plays of Molière and Racine, as well as to Shakespeare, in Sophia's letters, and long ago, as a young Princess, she had amused her mother by acting in a presentation of Corneille within the family circle. Perhaps she did not always read the books which were presented to her by Leibniz and less formidable scholars; but she was able to retain her reputation for gracious learning, and it was Leibniz himself who described Sophia as 'the oasis in the intellectual life of Hanover'.

It was Leibniz, too, who in August 1700 informed Sophia of the death of Anne's sole surviving child, the eleven-year-old Duke of Gloucester. 'Now more than ever is the time to be thinking of the English succession,' he added unfeelingly.[20] Sophia, however, had a warmer comprehension of grief. She knew that King William III, as well as the boy's parents, had idolized the young Duke, and she behaved with compassionate circumspection. Two months after Gloucester's death, Sophia and her daughter, Sophia Charlotte (wife of the Elector of Brandenburg) travelled to Holland and met William III at his favourite home, Het Loo, the palace he had built near Apeldoorn. Sophia was careful not to press her claims: she even proposed that soundings should first be made at St Germain to discover from her exiled cousin, James II, whether 'the Prince of Wales' might abandon his Catholicism and settle in England; and she made it clear to William that only if Jacobitism remained wedded to Rome would she personally seek the succession. At the same time, she gave the impression that 'her son was very happy as he was, and did not ask for a crown' – as she subsequently wrote to a kinswoman. Not surprisingly, the King was puzzled by her attitude and considered the possibility of introducing legislation in the British parliament which would have passed over the claims of both Sophia and her son in favour of her seventeen-year-old grandson, the Electoral Prince, George Augustus. Meanwhile, reports from the exiled court at St Germain made it clear that James II would not countenance a change of faith by his son; and in June 1701 the parliament at Westminster duly passed the Act of Settlement which vested the succession in the Dowager Electress Sophia and her Protestant heirs, if William III and Princess Anne died without children.[21]

News of the passage of the Act of Settlement pleased Sophia. Six months previously her son-in-law, the Elector of Brandenburg, made himself the first 'King in Prussia', with an impressive coronation at Königsberg; and her daughter was therefore by now a queen. This dynastic innovation was in Sophia's mind when she replied to William III's letter formally notifying her of the Act of Settlement. 'Although it is now the fashion for Electors to become Kings', she wrote, 'here we await that event without impatience, and with all our hearts we pray, "God save the King".'[22] The Electoral Prince at once began to learn English, and Sophia ordered the striking of a special medallion to emphasize the somewhat tenuous dynastic links between Hanover and England through fifteen generations. The medal showed, on one side, an unflattering profile of Sophia herself, while on the obverse appeared a representation of the twelfth-century English Princess, Mathilda, eldest daughter of Sophia's ancestor King Henry II and wife of the redoubtable Guelph Duke of Bavaria, Henry the Lion. The medallion was presented to Lord Macclesfield when, in August 1701, he came to Hanover with a formal copy of the Act of Settlement.

Despite the warm reception which his mother gave the Macclesfield mission, the Elector himself was far from happy about the terms of the Act. It was, in the first place, a measure carried only by the English parliament and could contain no guarantees for the succession in Scotland. Moreover, thirteen years of a Dutch Calvinist sovereign made parliament impose new limits on the power of a future monarch: he or she was to worship as a communicant member of the Church of England, appoint only native-born Englishmen to hold office under the Crown, and obtain parliamentary consent before leaving British shores; and the Act specifically stated that, on the death of Princess Anne, the soldiers and seamen of Great Britain should not be obliged to fight for Hanoverian interests. George even suspected crypto-Jacobites at Westminster of hoping to provoke him into downright rejection of the Act. But he was content to bide his time. He wished to concentrate on the war and on completing his father's mission in Germany – it was not until 1708 that the remaining states of the Empire finally recognized Hanover's electoral status. Succession politics George left to his mother, however much at times her attitude exasperated him.

But poor Sophia – by now in her seventies – found succession politics increasingly perplexing. It was not only that party affiliations were hard to follow; the 'Lady Anne' remained an enigma, as Princess and as Queen. When William III proposed that the Electoral Prince should visit London in the autumn of 1701, the Princess gave the King the impression that she was again pregnant, a false alarm which momentarily threw into question the usefulness of George Augustus's English lessons and kept him in Hanover, as Anne intended.[23] The deaths of James II in exile in September 1701 and of William III in London six months later hardly improved the situation. Though Queen Anne might add the Dowager Electress's name to the prayers for the royal family in the *Book of Common Prayer*, she had no intention of giving Sophia the title 'Princess of Wales' or of providing her with an establishment in the kingdom over which she might well be called to reign – for, despite the difference in their ages, Sophia was the healthier of the two ladies. Ailing childless monarchs dislike successors hovering in the antechamber, and on personal grounds Sophia would have been no more welcome at St James's

Palace in the winter of 1702–3 than her grandfather at Whitehall or Richmond a century before.

There was, too, a political consideration which influenced Anne but which Sophia never understood. Anne knew by experience the value to an Opposition of a rival court, a centre of disaffection for what would later be called the 'reversionary interest'. To have Sophia in England would pose problems enough; to have the Electoral Prince – a magnet for yesterday's rejects and tomorrow's self-seekers – would hamper any government seeking vigorous prosecution of the war according to an agreed strategic plan. Anne consistently opposed all moves which might have allowed a German successor to settle in England.

In one sense, a rival court already existed. But it was some 450 miles from Westminster, relatively inaccessible beyond the North Sea, the Weser and the Lower Saxon plain. Even so, from Christmas 1703 until midsummer 1706, the High Tories opposed to Marlborough and the Whigs were in contact with the Dowager Electress in Hanover; they exploited her sympathy for the sons of exiles she had known in her childhood, her ignorance of party faction, and the reluctance of her chief adviser, Leibniz, to recognize that he understood Westminster in-fighting as little as did his patron. Confused intrigues led the Archbishops of Canterbury and York, and other great dignitaries, to believe that the Dowager Electress wished to settle in England as soon as possible and that her son favoured her withdrawal from the life of the Electorate. Fortunately Hanover was well represented by George's envoy in London, Ludwig von Schutz, who was able to convince the Elector of the mischief behind the Tory invitation. George, for his part, settled the matter amicably in conversation with Marlborough when the Captain-General visited Hanover after his victory at Blenheim.[24] Although Sophia was disappointed at the outcome of the affair, the intrigues ultimately helped strengthen the prospects of a Hanoverian succession, for early in 1706 the predominantly Whig government in London passed a Regency Act, specifying arrangements for the transitional period between the death of the sovereign and the arrival of her successor. At the same time a Naturalization Act gave each Protestant member of the ruling family in Hanover the status of an English subject of Queen Anne. Lord Halifax, who was sent as a special envoy to Hanover in the summer of 1706 when the Queen was anxious to clear up misunderstandings with her German kinsfolk, found that the Electoral Prince 'had a mind to be an English duke'. Anne, although wary in case the Prince might wish to take his seat in the House of Lords, reluctantly agreed to the proposal; and in November 1706 George Augustus was created Duke of Cambridge. The Queen explained that she was pleased to honour both the Prince and his family; but she added, firmly and tactfully, that it was a pity the obstacles of war prevented his coming to England and sitting with the peers in parliament.[25]

The whole episode resolved lingering doubts in the Elector's mind over the feasibility of gaining the English succession. Until now the English Tories had believed George was reluctant to come to Britain. Many Whigs, too, shared their suspicions. There were persistent rumours that, if Sophia predeceased Anne, the succession would pass to the 'Duke of Cambridge' while George remained in Hanover and concentrated on building up his German inheritance. Perhaps, in his heart, this was what George most desired.[26] But the care with which the Regency Act was steered through parliament impressed him. So, too, did the reputed wealth in London's coffers. Moreover, in the last resort, he was as ambitious as any other member of the Brunswick family. If his brother-in-law the Elector of Brandenburg was now a crowned king in Prussia, why should he be content with the purple ermine cap his father had sought and won? By the end of 1706 the Elector sensed that succession politics were becoming too serious a business for Sophia and Leibniz to handle.

CHAPTER THREE

❧ Protestant Succession ❧

By the summer of 1708 popular sentiment in London was growing weary of the long campaign around France's northern frontier. Apart from an uneasy interlude between September 1697 and April 1702 Britain had been at war since the coming of 'Dutch William', for the Revolution of 1688 gave a new direction to foreign policy as well as to domestic affairs. Participation in a Continental alliance system was, however, alien to English political traditions. Moreover what had begun as a defensive policy to check the territorial greed of Louis XIV became under the military and political leadership of the Duke of Marlborough and the Earl of Godolphin an ambitious attempt to reshape the dynastic map of Europe. Small wonder if the public mood was beginning to question Britain's role on the Continent in a way which eluded most foreign observers, even the envoys sent regularly from Hanover to London.[1]

It was difficult for outsiders to understand England's new political pattern. Parliaments were short-lived: there were ten within twenty years, giving the country more frequent general elections than at any other time in history. Outwardly the politics of the hustings were already becoming a dichotomy. The Whigs, who were accepted abroad as the war party, believed that government depended on a contract between ruler and ruled; they sympathized with religious dissent and became identified with the privileged commercial corporations and the moneyed interest. The Tories grudgingly accepted constitutional monarchy, favoured traditional Anglicanism, and looked to the land as a source of true wealth. They were also more interested in maritime enterprise than in land campaigns to contain France, and gradually they emerged as the peace party. But the sovereign preferred, not a simple Tory or Whig government led by a party chief, but a 'mixed ministry' headed by 'managers', for she would rather have a coalition than the contentious faction fight of Whig or Tory. Thus although the General Election of June 1708 returned a Whig House of Commons, Godolphin remained Queen Anne's principal 'manager', while Marlborough, as Captain-General of the army, concentrated on the war against France. Such an arrangement well satisfied George of Hanover.

But it was all too easy to misread popular verdicts and attribute to the sovereign a consistency she did not possess. Voters, influenced by pulpit sermons and deft journalism, were both vocal and volatile. Soon after their election victory reckless conduct by a Whig junto who enjoyed a comfortable

Commons majority alienated the Queen: she complained that she was being browbeaten over ministerial appointments. At the same time, quarrels between Anne and her former bosom friend Sarah, the masterful Duchess of Marlborough, trivialized the conflict between the monarch and her ministers and jeopardized the Duke's control of war strategy. The influence of the new court favourite, Abigail Masham, counted against the Marlboroughs and for the Tory spokesman, Robert Harley, Abigail's kinsman. In partnership with the moderate Whig elder statesman, the Duke of Shrewsbury, Harley was able to oust Godolphin from office as Lord Treasurer in August 1710 and two months later win a resounding electoral victory for the Tories. Secret peace feelers were at once put out to Versailles, where they were received with interest.[2]

The ministerial revolution in London and the fickleness of English voters made a deep impression in Hanover. The Elector was unaccustomed to parliamentary conflict. Edmond Poley, an envoy sent to Hanover in 1705, anatomized the constitutional structure of the Electorate: 'As to the form of government,' he wrote, 'the authority of the prince is so great, as to have seldom need of assembling the States of the country but for the raising of money and on other important occasions.'[3] Reports of party manoeuvres in London puzzled George; and rumours of a separate peace made him look on the Tories as cynical betrayers of Britain's best interests.

Harley tried to reassure the Elector. In September 1710 he sent Lord Rivers to Hanover with renewed protestations of loyalty to the Protestant Succession. But George was suspicious. Why send a respected soldier so great a distance to voice conventional platitudes? The Elector remained uneasy. One of the ablest Hanoverian diplomats, Hans von Bothmer, was sent to Marlborough's headquarters with orders to accompany the Duke back to England; and when Marlborough landed near Southwold on Boxing Day 1710 a resolute, if somewhat seasick, Hanoverian envoy was thus at hand to share his carriage to London.[4]

Bothmer, a specialist in Dutch affairs, made a determined effort to master British politics. He stayed in England until midsummer 1711 and returned again in December. Parliament did not impress him. He thought poorly of members in both Houses and briefed the Elector on his views. Harley's power base was so fragile that in the Commons he was dependent on the votes of the 'country gentlemen', a pressure group who persisted in smearing Marlborough's reputation; they were, the Elector was told, a faction who 'live as their ancestors had done, when England took no part in continental affairs'.[5] Anne might show confidence in Harley by creating him Earl of Oxford in May 1711, but her second cousin was unimpressed. Bothmer confirmed his suspicion that the Tories were hell-bent on destroying the alliance against France.

On New Year's Day 1712 Marlborough was dismissed from his army commands. He was succeeded by the Duke of Ormonde, whom Bothmer considered a crypto-Jacobite, and with good reason. When Oxford imposed 'restraining orders' on Ormonde to prevent the launching of any new campaign, it became clear that Queen Anne's ministers were giving scant heed to Hanover's needs or to the Elector's representations. Throughout the year 1712 Marlborough and the Whigs waged a political campaign at Westminster complaining that the peace negotiations were ignoring Britain's Dutch and Hanoverian allies, whom the City of London had subsidized. But Marlborough could no longer stand above party affiliation, as in his days of power. The sudden death of Godolphin in September left him politically isolated. He settled for voluntary exile in Antwerp. From there, he could keep in touch with Hanover. With calculated impartiality he saw that a Jacobite door was left ajar for him by the Pretender at St Germain as well.[6]

The Electress Sophia had long admired Marlborough, and she remained his supporter until her death. Her son wavered. Suspicion of contact between Marlborough and the Pretender rekindled resentments from earlier campaigns. Moreover, George's advisers urged him to find supporters among the peers in England rather than back yesterday's exiled warlord. The Elector was prepared to give Marlborough power to defend the succession should the Stuart Pretender invade England on Anne's death. But at the same time he sent a new envoy to London, George von Schutz, with instructions to cultivate good European-minded politicians wherever they might be found. It did not matter if they were Whigs or Tories, only that they should be loyal to the Protestant Succession.

Schutz – whose father, Ludwig, had served in England from 1693 until his death in 1710 – arrived in London at a crucial time. Queen Anne's health was deteriorating. On Christmas Eve 1713 a sudden fever brought her close to death and threw her ministers into irresolute confusion. For several days alarming rumours swept the capital. Oxford ordered the immediate closure of all ports, although trusted messengers were allowed to cross to France. Schutz's couriers hired fishing smacks to smuggle them to the Dutch coast, where Bothmer was ready to intercept the reports and assess and comment on them before they went on to Hanover. If Anne had died that Christmas, Schutz and Bothmer were both convinced the Tories would have hustled the Pretender into the kingdom and proclaimed the accession of 'James III'. So long as Oxford remained in office, with Viscount Bolingbroke as his Secretary of State, the Protestant Succession was in peril.[7]

Oxford was fully aware of Schutz's astuteness and planned to counter his influence. Early in January 1714 he decided to send another envoy of his own to Hanover to reassure the electoral court. His cousin, Thomas Harley, had visited Hanover in the late summer of 1712 and was courteously received; now Oxford wished him to set out again for Germany. But Tom Harley was in no hurry: he left London in mid-February, lingered in Amsterdam until 6 April and took another week to reach the Electorate. Either he hoped Oxford's contacts at St Germain would induce the Pretender to abandon his Catholicism and make his mission unnecessary or he was waiting until Oxford was sure he could retain his primacy in a divided government. At all events, while Tom Harley was in Holland, the Electress Sophia and her son became tired of Oxford's prevarication. To them it seemed essential that a member of the dynasty should be established in London when Anne's health finally gave way. Two days before Tom Harley reached Hanover, George von Schutz unexpectedly called on the Lord Chancellor at Westminster and demanded issue of a writ summoning George Augustus, the Electoral Prince, to sit in the Lords as Duke of Cambridge.[8]

Oxford was convinced Schutz had blundered. 'I have suspected that the arts of some men who are restless for power would draw Mr Schutz unto some inconveniences,' he wrote gleefully to Cousin Tom. 'Some very zealous for the Protestant Succession have greatly complained at his conduct as what would in time reflect upon the House of Hanover.' The next day he added, 'I never saw Her Majesty so much moved in my life. She looked upon it as that she is treated with scorn and contempt.'[9] Anne certainly fussed: why had not Schutz consulted her rather than demanded a writ from the Lord Chancellor? She magnified the lapse in protocol so as to keep away the Electoral Prince since many believed that he, rather than his father or grandmother, would be designated her successor. Oxford willingly pandered to his sovereign's whim: Schutz was hurried out of the country without discovering whether or not the Electoral Prince would be invited to England. Hanover's interests in London remained in the hands of Carl von Kreyenberg, an accredited diplomat but less skilled than Bothmer or Schutz.

As the spring of 1713 passed into summer the Elector and his mother thought England on the verge of civil war. Every move by Oxford and Bolingbroke strengthened their conviction that the Tories would cast aside the Act of Settlement. George Augustus was ready to set out for England without delay. But the Elector was more subtle than his son. On 27 April he handed Tom Harley a 'memorial' asking Queen Anne 'for the security of her royal person, and for that of her kingdoms, and of the Protestant religion' to invite 'someone of the Electoral family' to England. The Elector, rightly suspecting that Tom Harley would be slow to transmit his message, made certain that copies intended for publication reached Bothmer in Holland as well as Kreyenberg in London.[10]

It was in fact Kreyenberg who first told Oxford of the 'memorial', as early as Wednesday, 5 May. The news was unwelcome and Oxford kept it to himself as long as possible, hoping his cousin would induce the Elector to change his mind.[11] Not that Oxford was a Jacobite, as Hanover suspected. Having by now recognized that the Pretender would never 'Protestantize', he would work for the Hanoverian succession – but on his own terms. 'Kingmaker Oxford' was the role he fancied for himself; and if a Hanoverian Prince settled in London, he would undermine Oxford's bargaining position. On that same Wednesday evening Oxford seems to have drunk himself silly, for he wrote nonsense to the Queen: secret reports, he told her, indicated that the Elector planned to back up his pretensions by landing thirteen regiments of hired Russians in Ireland and another thirteen more in Scotland.

By Friday morning the Queen was ill again, perhaps agitated by these tales. Over the weekend she was feverish and her answer to the 'memorial' was delayed until she was convalescent. Oxford then presented her with letters for the three generations of Hanoverian claimants: each letter emphasized that no member of the House of Hanover would be permitted to live in Britain during the Queen's lifetime.[12]

This unusually strong language caused consternation in Hanover, where the letters arrived at midday on Wednesday, 26 May (although by the Gregorian calendar in use in Germany it was 3 June). The Electoral Prince was so enraged that his wife 'feared for his health and even for his life'. But it was his grandmother, the Electress Sophia, who was most puzzled by their harsh tone. Late on the following Saturday afternoon, as she walked in the Herrenhausen gardens, she collapsed; she died before she could be carried back to the palace. 'Those letters . . . I verily believe have broke her heart and brought her with sorrow to the grave,' declared one of her attendants that afternoon.[13] But, at eighty-four, it is unlikely that Sophia's life was appreciably shortened by a perplexing letter from her sick kinswoman at Kensington Palace.

News of Sophia's death reached London six days later. When Anne's personal physician, Sir David Hamilton, asked the Queen on 5 June if the Electress's death 'added anything to her quiet or disquiet', he received a sharp answer. 'Princess Sophia was chipping porridge,' a thing of no importance, and her death 'would neither give more ease nor more uneasiness'.[14] This seems a callous comment on the passing of an heir-apparent for whom the church had dutifully prayed Sunday after Sunday for twelve years. But Anne, sensing her reign was nearly over, was out of patience with what Oxford represented as Hanoverian importunity. She was also, though he did not know it, running out of patience with her Lord Treasurer as well. When the Elector again asked for a member of his family to be received in London and announced that the formidable Bothmer would cross to England to replace Schutz, the Queen recognized that the Harley family had no influence whatsoever in Hanover. She began to give her confidence to Oxford's rival in the government, Bolingbroke; and, as if emphasizing her low opinion of all Harleys, she sent her own cousin, Lord Clarendon, to Hanover to supersede 'Cousin Tom'.

Anne's pathetic life closed, not tranquilly, but in high political drama. On

27 July she proposed to Sir David Hamilton that he find a pretext for visiting Hanover, for she wished to assure the Elector of her sincere friendship and urge him to come in person to England 'for three or four weeks, by which means he would have satisfaction and she quiet'.[15] On that same evening the Queen dismissed Oxford. But she gave no indication of whom she wished to succeed him. Bolingbroke – who, at thirty-six, was fourteen years younger than Oxford – confidently believed he could ensure a smooth succession, provided he lived down his reputation for Jacobitism and won Marlborough's support. He did not realize that the Hanoverians believed that he, rather than Oxford, was responsible for the harsh letters; and he may not have known that in late June the Queen sent a secret message to Marlborough that she would welcome his return from exile. The Duke was expected from Flanders at any moment. This time, however, the Protestant wind failed to blow; he was becalmed in Ostend for twelve vital days.

The Queen's health was failing more speedily than she or her physicians realized. Was it any good waiting for Marlborough? By Friday 30 July her privy councillors were desperately hoping their ailing monarch would have a lucid moment in which to appoint a successor to Oxford. When that Friday afternoon she rallied sufficiently to regain consciousness, the Lord Chancellor urged her to appoint Shrewsbury, the last active survivor of the Glorious Revolution, as head of her government. She showed her approval and Shrewsbury at once organized the Privy Council to defend the realm, for it was thought the Queen would die before the morning. A courier was sent to Hanover, a naval squadron ordered to the Dutch coast to escort the Elector to England, and arrangements were made to bring home troops serving in the southern Netherlands so as to reinforce the defences against a Jacobite incursion from France.

To his surprise Shrewsbury was given one more day in which to safeguard the Hanoverian succession, for the Queen defied death until a quarter to eight on the Sunday morning (1 August). While she was still alive – at eleven o'clock on Saturday – the Privy Council met at Kensington; both Bothmer and Kreyenberg were invited to attend so momentous a session. Forty members duly signed the famous appeal to 'the Elector of Brunswick Lüneburg' urging him to set out from Hanover for London as soon as possible. Next morning a list of regents, drawn up secretly by the Elector a week after his mother's death, was read out to the Council. Only three members of the interim government found their names on the list: the Archbishop of Canterbury, the Lord Chief Justice and Shrewsbury himself. The remaining fifteen regents were mainly Whigs: there was no Lord Oxford, no Viscount Bolingbroke and no Duke of Marlborough. But the transfer of authority to the regents was peaceful and orderly. Barely eight hours after Queen Anne's death, the heralds proclaimed 'the High and Mighty Prince George Elector of Brunswick Lüneburg ... George by the Grace of God King of Great Britain, France and Ireland'. The new King did not learn of his accession until the following Friday.[16]

George's nominated council of regency ruled Great Britain for seven weeks. Despite fears of civil war, there was no murmur of Jacobite rebellion. Stocks in the London money market stood high throughout the seven weeks, a sure sign of confidence in the new order. Fulfilment of the Act of Settlement was a guarantee of stability: Hanoverian rule would offer no challenge to constitutional monarchy, to religious tradition or to an expanding economy. No one awaited the coming of the 'Brunswickers' with starry-eyed enthusiasm: embellished accounts of the Königsmarck affair ensured that gossip was ungenerous to the Elector-King's reputation even before he sailed for England. But in the taverns the beer drinkers were willing to toast the health of 'Royal George' as a scourge of the papists; continuity of the Protestant Succession seemed to matter more than any new-fangled German royal connection.[17]

Some decisions George I resolved speedily: Anne's funeral was to take place 'privately' as soon as possible; and Bolingbroke was dismissed from his post as Secretary of State for the South, his papers being sealed as the King suspected him of treason. But other matters could not be hurried. George had to settle the management of the Electorate's affairs before he left for London. The Electoral Prince and his comely wife, Caroline of Ansbach, would reside in England. George I's youngest brother (Ernest Augustus) was to remain in Hanover; he became Prince-Bishop of Osnabrück a year later. The King also insisted that his seven-year-old grandson, Frederick, should be brought up in the Electorate, receiving a good sound German education from tutors supervised by Ernest Augustus. Routine matters of government in the Electorate were left to George's financial expert, Friedrich von Gortz, a Hessian who had been in his service for twenty-eight years; he came to England for the coronation but returned home and became virtually a viceroy. Three of George's most experienced counsellors served George in London: the Minister of State, Andreas von Bernstorff, was known only to those Englishmen who had made the journey to Hanover; Jean de Robethon, the King's political secretary, was a Huguenot who knew London in William III's time; and Bothmer was already familiar with Westminster politics. Predictably the 'German ministers' soon became unpopular with George's new subjects. It was believed that Bothmer and Robethon encouraged the King to favour the Whigs even before he left Hanover.

This was an over-simplification. Temperament inclined George I to rely on English politicians who had backed the war and to frown on any who supported the Utrecht peace. Moreover others, besides Bothmer and Robethon, tendered him good advice. Lord and Lady Cowper, staunch Whig friends of the Schutz family, corresponded with Bernstorff, who passed on to the Elector-King Lady Cowper's French translation of her husband's *An*

Impartial History of Parties, a lengthy and inappropriately named document which recommended the establishment of a Whig ministry; and the 'Hanoverian Tory', Lord Nottingham, wrote to Bernstorff suggesting that the King would more easily collaborate with the Whigs than the Tories. George, however, wished to appear correct. He would not, he declared, think of the words 'Whig' or 'Tory' when appointing his ministers, but would select them on merit. This principle, admirable in an enlightened autocrat, suggests a certain unfamiliarity with the embryonic party system.[18]

The King was expected in London on 10 September. Like Marlborough a few weeks before, he was delayed by contrary winds and spent eleven days in the Netherlands, finally embarking in the royal yacht on Thursday, 16 September. The crossing was rough, and when the yacht and its escorting flotilla reached the Nore they found the Thames estuary shrouded in fog. It was past six on Saturday evening before George stepped ashore from the royal barge at Greenwich; he was in no mood to appreciate the torchlit ceremonies improvised in front of Wren's magnificent waterside palace. Formal presentations were postponed until next morning. His Majesty seemed courteous, greeting Marlborough affably and reinstating him in his army commands. But occasionally George's blue, bulbous eyes clouded with lack-lustre contempt, as when the Lord Chamberlain declared, 'Here is the Earl of Oxford, of whom Your Majesty will have heard.' A royal hand was offered for Oxford graciously to kiss: not a word was said.[19]

There followed an impressive processional journey to Westminster. More than 200 coaches and a troop of Life Guards escorted the King and his son through Deptford and Southwark to London Bridge, where the Lord Mayor greeted his sovereign. Thousands cheered the Elector of Hanover and his courtiers. Not everyone was in the London streets, though. 'I sat at home yesterday, very contently when all the town was gazing at the fine show,' Lord Oxford's daughter wrote to her aunt on 21 September. 'It was so contrived that it was dark when the King came into the Strand, so from thence to St James's they had not the satisfaction of seeing His Majesty. The show altogether was very fine, but a vast mob and crowd; there were great bonfires and illuminations at night.'[20]

A collective sense of relief continued to bring out cheering crowds for several weeks after the King's coming. They were in the streets again on Wednesday, 13 October, to greet the new and vivacious Princess of Wales, Caroline of Ansbach, as she arrived from the Netherlands with her daughters Anne and Amelia; and there were more celebrations a week later when Archbishop Tenison crowned George I 'undoubted King' in Westminster Abbey. But while heralds trumpeted the triumph of an ambitious dynasty, the Whigs too had cause for satisfaction. George's hopes of a 'mixed ministry' in which a leavening of moderate Tories would curb Whig impetuosity came to nothing. Apart from the egregious Nottingham, the Hanoverian Tories refused to serve unless they received half the posts. The new government was therefore overwhelmingly Whig: Viscount Townshend, whose appointment as Secretary of State for the Northern Department was announced even before George landed in England, was confirmed in office while James Stanhope replaced the disgraced Bolingbroke as Secretary of State for the Southern Department. Lord Halifax became nominal head of the government as First Commissioner of the Treasury; and Townshend's brother-in-law, Robert Walpole, was given the influential post of Paymaster-General. The Whigs were jubilant: fortune was smiling again on ordered liberty and Protestant orthodoxy; and they rejoiced in a monarch who resented the humiliations of the recent Tory past as much as they did themselves.

The political honeymoon, strained at times, lasted until the summer of 1716. The Whigs exploited every advantage at the General Election in January 1715, not least the public pronouncements by the King which associated the Tory leaders with Jacobitism. The flight of Bolingbroke to the Pretender's court in France and the Jacobite rebellion in Scotland in the autumn again raised fears of papist subversion. With royal backing, the Whigs imprisoned Oxford in the Tower and took rigorous action against other peers tainted with Jacobitism. Moreover by insisting that frequent elections were dangerous when 'a restless and Popish faction' was liable to exploit 'violent and lasting heats and animosities', the Whigs lengthened the life of parliament from three years to seven years, thus consolidating their mastery of the Commons.[21] George I, too, benefited from the Crown-Whig partnership: the clause in the Act of Settlement forbidding the monarch to leave the kingdom without parliament's consent was repealed. Theoretically George could now return to his beloved Electorate as often as he wished. In practice, he felt unable to leave England until the embers of Jacobitism were stamped out.

The King was at heart a brusque soldier. He made no bid to gain popularity in London, and he never won it. The diary of Lady Cowper – whose husband became Lord Chancellor – illustrates the antipathy between German and British courtiers during the first year of the reign. But hostility towards the new German connection was not confined to Kensington and St James's. Londoners despised George's German mistresses, the 'old ugly trolls' whom he created Duchess of Kendal and Countess of Darlington. Both were suspected of taking bribes to ease the rise to office of ambitious peers, and both were notoriously avaricious. So, too, it was alleged, were the trio of German ministers. Yet much of the criticism was unjustified, a prejudice fired by the xenophobic insularity skin-deep among George's new subjects. None of the Germans milched the British so ruthlessly as William III's Dutchmen in the previous generation, and the King was cautious in rewarding the friends who accompanied him across the North Sea.[22]

George, however, never hid his preference for Hanover or his continued interest in Germanic affairs. 'His views and affections were singly confined to the narrow compass of the Electorate; England was too big for him,' wrote Lord Chesterfield, the urbane man of letters who was later to marry the King's bastard daughter.[23] Inevitably the worst friction between George and his English ministers arose over foreign affairs. Until 1710 Britain and Hanover were drawn towards each other by a common strategic objective, the containment of France. But the Utrecht settlement, by bringing peace to western Europe, accelerated the centrifugal pull of differing interests. While the British were increasingly concerned with maritime enterprise, the King still sought to realize narrowly Hanoverian territorial ambitions, especially in northern Germany and the Baltic. Townshend, George's first choice as Secretary of State, cared little about the Baltic, even if technically it fell within his area of responsibility in foreign affairs, the 'Northern Department'; he suspected that the King wished to commit the Royal Navy to action in the Great Northern War, the chronic Russo-Swedish contest from which the German states sought to benefit. But Townshend's colleague, Stanhope, Secretary of State for the Southern Department, the soldier son of a diplomat, had spent more of his life on the Continent than at home and possessed a broader vision than Townshend and his Little Englander friends. Stanhope was a natural courtier, sophisticated, cultured and fluent in French, whereas Townshend and Walpole affected a bucolic patriotism, knowing no German at all and speaking French with the appalling clumsiness of most of their compatriots. Small wonder if George, despairing of their insularity, turned more and more to the Stanhope Whigs, with their sense of Europe's identity. Among them was even that rare phenomenon: a young English nobleman who was prepared to speak German, Baron Carteret. By the end of the year 1715 Stanhope and Carteret had gained the King's confidence, and they never lost it.

The political novelty in British life was the opportunity for disappointed and disaffected office holders to find consolation in the rival court of a Prince and Princess of Wales. No doubt the rift between the sovereign and his son dated from the banishment of Sophia Dorothea, but it was intensified by the King's resentment that the new Prince of Wales spoke English. Moreover, through the skilful coquetry of his wife, the Prince was able to establish a primacy in London society which his stolid father could never attain. English politicians exploited the quarrels in the royal family.

The Prince and Princess genuinely suspected that the King and his favourite ministers were plotting against their interests. When George I was preparing to return to Hanover for the first time since his accession the Princess consulted her lady-in-waiting, Charlotte Clayton, over the possibility of employing an informant. She thought that William Benson, the Surveyor-General who accompanied the King to Hanover on his first two journeys, might be of service. 'May we trust Benson enough to employ him on the journey to Hanover to give an account of what passes?', the Princess asked

Mrs Clayton, apparently in May 1716.[24] The Princess certainly acquired a good informant, for later in the year she was able to tell her lady-in-waiting of a letter from Hanover 'which assures me that Mr Stanhope has more credit than ever and that, on his insistence, the King caused Mr Robethon to be arrested by four soldiers. . . . He is at liberty in Hanover but is in disgrace.'[25] It was important that the Prince of Wales, 'Guardian of the Realm' in his father's absence, should be able to gauge the King's mood: if he was listening to an English minister in Hanover rather than to his old political secretary, then Stanhope had certainly achieved a remarkable personal ascendancy.

The King returned from Hanover suspicious of the politicians who had worked closely with the Guardian of the Realm while he was away. He was pleased to accept the resignation of the two most prominent figures among them, Townshend and Walpole. The fallen ministers maintained that the King and Stanhope had conducted negotiations with the French while they were in Germany and had given the interests of Hanover a higher priority than the interests of Britain. This accusation, with minor variations, became the stock-in-trade of every aggrieved political leader in Opposition over the next half a century, and Walpole himself was later to suffer from it. But in 1716–17 there was a grain of truth in the charge. In a heated debate in parliament on 8–9 April 1717 Stanhope had difficulty in refuting accusations that George's 'German ministers' were using British funds to safeguard the Elector's acquisition of Bremen and Varden; and the Commons failed to understand that London, too, benefited commercially from trade concessions won for Hanover in the Baltic.[26] Nor was the political storm confined to Westminster. The King was angered by courtesies shown by the Prince of Wales to Whigs who attacked the government. He felt that he could not trust his son. Rather than risk the Prince's exercising even limited authority in London during the sovereign's absence abroad, George abandoned plans for an autumn visit to Hanover.

Self-deprivation did not improve the King's temper. On 28 November 1717 there was an absurd incident at the christening of the Princess of Wales's second son. The young Duke of Newcastle, who was Lord Chamberlain and a supporter of the King's German policy, complained that the Prince had threatened his life by challenging him to a duel. In reality the Prince had been commenting, in heavily accentuated English, on the Duke's 'rascally' behaviour in accepting his sovereign's command to stand as godfather to the child against the wishes of its parents. The King reacted sharply to his Lord Chamberlain's complaints. For four days the Prince of Wales was placed under house arrest, and he was subsequently banished from St James's Palace. Tactically this was a mistake on the part of the King: it enabled the heir to the throne to establish himself half a mile away, at Leicester House, where he held court to the political opposition with much greater freedom than at his father's palace.[27]

Despite a formal reconciliation in the spring of 1720, King and Prince remained 'gravely out of humour', as a contemporary observer commented. The rift ran deeper than any ordinary family quarrel. Some eight weeks after banishing his son, George I sought the opinion of his ten senior judges on three questions of constitutional law: whether a king had the right to prescribe the education of his grandchildren; whether it was possible to give males precedence over females in the British succession; and, most significantly, whether the dynastic union between Britain and Hanover could be dissolved if the King drew up a will leaving his electoral title to one prince and his British crown to another. The judges were in no hurry to reply. Eventually, sixteen months later, they submitted their considered opinions: the King could settle his grandchildren's education; he could, if he wished, favour the rights of princes over princesses; but to end the personal union of Britain and Hanover would raise far graver problems. Separation might, they said, imperil the Protestant Settlement as well as question the accepted English principle of immediate succession: 'This scheme seeks to look very far into futurity,' they declared with a hopeful touch of non-committal finality.[28] George, however, did not give up his idea of dissolving the union. If British jurists were unhelpful, he would seek support from the Emperor in Vienna and pay money to have the electoral title conferred on a second grandson of his line. Anything seemed better to him than the prospect that Hanover might eventually be treated by England's Whig politicians as though it were an additional province of the United Kingdom. A codicil added to George I's will in 1720 assumed that personal union would not pass into the third generation.

In 1720 it seemed unlikely George himself would live many more years. He was only sixty that spring, but he had been ill in the autumn of 1716 and, although his mother reached her eighties, none of his uncles managed sixty-five. Moreover in that summer he was faced with a grave financial crisis in England: the bursting of the South Sea Bubble threatened the London stock market with disaster and there was a danger of embarrassing questions being asked in parliament over the amount of stock held by the monarch and his two mistresses. Although the King mistrusted Walpole, he now recognized his skill as a parliamentary manager, for it was Walpole – having only returned to the government two months before – who prevented a Commons inquiry, thus making himself indispensable to his sovereign. The sudden death of Stanhope in February 1721 robbed George I of his one statesman of vision and integrity, although until 1724 Carteret remained Secretary of State for the Southern Department. But it was now to Walpole and Townshend that the King turned. He could have fared worse. When, in April 1721 Walpole accepted office as First Commissioner of the Treasury, he was beginning a term of twenty-one continuous years as Prime Minister.

George I concerned himself little with the day-to-day running of government affairs. He took a professional interest in the army and insisted the navy was kept up to strength, with fast vessels capable of reaching the Baltic speedily. The textbook legend that cabinet government developed in George's reign because the King's ignorance of the English language made his presence in the council chamber superfluous is now discredited: there is evidence that he could speak some English and that he presided over cabinet councils at least until 1723, probably longer.[29] But from 1721 onwards he was essentially a perplexed observer of Whig government. The independent authority of the cabinet increased, not because of the monarch's linguistic limitations but because he could never begin to understand the fragmentation of a one-party oligarchy.

George's chief delight as King was to escape to his Electorate. He left England for Germany six times in all after his accession, in 1716, 1719, 1720, 1723, 1725 and 1727. Most visits were marked by festivities which brought to the Herrenhausen and his other electoral palaces a touch of exuberance lacking at St James's or Kensington. When Townshend and Carteret accompanied George in 1723 they were amazed at the lavish entertainment and the change in mood of their sovereign: the sight of familiar places and faces seemed to unshackle inner restraints.

He looked forward to the visit of 1727 with particular eagerness.[30] His daughter, the Queen of Prussia, was to visit him at the Herrenhausen to discuss double marriage plans which would have linked the Brunswick and Hohenzollern dynasties; and George also wished to inspect progress made in landscaping the avenue of linden trees which he had approved on his last visit and which he hoped would form an impressive route between the Herrenhausen and the city. But he was never to see daughter or linden trees. He left London on 3 June and landed in Holland on the evening of 7 June, setting out at once for the Electorate. On the second morning, after barely an hour and a half in his carriage, he felt ill. His companions realized he had suffered a stroke but, when he regained consciousness, a doctor in the party resolved to continue the journey to Osnabrück, which was reached late in that evening. There, in the room he had occupied as a child, George I died soon after midnight on 11 June (locally 22 June). He was buried beside the Electress Sophia's tomb in the Leine Palace chapel at Hanover, although after the palace was destroyed by American incendiary bombs in 1943 the sarcophagi of mother and son were moved to a mausoleum in the gardens facing what remained of the Herrenhausen. There was never any thought, in the eighteenth century or the twentieth, of bringing George I's body back to what was for him always a largely alien kingdom.

The news reached London on 14 June and Walpole hastened to Richmond to inform the Prince of Wales of his accession. True to form, the new King refused to believe his father's chief minister: 'Dat ees vun beeg lie,' he exclaimed in his best English. It was, he decided, a trap set by his enemies; they were spreading reports of George I's death so as to tempt him into follies which would lead to violent quarrels when his father returned. Fortunately the new Queen, Caroline of Ansbach, was better fitted than her husband to sift the reality of official despatches from mere rumour, and George II's accession was proclaimed at St James's Palace on 15 June.

At his first Privy Council Archbishop Wake handed the King a copy of his father's will. George II said nothing and placed it in his pocket. Any plans his father may have had for dissolving the dynastic union were not to be made public. Even the copies deposited in Brunswick and Vienna were acquired by George II and buried in the Hanover archives.[31] It might, in time, become necessary to resolve the problems of succession to two markedly different inheritances. For the moment George II refused to be tied by the dead hands of a father with whom he had habitually quarrelled. Past affronts loomed in his memory, and he was content to rule both as Elector and as King.

CHAPTER FOUR

❦ Fathers and Sons ❧

The accession of George I inevitably broadened the interest of British politicians in German affairs. For more than a century London had been concerned with events in the Rhineland and the future of the great trading cities of the north but, beyond the Elbe, the eastern marchlands of Brandenburg seemed almost as remote as Siberia and commercially quite as unrewarding. The strategic conjuring trick by which the Hohenzollerns of Brandenburg won a foothold on the lower Rhine in 1609 and possession of the Duchy of Prussia as a fief from the Kings of Poland had passed almost unnoticed in Jacobean England. Only after 1688 – with William of Orange in London and his first cousin in Berlin – were Britain and Brandenburg-Prussia drawn together in the struggle against France. Even then, contact between the two allies was never close. The Prussian inheritance forced Frederick I and his son to look to the east, to relations with Russia, Poland and Sweden and away from the conflicts of western Europe which loomed so large in English policy. London was puzzled by the constitutional fiction by which, in 1701, Frederick I crowned himself 'King *in* Prussia' while remaining Electoral Prince of Brandenburg for his lands within the Empire. When, two months after his accession, Frederick William I accepted the Peace of Utrecht as King in Prussia, he continued for another year to keep his armies ready for battle against the French in his capacity as an Electoral Prince. These niceties of German politics merely exasperated the English Tories.

George I, however, understood such careful distinctions. Apart from the broad barrier of the River Elbe, only 175 miles of heath and open fields separated Hanover from Berlin and there had long been close contact between the two Protestant courts. George's sister, Sophia Charlotte, married the future King Frederick I in 1684; and, at the time of George's accession, his daughter, Sophia Dorothea, was Queen-Consort of Prussia, having married her first cousin, Frederick William, in November 1706. But, despite the marriage links, the Guelphs of Brunswick-Lüneburg consistently looked down on the Hohenzollerns as ambitious *parvenus*; they might, it was felt, found garrison towns and surround them with defensive walls but, as a family, they seemed to possess no more feeling for architecture than for books or music; and the Berliners could thank their sovereigns' wives for every civilizing influence around them, from the long line of linden trees and the parks of Charlottenburg to the foundation of the Academy of Science.[1]

This assumption of cultural superiority left the Hohenzollerns ruffled at Guelph arrogance, for Frederick I delighted in commissioning prestigious palaces worthy of his family's rising fortunes. He it was who, in 1709, adorned his father's functional *Schloss* in Potsdam with a marble ballroom and ornate portals to welcome the rulers of Poland and Denmark. It is true that Frederick's successor was a natural philistine who deplored such extravagance and liked to pass his leisure hours with his beer-swilling, pipe-puffing army commanders; but even Frederick William allowed his chamberlain all the trappings of regal ceremonial to impress the King of England when George I, with a flock of English and Hanoverian courtiers, arrived at Charlottenburg in October 1723. He might care little for his Hanoverian father-in-law but he was determined to trim that 'pride and haughtiness of the House of Hanover' of which his daughter, Wilhelmina, was to complain in her memoirs. It was ironic that George I should have marred the festivities by collapsing at the supper table within an hour of his arrival, although he recovered next morning.[2]

George spent six days at Charlottenburg, Berlin's 'Kensington Palace', a *Schloss* created by his sister and perpetuating her name. The visit held high promise for the future, both politically and dynastically. Britain and Prussia concluded a defensive alliance, hailed somewhat extravagantly by Townshend as bringing together the strongest naval and military powers in Europe. At the same time Queen Sophia Dorothea won her father's approval of a marriage project to broaden the Anglo-German connection. Ever since the birth of her daughter, Wilhelmina, in 1709, Sophia Dorothea had worked for the child's betrothal to her first cousin, Frederick of Hanover, a union which Sophia Dorothea assumed would one day make Wilhelmina Queen-Consort of England. A few years later, after George I's accession, Sophia Dorothea began to expand her marriage project: she now suggested that her brother's second daughter Amelia might, at the same time, marry Prussia's Prince Royal, the future Frederick the Great, who was six months younger than his proposed bride. Without consulting the Prince and Princess of Wales, George told Sophia Dorothea that he welcomed her marriage plans for his four grandchildren. But since the eldest, Frederick of Hanover, was only sixteen at the time of the Charlottenburg visit, the King assumed there was no hurry. To Sophia Dorothea's chagrin, his ministers subsequently encouraged him to prevaricate, hoping to strike better political bargains with the Prussians. With mounting impatience she travelled to Hanover in August 1725 and urged her father to fix a date for Wilhelmina's marriage. George insisted that 'the children' were still too young and pointed out that he had not yet gained parliament's approval for the betrothal. Nevertheless he assured his daughter that the marriage would be solemnized during the next visit to his German lands. But George did not set out again for Hanover until midsummer 1727, and it was on this journey that he died before reaching his destination. The marriage contract remained unratified, not least because the new King of England had doubts over the close kinship of the marriage couples: was it, he wondered, wise for a son and daughter to marry first cousins who were themselves the offspring of first cousins? He had a low opinion of his eldest son and feared that Princess Wilhelmina might have inherited the mental instability which, he had long believed, shaped Frederick William's actions. He did not think 'ingrafting my half-witted coxcomb upon a madwoman would improve the breed'.[3]

Frederick William, too, hesitated. A princess brought up at the English court would wish to play politics, he complained. Already he was in conflict with his eldest son, whom he criticized for liking 'comedies, opera, ballets, masquerades and . . . godless things increasing the kingdom of the Devil'. He had no wish to provide the Prince Royal with a wife who would strengthen his rebellious obduracy. There was, too, a personal antipathy between the two Kings. 'Although brothers-in-law, they could never abide each other even when children,' Frederick the Great was to write, 'the King of England used to style the King of Prussia, "My brother the Sergeant" and the King of Prussia would call the King of England "My brother the Dancing Master".'[4] In reality George and Frederick William were more akin in character than either would admit. Both raged in splenetic frustration at affronts, real or imaginary; and both, without realizing it, were ruled by their wives. In March 1730 Queen Caroline encouraged George to send Sir Charles Hotham to Berlin to complete the double marriage arrangements once and for all; and Sophia Dorothea induced Frederick William to receive Hotham 'in the most obliging manner and the height of good humour'.[5] Wilhelmina and Frederick assumed the matter was settled at last, and were well pleased.

They were soon disillusioned; no one allowed for Hotham's incompetence or Frederick William's irascibility. There was an extraordinary scene in Berlin on 14 July 1730: Hotham had intercepted letters which he hoped would discredit the King's chief minister, Grumbkow, who was thought to be in Austrian pay and therefore hostile to British commercial interests; but when he presented the evidence to Frederick William, the King lost his temper, furious that a foreigner should interfere with his minister's mail. He threw the letters at Hotham's head and stalked angrily out of the room. Hotham, as indignant as the King, announced that he would return to London. So far as he was concerned, the negotiations were at an end; there would be no Anglo-Prussian nuptials, single or double.

The news was a bitter blow to 'young Fritz'. By now life had become intolerable for him: Frederick William was treating his son brutally in public, hitting out wildly with his rattan and kicking him. Hotham's return to England convinced Frederick he would never gain the independent establishment to which he considered that at eighteen an heir to the throne was entitled. Less than a month after the quarrel between Hotham and his

father, the Prince revived a scheme he had earlier discussed secretly with his
sister: he would flee to England where he hoped his uncle, George II, would
give him sanctuary. Before daybreak on 4 August he attempted to make his
escape, while travelling with his father down the Main and the Rhine.

Everything went wrong. Although little more than forty miles from the
French frontier, Frederick could not find horses to carry him across the
border; soon he was under the escort of two of his father's most trusted
colonels. King Frederick William accused his son of desertion and placed him
under close arrest, threatening to have him beheaded. His life was spared, but
from the window of a cell in Kustrin Castle he was forced to witness the
execution of his closest friend, Hans Hermann von Katte, a twenty-six-year-
old officer whom the King held responsible for the madcap escapade.

Frederick William blamed his daughter and his brother-in-law in London
for encouraging the Prince to flee the country. There was no English
bridegroom for Wilhelmina: in November 1731 she was married off to the dull
and earnest Margrave of Bayreuth. And in the summer of 1733 Frederick was
married to Elizabeth Christine of Brunswick-Wolfenbüttel, the plump, plain
and uncultured offspring of the less distinguished ducal line of the House of
Guelph. Frederick's attempted escape soured every aspect of Anglo-Prussian
relations for the remaining ten years of his father's reign. There is no doubt the
King trivialized genuine conflicts of interest by concentrating his rage against
George II personally, as the diplomats in Berlin were quick to see. 'The King of
Prussia', Hotham's successor wrote home in December 1739, 'would sooner
decline the most advantageous offers on our part than the pleasure of giving
our royal master some mortification if he had an opportunity to do it.'[6]

The Katte tragedy confirmed George II's belief that Frederick William was a
brutal martinet. Yet, in English eyes, George's treatment of his own eldest son
was almost as deplorable. For more than fourteen years, from the age of seven
until the eve of his twenty-second birthday, Frederick of Hanover saw nothing
of his parents or his three elder sisters. His two younger sisters and his brother,
William, were all born at Leicester House and Frederick did not meet them
until the King summoned him to London in December 1728. By then William,
who was created Duke of Cumberland at the age of five, had become a spoilt
child of seven; and the brothers never liked each other. Frederick was already
titular Duke of Cornwall, and the King created him Prince of Wales on 8
January 1729, but neither his father nor his mother showed much affection for
him. His requests for a London residence were brushed aside by his father
who, at first, expected him to share the 'schoolroom' apartments at St James's
Palace with his sisters and young Cumberland. Small wonder if, once he
discovered how to slip unobserved from the palace, he won a rakish
reputation. This was, after all, the London of William Hogarth; and the
Hanoverian-born Frederick was eager to show the young bloods in the English

aristocracy that he could dissipate with all the animal zest which they themselves possessed. It was an expensive way of life, and one that ran him headlong into trouble with his mother and father; for George II was determined to keep his son short of money. Grudgingly he allowed him £24,000 from the revenue of the Principality of Wales. It was not enough. By December 1731 the Prince of Wales was heavily in debt.

Frederick's fury at his father's firm grip on the purse-strings brought the quarrels of the House of Hanover into party politics. From his wealthy friend, Bubb Dodington, the Prince borrowed sufficient money to purchase Carlton House in Pall Mall. By 1733 it was becoming a favourite resort of the factious Whig Opposition, members of both Houses of Parliament who resented the seemingly endless rule of Sir Robert Walpole and his 'Robinocracy', the Establishment Whigs. As Duke of Cornwall, Frederick controlled enough pocket boroughs to disturb Walpole and by assuming a 'Britain first' pose he could win easy popularity as an opponent of Hanoverian influence at court. Hostility to Walpole angered Queen Caroline, the Prime Minister's consistent champion; and hostility to Hanover angered the King who, having been ostentatiously 'English' throughout George I's reign, reverted to a sentimental love for the Electorate upon his accession. The rift between father and son widened with each malicious pinprick the one sought to inflict on the other.

The Opposition leaders – the 'Boy Patriots' as Walpole contemptuously labelled them – encouraged Frederick to demand marriage and the increased income which should come with family responsibility. His father duly looked for a bride, and suggested an unfortunate Danish Princess, who was mentally sub-normal and deformed. Frederick refused, and even Walpole backed him up. In the spring of 1735, during George II's biennial visit to Hanover, the fifteen-year-old Princess Augusta of Saxe-Gotha was presented to him. Augusta was gawky, her good looks marred by smallpox scars, and she spoke no other language than German, but she seemed dutifully modest and the King decided she would make an admirable bride for his tiresome son. Gotha was one of five scattered districts (all prefixed by the word 'Saxe-') ruled by Protestant members of the Wettin family, whose most famous branch formed the reigning House of Saxony; and George was pleased to counter the dynastic ambitions of Prussia by strengthening the royal connection with Lutheran central Germany. Frederick raised no objections but the marriage did not take place until Augusta arrived in London in May 1736. Her mother, meanwhile, thought it superfluous for Augusta to learn English. After twenty-two years of the House of Hanover, she assumed that German would be the natural language of the ruling classes and there seemed no reason why her daughter should familiarize herself with the vernacular of the lower orders.[7]

Marriage merely deepened the quarrels in the royal family. Frederick demanded an income of £100,000 a year, the sum his father had received as a married Prince of Wales; he was allowed only half that sum. When parliament

met in February 1737 the 'Boy Patriots' raised the question of the Prince's
income in the Commons and almost toppled Walpole's ministry. Lord
Hervey, a venomous critic of the Prince of Wales, recorded how, on the
morning of the debate, he was talking with Queen Caroline when she noticed
her son walking across the courtyard beneath her window. 'Look, there he
goes! That wretch! That villain!', she angrily exclaimed. 'I wish the ground
would open this moment and sink the monster to the lowest hole in Hell.'[8]

For five months after the debate no words were exchanged between
Frederick and his mother or sisters. When, on 5 July, he formally notified his
parents that Augusta was six months pregnant, the King ordered the Prince
and Princess to join the family at Hampton Court, since Queen Caroline had
convinced herself that Frederick was impotent and feared that any supposed
child of the marriage would be a changeling. But at Hampton Court the
tensions within the family were unbearable and when, on the evening of 31
July, Augusta unexpectedly went into labour, Frederick resolved that the child
should be born at St James's Palace, for he was determined that Augusta
should not be troubled by the presence of his mother at such a time. The
Princess of Wales was duly smuggled out of Hampton Court and hurried in
a rattling carriage twelve miles to St James's, the birth starting as the coach
swung into the palace courtyard. Remarkably the child, a princess named
after her mother, lived – surviving indeed for another seventy-five years.

The incident fanned the flames of the family quarrel. Caroline, who was
valiantly concealing from her husband and daughters the suspicion that she
was mortally ill, declared she would never again see her son; and on her
deathbed, four months later, refused to receive him. A letter preserved in the
Windsor archives shows that George II, though angry with Frederick, was at
first prepared to observe the courtesies. The Prince was told that 'his Majesty
most heartily rejoices at the safe delivery of the Princess, but that your carrying
away Her Royal Highness from Hampton Court . . . without acquainting His
Majesty or the Queen with the circumstances the Princess was in . . . is look't
upon by the King to be such a deliberate indignity offered to himself and to the
Queen . . . that he resents it to the highest degree'.[9]

With Frederick perfunctory in apology, the King's tone grew sterner. 'The
whole tenour of your conduct for a considerable time has been so entirely void
of all real duty to me that I have long had reason to be highly offended with
you,' he wrote on 10 September, 1737.[10] The Prince and Princess were
thereupon told that they had no right of residence in any royal palace nor
would they receive the protective honour of Foot Guards outside their home. At
the same time the court was instructed to ostracize them. When, nine months
later, Augusta gave birth to her second child – the Prince who became George III
– they were living in a house leased from the Duke of Norfolk in St James's
Square. Four more boys and three more girls were to follow over the next
eleven years; none of the previous fourteen Princes of Wales had been so

prolific. Whatever his other failings, Frederick at least ensured the continuance of the Hanoverian dynasty. His only surviving brother, Cumberland, never married.

These stormy scenes of royal melodrama were no novelty; it was only twenty years since the scandal-mongers had been gossiping over George I's banishment of the present King from St James's Palace. Now, as then, disappointed politicians looked on the heir to the throne as spokesman for the next generation, expecting him to share their views on the issues of the day. It never seemed to them illogical that a Prince who had spent most of his life in Hanover should complain of the iniquities of the Hanoverian connection or the use of German troops in British pay. Nor indeed did the inconsistency trouble Frederick himself. He gained a political victory at last in February 1742 when his faction in the Commons tipped the balance of votes against Sir Robert Walpole and the Prime Minister was forced from office. Significantly, after four and a half years of ostracism the King now thought a family reconciliation expedient. Even the Prince's Foot Guards were restored to him.

It was, however, a brief hour of triumph, for Frederick was no political leader. His temperament did not impress contemporaries. No doubt the hostile verdicts of the memoirists must be toned down because to a man they disliked him, but even from the diary of his friend Bubb Dodington he emerges as an irresolute, vindictive lightweight.[11] The family feud also allowed the politicians to take the measure of the King. They could see that however much George II might splutter indignantly about 'that damned House of Commons' or the crypto-Jacobitism of bishops in the Lords, he was too weak and querulous to assert the executive authority of the sovereign. He lacked the patience to accommodate his prejudices within the loose framework of a constitutional monarchy. 'I am sick to death of all this foolish stuff', Hervey records him saying in a characteristic fit of petulance, 'and wish with all my heart that the devil may take all your bishops, and the devil take your Minister, and the devil take your Parliament, and the devil take the whole island, provided I can get out of it and go to Hanover.'[12]

When in the spring of 1740 he set out once more for the Electorate, despite the naval war with Spain, his ministers accepted their King's need to spend six months of the year away from the restraints of London. By now they understood that he was a king who would sit contentedly on his throne in England so long as he might actively reign with paternal benevolence in his German lands. It remained anyone's guess what would happen when the interests of the King of Great Britain ran into conflict with the needs of the Elector of Hanover. That Gilbertian dilemma George was soon to face.

While George was enjoying the summer at the Herrenhausen early in June 1740 he heard that his brother-in-law, 'the Sergeant King', had died in Potsdam. Frederick William was succeeded by his ill-used eldest son, the

Prince Royal, who acceded as Frederick II. At first George was well-satisfied with the news, even though he sought to console his widowed sister. Secretly during the last years of Frederick William's reign, George had subsidized his nephew and he hoped to draw on the new King's gratitude. But, as George's envoy was told later in the year, Britain, like France, was too inclined 'to bring other princes under tuition'.[13] The money was speedily repaid, for Frederick possessed a strong army and a full treasury; and he had every intention of showing his independence. Whatever may have been the policy of his father and grandfather, he would never allow Prussia to accept patronage from the older Powers of Europe.

A freak of fortune helped him in this resolve. Five months after his accession Frederick II suddenly found himself master of the only stable autocracy east of the Rhine, for in October – within ten days of each other – the Emperor Charles VI died in Vienna and the Empress Anna of Russia suffered a fatal stroke. Russia was nominally ruled by an infant of four months while Maria Theresa, a pregnant Archduchess of twenty-four, claimed the Habsburg inheritance and the imperial title remained in dispute. Since it had long been accepted that only a prince could be imperial sovereign of the German nation, Maria Theresa could not be elected 'Empress', but Charles VI had spent some twenty years of his life seeking recognition of his daughter's claim to the ex- clusively Habsburg lands by the so-called 'Pragmatic Sanction', while he had hoped her husband, Francis of Lorraine, would succeed him as Emperor. Great Britain and Prussia were among the Powers who recognized the Pragmatic Sanction during Charles VI's lifetime. Frederick II, however, anxious to raise the status of the kingdom he had inherited, took advantage of the confusion into which Charles's sudden death threw central Europe. He made his support for Maria Theresa and for Francis's imperial pretensions dependent on the cession of Silesia, a province to which the Hohenzollerns had a tenuous claim. On 16 December 1740, before Vienna could reply to his demands, Frederick led 40,000 men across the imperial frontier and into the coveted province. Thus began a military contest for Prussian mastery of Germany which was to remain unresolved for a century and a quarter.

The fate of Silesia was of little importance to the politicians at Westminster. But George II and his ministers agreed that any reduction in Habsburg power would create a vacuum in Germany which Britain's traditional rival, France, would readily fill. From April 1741 onwards the British therefore paid regular subsidies to Maria Theresa, a decision which seemed justified when a few weeks later France began to build up an anti-Habsburg coalition in Germany. Yet when George again spent his summer in Hanover he became concerned for the safety of the Electorate; his lands seemed threatened by Prussia to the east and France to the west. In July 1741 he concluded a convention with the French in his capacity as Elector without consulting the King's ministers in London: the neutrality of Hanover was assured, provided that the Elector would cast his vote to support the imperial claims of France's candidate, Charles Albert of Bavaria, rather than the Anglo-Austrian candidate, Francis of Lorraine. Charles Albert, backed by the King of France and the Electors of Brandenburg-Prussia and Hanover, duly became Emperor in February 1742, against the wishes of the British.

Four days after the imperial election the King-Elector was rescued from the confusion and contradiction of his German policy: Lord Carteret, the most gifted diplomat of his age, returned to the Secretaryship of State from which the intrigues of Walpole and Townshend had ousted him in the spring of 1724. Twenty-three years before, George's shrewd consort perceived the need to win Carteret's support and wrote to her friend, Mrs Clayton, 'Pray see what can be done with Carteret; I am afraid of him.'[14] Queen Caroline, with her partiality for Walpole, had never been at ease with Carteret and mistook his Cornish aloofness for haughty contempt. But, after his wife's death, George II welcomed Carteret back as someone who spoke German and French fluently and understood the structure of the Germanic Empire. Carteret not only increased the subsidy to Maria Theresa; he induced the King, who had last fought at Oudenarde a third of a century ago, to take the field once more against a French army covering northern Bavaria, along the River Main. And on 27 June 1743 – 16 June by calendars in England – George II led the 'Pragmatic Army', a motley force of British, Hanoverians, Hessians, Dutch and Austrians, to a victory over the French at Dettingen, a village some twenty miles upstream from Frankfurt and seven miles north of Aschaffenburg.

Dettingen is a strange episode in British military history: it occurred while France and Britain were still technically at peace; it was the last occasion upon which the sovereign led his troops into battle; and it was fought many miles from any lands ruled directly by George II as King or Elector. The battle began with George outmanoeuvred, exposed to heavy French cannon fire and cornered between hills, swamp and river. From this ominous position he was saved by his own calm confidence and by the steady musketry of the Pragmatic allies' infantry, which halted French frontal assaults until British cavalry charges drove the enemy back into Dettingen itself, scattering them in spectacular rout. George found, at the end of the day, that he had won a tactical victory, although it proved to be one without any strategic significance whatsoever.

News of the royal victory suddenly raised the King's stock in London. Seven months before, Carteret's insistence on taking Hanoverian and Hessian troops into British pay had provoked Pitt's famous complaint that 'this formidable Kingdom is considered only as a province of a despicable Electorate'. Now, when George returned to England in November, he found himself a popular hero. 'They almost carried him into the palace on their shoulders,' wrote Horace Walpole, 'and at night the whole town was illuminated and bonfired.'[15] With greater dignity, Handel celebrated the royal victory with his

Dettingen Te Deum. The King was gratified by his reception but took pains to praise the courage of his favourite son, William of Cumberland, who commanded a corps at Dettingen and was slightly wounded on the battlefield. In March 1745 Cumberland was appointed Commander-in-Chief of the Pragmatic Army in the field and created Captain-General of British Land Forces. He was then a month short of his twenty-fourth birthday; Marlborough, by contrast, was fifty-two when he was made Captain-General, with the experience of six campaigns behind him.

The Prince of Wales, too, had sought an army command, but his father thought him ill-disciplined and lacking in military training. It was galling for him to observe the rapid preferment of a brother fourteen years his junior, and the Prince gave credence to any report which dimmed the lustre of Dettingen. Thus when Lord Derby commented that, as a victory, Dettingen was 'not so complete as a good Englishman would wish, or else the French would not have been suffered to pass the Main so easily', his criticism found its place among the Prince's papers.[16]

Such crumbs of information brought Frederick small comfort. After the Boy Patriots' unexpected success in toppling the Robinocracy, the Prince's cause failed to prosper. He established his headquarters in his new home, Leicester House, but his political supporters became more and more factious. Most of his Patriot friends found minor posts in the governments of Walpole's successors: Lord Wilmington (who, until his death in July 1743, was nominal head of the ministry dominated by Carteret) and Henry Pelham (Prime Minister from 1743 until he, too, died in 1754). John Carteret himself, the loyalest of king's men over everything German, wasted no time on Leicester House politics; and Pitt, who remained Groom of the Chamber to the Prince until 1745, was too much 'the Voice of England' against Hanover to back Frederick with any relish. Moreover politically the Prince, too, was mellowing. He became less eager for immediate political advantage; rather he would plan for the future, watching as his father grew older and waiting until a 'flying squadron' of newly discontented Whigs should join him at Leicester House in readiness for a call to the throne. If Cousin Fritz in Berlin had broken dramatically with the past upon his accession, why should not King Frederick I of England? There was talk at Leicester House once again of separating Britain and Hanover, with Frederick's second son becoming Elector; and this time it was suggested that his youngest son should be created 'Duke of Virginia' and eventually sent to the Caribbean as Viceroy for the British Americas.[17] More than any other member of his family, Frederick of Wales appreciated the popular prejudice against Continental entanglements and in favour of naval and colonial war on the two Bourbon Powers, France and Spain.

So long as Carteret was an active Foreign Minister George II's government in London maintained an interest in German affairs. But, after Wilmington's death in June 1743, Carteret was isolated from his colleagues and he was extremely unpopular in parliament, where it was believed he conducted secret diplomatic negotiations whenever he accompanied the King to Hanover. Carteret could defend himself ably in the Lords, but in the Commons he was constantly denounced by Pitt for having placed Hanoverian and Hessian troops on the British payroll. To Pitt he was not merely 'the Hanoverian troop-minister' but an 'execrable sole minister who . . . seemed to have drunk the potion . . . which made men forget their country'.[18] The unpardonable characteristic of Carteret's statecraft was his subtlety. He was too clever by half for the lawyers, country gentlemen and serving officers who sat in the Commons; and when, in November 1744, he appeared to be neglecting British interests in the Mediterranean to concentrate on the affairs of Germany, his cabinet colleagues secured his resignation.

Rather unexpectedly, Carteret's departure was followed – at least on paper – by a strengthening of Britain's Continental commitment. At the end of the year a formal Quadruple Alliance bound the British, the Dutch, the Austrians and the Poles against Prussia, while the agreements between London and Vienna were made more precise in the early months of 1745. Yet, though the Pelham administration kept a Pragmatic Army in the field, it was by now fighting, not in Germany, but in the traditional Belgian cockpit. Even here its record was unimpressive, for within a month of becoming Captain-General, young Cumberland was defeated by Marshal Saxe at Fontenoy, leaving Flanders open to a French invasion. Pride, prestige and habit insisted that the British and Hanoverian contingents should seek to hold the line of the Scheldt and defend the Dutch Republic. But all these good intentions were thrown into disarray through the success of the most effective sideshow on the cheap ever conceived by the grand strategists of Bourbon France. Nine weeks to the day after Fontenoy, Prince Charles Edward, the 'Young Pretender', landed in the western Highlands and raised Scotland in revolt.

News of Charles Edward's landing only reached London in mid-August and had then to be conveyed to George II, who was in Hanover. For once, he cut short his German visit and was back in England by the end of the month. So, too, were most of the British contingents from the Pragmatic Army, together with several thousand Dutch troops and Hessian mercenaries. By the end of the year the Captain-General himself had returned to take command against the Highlanders. For once, the Westminster politicians had no option over choosing the main theatre of operations for George II's army: it was to be neither in the colonies nor on the Continent but within the British Isles. There was little now to prevent Marshal Saxe from mopping up Brabant as well as Flanders. Brussels fell in January 1746, Antwerp six months later.

Cumberland gained his victory against the Jacobites at Culloden in April 1746, acquiring thereafter the reputation for callousness which has earned him the enduring nickname of 'Butcher'. At the time, however, he was almost as popular a hero as his father in the weeks following Dettingen. William of Cumberland was unquestionably a Prince of character, a forceful personality eager to 'Prussianize' an army which he regarded as administratively unprofessional. Was he potentially something more than a commander in the field? There was uneasiness at Leicester House, where no one had ever doubted the King's preference for William over all his other children. Intermittently during the following fifteen years successive Whig politicians conjured up the bogey of a 'military tyranny' with Cumberland becoming, if not a Cromwell, at least a Protestant James II reasserting the authority of the Crown at the expense of parliament.[19] But this was always a groundless fear. Cumberland lacked the two prerequisites for such a role: the support of his officers, and a succession of victories. His systematic reform of the structure of command in the army made him unpopular both politically and personally; and when, after the Jacobite panic, he once more took the field in the Netherlands, with 100,000 men at his command, he was defeated yet again by Saxe in the battle of Laffeldt and his men almost put to rout.

Cumberland's elder brother thought little of the improvised strategy of a muddled Continental war. He favoured all-out assistance to Maria Theresa, especially when her troops cleared northern Italy of the Franco-Spanish armies and threatened to invade Provence. 'No news but the great Empress's successes in Italy, who has shown Herself a true friend to us,' Frederick wrote to a supporter in the Commons in October 1746. 'She'll teach 'em what England through her National Allys and her money can do.'[20] It was a point of view on which, oddly enough, his father would have agreed with him. But the politics of the past twelve months had shown that neither the King nor his sons had sufficient influence in the Commons to control parliament. Royal initiatives in foreign affairs were countered by Pelham's insistence that his cabinet would resign in a body rather than accept pressure from the palace. When, in February 1746, George II tried to make his old friend Carteret (now Earl Granville) Prime Minister, he found that Pelham and his brother, the Duke of Newcastle, had sufficient voting strength to prevent a government that believed in a policy of Continental alliance from remaining in office for more than three days.

By then the 'War of the Austrian Succession', confused from its very beginning in character and purpose, was rapidly dissolving into a series of totally unrelated campaigns. The original issue, the possession of Silesia, was decided by Frederick II in two wars against Maria Theresa, fought independently of the major European struggle, from December 1740 to June 1742 and from August 1744 until December 1745. The victories which made Frederick the Great's military reputation – Mollwitz, Chotusitz and Hohenfriedberg – aroused little interest in London, although significantly George II hastened to make his own agreement with his nephew in August 1745 after Hohenfriedberg and thereafter put pressure on Maria Theresa to end the war. A Prusso-Austrian peace treaty was duly signed at Dresden on Christmas Day in 1745: Frederick II secured the formal cession of Silesia in return for recognizing Maria Theresa's husband, Francis I, as Emperor in succession to Charles Albert of Bavaria (Charles VII), who had died after only three years on the imperial throne. If the War of the Austrian Succession dragged on until the autumn of 1748, it was largely because the British were by now primarily concerned with waging a commercial and colonial contest against France and Spain. It was for this cause, rather than for the dynastic balance of power in Germany, that subsidies continued to be paid from London to George II's Continental allies over the three years following the Treaty of Dresden.

Yet, curiously enough, when peace was finally agreed, at Aix-la-Chapelle (Aachen) in October 1748, the one clear consequence of eight years of warfare in three continents was the changed order within Germany implicit in the Dresden peace. Most of the conquered lands in Europe – and, indeed, in India and North America – were restored, but not the province where the European war had begun; Silesia was never again to come under the Habsburgs. At Aix-la-Chapelle Europe acknowledged Maria Theresa's right to rule in Vienna, Budapest and Prague as well as her husband's imperial title. But the novelty was the style accorded to the ruler in Berlin. In September 1742 Frederick II celebrated his first victories by amending his title from 'King *in* Prussia' to 'King *of* Prussia'; and that assertion of independence was at Aix accepted by all the European Powers. George II, with Hanover lying between the core of Frederick's kingdom and the isolated Prussian outposts on the Rhine, could hardly welcome his nephew's aggrandizement. Aix-la-Chapelle was a poor peace, which no one expected to last.[21]

George II's preference for life in Hanover over life in London was, by the end of the wars, beginning to interfere seriously with the conduct of British political business. At first it had been anticipated he would spend every other summer in the Electorate. If now he could not get away from England, he became peevish and complained that his ministers were keeping him 'in toils'. At least one secretary of state was expected to follow him to Hanover so as to keep him in touch with developments in the kingdom. Thus the Duke of Newcastle, as Secretary for the Northern Department, was with him in Germany from May to late September in 1748 while the peace negotiations were slowly continuing at Aachen. Newcastle's brother, Prime Minister Pelham, found the King's absence exasperating, especially with the prospect of an important parliamentary session opening in the autumn. 'How can anyone form a speech without receiving His Majesty's particular commands?' he wrote plaintively to his brother in September. The Duke, who had never been the most tactful of men, found his sovereign reluctant to return. 'He said a great many things I need not repeat,' Newcastle told Pelham.[22] Grudgingly, however, the King was back in time to open parliament. But not for long. A letter from one of the Prince of Wales's parliamentary nominees to his patron in March 1749 shows the pressure placed by the King's movements on members of the Commons. 'We are finishing all parliamentary business in the greatest hurry,' he wrote. 'The King is to go abroad in Easter Week and the House to be up by the 12th of next month.'[23] The Hanoverian system of government, George explained to his Lord Chancellor, was much more to his liking: 'There the government is military, as here it is legal.'[24] Strictly speaking the government of the Electorate was oligarchic rather than military, a few land-owning families dominating the Estates; but, after Dettingen, George tended to think of himself as a somewhat ill-used retired general, especially in the presence of English jurists.

The King was in England at the end of March 1751 when his eldest son died unexpectedly from pleurisy. Frederick's death posed a major constitutional problem. His heir – the future George III – was not yet thirteen and even his highly possessive mother regarded him as backward for his age. George II was sixty-seven, astonishingly robust during his Hanover visits but a crabbed valetudinarian for much of the winter at St James's Palace and Kensington. Who would be regent if, like his father and grandmother, he were suddenly to die? George never doubted that the regency should pass to his favourite, 'Butcher' Cumberland. But the young prince and his mother feared Uncle Cumberland, and pamphlets were circulated which recalled the alleged fate of Edward V in language which maligned the Duke – and, for that matter, King Richard III too. George II bitterly resented these attacks, but the combined representations of the Prime Minister, the Secretaries of State and the Lord Chancellor convinced him that Cumberland was too unpopular to head any regency; and before he next departed for Germany parliament carried legislation providing for the widowed Princess of Wales to become Regent, but with a twelve-man advisory council to assist her, under Cumberland's presidency. Young George, who was created Prince of Wales a month after his father's death, remained personally scared of his uncle and mistrustful of his powers until he was himself safely on the throne.

Relations between the Prince and his grandfather were frequently strained, largely because he accepted his mother's views on public questions and she turned for advice to her dead husband's friends. Soon George II was indulging in the familiar game of dynastic matchmaking. While in Hanover in the summer of 1755 he met his niece, Frederick the Great's sister, the Duchess of Brunswick-Wolfenbüttel. She presented to him her two unmarried daughters, Sophia Caroline and Anna Amalia. A marriage link between Brunswick and Hanover, the two ducal branches of the Guelphs, made admirable political sense: their territories were contiguous and the Brunswickers were held in high esteem by the dangerously volatile ruler in Berlin. Although Anna Amalia seemed too precociously intelligent for the court of St James's, her elder sister had everything to commend her. At seventeen Sophia Caroline seemed to her royal great-uncle admirably suited to become a Queen of England. 'He wished to make her his granddaughter being too old to make her his wife,' drily commented James Waldegrave, governor of the Prince's household.[25]

It was all in vain. Neither the Prince of Wales nor his mother would have anything to do with the proposal. Why tie Britain yet closer to the duchies of the North German plain? Moreover young George was by now developing sufficient character to resent the imposition of a wife hand-picked by his septuagenarian grandfather. Poor Sophia Caroline eventually succeeded an earlier reject for the English throne, her Aunt Wilhelmina, as Margravine of Bayreuth and passed into obscurity. Of all these German princesses it is Anna Amalia who is best remembered today, as patroness of Goethe, Schiller, Herder and Wieland in Weimar's golden age.

Wife-hunting for the Prince of Wales was only one among many diplomatic activities in which the King-Elector indulged during this last long visit to Hanover. In early September 1755 he concluded an alliance with Russia which guaranteed Tsarina Elizabeth a British subsidy so long as she kept an army of 55,000 men on Prussia's eastern frontiers to deter Frederick II from attacking Hanover in the west. A second treaty provided for London to pay Hessian mercenaries to defend Hanover's borders. Both of these treaties were savagely denounced by Pitt in the Commons because, by placing the Electorate's needs first, the government was ignoring obligations to defend the American colonists against French and Spanish incursions. This was a familiar grievance, but an essentially demagogic one: for while the defence of the Electorate was certainly a burden for the taxpayer, possession of Hanover gave the British a springboard in Continental Europe which, if rightly used against the Bourbons, could prevent France from sending large armies to threaten England's colonies in America and the West Indies. Within eighteen months Pitt was to see this for himself, and make it the key to his global strategy.

For the year 1756 saw the famous 'diplomatic revolution' which brought the Protestant Powers together against Catholic France, Austria and Spain. It was largely from fear of Russia that Frederick the Great responded to British proposals for a mutual guarantee of frontiers, together with a joint pledge to resist the incursion of foreign armies on German soil. At the same time the new Austrian Chancellor, Anton von Kaunitz, ended the traditional hostility between Bourbons and Habsburgs by negotiating an alliance with France. When at the end of August 1756 Frederick launched a preventive strike against Austria's ally, Saxony, the contest for central Europe was thus resumed after a seven-year interlude; but with the old rivals, Prussia and Austria, finding different partners.

There were no early victories for the Protestant allies and George II allowed his government to bring Hanoverian and Hessian troops to England to strengthen the home defences. By the end of the year the King was accustoming himself to the presence of Pitt in a senior government post as Secretary of State for the Southern Department. But the Duke of Cumberland was less accommodating: he feared that his 'British army of observation' in Hanover would be starved of financial and military support from a minister resolutely opposed to everything Hanoverian.

George II professed every confidence in his son, William of Cumberland, when he took the field to check a French invasion of the Electorate. But an uneasy note crept into the King's letters even before the first shots were fired. George was worried over the disposition of the troops: did William realize his first task must be the protection of Hanover itself? 'Knowing your affection for me, I shall not impute to you the negligence of those old fools by whose stupidity you find yourself distressed,' the King wrote to him, somewhat cryptically, on 5 May.[26] Seven weeks later Cumberland's army was overwhelmed by the French at Hastenbeck, on the River Weser, some forty miles south of Hanover city. The King could hardly believe the news. He hoped the army of observation would reform and check the French advance; but by the beginning of August poor Cumberland was almost encircled. The King realized that, humiliating though it might be, he would have to sue for peace as Elector of Hanover. 'I have just received your letter of 2 August by which I note the distracted condition of my affairs in Germany,' the King wrote to Cumberland on 9 August in a firm and clear hand. 'I am convinced of your sense and capacity and zeal for my service. Therefore you will receive powers to get me and my country out of these difficulties at the best rate you can by a separate peace as Elector. . . . It seems fate is everywhere against me. . . . As in the case of war I depend upon your courage and skill, so now I depend on your affection, zeal and capacity to extricate yourself, me, my brave army and my dearly beloved subjects out of the misery and slavery they groan under.'[27] The King added two postscripts: he was concerned for William's health ('When you have settled everything, come to a father who esteems and loves you dearly'); and he mistrusted French skills in drawing up the peace terms ('Take care in your negotiations about cavils and there thus may be no tricks played, either to my troops or the troops of my Allies').

His loving father sent William no advice on how to strike such a bargain; and what followed was the deepest humiliation for the Hanoverian Guelphs since fortune first smiled on them a century before. For on 8 September 1757 Cumberland was forced to sign the Convention of Klosterzeven: Hessian and Brunswick troops were to be disarmed and sent home; the Hanoverian contingents were to retire to the northern regions of the Electorate; and the French were to occupy the city of Hanover and several other towns. George II was furious, alternating between fits of rage at the ineptitude of his 'rascally son' and tears of self-reproach. For William of Cumberland, still only thirty-six, Klosterzeven marked the end of his public career. His father was implacable. 'Here is my son who has ruined me and disgraced himself,' George announced to anyone within earshot when Cumberland appeared at a court levee on his return from Germany.[28] The Duke, with some dignity, resigned as Captain-General and handed over all his military commands.

Not least among George's concerns was the effect of Klosterzeven on his Prussian nephew, for Frederick had already complained, immediately after Hastenbeck, that 'it was his misfortune to have allied himself with England in her decadence and to have been used as no ally of England ever was'.[29] The war was going badly for the allies. Frederick was defeated at Kolin in the summer and, for three days in October, a raiding column of Hungarians even held Berlin. But in November the tide turned: Frederick defeated a Franco-Austrian army at Rossbach in Saxony and a month later gained what Napoleon considered his outstanding victory, at Leuthen in Silesia, 200 miles east of Rossbach. The sustained winter campaign prompted George II to disavow Klosterzeven and establish 'His Brittanic Majesty's army in Germany', under the command of Ferdinand of Brunswick. Like Frederick the Great (his brother-in-law), Brunswick broke accepted convention by waging war in the depth of winter. The French were ejected from Hanover at the start of the year and within two months Brunswick was on the Rhine, threatening France with invasion.

'His Brittanic Majesty's army' mainly comprised Hanoverians and German mercenaries, subsidized from London; British troops did not augment the force until the autumn of 1758. The English public therefore took little interest in Brunswick's painstaking campaign. But Frederick the Great's victories were so dramatic that they gained the King of Prussia astonishing popularity almost overnight. Several English towns rowdily celebrated his forty-sixth birthday at the end of January 1758; his name was usurped by taverns and coaching-inns; enterprising manufacturers moulded his profile to decorate beer-mugs and teapots; and the great Methodist evangelist, George Whitefield, drew hundreds of Londoners to his Tabernacle in Tottenham Court Road to thank the Almighty for Frederick's triumphs over the papist armies. The mood was similar to the vociferous frenzy with which the English hailed another Frederick as their 'Protestant Hero' when James I seemed slow to back the true cause. Pitt made no such mistake: the London Convention of April 1758 assured Frederick of a generous annual subsidy, together with a pledge of alliance by which neither government would engage in separate peace negotiations. So long as the alliance continued, Frederick could count on Brunswick's army to guard his western frontier against the French.[30]

By January 1759 Brunswick was tying down some 90,000 Frenchmen in Hesse with an army still nine-tenths German in composition and larger than any forces engaged that year in the famous campaign up the St Lawrence River or in the seizure of France's sugar-rich Caribbean island of Guadeloupe.

In April it seemed as if Brunswick had stumbled into defeat in the foothills of the Taunus and he pulled back northwards. George II was alarmed at a new threat to Hanover, but on 1 August Brunswick turned and faced the French commander, Contades, outside the fortified town of Minden, on the Weser forty miles west of Hanover. The British and German infantry stood firm against successive waves of French cavalry until Contades ordered a southward retreat out of George II's German lands. Forty-four years were to pass before invaders again ravaged Hanover.

Minden pleased the King more than any of the other victories of that year. For as he grew older what happened in the land of his birth mattered to George intensely. It vexed him that his grandson, the Prince of Wales, again rejected marriage offers from the Brunswick family and seemed to give only grudging support to the continuance of the war. Not that the veteran of Oudenarde and Dettingen took decisions over campaigns any more. His eyesight was failing, his hearing almost gone; only his choleric peevishness remained constant and was perhaps intensified when the march of armies denied him summer calm in the spaciousness of the Herrenhausen. There were still threats to quit London and end his days in Hanover. But Brunswick's victories lifted his life to a plateau of contentment. For fifteen more months after Minden, eventless weeks succeeded each other at St James's and Kensington Palace. Then early one Saturday in October 1760, five days after George's seventy-seventh birthday, his valet heard a crash and a groan from the bedroom and found his master lying on the floor beside his close-stool. A doctor declared the King-Elector was dead. His successor was born in London. Never again would a British sovereign concern himself so intimately with the princely politics of Germany. 'Hanover was no longer the native soil of our Princes,' Horace Walpole wrote. 'The prejudice against his family as foreigners ceased in his person.'[31]

CHAPTER FIVE

Glorying in
✑ the Name of Britain ✑

George III, the longest lived of British kings, may well have been the most insular. All the rulers from whom he was descended in the Anglo-Scottish line had known foreign courts and seen the play of politics in capitals other than their own. So, too, did his successors. But George's range of vision was limited. The lands of Continental Europe he knew only by hearsay. Although styled Duke of Brunswick-Lüneburg and Elector and titular Archtreasurer of the Holy Roman Empire until that institution ceased to exist, he never set foot on German soil nor did he even cross the Channel. In Hanover he remained as much an absentee sovereign as in his thirteen American colonies.

There was, however, in the Electorate no sense of alien rule to kindle resentment or rebellion. As their community was run smoothly and noiselessly by oligarchs who kept the taxes low, the people of Hanover saw no need for representation in government. Nor did they grieve unduly for a monarch they did not know, for a resident Elector would require the expensive trappings of court life. A good succession of envoys to the Hanoverian Chancery in London ensured that the Elector was told all he needed to know of German affairs. Their chief fear was that George's isolationism would leave the Hanoverians powerless to check the inroads of their neighbours. But of this there seemed little danger in the early years of George's reign; for, whatever he might say to win easy applause in London, the King accepted the reality of the German connection. He took his responsibilities to the Electorate too seriously to weaken bonds of personal union. It was his European allies, especially Prussia, who suffered from his desire to shake off the commitments of his grandfather's reign.

'Born and educated in this country, I glory in the name of Britain,' George told his first parliament three weeks after his accession. The famous phrase – with 'Britain' erroneously printed as 'Briton' in the speech's published form – was written in the young King's own hand and may still be seen today exhibited among the royal autograph letters in the British Museum.[1] There is no doubt George was striving to express sentiments of which he was genuinely proud. But, though the words were George's, they were inspired by the young King's former tutor and 'dearest friend', the Earl of Bute, a Scottish peer whom Frederick of Wales advanced to backstairs eminence at Leicester House in the last four years of his life. For at twenty-two George still held few opinions of his own, only the prejudices imparted by his mother and his tutor. He dreamt of purging a corrupt government of vicious men, but he was not sure how it was to be done or whom his earnest reproaches were to cast into Opposition. Six months before his grandfather's death George wrote to Bute, 'As to honesty, I have already lived long enough to know you are the only man who possesses that quality'; and some five hours after his accession he alarmed his Prime Minister with the assurance, 'My Lord Bute is your good friend. He will tell you my thoughts at large.'[2] Before long the Duke of Newcastle and even Pitt were looking back nostalgically to 'the good old king' whose tantrums they had at least understood.

Throughout the first two and a half years of his reign George III consulted Bute daily over matters great and small. He immediately accepted that there was now an urgent need for him to find a wife, preferably in time for a joint coronation. Despite his anti-Hanoverian affectations, George never seriously considered looking for a non-German bride. This is not surprising: English law stipulated that he could not marry a Roman Catholic; and the laws of the Empire stipulated that an Elector must marry into one of the princely houses. In the winter before his accession George therefore set himself the task of 'looking in the New Berlin Almanack for Princesses' and he mentioned to Bute the need 'by some method or other' to 'get some account of the various princesses in Germany', although he still vetoed the Brunswick-Wolfenbüttels. ('I would never consent to take one out of that house.')[3] The search was resumed after his accession: he wanted a sympathetic, easy-going woman who would bear plenty of children, keep out of politics and not assume intellectual poses beyond his comprehension. To find this Protestant paragon was the secret task of two brothers, much respected in the Hanoverian bureaucracy; they were members of the ancient North German noble family of Munchhausen, and one of their kinsmen was, at that time, acquiring an enduring reputation as a raconteur of tall stories.

With astonishing speed, the Munchhausens supplied the King-Elector with six names. It was not, on the whole, a promising list. The best prospect was yet another of the Wolfenbüttel girls, Elisabeth Christina Ulrike; blackballed as Queen of England she married her cousin, the heir to the Prussian crown, but was divorced after four years – although not before she had given birth to the daughter who was to marry George III's second son. Of the Munchhausens' other candidates, two were eliminated because their recent family history was tarnished with misalliances; two more were reputedly stubborn and bad-tempered; and a Saxe-Gotha cousin was rejected as partially deformed and inclined to dabble in philosophy.

At this point George asked the Munchhausens for more names. A Danish princess occurred to them, but they rightly suspected she had a prior engagement to a cousin in Hesse. In some desperation they then added the

name of a fatherless princess of whom they knew nothing since her ruling brother's *Residenz* was amid the woods and marshland of eastern
Mecklenburg. It was this last nomination that finally satisfied the royal suitor.
Subsequent reports rated Princess Charlotte of Mecklenburg-Strelitz highly
for character but lower for beauty. 'I own 'tis not in every particular as I could
wish,' George told Bute, 'but yet I am resolved to fix here.'[4] In June 1761 a
special emissary left London for Neu-Strelitz to inform the Duchess of
Mecklenburg that King George III was interested in marrying her daughter.
Within three months the seventeen-year-old Charlotte had landed at
Harwich. They were married at St James's Palace on 8 September, six hours
after meeting each other. Sixteen days later they shared the splendours of
coronation in Westminster Abbey. Thus began a close dynastic link between
London and remote Strelitz which was to last through three generations and
even defy the barriers of world war.

In the first ten years of married life Queen Charlotte bore five sons and three
daughters. Four more sons and three more daughters followed over the next
thirteen years. Only the two youngest boys died in childhood. Of the others,
six sons and two daughters eventually married into German dynasties. As
George had wished, Charlotte neither intervened in politics nor weighed him
down with any cultural burdens. Although as staid a model of Protestant piety
as her husband, she appears to have made him less prudishly censorious;
unobtrusively she may even have encouraged him to become scientifically
bookish, stimulating his interest at least in agriculture and botany. Certainly
Charlotte countered George's insularity. Within the family circle husband and
wife spoke German and four of their sons studied at the university which their
great-grandfather had founded in Göttingen. In the year that George and
Charlotte celebrated their silver wedding, the King was even heard to
comment proudly on the good German blood that pulsed through his veins.[5]
But by then his Scottish 'dearest friend' had been twenty years out of favour.

Bute was, however, still in the ascendant at the time of George's coronation. In
March 1761 he entered the Newcastle coalition as Secretary of State for the
Northern Department and for six uneasy months tussled with his formidable
colleague in the Southern Department, Pitt. Newcastle, alarmed at the cost of
the long war, was anxious to negotiate peace. So, too, was Bute. Pitt, however,
thought the scope of overseas operations should be broadened by an
immediate declaration of war on France's ally, Spain. This was too much for
George III and the court party in the Commons; in October Pitt was forced out
of the government over this issue.

Pitt had been the leading spirit in the administration for the past four
years and Newcastle found himself isolated in a cabinet dominated by Bute
and his nominees. What followed was more than a conflict between non-
personalities for Bute favoured not merely a rapid ending to the war but total

disengagement from all European commitments as well. In December 1761 the existing subsidized alliance treaty with Prussia was allowed to expire. Bute thereupon made renewal of financial support dependent on Frederick the Great's acceptance of conditions which would have limited his freedom of action in central Europe. This proposal thoroughly alarmed Andrew Mitchell, the British envoy in Berlin. 'Nothing would more disgust' Frederick 'than if he should be treated as a pecuniary dependent', Mitchell warned Bute. 'He will not easily forget; and the first opportunity that offers, he will not fail to take his revenge.'[6] Mitchell was right: Frederick railed against Bute's high-handed behaviour. The discovery that Bute was, at the same time, negotiating with the Russians in an attempt to limit Prussian control of the southern Baltic shores convinced Frederick that George III had thrust into office a minister who was willing, not simply to betray an alliance, but to conspire with his enemies. He strongly suspected that Bute's emissaries were also making advances to Britain's old ally, Maria Theresa. It was this clumsy diplomacy, rather than the protracted peace negotiations with the French and Austrians, that soured Anglo-Prussian relations for more than a generation.

Newcastle, perturbed by his Secretary of State's treatment of the irascible King of Prussia, left office on 26 May 1762, and the King invited Bute to head the government. The experiment of a prime minister dependent solely on royal favour proved a disaster. Bute achieved his immediate ambitions: the Peace of Paris, though denounced by the Pittites as an inadequate reward for a Seven Years War, ended the financial burden of campaigns in three continents and secured more colonial gains for Britain than any previous settlement; and Bute could claim that he set British foreign policy on an entirely new course. But he found his skills in the cynical game of high politics were limited and he resented hostile demonstrations both against the peace terms and against his Chancellor's proposal to introduce a cider tax. The first boo of autumn in a London street tempted him to resign, for he was much too thin-skinned for public office. The King persuaded him at least to see the winter out. He went, thankfully, on 8 April 1763. For three more years George III consulted Bute intermittently, until even he could sense the poverty of his old tutor's judgement.

'The King of England', Frederick the Great scornfully remarked, 'changes his ministers as he changes his shirts.' There was some truth in the gibe: the average life-span of a government in the first decade of George III's reign was twenty months; there were nine Secretaries of State for the Northern Department and seven for the Southern in these ten years. Short-lived administrations made continuity in British policy abroad impossible during the period that the European monarchies were beginning to build up professionalized foreign ministries. The twelve bumbling years of Lord North's premiership, from 1770 to 1782, lowered still further British prestige on the Continent. The radicalism of Wilkes, the Gordon Rioters in London,

the rebellious character of the Irish, the problems of India and of America
were all topics of only peripheral interest to Frederick the Great and the lesser
princes of Germany; it seemed as if British history was shaped to follow a
course different from anything in their experience. But the German states
possessed two indispensable necessities for a ruler trying to hold together the
first British Empire – men and horses. Both found their way to America as
the long dispute between the colonists and their governors turned to armed
rebellion.

'King George's German mercenaries' stand high in the list of villains in the
folk mythology of the American Revolution. When George Washington
crossed the Delaware in the Christmas snows of 1776 he surprised and
captured 1,000 Hessians at Trenton; and when, in the following August, John
Stark ambushed a column in the Green Mountains of Vermont, his victims
were principally Brunswickers. It was Frederick the Great who remarked that
George III seemed to believe he could buy and sell foreign troops like cattle. But
George was genuinely conscientious in observing 'the laws of Germany'; thus
he rejected proposals from Colonel Fawcett, his principal recruiting agent in
Brunswick and Hesse-Cassel, because 'in plain English' they 'are turning me
into a kidnapper, which I cannot think a very honourable occupation'.[7] He
was anxious for Fawcett to show tact on his mission. 'Though brave on shore',
George told Lord North in discussing Fawcett's task, 'Continental forces fear
the sea, and he must preach the little difficulties that will arise in their voyage.'
Remembering his German loyalties, he added, 'I should not do justice to my
Electoral troops if I did not express hope that they show the same zeal for my
person they have ever shown for my ancestors.'[8]

It would be a mistake to exaggerate the numbers of Germans who fought in
defence of George's possessions. At the peak of the war they may have formed
a third of the army. But Hanover also provided troops for duties outside
America, releasing British forces for service across the Atlantic. In July 1775
George informed North that as Elector he was willing to supply five battalions
to garrison Gibraltar and Minorca. 'By these conditions Great Britain obtains
a corps of 2,355 men much cheaper than if raised at home,' for the Elector of
Hanover would treat the King of England's Treasury magnanimously;
'Nothing but to be reimbursed all expenses', he explained.[9] He was anxious
that Hanoverian and Hessian troops who were stationed in England should
not be used to discipline demonstrators, a point on which North emphatically
agreed with his sovereign. On 8 June 1780 – the day on which the water supply
in Holborn was running alcohol because the Gordon rioters were sacking
distilleries – the King's sixteen-year-old son, Prince Frederick, wrote to the
Commander-in-Chief of the Horse Guards proposing to fit out a corps of
Germans and Swiss in London 'and to lead them myself against the
seditious'.[10] The offer was hastily turned down. Nothing could make the
German connection unpopular so swiftly as tales of armed foreigners buffeting

the anti-papists of the capital. Rumour would not stop to inquire if the rioters were sober or gin-soaked. It is not surprising that six months later a morning news-sheet announced, 'His Royal Highness Prince Frederick, His Majesty's second son, has left for the Continent.'[11]

By 1780 the familiar Guelph conflict of generations was again in full flood. The Prince of Wales – the future George IV – was a natural rebel who, as his father noted on his twelfth birthday, had 'a bad habit of not speaking the truth'. Now, six years later, the King complained of the regularity with which the 'public papers' were commenting on his love of dissipation. He imposed strictly regulated rules of conduct on his eldest son and, at the same time, decided to break up the close companionship between George and Frederick, twelve months his junior. The King thought highly of his second son, a soldierly young man, industrious and affectionate, who deserved to be saved from his elder brother's wayward influence. If he wished to be a soldier where better could he learn his profession than in Germany? He therefore set out for Colchester, Harwich and Hanover at Christmas 1780 with the rank of colonel.

Nursery rhymes recall Frederick as 'the grand old Duke of York who had ten thousand men' but it was not until November 1784 that an indulgent father created him Duke of York and Albany and Earl of Ulster. Yet by one of the old Germany's more charming constitutional anachronisms Frederick already enjoyed a certain status in Hanover: he came to the Electorate as Prince-Bishop of Osnabrück. To this dignity he had been raised by election at the age of six months when, in February 1764, it again became his family's turn in the rota to supply a ruler for the ecclesiastical principality. The episcopal mantle suited him as little as the Roman toga which envelops his sculpted figure on the Duke of York's column above London's West End. Frederick was, in fact, the last of the Prince-Bishops, for the ecclesiastical principalities were swept away in Napoleon's re-ordering of Germany; but when the blow fell he did not grieve unduly, for he had never taken his responsibilities in Osnabrück too seriously.

To the elderly officers whom his father sent as restraining advisers for the young Prince it seemed, indeed, as if Frederick took nothing too seriously; and Mirabeau, the 'enlightened' French cavalryman turned diplomat, complained that he hunted and drank too much and delighted in boorish horseplay.[12] But this was an unfair assessment. Frederick handled the prickly problems of German politics with remarkable dexterity during the six and a half years in which he remained on the Continent. At first he was fêted so exuberantly in Hanover and Osnabrück that it is not surprising if his head was turned. He was made especially welcome at the home of his uncle by marriage, the Duke of Brunswick, who had recently succeeded his father, a brother of the commander-in-chief of 'His Britannic Majesty's army in Germany' during the Seven Years War. Since the new Duke, too, was a veteran soldier, Prince

Frederick acquired a good grounding in the military sciences. He also struck up a friendship with his hoydenish cousin Caroline, whom he came to know all too well in later years as a sister-in-law.

The Duke thought sufficiently highly of the Prince to send him in the autumn to Potsdam, and for several years young Frederick attended his great namesake's manoeuvres and those interminable reviews of what was still rated as the finest army in Europe. By now the King of Prussia seemed to the younger officers of his army a soured, terrifying old man who would entertain them to a banquet in his vast Neues Palais and expect them to catch the quiet monotones of his voice and comment sensibly on whatever subject was passing through his sardonic mind. Thus when the nineteen-year-old Prince William – the future William IV – was invited to accompany his elder brother to Potsdam, Frederick the Great started to talk to him about Voltaire (of whom it is unlikely William had heard) and reprimanded him for not having read *Candide*. But the Duke of York was evidently a dutiful listener as well as a good military pupil; and at times the King took him into his confidence. In 1785, without realizing what he was doing, the young Duke promoted a recon-ciliation between his father's court and Potsdam and thus began to thaw the icy suspicion which had kept the two Kings at arm's length since Bute allowed the subsidy treaty to expire nearly a quarter of a century before.

In November 1780 Frederick the Great's old enemy, Maria Theresa, died in Vienna. Technically her son, Joseph II, had by then been associated with her sovereignty in the Austrian lands as co-Regent since his father's death fifteen years before. Joseph, who modelled himself on the King of Prussia, was a reformer by conviction and a methodical autocrat by character. So long as his mother lived, Joseph had to contain his desire to tidy up Austria's empire. But foreign princes who met him, even the Duke of York, were impressed by his determination and orderly mind. The German states feared that sooner or later he would sweep aside the counter-weights in the imperial constitution and tilt the balance in favour of the Habsburgs once more. His particular brainchild, a project for allowing the Elector of Bavaria to reign in Brussels while the Habsburgs absorbed Bavaria as compensation, induced Frederick the Great to seek the leadership of Germany as head of a 'League of Princes', pledged to uphold the traditional structure of the Empire. The Duke of York was pleased to commend the League by letter to the Elector of Hanover.

George III's attitude to his German possessions mellowed year by year. At the same time defeat in America and the prospect of a Whig government made him despondent, and in March 1783 he even drew up an abdication speech, ready to send to parliament: he would, he said, resign his royal crowns and 'retire to the care of my Electoral dominions, the original patrimony of my ancestors'.[13] The speech was never delivered, but its text was not destroyed. For so long as Germany was undisturbed, Hanover remained an idealized sanctuary for him, a happy little court to which he could escape, free from wavering politicians, parliamentary patronage and all the worrying imponderables of a general election. He therefore welcomed Frederick II's proposed League of Princes and gave it his warm support. Moreover, as Elector of Hanover, he was content to keep his British ministers informed of what he was doing. Why, he wondered, need he consult them about German matters which were primarily the concern of his Electorate? It was the type of argument his grandfather would use in dispute with the Duke of Newcastle at the beginning of Frederick the Great's reign. Now, at the end of it, the younger Pitt accepted George's distinction between royal responsibilities and electoral responsibilities without demur; Hanover was no longer a contentious issue in British politics.[14]

The League of Princes, and the hostility of France, made Joseph II abandon his favourite project of exchanging the Austrian Netherlands for Bavaria. It was therefore a diplomatic victory for the King of Prussia, the Elector of Hanover and for the familiar order within the Empire. But it was a victory which Frederick the Great had no opportunity to exploit. Throughout the winter of 1785 and 1786 his health deteriorated and he died at Potsdam in August 1786. He was succeeded by his nephew, Frederick William II, an indolent hedonist with no ideas of his own on policy. The new King retained many of his uncle's specialists in foreign affairs even if he was incapable of giving them clear directions for the course he wished to take. Nevertheless relations between Berlin, Hanover and London continued to improve and in April 1788 a defensive alliance was concluded between Britain, the Netherlands and Prussia which provided for collaboration to check Bourbon infiltration into the Low Countries. The triple alliance seemed a familiar gesture, recalling the days when Marlborough and the Dutch and German Protestants bolted the shutters against Louis XIV's France; but 1788 was not 1688, and when next year a gale rose fast in Paris the old allies were slow to fasten the rattling windows around her borders.

George III summoned the Duke of York home in the summer of 1787, but three of his brothers remained in the Electorate: the future Duke of Kent was learning soldiering on Lüneburg Heath; and the future Dukes of Cumberland and Sussex were studying intermittently at Göttingen. On his return to London Frederick found his father in indifferent health and his elder brother secretly (though not legally) married to the widowed Maria Fitzherbert; he also discovered that gaming tables were more plentiful than in Germany, if less personally rewarding. A year later George III suffered a total breakdown, at first physical but by early November leaving him mentally confused and liable at times to violent gusts of passion. For some weeks a regency headed by the Prince of Wales seemed imminent and the Whigs believed they stood on the threshold of office, for the Prince had never hidden his dislike of Pitt's moderate Tory administration or his enthusiastic support for Fox and his 'Buff and Blue' followers. Had a regency been established George III, so he later remarked, would on his recovery never have resumed sovereign authority within the British Isles but would have settled in Hanover. Pitt, however, skilfully delayed the passage of a Regency Bill through parliament, and in the last week of February 1789 the King was officially pronounced restored to health. There was to be no regency until 1811 and no Whig government for two decades after that.

The King's illness emphasized, particularly to Queen Charlotte, the need to ensure the line of succession to the throne. The Prince of Wales had frequently indicated he had no intention of marrying a foreign princess and there seemed no prospect he would have any legitimate heir. As far as he was concerned, the succession might safely be left to the eldest of his brothers. But Frederick, too, was in no hurry to marry and it was not until the early summer of 1791 that the joint pressure of his parents and his debtors inclined him to look for a wife and the improved revenue that would come to him as a married man. The Duke possessed, if not a romantic longing for a dream princess, at least a clear idea of where to find his wife. He set out again for Germany, travelled to Berlin and at Michaelmas 1791 married the King of Prussia's daughter, Frederica, in the palace of Charlottenburg. She was almost four years his junior; he had met her in Berlin shortly after her father's accession and found her intelligent, modest and easy-tempered. No one could say she was a beauty, although she was to make tiny feet fashionable when she reached England; but the Duke told his elder brother that, having met her again after four years of separation, he had 'grown more attracted to her' and was, indeed, 'over head and ears in love'.[15]

So attentive was the bridegroom for his wife's comfort that, to spare her the long North Sea crossing to England, he headed for Calais and the Channel coast. But in the autumn of 1791, four months after Louis XVI's abortive flight to Varennes, to seek a passage across northern France in a carriage with royal arms on its panels was the height of folly. As they passed through Lille, a hot-tempered crowd surrounded them and would not allow them to continue to the coast until the offending insignia were removed. By the end of the third week in November the Duke and Duchess were safely in London, where they were wedded a second time at the 'Queen's House' (not yet known as Buckingham Palace). The royal marriage was popular in the newspapers; and the Duke was gratified to find that parliament increased his income by more than fifty per cent to £70,000 a year. Allowing for changes in the value of money, this sum is equivalent to over a million pounds by today's reckoning, a far more generous financial arrangement than is enjoyed in the 1980s by any beneficiary from the Civil List except the sovereign.

Fifteen months after the London marriage celebrations the Duke left England again. George III – like his grandfather after Dettingen – insisted that his favourite son should be given command of the army Pitt was raising to co-operate with Austria in resisting revolutionary France. The appointment was unpopular: Frederick of York was a Major-General of twenty-nine, well-schooled in warfare from manoeuvres in Silesia but without battle experience; the older veterans among his brother officers resented his rapid advancement. Yet perhaps they should have felt relief at being passed over; for the Flanders Front in 1793–4 was a natural graveyard of military reputations. The Duke was given the task of besieging Dunkirk with an army of slightly more than 6,000 British troops, twice as many Hanoverians, 15,000 Dutch, a promissory note for 8,000 hired Hessians, and not a single siege gun. He was defeated at Hondschoote in September 1793 and at Tourcoing the following May, where he narrowly escaped capture. Some six weeks later, on 5 July 1794, the Duke attended an inter-allied Council of War at a village twelve miles south of Brussels. The Duke suggested to the Austrian commander-in-chief that a ridge a mile south of the village offered an ideal position for the British, Austrians, Hanoverians, Hessians and Dutch to seek to stem the French advance. But the allies moved too slowly: the Austrians retreated eastwards, the Duke's army falling back towards the Scheldt and the lower Meuse. There was, however, nothing wrong with Frederick of York's strategic sense: for the locals called their village 'Waterloo'; the ridge was marked Mont St Jean on the maps; and a Lieutenant-Colonel Wellesley, then commanding the Thirty-Third Foot at Antwerp, was to chose it twenty-one years later as the defensive pivot of his most famous battle.[16]

The Duke of York settled down to a winter war among the ice-bound polders of the Netherlands. No one seriously doubted his courage, nor that of two of his brothers, the future Dukes of Cumberland and Cambridge, both of whom were slightly wounded while serving with the Hanoverian troops. But there was a growing conviction at Westminster that the inexperience of the royal commander-in-chief contributed to allied disasters. York was recalled to England in December 1794.[17] Four months later what was left of the British force was evacuated from Bremen, while the Hanoverians were left to follow the example of Prussia and Holland and seek terms from the French Republic. It was a humiliating episode in the tangled history of British involvement in Continental affairs. There were accusations of bad faith all round. The German Princes felt deserted and the connection between Hanover and London was left weaker than at any time since the death of Queen Anne.

It was during this disastrous winter of 1794–5 that the Prince of Wales decided he would, after all, take a foreign princess as his wife and cut his links with Maria Fitzherbert. The Earl of Malmesbury (who, as Sir James Harris, had served in Berlin successfully as a diplomat) was sent to Brunswick to negotiate the Prince's marriage with his first cousin, Caroline, the youngest daughter of the Princess Augusta whose birth in 1737 had led to the great breach between Frederick of Wales and his parents. Queen Charlotte, who had a deep-rooted Mecklenburg antipathy to the Brunswicks, did not approve of the proposed marriage but the King could see nothing against it, even though Caroline was not only his niece but also a niece of the three Brunswick-Wolfenbüttel princesses for whom, on hearsay, he professed so marked a distaste in his youth. Caroline was, indeed, an odd choice for a fastidious prince to have made. Malmesbury could have listed a host of faults in the twenty-four-year-old woman long before he left Brunswick for home:[18] she was gauche and tactless; and even her father, the soldier-duke who shaped Frederick of York's military career ten years before, was afraid of the impression his daughter would create in London. Yet no doubts crept into Malmesbury's reports: he was told to arrange the marriage and bring the bride safely across the North Sea, travelling well out of reach of French marauders; and this task he accomplished. Caroline arrived in England on 5 April 1795: that day, at Basle, Frederick William II made peace with the French regicides and thereby took Prussia, and his North German client states, out of western Europe's affairs for eleven momentous years. All in all, the spring of 1795 was a poor time for Anglo-German dynastic nuptials.

Predictably the Prince of Wales was disappointed with his bride and drunk throughout the wedding ceremony. He was disappointed, too, with Pitt for not persuading parliament to settle his outstanding debts. Within a few months, the mutual repugnance the Prince and Princess felt for each other was common knowledge in London. Yet, in one sense, it was a more successful marriage than the Duke of York's: a daughter, named Charlotte after the Queen, was born in January 1796. The Princess was the only grandchild whom George III ever knew, for none of his other fourteen sons or daughters had legitimate children until long after the thread of reason snapped in their father's senile mind. Throughout her life Charlotte stood second in succession to the crown of the United Kingdom, as England, Wales, Scotland and Ireland were collectively known from 1801 onwards. But Charlotte could never succeed to her grandfather's Hanoverian titles, for the Electorate accepted the clauses in the old Frankish *Lex Salica* which declared that women had no rights of succession since they could not inherit land. Hanover would therefore pass eventually to an uncle or male cousin.

But would there still be an Electorate of Hanover for the next generation to inherit? It seemed unlikely. The Treaty of Campo Formio, which in October 1797 ended Austrian participation in the War of the First Coalition, provided for a congress to meet at Rastatt, where the future of the German lands would be discussed. Before the Congress opened, General Bonaparte made a swift visit to Rastatt to let the German rulers hear his views: no more ecclesiastical Electors, and increased power for those intermediate dynasties who, like Hesse-Cassel and Württemberg, had made peace with the French; but there was little hope of survival for the Electorate whose ruler was also sovereign of his most persistent enemy. Yet, as the Rastatt Congress dragged on through fifteen months of inconclusive diplomacy, it became hard to see whether

Hanover was menaced more by George's foes or by his friends. Frederick William III, who succeeded his father as King of Prussia in December 1797 on the eve of the Congress, was committed to protecting Hanover's neutrality, but the Prussians coveted George's German lands and made no secret of their ambitions. At the beginning of 1801 Prussia occupied Hanover, allegedly to forestall a French invasion. George's youngest surviving son, Adolphus, Duke of Cambridge, was at the time in Hanover. He protested in person to Frederick William III and was assured that Prussia had no intention of annexing his father's lands. He wished to protect the city – which was, as it happened, the birthplace of his wife, Prussia's valiant Queen Louise. In March 1802, when the Treaty of Amiens brought a prospect of peace in the long Anglo-French conflict the Prussian troops were, indeed, withdrawn. The Hanoverians hastily made public professions of their total neutrality.

The 'Peace of Amiens' proved no more than a fourteen-month interlude of non-belligerency. When war was renewed, Napoleon concentrated his 'Army of England' around Boulogne, and for the next three summers there was a risk of cross-Channel invasion if the French could only 'be masters of the Straits for six hours'. The threat stimulated a mood of patriotic loyalty throughout the United Kingdom. The King refused the Prince of Wales's request to be given a military command but assured him that, if invasion came, father and son would meet the French in battle together, in Kent or Essex. Meanwhile the Duke of York, as Commander-in-Chief from 1795 to 1809, was completing reforms in army administration initiated by his great-uncle, William of Cumberland, half a century before. No one doubted the warlike spirit of the House of Hanover, only at times its good sense.

These virtues and faults were well exemplified in the conduct of the young Duke of Cambridge, who had remained in Hanover during the Prussian occupation. Renewal of the war induced Napoleon, in May 1803, to order the immediate occupation of the Electorate, despite its neutral status. The Hanoverians showed little will to fight an isolated campaign against General Mortier's invaders and the Hanoverian commander, General Walmoden – an illegitimate son of George II – recommended an early capitulation, on honourable terms. The Duke of Cambridge was astonished at such pusillanimity. 'Rest assured that I will sacrifice my blood and life for a country to which I am so much attached,' he declared; and Walmoden had difficulty in preventing him from launching a reckless attack on the French. The Duke was hustled out of Cuxhaven before Mortier's men closed in on the port.[19]

Napoleon used Hanover as a bait to entice Frederick William III away from the new coalition which the younger Pitt was subsidizing to curb French imperial power. At first Prussia refused the offer and prepared to enter the war as an ally of Russia and Austria. Napoleon's victory at Austerlitz made Frederick William modify his policy. He was told that if he ceded the French two small enclaves, Prussia could receive Hanover in exchange. The offer seemed irresistible. France's tricolour was lowered and the Prussian flag rung up in Hanover at the end of February 1806. But Prussia had blundered: George III was slow to forgive Frederick William; and the other German states saw him as an arch-appeaser, unable and unwilling to protect them against France. In becoming a beneficiary of Napoleon's latest exercise in map-making, Prussia hastened the disappearance of the old Germany.

The enormity of Prussia's error became clear before the coming of autumn. For 1806 was the year of transformation in Germany. On 7 July it was announced in Paris that Napoleon had consented to become 'Protector' of a Confederation of the Rhine, which would include sixteen of the states in the old 'Holy Roman Empire of the German Nation', among them Bavaria, Württemberg, Hesse-Darmstadt and Baden. Four weeks later Francis I, who had assumed the title 'Emperor of Austria' in April 1804, abdicated as Holy Roman Emperor because in the changed order of Europe he found it impossible to fulfil his obligations to Germany as a whole. Thus was swept away an institution which, in varying forms, had survived for a thousand years; and the Emperor in Paris replaced the Emperor in Vienna as effective arbiter of Germany's destiny.

George III, as Elector of Hanover, refused to recognize the dissolution of the old Empire, and he was supported by his British ministers, so long as the war continued against Napoleon. There was no reason why the abdication of an emperor should mean the extinction of the body over which he was elected to rule. But the old Empire was too cumbersome a relic to win many champions; significantly, neither the basic constitutional act of the Rhine Confederation nor Emperor Francis's Instrument of Abdication use the phrase 'Holy Roman Empire' but refer to it as the 'German Empire' (*Deutsches Reich*).

In Berlin, the Prussian reaction to these changes was swift and desperate. Rather than recognize French hegemony in Germany, Frederick William III resolved on war. On 26 September 1806 Prussia demanded that all French troops should retire from Germany east of the Rhine. Napoleon's response was a march across Saxony towards Berlin. On 14 October the Prussian army was virtually destroyed in two battles fought within fifteen miles of each other, at Jena and Auerstädt. The septuagenarian Duke of Brunswick, commanding Prussia's largest army, was wounded at Auerstädt and died a month later at Altona. By then all northern Germany was overrun, apart from isolated garrisons resisting in Pomerania, Silesia and East Prussia.

These victories of Napoleon finally snapped the German connection as it had existed in the eighteenth century. From 1807 to 1813 Prussia survived as a French satellite state and Hanover was absorbed in the Kingdom of Westphalia, a Napoleonic improvisation ruled by Jerome Bonaparte, with his capital at Cassel. Yet the dynastic union was still of value to George III. For, as acknowledged sovereign of Hanover, he could maintain diplomatic contact with Austria and Prussia. Count Münster, head of his Hanoverian Chancery in London, sent messages to and from the courts of Berlin and Vienna despite the official severance of their relations with Britain, and these helped prepare for the 'War of Liberation' which, in the course of 1813, turned northern Germany against the French. At the end of the year the Duke of Cambridge was welcomed back in Hanover as his father's representative. The subsequent peace settlement recognized Hanover as a Kingdom within the German Confederation.

George III was duly proclaimed King of Hanover on 12 October 1814. The new title meant nothing to him. Two years before, as the royal family at Windsor quietly celebrated the fiftieth anniversary of his accession, he became agitatedly loquacious, with a 'dreadful excitement in his countenance'. The 'royal malady', which assailed the King so dramatically in the winter of 1788–9, had returned; and at seventy-two there seemed little prospect of recovery. By Christmas it was thought George was dying, but within a month he was walking on the North Terrace, wrapped up against the clawing January winds. His doctors, drawing fine distinctions for the benefit of select committees from parliament, insisted that he was not insane but mentally deranged, subject to delusions which would pass from time to time. But all realized his reign was over. On 5 February 1811 the Prince of Wales was sworn in as Regent of the United Kingdom before the Privy Council, gathered at Carlton House. It was 'Prinny' who presided over the victory revels of 1814 and marked the centenary of the accession of the House of Hanover by staging a mammoth popular fête in London's Green Park. George III, a white-bearded Lear drifting into a world of his own, outlived his Queen, the grandchild he knew, and his fourth son, Edward of Kent. It was said that, in his delusions, he even assumed he had outlived himself.[20] No one around him could tell where his spirit wandered in those rare moments when light flickered through the darkness of oblivion. He could still strike the keys of his harpsichord as late as the autumn of 1819. Mercifully, four months later, the light was extinguished altogether.

The House of Coburg
(ruling dukes in bold type)

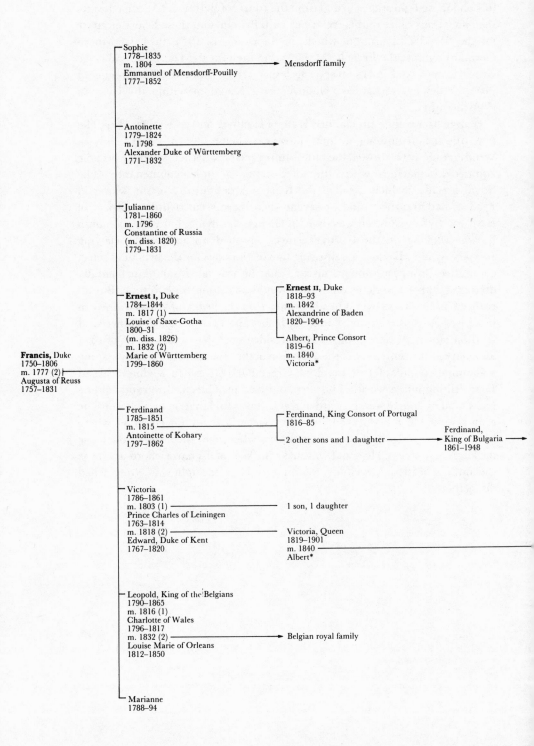

Sophie
1778–1835
m. 1804 ⟶ Mensdorff family
Emmanuel of Mensdorff-Pouilly
1777–1852

Antoinette
1779–1824
m. 1798 ⟶

Julianne
1781–1860
m. 1796
Constantine of Russia
(m. diss. 1820)
1779–1831

Ernest I, Duke
1784–1844
m. 1817 (1) ———
Louise of Saxe-Gotha
1800–31
(m. diss. 1826)
m. 1832 (2)
Marie of Württemberg
1799–1860

Ernest II, Duke
1818–93
m. 1842
Alexandrine of Baden
1820–1904

Albert, Prince Consort
1819–61
m. 1840
Victoria*

Francis, Duke
1750–1806
m. 1777 (2)
Augusta of Reuss
1757–1831

Ferdinand
1785–1851
m. 1815 ———
Antoinette of Kohary
1797–1862

Ferdinand, King Consort of Portugal
1816–85

2 other sons and 1 daughter ———
Ferdinand,
King of Bulgaria ⟶
1861–1948

Victoria
1786–1861
m. 1803 (1) ——————— 1 son, 1 daughter
Prince Charles of Leiningen
1763–1814
m. 1818 (2) ———
Edward, Duke of Kent
1767–1820

Victoria, Queen
1819–1901
m. 1840 ———
Albert*

Leopold, King of the Belgians
1790–1865
m. 1816 (1)
Charlotte of Wales
1796–1817
m. 1832 (2) ⟶ Belgian royal family
Louise Marie of Orleans
1812–1850

Marianne
1788–94

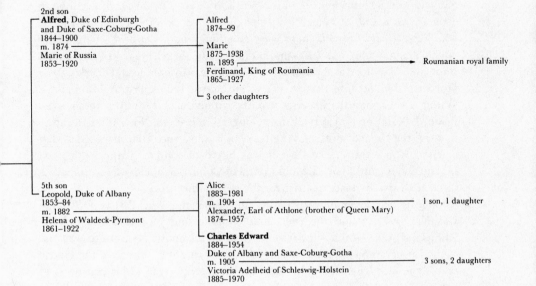

2nd son
Alfred, Duke of Edinburgh
and Duke of Saxe-Coburg-Gotha
1844–1900
m. 1874
Marie of Russia
1853–1920

Alfred
1874–99

Marie
1875–1938
m. 1893
Ferdinand, King of Roumania
1865–1927

→ Roumanian royal family

3 other daughters

5th son
Leopold, Duke of Albany
1853–84
m. 1882
Helena of Waldeck-Pyrmont
1861–1922

Alice
1883–1981
m. 1904
Alexander, Earl of Athlone (brother of Queen Mary)
1874–1957

1 son, 1 daughter

Charles Edward
1884–1954
Duke of Albany and Saxe-Coburg-Gotha
m. 1905
Victoria Adelheid of Schleswig-Holstein
1885–1970

3 sons, 2 daughters

CHAPTER SIX

⨎ Coburg ⨎

On 6 June 1814 the cliffs of Dover echoed the boom of ceremonial salutes from warships and the cannon of the castle; HMS *Impregnable*, with the Duke of Clarence in command, was bringing the Tsar of Russia, the King of Prussia and a host of other distinguished visitors across from Boulogne to share Britain's celebration of a victorious peace. An imperial and royal visitation on such a scale was a novelty and, over the following three weeks, curious crowds flocked to see the foreign rulers and their military commanders. Tsar Alexander stole the show. By contrast Frederick William III of Prussia, a dull widower in his mid-forties, aroused little interest, while onlookers scarcely noticed his dutiful soldier son, Prince William, a veteran of seventeen who in 1871 was to become the first German Emperor. London was so crowded with old campaigners in exotic uniforms that it became hard to spot princes with a future from princes with a past.

Yet one staid and sober member of the Tsar's suite soon caught the eye of the court. Prince Leopold, third son of the reigning Prince of Saxe-Coburg-Saalfeld, was a handsome and intelligent Lutheran of twenty-three. Although economy made him seek cheap lodgings over a grocer's shop at 21, Marylebone High Street, there was something about Leopold's personality which singled him out in fashionable society. Seven years back he had impressed Napoleon at the Tuileries, the Empress Josephine and her daughter Hortense spoiling him that spring when he was their guest at Malmaison. Within twelve months he attracted the attention of Tsar Alexander, who beamed affably on him at the Erfurt Congress of Princes. Now, at midsummer in 1814, the Duke of York and the Duke of Kent seemed well-disposed and at Carlton House the Prince Regent was heard to commend him as 'a most honourable young man'. Leopold of Saxe-Coburg-Saalfeld was to remain a force in British dynastic politics for the next half century.[1]

Coburg was a small principality in Thuringia, lying between Roman Catholic Bavaria and the even smaller dukedoms of Franconia and the Rhineland. Like Gotha – the home of George III's mother – Coburg was one of the Lutheran Saxon duchies ruled by the 'Ernestine' branch of the House of Wettin. But when Leopold was born in December 1790 his prospects of worldly success looked poor: he was the eighth child of the heir to a duchy whose ruler was grossly extravagant. Materially the outlook remained bleak during his boyhood, for Leopold's father, Francis Frederick, succeeded to the ducal dignities in September 1800 only to find his authority challenged throughout a short reign by the pretensions of Bonapartist France. When Francis Frederick died, ten days before his son's sixteenth birthday, Coburg was in French hands and seemed certain to lose its independent sovereignty.

But in 1777 Francis Frederick had had the good sense to marry one of those intelligent and formidable princesses who, over the centuries, so often strengthened the life-blood of German dynasticism when it was running thin. As a young woman Augusta of Reuss-Ebersdorf impressed Catherine the Great in St Petersburg, ensuring Russian protection for her husband's scattered territories by marrying off her third daughter to the Grand Duke Constantine. In widowhood Augusta was not too proud to importune Napoleon; and as a vigorous septuagenarian she still retained such character that forty years later Queen Victoria vividly recalled from nursery days her grandmother's 'almost masculine mind, accompanied by great tenderness of heart and extreme love for nature'.[2] From 1806 to 1844 Coburg was ruled by Duke Ernest I, her eldest son and Leopold's brother, but for twenty-five of those thirty-eight years the wisest of Ernest's counsellors in Coburg was his mother.

It is hardly surprising that Leopold, Augusta's youngest surviving child, was her favourite: he was good-looking, courageous and politically astute. Even before his fifteenth birthday he reported to Russian field headquarters in Moravia, Catherine the Great having gazetted him among noble cadets in a crack Guards regiment when he was five. But the battle of Austerlitz swung the war in France's favour and Leopold returned to Thuringia. He assisted his eldest brother in diplomatic encounters with Napoleon and Talleyrand in Paris and at Erfurt, a taxing apprenticeship in statecraft. Briefly Leopold gave the impression he would like to attend Napoleon as a personal aide-de-camp, but the Emperor was suspicious of a German prince with close connections in St Petersburg, and by the spring of 1813 he was serving with the Russian cavalry in Silesia and Saxony. He fought against the French at Lützen and Bautzen, made himself known to Metternich during the negotiations which preceded Austria's entry into the war, gained Russian and Austrian decorations for valour at the battle of Kulm, played a modest role in the 'battle of the nations' at Leipzig and made certain he rode at the head of his Russian regiment when it followed the Tsar triumphantly into Paris on 31 March 1814. Ten weeks later he was in London eager, so he told the Prince Regent, 'to see a country which for a long time I have wished to come to know'. He remained attached to Alexander's suite, but merrymaking postponed all serious discussion of German affairs and in three weeks he had only one brief audience with the Tsar.

Soon after his arrival in London, the Tsar's sister, Grand Duchess Catherine, presented Leopold to Princess Charlotte, the Regent's daughter, at one of the grand receptions for visiting dignitaries. It was a formal encounter,

unremarkable in either of their memories. In Paris, before setting out for
Boulogne and Dover, Leopold had discussed with his brother, Duke Ernest,
the possibility of paying court to Charlotte. Neither Coburger rated Leopold's
chances highly. It was well known that for several months the Regent had been
pressing Charlotte to accept marriage with William of Orange, a Dutch Prince
who had fought under Wellington in the Peninsula. Although a marriage
contract was drawn up in the spring of 1814 Charlotte found her 'Young
Frog' unattractive. She told her father that it was not right for an heiress
presumptive to the British throne to live in Holland; and the Whig parliamentary Opposition, always ready to embarrass the Regent, agreed with
her.

Charlotte's reluctance to marry William of Orange hardened during the
visit of the foreign princes. She was attracted by other, more handsome suitors
and she saw for herself the flaws in Orange's character. Every gossip in
London society that summer had tales of his drunken escapades, especially
when the princes returned from Ascot Races, on 10 June. Six days after Ascot,
Charlotte wrote to Orange informing him that she considered the engagement
at an end.

Her father, however, refused to give up a marriage project which his
ministers insisted would increase British influence in the Low Countries. Over
the following three weeks the Regent persistently urged Charlotte to accept
Dutch William. His correspondence shows he still had hopes his daughter
would change her mind eight months later. But Charlotte was too self-willed to
give way meekly to a father's wishes. She enjoyed the company of princes who
paid courtesy calls at Warwick House: the King of Prussia's nephew, Prince
Frederick, and his cousin, Prince Augustus; and the King of Württemberg's
nephew, Prince Paul. The Regent thought all three princes were ambitious
rakes. He particularly disapproved of Augustus, who twice secretly met
Charlotte at her London home, Warwick House, which was virtually an
annexe of her father's residence, Carlton House.

Character and experience inclined the Coburg Prince to greater circumspection, although gossips bandied around Leopold's name soon after
the Princess broke with Orange. On 10 July he gave an account of his first
private meeting with the Princess in a letter to her father, seeking to dispel
rumours that he had stiffened Charlotte's opposition to the Orange marriage.
He claims that he met Charlotte on the afternoon of Tuesday, 21 June,
escorting her to her carriage in Albemarle Street after she had called on the
Tsar's sister, Grand Duchess Catherine. According to Leopold, Princess
Charlotte chided him for having avoided her company. 'You have not been at
all polite, for not once have you visited me,' she said; and she hoped that, if he
were planning to stay on in London, he would in future be more polite.
Leopold says that he then received permission from the Tsar to remain in
London and that, on the following Tuesday afternoon, he dutifully presented

himself to Charlotte at Warwick House. The Regent was repeatedly assured that Leopold had at no time spoken to his daughter about 'an arrangement in the future'. It was, commented the Regent to Charlotte's principal chaperone, 'a letter which perfectly justified himself'.[3] So indeed, as Prinny was to discover over the years, did most of Leopold's letters.

Was this self-righteous tale disingenuous? Did Leopold really see more of Charlotte during these few weeks? The evidence is inconclusive. The Princess's chaperone, Cornelia Knight, a middle-aged confidante of the Queen, says that Leopold 'paid many compliments to Princess Charlotte' on his first visit to Warwick House but that she 'only received him with civility'. 'When we drove in the Park he would ride near the carriage and endeavour to be noticed,' she wrote; adding cryptically, 'There were many reasons why this matter was by no means agreeable to Princess Charlotte.' The Princess seems to have been displeased at news of his letter to her father. But there is no doubt that Leopold had decided to make a bid for the English marriage connection when, on 21 June, he received the Tsar's permission to stay on in London after Alexander and his sister returned to the Continent. Leopold wrote to Duke Ernest, explaining that he had only decided to remain in England 'after much hesitation and after certain very singular events made me glimpse the possibility, even the probability, of realizing the project of which we spoke in Paris'. He still thought the Regent's partiality for Orange left his chances 'very poor' but, he added, 'I am resolved to go on to the end, and only to leave when all my hopes have been destroyed.'[4]

Despite these fine sentiments he set off for Coburg on 14 July with nothing settled. The death of his brother-in-law, the Prince of Leiningen, on 4 July, had left Leopold's favourite sister, Victoria, with a young son and daughter in need of an uncle's care. But the timing of Leopold's departure is significant. Two days previously Charlotte's tearful quarrels with her father reached a dramatic climax: the Princess stormed angrily out of Warwick House, hailed a hackney cab and hurried to consult the Whig lawyer, Henry Brougham, over her right not to be forced into marriage with Orange. Public sympathy was, as ever, on Charlotte's side and when her father banished her to Cranbourne Lodge, Windsor, the Regent's political enemies had no difficulty in representing him as a heartless bully. In reality he was fond of his daughter and concerned for her health and her safety. When, on Christmas Day, Charlotte casually remarked to the Regent and his sister Mary that her mother had, from time to time, left her in a locked bedroom with a Light Dragoon officer who was thought to be the Duke of York's bastard, it was decided that marriage to a European prince was desirable, with or without political advantages. 'God knows what would have become of me if he had not behaved with so much respect to me,' the Princess reflected, with an innocence too disarming to be true.[5]

Charlotte herself seems momentarily this Christmas to have held high hopes of Prince Frederick of Prussia. But soon after the turn of the year he disappointed her, and on 23 January 1815 she was writing to her friend, Margaret Mercer Elphinstone, in resigned tones of Leopold as a suitor: 'After all if I end by marrying Prince L., I marry the *best* of all those I *have seen*, and that is some satisfaction.' A few weeks later Charlotte showed a little more enthusiasm: 'I don't at all see why in the *end*, when once tacked to him, that I should not be very comfortable and comparatively happy,' she told Margaret.[6] Her father was, however, cautious and mistrustful. For, unlike Charlotte's other suitors, Leopold had shown some interest in Westminster politics while he was in London, and the Regent was disturbed to hear he had become friendly with the eccentric Whig lawyer, Lord Lauderdale. But Leopold had two champions among Prinny's brothers. His discreet charm and pleasing social deference had favourably impressed the Dukes of York and Kent the previous summer. York already held the Coburg family in high esteem, having served in Flanders under 'old Coburg', Leopold's distinguished cousin, Prince Frederick Josias (who died early in the New Year). Kent, who retained a number of Whig friends, was strongly in favour of his niece's marriage to Leopold. It was Kent who, during the Congress of Vienna, ensured that a trickle of letters reached Leopold from Charlotte. By the end of January 1815 his chances of becoming Prince Consort of Great Britain were far better than when he had first discussed the project with Duke Ernest in Paris.

Yet it was by no means clear if Leopold still sought an English marriage alliance. He was far from being a dull nonentity like George of Denmark, the last consort of a British queen. The Vienna Congress sharpened his intelligence and broadened his understanding of Continental politics. The brothers, Ernest and Leopold, were in Vienna from October to March, seeking to enhance Saxe-Coburg's status and ensure that any re-tracing of German state boundaries brought cohesion to the Duke's scattered territories. But it was Leopold rather than Ernest who handled the delicate diplomatic negotiations, pressing Tsar Alexander to show lenience towards the King of Saxony (who had remained loyal to Napoleon inexpediently long) and opposing the enlargement of Prussia on Coburg's Saxon borders. Even if Metternich was suspicious of Leopold's friendship with the Emperor of Austria's allegedly liberal brother, Archduke John, he was impressed by his quiet persistence over the Saxon Question. So, too, was Castlereagh, the British Foreign Secretary. By his reckoning there was much to say for a German Protestant Prince who was hostile to Prussia, sympathetic to the Habsburgs and politically mistrustful of Russia. By the time Castlereagh returned to London from Vienna in February 1815 he, too, favoured a Coburg dynastic link. Hanover and Coburg together would be useful counter-weights within the new German Confederation, tipping the balance, if needed, against Austria or Prussia or even Bavaria.

Indirectly, Napoleon's Hundred Days settled Leopold's personal fate by destroying the influential position which he had won for himself at the Congress. In the campaign he once more commanded a cavalry division in the Tsar's army; but he saw no action, for Waterloo was the greatest of joint Anglo-Prussian victories. It was fought and won without Russian aid. When Leopold returned to Paris to resume discussions over Germany's future he found the Prussian mood harder than in Vienna, largely because of Blücher's triumphs in this last campaign. At Vienna the Prussians had agreed to exchange districts along their Franconian frontier for Coburg enclaves on the Rhine. Now nothing more was heard of the proposal. Leopold was exasperated at this first failure of his diplomatic career. From Paris he went back to his homeland and, early in the New Year, travelled to Berlin in the hopes of putting further pressure on Prussia. There, late in January 1816, a King's Messenger sent on from Coburg brought an invitation from the Prince Regent to visit England as soon as possible. Leopold was left in no doubt over the reason for the summons. It was welcome after all the frustration of German mini-diplomacy.

A gently ironical note from Charlotte to her father in late December had informed him that 'I no longer hesitate in declaring my partiality in favour of the Prince of Coburg – assuring you no one will be more steady or consistent in this the present and last engagement than myself.'[7] But family tension over Christmas and a subsequent attack of gout delayed the Regent's invitation to Leopold. Perhaps, too, he wished to test his daughter's resolution. Charlotte, however, had indeed made up her mind. 'I consider myself as much German as English,' she told the Austrian ambassador at Brighton on the eve of her twentieth birthday, the first occasion upon which she had been a guest in her father's Royal Pavilion for eleven years. When, at the end of the first week of February, news came that Leopold was setting out for England, Charlotte visited the Queen at Windsor 'with the happiest face imaginable'. He arrived in London a fortnight later and was taken to Brighton by Castlereagh on 23 February, finding his prospective father-in-law so gout-ridden that he could only move down the long corridors of the Pavilion in a wheeled chair. Soon Charlotte, too, came to Brighton and the courtship proceeded, decorously. Within a week the marriage contract was ready; within another month Leopold was a British subject and a General in George III's army. The wedding took place at Carlton House on the evening of 2 May, with all the splendour in which Prinny delighted. When Leopold repeated the ritual phrase, 'With all my worldly goods I thee endow', his bride tittered with laughter.[8]

The marriage, originally a calculated act of political convenience, soon became a love-match. It was extremely popular, partly because people believed Charlotte had chosen a husband of whom her much-criticized father did not approve. Parliament voted the couple £60,000 a year with 'unanimous approbation', together with a capital sum of the same amount to establish themselves in a manner 'suitable to their rank and station'. This generous gesture included provision for an annuity of £50,000 to Leopold should he be left a widower. In London the royal couple were given Marlborough House, and Claremont House, a Palladian mansion near Esher in Surrey, was also settled on them. Hardly a murmur was heard in the Commons at such expenditure. Leopold had his critics at court: there were murmurings about a 'damned humbug' from the Duke of Clarence's illegitimate offspring; the Duke of Cumberland detested him; and it was his father-in-law who nicknamed Leopold the *Marquis Peu-à-Peu*. But, for most Londoners, bride and bridegroom were the darlings of the summer. George Dawe painted flattering portraits, soon available as cheap prints; and the Coburgs encouraged publication of a book by Frederic Stoberl to enable the British reading public to discover the history of an 'unknown' German duchy and its dynasty. The librarian of Carlton House, writing on behalf of the Regent to thank Jane Austen for the dedication of *Emma*, suggested that 'perhaps when you again appear in print you may choose to dedicate your volumes to Prince Leopold; any historical romance illustrative of the history of the august House of Coburg would just now be very interesting'. 'I am fully sensible that an historical romance founded on the House of Saxe-Coburg might be much more to the purpose of profit or popularity than such pictures of domestic life in country villages as I deal in', Jane Austen replied, but she added, 'I could no more write a romance than an epic poem'. Fortunately instead there next appeared in print *Persuasion*.[9]

The librarian, the Reverend James Clarke, had sound personal motives for his suggestion: the Regent had just appointed him principal English secretary to His Serene Highness. Leopold, however, possessed a far wiser personal adviser than this former naval chaplain. Christian Stockmar, the son of a lawyer of Swedish descent, was born in Coburg three years earlier than Leopold. He was educated at the famous Coburg Gymnasium, across the road from the ducal Ehrenburg Palace, and studied medicine at Würzburg and Jena before returning to his birthplace, where he practised as a physician. In the winter of 1812–13 he established a military hospital at Coburg, but it was not until the beginning of 1814 that Leopold met him, and by then he was attached to a field hospital at Worms. The Prince was told of an obstinate Coburger who, against the wishes of the senior medical officer, wished to serve all the sick and wounded alike rather than give priority to the allied soldiers over their French enemies. Leopold spoke to Stockmar and was deeply impressed by the warm humanity with which he tempered his conviction of the need for a unified and liberal Germany. Later Leopold discovered that he was an Anglophile, although the Britain Stockmar admired was an idealized community cherishing Locke's beliefs in compromise and ordered freedom with Milton's puritan fervour. It says much for Stockmar's faith in British traditions that when, in March 1816, Leopold invited him to London as his personal physician, he was far from disillusioned by what he saw around him at court and in the capital. Beneath the light-hearted magnificence of Regency England Stockmar sensed the residue of moral responsibility from which a continuing society might mould the destiny of a liberalized monarchical Europe. Nobody before him had brought such a sense of mission to the forging of links between the dynasties of Britain and Germany.

Stockmar became Leopold's principal personal adviser, a post he held for fifteen years. Charlotte came to trust 'Stocky' who, in his turn, realized her need for a husband to steady her self-control and allay her sense of insecurity. Leopold handled his emotional young wife well, even though she suffered two miscarriages during their first year of married life. 'We have a mutual confidence and harmony which it would be very difficult for any evil-disposed person to disturb,' Leopold wrote to the Archduke John in September. So happy was Charlotte that, with her husband's backing, she began to encourage her uncle, the Duke of Kent, to seek a Coburg bride. Leopold, as he later told Queen Victoria, looked upon Kent as 'the chief promoter' of his own marriage because he had safeguarded the secret correspondence between his niece and her eventual husband during the difficult months when the Regent was still backing William of Orange. For Kent to marry Leopold's widowed sister, Victoria of Leiningen, would have delighted the young couple at Claremont. The Duke, who was approaching fifty, travelled to Amorbach, near Darmstadt, Victoria's principal residence, in late August 1816. He admired Victoria's charming manners, expressed delight at an evening 'concert of wind instruments', and sent the Princess a letter proposing marriage. To his surprise, she turned him down, for she was uneasy over the guardianship of her son and daughter. Puzzled, but not particularly dismayed, Kent returned to England. He left a good impression at Amorbach, Leopold tactfully assured him.[10]

Charlotte, who like her grandfather never once left England, maintained a lively correspondence with her sister-in-law at Amorbach. She praised Leopold, she spoke well of the Duke of Kent, she wrote excitedly of her coming confinement. Such harmony reigned at Claremont that Stockmar believed he was counsellor to the happiest of unions. But the idyll ended with tragic abruptness on 6 November 1817: Charlotte died from convulsions four hours after she was delivered of a still-born son. She had been married for a mere 553 days.

Charlotte's death was a personal disaster for Leopold, scarring his personality. He had been a solemn and serious young man with deep feelings which his wife alone could fire. His first instinct was to retire to his homeland, taking up the threads of political life in the new German Confederation. From this he was dissuaded by Stockmar – and, no doubt, by the attractions of Marlborough

House, Claremont, and his generous annuity. From September 1818 until May 1819 he did indeed remain on the Continent. But, during a brief stay in Coburg, he became impatient, chafing at the slow pace of social life in a small German duchy. 'John Bull, who has his own ideas, does not like my long absence,' he told Archduke John in the spring of 1819.[1] It did not occur to him that, just possibly, John Bull had fickle sentiments and might even have forgotten him.

For in the months which followed their niece's death the behaviour of the Regent's brothers provided London's caricaturists with ready material for their satire. The early summer of 1818 proved a fine season for belated royal nuptials: there were four between April and July, each bringing closer to the court of St James's some minor constellation in Germany's dynastic firmament. The Dukes of Kent, Cambridge and Clarence were ready to settle for respectable domesticity, the expectation of larger allowances from parliament, and a prospect of fathering an heir to the throne.

Yet the earliest of these ceremonies was, in fact, the marriage not of one of George III's sons, but of his third daughter, Elizabeth, who on 7 April became the wife of the Landgrave of Hesse-Homburg. No sooner had Elizabeth left for her Landgrave's *Residenz* amid the dark hills of the Taunus than her brother, Edward of Kent, at last set out for Coburg to claim his bride. The Prince Regent had guaranteed to protect Victoria of Leiningen's two children and, with his assurance, she became the Duchess of Kent at a Lutheran ceremony in the hall of Coburg's Ehrenburg Palace. Meanwhile Adolphus of Cambridge, who was living as Governor in Hanover, travelled to Cassel to marry Princess Augusta, third daughter of the Landgrave of Hesse-Cassel.

By now only William of Clarence remained a bachelor, for Ernest of Cumberland had married his first cousin, the twice-widowed Frederica of Mecklenburg-Strelitz in 1815, when the armies were gathering for the Waterloo campaign. Clarence, who at fifty-two was nine years older than his brother Adolphus, was content for young Cambridge to take advantage of his presence in Germany to arrange a marriage for him with Adelaide of Saxe-Meiningen. This meek and modest twenty-five-year-old was resolved to make her habitually casual husband regally presentable. They met for the first time at Grillons Hotel in Albemarle Street on the evening of Adelaide's arrival in London, and a week later, on 11 July, were married in the drawing-room at Kew Palace. The ailing Queen Charlotte, who was to die before the end of the year, was there. So, too, were the Duke and Duchess of Kent who, having stayed less than a week in Coburg, were now again 'pronounced man and wife', on this occasion with the authority of the Archbishop of Canterbury.

Most of these marriages aroused new tensions within the royal family. No one except the Regent had a good word to say for Cumberland's choice, Frederica, who had once been engaged to his brother, Adolphus, but contracted out on finding herself pregnant by Frederick of Solms-Braunfels (who became her second husband). Although Cumberland and his Duchess remained in London from August 1815 to July 1818 Queen Charlotte refused to receive her daughter-in-law (and niece). Nor was the House of Commons any more generous, rejecting the government's bill to increase the Duke's annual allowance by £6,000 to £24,000 now that he had taken a wife. 'The marriage was an improper one, however much the parties might be suited to each other from their habits and morals,' declared one Whig MP with caustic irony.[12] Living was cheaper in Germany than in England and the Cumberlands, who were indeed a loving and devoted couple, settled in Berlin. There a son was to be born in 1819, three days after Cumberland's elder brother's daughter, the future Queen Victoria. The unfortunate Prince lost his eyesight in an accident when he was thirteen years old, and became known to history as the 'blind King', George V of Hanover.

The House of Commons grudgingly allowed both the Dukes of Clarence and Kent an additional £6,000 a year, but this was insufficient to pay off debts or to allow themselves to set up suitable homes in England. The Clarences went off to Hanover, where Adolphus of Cambridge offered them the compact and elegant Fürstenhof. William, however, had never liked 'detestable and unhealthy' Hanover. 'Necessity and not inclination keeps me here till I can live without incurring fresh debt,' he wrote frankly to his eldest illegitimate son six months after his arrival.[13]

The Kents left for Amorbach in the first week of September 1818. By the time they reached the little castle in the wooded hills, the Duchess was pregnant. So, for that matter, were her sisters-in-law of Cambridge, Clarence and Cumberland. Adelaide and Augusta decided to await their lyings-in at Hanover. But Edward of Kent – long convinced that he, rather than his brothers, would provide for the royal succession[14] – was determined his child should be born in London, provided he could find money to pay for the journey home. The Prince Regent, who had little liking for Edward, refused to assist him. No loan came from Leopold, probably because he did not think his sister should be encouraged to make such a journey when she was expecting a child; but the Duke's friends in England, who included Whig champions of the Regent's estranged wife, raised £15,000 and this seemed sufficient backing for the journey.

The Duke of Kent set out for England on 28 March 1819, heading the ten-coach cavalcade by taking the reins of his wife's phaeton. As the Duchess was eight months pregnant, they moved at a steady twenty-five miles a day, with one day in four spent resting. On the insistence of the Duchess's mother Fräulein Siebold, a German obstetrician who had qualified as a physician at Göttingen, travelled in the fourth coach. Three weeks after leaving Amorbach the Channel coast was reached at Calais. Regular steam-packet services between Calais and Dover did not begin for another year, and the Duke's party was therefore forced to wait for a favourable wind, like so many earlier travellers from Germany. During the six-day delay, the Kents heard that in Hanover the Duchess of Cambridge had given birth to a son on 26 March, but that the daughter born to the Duchess of Clarence a day later had lived only seven hours. This sad news increased the significance of the Duchess of Kent's confinement because any child, whether boy or girl, born to the wife of George III's fourth son would be the first of its generation in the line of succession. The Duchess arrived safely at Kensington Palace on 24 April. Her baby, Princess Victoria, was born there on 24 May, with Fräulein Siebold in attendance as midwife.

Some fifteen hours later a courier set off from Kensington for Coburg to take the news from the Duke to his mother-in-law. 'Thank God the dear mother and the child are doing marvellously well,' Kent wrote; the baby Princess, he declared 'is truly a model of strength and beauty combined'. It was only eighteen months since another courier had brought the Dowager Duchess an account of the 'gigantic tragedy' at Claremont. Now she hoped her daughter would know the happiness denied 'poor, poor Leopold' and that she would herself eventually become, as she had already once assumed, grandmother to a sovereign of the United Kingdom.[15]

Of that possibility the Duke of Kent had no doubt whatsoever. Stockmar was drily amused at the Duke's habit of constantly showing the baby 'to his companions and intimate friends with the words "Take care of her for she will be Queen of England" '.[16] These displays of paternal pride were galling to the Prince Regent, who had long found his brother Edward exasperating company. The Regent insisted that 'Charlotte' should not be one of the child's names and that the baptism should be private, rather than the public ceremony Edward would have liked. Prince Leopold, who returned to England three days before his niece's birth, was in the Cupola Room of Kensington Palace on 24 June for the baptism. His sister noted that at first he could hardly bring himself to look at the infant Victoria from memory of that dreadful night at Claremont. It was not a happy christening. Apart from Leopold, the Duchess of Kent and the Prussian-born Duchess of York, only English-born members of the royal House were present; and by now they were beginning to treat the Coburgs, brother and sister, as ambitious outsiders. The public, too, had lost interest in Leopold. As he wrote to Archduke John, he was happier with country life at Claremont than in London.[17]

At Coburg in the previous winter Leopold met, for the first time since her infancy, his sister-in-law and distant cousin Louise, who had married Duke Ernest in July 1817. So far as the duke was concerned the marriage was primarily an act of state: Louise was heiress to Saxe-Gotha and he hoped eventually to add her Duchy to his own. But Louise, as the Dowager Duchess readily perceived, deserved a happy family life. She was an attractive bride, a small and pretty romantic of sixteen, popular with the Coburgers. A son, named after his father, was duly born in June 1818, and by Christmas Louise was again pregnant. On this occasion the Dowager Duchess encouraged her to escape from the bustle of central Coburg; she chose, as birthplace for her second child, the Rosenau, a small fifteenth-century *Schloss* in parkland some four miles east of Coburg city. On 26 August 1819 the Dowager Duchess was able to send happy news to the Duchess of Kent. 'Louischen', she wrote, 'was yesterday morning safely and quickly delivered of a little boy. Siebold, the *accoucheuse*, had only been called at three, and at six the little one gave his first cry in the world, and looked about like a little squirrel with a pair of large black eyes. . . . Louise is much more comfortable here than if she had been laid up in town. The quiet of this house, only interrupted by the murmuring of the water, is so agreeable. . . . No one considered the noise of the palace at Coburg, the shouts of children, and the rolling of the carriages in the streets.' The Prince, she added, would be called Albert; and she closed her letter with a reference to her granddaughter in Kensington. 'How pretty the May Flower will be when I see it in a year's time. Siebold cannot sufficiently describe what a dear little love it is.'[18]

It was, of course, natural that the Dowager Duchess Augusta should be the first person to link in writing the destiny of two grandchildren, born within three months of each other; and the marriage of these first cousins became an obsessive theme of her correspondence. Thus shortly before Albert's second birthday, at a time when his Uncle Leopold was visiting Coburg, she could write to the Duchess of Kent stressing how 'the little fellow is the pendant to the pretty cousin; very handsome, but too slight for a boy; lively, very funny, all good nature and full of mischief'.[19] Soon she was enlisting the backing of Leopold and Stockmar for her dream project.

But while a family union of this kind was for the Dowager Duchess primarily a matter of sentiment, to her politically astute son a third Anglo-Coburg marriage called for careful planning and timing. Kent's marriage to Leopold's sister had brought out the Regent's latent suspicion of his son-in-law's ingratiating good manners and calculating behaviour. Court and parliament in England were growing suspicious of what later generations would have called a Coburg takeover bid. He could not risk the social rebuffs of failure; and there were several occasions over the following sixteen years when he wondered if this union of cousins was practicable or desirable.

The sudden death of the Duke of Kent at Sidmouth in January 1820 gave Leopold fresh and unexpected responsibilities. For a second time he had to sustain his widowed sister. Moreover the Duke had leased Woolbrook Cottage largely because south-east Devon was remote from his growing army of creditors; and when he succumbed to pneumonia in the little two-storeyed white house beside the sea, Leopold was left to rescue the Duchess from debt as well as ensuring that she returned safely to London with her two children, the infant Princess and her half-sister Feodora of Leiningen.

To accommodate the Duchess and her family at Claremont was impossible: there was an epidemic of measles among the domestic staff in that unlucky house. Leopold had to seek permission for his sister to return to the apartments at Kensington Palace which the Regent had grudgingly leased to Kent nine months before. When the Duchess reached Kensington, she found confusion in the royal family. George III had died six days after her husband, and now 'Prinny', a king at last, was so ill with pleurisy that the Duchess believed Victoria might any day become second in line of succession. Metternich in Vienna even misinformed his Emperor of George IV's death. When the new King recovered, he declined to offer the Duchess any financial assistance. She might retain her Kensington apartments for the time being; but he was determined she should return to Amorbach with her children. In sunnier moments he hoped Leopold and the whole Coburg troupe would accompany her.

Left to herself, the Duchess might have gone, for she was unhappy in London and, unlike her brother, had great difficulty in learning English. Amorbach, however, was in poor repair and Leopold, although exasperatingly devious in advice, seemed to wish her to remain in England. But Leopold's financial help could not keep the Duchess free from debt. At times the exchanges between brother and sister became tense and strained. So, indeed, did most of Leopold's personal relationships. Old friends now found him, in Countess Lieven's words, 'a Jesuit and a bore'.[20]

The return from six years' voluntary exile of George IV's consort, Caroline of Brunswick, upset Leopold's political calculations and threw him into confusion. For the first four months of his mother-in-law's stay in London he made no attempt to call on her, fearing the wrath of the King who was angered by his wife's attempts to claim the status of a Queen. But when, in late October 1820, the Whig campaign to vindicate Caroline seemed near success, Leopold stopped his carriage outside the house she had leased in St James's Square, only to find that Caroline refused to see him. Less than a fortnight later, when the Prime Minister induced the King to drop his attempt to have the Queen's conduct condemned by parliament, Leopold's London residence, Marlborough House, was among the great mansions illuminated to celebrate the Queen's 'acquittal'. In the following spring Caroline sought to lease Marlborough House from the Prince; he kept her lawyers waiting three months before declining her offer. Leopold thus succeeded in offending the rival factions: George IV was incensed that he should even have made contact with Caroline, while the Queen's party despised him for his inconsistency. Alderman Wood, Caroline's most outspoken champion, had befriended the Duke and Duchess of Kent – and indeed was largely responsible for the leasing of Woolbrook Cottage in his native Devonshire. In offending Matthew Wood, Leopold lost the support of the City of London Whigs.

'The incessant intrigues of the metropolis' were too much for Leopold. In August 1821 he crossed to France, resolved to remain on the Continent for at least a year. Hardly had he reached Paris than he heard that Caroline of Brunswick had died suddenly in Hammersmith. 'I am glad I am out of all the trouble,' he told Archduke John.[21] For eighteen months he kept away from Britain. Coburg fortunes were at a low ebb: Leopold was out of favour, his sister grudgingly patronized as the royal family's poor relation, his niece unsure of the succession so long as the Clarences might have healthy children. The Dowager Duchess's ambitious dream for her favourite offspring had become a passing fantasy, as unobtainable as the promised realm which beckons the youth and the lily in Goethe's supernatural *Das Märchen*. But this was, after all, the Age of Romanticism; and in the best fairy tales the chosen couple must always combat torment and frustration before attaining the happiness of triumphant love.

Hanover tree (2) the kingdom of Hanover (1814–66)
(kings in bold type)

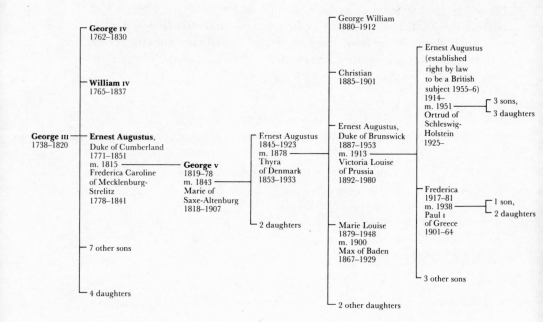

George III
1738–1820

George IV
1762–1830

William IV
1765–1837

Ernest Augustus,
Duke of Cumberland
1771–1851
m. 1815
Frederica Caroline
of Mecklenburg-
Strelitz
1778–1841

7 other sons

4 daughters

George V
1819–78
m. 1843
Marie of
Saxe-Altenburg
1818–1907

Ernest Augustus
1845–1923
m. 1878
Thyra
of Denmark
1853–1933

2 daughters

George William
1880–1912

Christian
1885–1901

Ernest Augustus,
Duke of Brunswick
1887–1953
m. 1913
Victoria Louise
of Prussia
1892–1980

Marie Louise
1879–1948
m. 1900
Max of Baden
1867–1929

2 other daughters

Ernest Augustus
(established
right by law
to be a British
subject 1955–6)
1914–
m. 1951
Ortrud of
Schleswig-
Holstein
1925–

3 sons,
3 daughters

Frederica
1917–81
m. 1938
Paul I
of Greece
1901–64

1 son,
2 daughters

3 other sons

CHAPTER SEVEN
❧ Dual Kingship ❧

'Why *should* we have Germans to rule over us?' the Countess of Jersey suddenly exclaimed at dinner in Woburn towards the end of George IV's first year on the throne.[1] The vehemence of the rhetorical question surprised her companions at table, even in so traditional a Whig household; only six years back, Lady Jersey was vying with her rivals in society to help celebrate the centenary of the Hanoverian dynasty. But by 1821 the sobering influence of Saxe-Coburg and Saxe-Meiningen and Hesse-Cassel on court revelry and the absurd wrangles over Queen Caroline's status were arousing a dormant xenophobia in the English aristocracy; and, in the year that Napoleon died on St Helena, Germans and Russians were more unpopular than the French.

George IV sensed this mood during the so-called 'Queen's Trial'. Frustration made him contemplate the escape which had appealed to his father and his great-grandfather on being thwarted by their ministers; and, when, in October 1820, the government dropped the Bill of Pains and Penalties which would have denied Caroline her rights, George was said to have 'serious thoughts of retiring to Hanover, and leaving this Kingdom to the Duke of York'.[2] Instead, with fickle public sentiment veering back in his favour, he found consolation in a magnificent coronation and planning a series of state visits. The Habsburg cities attracted him; but he knew that, if he set foot on the Continent at all, he must first go to Hanover, where no sovereign prince had stayed in residence for sixty-six years. He had wished to visit the Kingdom of Hanover in 1815, soon after it acquired this new status, but Napoleon's return from Elba precluded foreign excursions that year. Now that he was King in person, rather than regent for a senile father, he would wait no longer. As he told Countess Lieven, wife of the Russian ambassador, he might journey on to Berlin and Karlsbad and Vienna.

In retrospect, George IV numbered his Hanover visit among the three great occasions of his reign, comparable to the Westminster coronation and his triumphant fortnight in Edinburgh the following summer. He set out for Brussels and Germany in good spirits, crossing from Ramsgate to Calais on 24 September 1821, with Castlereagh (now, technically, the Marquess of Londonderry) as minister in attendance and the Duke of Wellington to conduct him around the battlefield of Waterloo. At Düsseldorf so warm was the welcome accorded him by the troops of his 'Waterloo ally' (Prussia) that he was looking forward to an extended sojourn abroad. But dreams of a grand

German itinerary soon dissolved after a few hours travel north-eastwards into his Hanoverian lands: the roads were so poor and rutted that horses were changed every five miles, twenty-two times between Düsseldorf and Osnabrück. His loyal subjects in Osnabrück welcomed their King with floral arches, illuminated buildings, banners from the windows, flag-waving and cheering. Sir William Knighton, the King's physician and unofficial personal secretary, thought the townsfolk 'almost mad with joy'.

Adolphus of Cambridge, Governor-General of the Kingdom, accompanied his brother into the city of Hanover on the evening of 7 October. The bells, cheers and gun salutes made the arrival at the Herrenhausen seem like the return of a victorious warrior. On the following days there was a military review and a second coronation, an improvised Lutheran ceremony at the principal church in the old town. In all, George remained in his Germanic Kingdom for three weeks. He travelled out to Göttingen, the university founded by George II, and was so moved by the address of welcome that tears coursed his jowls. The Royal Hanoverian Guelphic Order of chivalry was instituted and generously distributed to worthy citizens, the sovereign wearing no other insignia throughout his visit. Briefly, Hanover assumed importance in European affairs, for the Austrian Chancellor, Metternich, came to the city to talk high politics with the King and his Foreign Minister – and to resume his friendship with Dorothea Lieven, who had followed George IV to Hanover while her husband was conferring in St Petersburg. At times the King, like his brother Clarence before him, found the solemnity of Hanoverian life tedious, and he suffered agonies from chronic gout, but he was later to talk at length of the loyalty of his German subjects, in contrast to the ingrates of London.[3]

Poor health ruled out a longer stay abroad and George was back in London by the end of the second week in November. A month later, from the Royal Pavilion at Brighton, Dorothea Lieven was to write to Metternich, 'At table we heard of nothing but Hanover.' Yet, though for the last nine years of his reign George remained conscious of his dual kingship, to the disappointment of his Governor-General the King did nothing to improve the social or political life of his Hanoverian subjects.

Apart from occasional visits to England, the Duke of Cambridge continued as a conscientious representative of the absentee King for over twenty years. Unlike Clarence, who had brought his Duchess back to England after the loss of their first child, Cambridge enjoyed life in Hanover. Two daughters were born to his wife there, Augusta (who was to survive until 1916) in July 1822 and Mary Adelaide (the mother of Queen Mary) eleven years later; and, although his son spent his boyhood in England, the Duke insisted that both his daughters should pass their earliest years among the 'beloved inhabitants' of Hanover. On several occasions the Duke urged his eldest brother to grant his German Kingdom a constitution, but George IV turned for advice to Count Münster, the Hanoverian Minister in London, who was the most Tory of

Tories. Preservation of the old order seemed to Münster the surest guarantee of his homeland's independence within the German Confederation, for the Kingdom would then appear more politically reliable than larger states troubled by liberal student unrest. Münster advised George IV to change nothing, not even to give his youngest brother the status of a viceroy. All that Hanover received from its crowned sovereign was its first and last order of knighthood.

By 1824 it began to look certain that the era of dual kingship would be short-lived. For, although Hanover had become a Kingdom in October 1814, the traditional Salic Law of the Electorate was still valid: the crown of the United Kingdom of Great Britain and Ireland might pass to a woman; the crown of Hanover could not. Unless the two widowers, George IV and the Duke of York, re-married and fathered at least one son or a son was born to Adelaide of Clarence (which her husband by now thought unlikely) the British succession would eventually pass to the Princess Victoria of Kent and the Hanoverian succession to the Duke of Cumberland or his son. George IV was still reluctant to recognize the Duchess of Kent as a person of stature in his kingdom; nor did he show any greater warmth towards her brother when, early in 1823, Leopold returned to England. But with his niece herself George was invariably generous and bearishly avuncular. He had always been fond of children.

There is, however, no doubt Victoria had a sad, isolated upbringing. It was relieved, when he was in England, by visits to 'dear Uncle Leopold'. 'Claremont remains as the brightest epoch of my otherwise rather melancholy childhood,' she wrote in an autobiographical fragment half a century later.[4] But there were far fewer trips to Claremont than Victoria or her half-sister, Feodora, would have liked. The Duchess of Kent did not wish to increase her unpopularity at court by appearing too dependent upon her brother. Instead she turned increasingly for advice to her husband's former equerry, the plausible Irishman John Conroy. For the moment the association mattered little. Nor, indeed, did the growing influence in the nursery of Louise Lehzen, Feodora's governess. Lehzen, a woman of principle and purpose, had much to commend her and in 1827 the King willingly created her a Hanoverian Baroness. This was appropriate, for she was a daughter of the Lutheran pastor at Langenhagen, which was then a village outside Hanover and close to the Herrenhausen palace. Victoria, as she wrote in later years, had 'great respect and even awe' of the Baroness, 'but with that the greatest affection'. Yet there is no doubt that both Lehzen and the scheming Conroy – who was knighted in the year she was ennobled – were jealously possessive of Victoria, although fortunately in conflict with each other. Leopold was to find Lehzen an occasional ally, who sent him confidential reports from Kensington Palace; but he hardly needed Stockmar to convince him Conroy was a persistent enemy.[5]

* * *

Some 500 miles from Claremont Victoria's first cousin, Albert, also delighted
in his uncle's company. This is not surprising. Both children were denied
family life even more than most princes and princesses of their generation. For,
if death had deprived Victoria of a father she could never remember, marital
discord robbed Albert before he was five years old of a mother to whom he
remained deeply devoted. Neither Duke Ernest nor Louise were blameless, for
they had long since lost all affection and understanding for each other. But
Ernest was more tolerant than George I had been: he made no attempt to
imprison Louise in some Thuringian Ahlden, and his sons did not in
consequence feel so bitterly towards him as had the Hanoverian children
towards their father a century before. Louise was allowed to leave Coburg in
1824 and, once her husband made certain of receiving her Gotha inheritance
in November 1826, he raised no objection to her divorce and re-marriage. For
Prince Albert of Saxe-Coburg and Gotha – as he now became – the great
sorrow was that his mother survived only for five more years, dying at the age
of thirty, before he had left the schoolroom.

Apart from any personal scar on a child's emotional development, the
departure of his mother from Coburg had a double effect on Albert's life. It
meant that the ageing Dowager Duchess Augusta, so far as she could, acted as
the Prince's surrogate mother; and, impatient with her eldest son's selfish
extravagance, turned to her favourite, Leopold, for good advice. More
seriously, the scandal encouraged prurient gossips in Coburg to speculate on
past marital infidelities. Since there was a marked difference in character and
appearance between Louise's two sons, Albert's paternity was questioned:
some said his father was a Jewish court chamberlain, whose company had
certainly pleased his mother when she found ducal life tedious; and, since he
had been staying in Coburg nine months before Albert was born, others
maintained that Leopold, and not his brother, was the younger Prince's father.
Inevitably these tales – for which there is no shred of evidence – reached
London. They were soon embellished by groups in society envious of 'lucky
Coburg' and that generous annuity he received from the British taxpayers.

It was therefore natural that Leopold should have more influence on
Albert's training and education than on his niece's upbringing in Kensington.
At his mother's request Leopold sent Stockmar home to Coburg even before
Louise's departure from the Duchy in order to report on the two young
Princes and suggest a fitting system of education for them; and Albert
later maintained it was during these earliest years that he discovered he was
expected to marry his cousin in England. Stockmar recommended as a tutor
for the boys a young fellow Coburger, Christoph Florschutz, who was to serve
the ducal family for fifteen years.

The influence of Florschutz on the formation of Albert's character has been
consistently underrated. This is not surprising; he seems in so many respects a
clone of Stockmar, who was to write at such length of the Albert he had

created. The two men came from a similar background, optimistically liberal and Anglophile, proud of their Duchy's Lutheran heritage but conscious that Saxe-Coburg remained a small state, off the Grand Tour routes of European culture. Florschutz, who enjoyed the status of councillor (*Rath*) in his native Duchy, was less cosmopolitan than Stockmar but he at least knew Vienna, having for some years been a tutor in the household of Count von Mensdorff-Pouilly, who had married Leopold's eldest sister. From Florschutz, Albert and his brother were to acquire the conviction that full education comprised three essentials: formal learning, meticulously regulated according to a daily timetable which their father's social whims constantly disrupted; physical exercise in the good, mountain air of the surrounding countryside; and recreational 'self-imposed studies', which less pedantic minds might even have categorized as hobbies. By Stockmar's standards this programme was superficial; it lacked the moral purpose which would fire ambition and steel the will to succeed. It was on Stockmar's prompting that, for the sake of Albert's training, Leopold persuaded Duke Ernest to allow his sons to round off their education with a year at the liberal and enlightened University of Bonn. But Stockmar does not seem to have been surprised when in later years the elder pupil lapsed into the selfish, calculating hedonism of his father and namesake. Albert remained true to Florschutz's ideals; but it is not fanciful to see in the stiffness and reserve of the Prince Consort a conscious striving for a higher level of moral excellence than his boyhood tutor had held out to him as readily attainable.[6]

Leopold led a cosmopolitan life for most of the reign of George IV. He generally wintered in Italy and, although he continued to maintain Claremont and Marlborough House, he came only occasionally to the country whose taxes funded his annuity. At Potsdam, in September 1826, he became infatuated with an actress whom he first saw in the small theatre at the Neues Palais. Caroline Bauer bore a physical resemblance to Princess Charlotte and was first cousin to the ubiquitous Stockmar, who did not approve of her. Leopold installed her in a villa in Regent's Park which Caroline herself described in her memoirs as 'a charming golden cage'. Perhaps a morganatic marriage was contemplated, at least by Fräulein Bauer and her mother. But Caroline's presence in England was an embarrassment to Leopold's political ambitions and, after a year, the Bauers were packed off to the Continent. They were assisted, it would seem, by the diplomacy of Cousin Stocky and a lump sum of money from his master.[7]

Both Leopold and Stockmar were, however, concerned with weightier matters than Caroline Bauer or, indeed, the education of the Coburg Princes. As early as 1822, when the Greeks of the Peloponnese formally asserted their independence of the Ottoman Empire, Leopold was mentioned as a possible King of Greece; and for eight years he maintained contact with John

Capodistria, the astute Greek statesman, whom he knew well when both men
were serving Tsar Alexander I. Sometimes, notably in the late summer of 1827,
Capodistria and Leopold were in London at the same time, and the Prince's
Hellenic ambitions were well known. George IV contemptuously asked
Ellenborough, his Lord Privy Seal, how the politicians could be 'such fools as
to think *he* could be of any use'; Wellington, as Prime Minister, considered
'there never was such a humbug as the Greek affair'; and in Kensington Palace
the young Victoria was 'in despair at the thought' of her adored uncle's
departure for so distant a throne.[8]

Leopold himself had reservations. The possibility that he might, like his
third sister, be forced to accept the Orthodox faith does not seem to have
troubled him. He was, however, concerned over what should, or should not, be
included within the boundaries of the new kingdom and whether the Greeks
would, or would not, welcome him. Eventually, on 28 February 1830, he wrote
to Capodistria from Marlborough House telling him he was willing to accept
the Greek crown; and Capodistria urged him to come, as swiftly as possible, to
Nauplia, the provisional capital. By late April he was in Paris seeking a second
wife – for Greece, he felt, needed a queen – and hoping for a loan to finance his
new kingdom. In Paris news reached him that his father-in-law was seriously
ill. At once he returned to Marlborough House. From there, on 21 May, he
sent a letter to Capodistria withdrawing the acceptance he had made less than
twelve weeks before. So furious was George IV on hearing of this latest
vacillation that 'he had a seizure which threatened to be fatal'. In fact, with
astonishing resilience, he survived for another month; it was not until the
small hours of 26 June that a heart, which doctors believed was diseased even
when he was unwell in Hanover, finally ceased to function.[9]

Why did Leopold change his mind about Greece? Did reports of George's
fatal illness make him believe he could win a new ascendancy over the royal
family in London? Many people thought so at the time, including the French
ambassador. Leopold explained away his weak conduct by emphasizing that
he had failed to gain support from a tottering government in Paris and that he
thought his candidature was unpopular in Greece. Yet there is no doubt that
the Duchess of Kent wanted Leopold in England when the Duke of Clarence
succeeded to the throne and Victoria became heiress-presumptive. No one
supposed that William IV, although fond of Victoria, would listen any more
readily to the Coburgs, brother or sister, than George had done. But William
was sixty-five. Two years before, there were fears (so Ellenborough wrote in
his diary) that 'Fatigue will kill him' and, Ellenborough added with some
exaggeration, 'He is now and then mad – or very nearly so.'[10] It was moreover
only ten months since William enlivened the Lords debate on Catholic
Emancipation (which he favoured) by a verbal attack on his brother, the Duke
of Cumberland, an ultra-Tory about whom sinister stories were in circulation.
Yet if apoplexy carried William to his grave or delusions left him in a world of

his own at Windsor, it was Cumberland, the most feared and unpopular of George III's sons, who would become Regent and guardian for Princess Victoria. Leopold's sister needed her brother's counsel and support during the three months from mid-July to late October, when parliament stood prorogued and the country was in the grip of election fever.

It was a needless scare, the first of many alarms in which Cumberland was bogey-man over the next seven years. On 15 November the Lord Chancellor declared, 'It is the recommendation of His Majesty's Ministers that, in the event of the demise of the Crown. . . . Her Royal Highness the Duchess of Kent should be appointed sole Regent.' There was much friction between William IV and his sister-in-law for the remainder of his reign, not least over her daughter's use of a non-English name ('not even German, but of French origin'); but the Duchess had won the crucial battle.[11] It was, significantly, in that same week of November 1830 that Leopold first showed interest in offers of another crown. From Brussels a Coburg might feel the pulse of Europe better than from Nauplia or Athens.

By chance, William IV's accession coincided with a convulsion of political excitement on the Continent. In July 1830 a revolution 'stopped half-way' in the streets of Paris enabled Louis Philippe, the liberal Duke of Orleans, to become King of the French; and in August the Belgians rose in revolt against the Kingdom of the United Netherlands. There were risings in Italy and a rebellion in Russian Poland. The German lands responded more slowly but, as early as 7 September, a mob in Brunswick marched upon the *Residenz* of their young and unpopular Duke Charles III, burnt the palace, and forced him to flee for his life. Brunswick was a mere fifty-five miles from the city of Hanover, where the Governor-General, Adolphus of Cambridge, was a kinsman of the ousted Duke. Indeed after the Duke's father was killed fighting at Quatre Bras in 1815, Brunswick had been virtually a protectorate of Hanover, with George IV as absentee Regent, until October 1823 when Charles, at nineteen, came of age. There was a risk in the autumn of 1830 that unrest would spread across Hanover's borders, even though Cambridge personally was liked and respected by William IV's German subjects. Disorder spread that winter to Hesse-Cassel and Saxony. As in Britain, where the Whigs returned to power after a quarter of a century in opposition, there was throughout Germany a sentiment in favour of what Metternich castigated as 'French constitutionalism'.

William IV responded sensibly to the German emergency. Count Münster was retired as Hanover's Minister in London; his successor, Baron von Ompteda, made no attempt to follow Münster in shaping his country's policies at long range. William accordingly raised the status of the Duke of Cambridge, by making him Viceroy, and authorized him to prepare reforms for the German Kingdom in consultation with the Hanoverians themselves. A basic Constitutional Law in September 1833 considerably extended the functions of the old consultative assemblies of Estates, giving them new legislative and financial powers, and in the same year a National Property Law satisfied a widespread, but largely illusory grievance, that 'London' was exploiting Hanover.[12] At a time when Prussia was beginning to unify Germany economically through the *Zollverein*, road construction and (later) the spread of railways, it was essential for the Hanoverians to be able to safeguard their commercial and agrarian interest. The reforms of 1833 so effectively separated the interests of Great Britain and Hanover that the ending of dual kingship four years later had, at the time, a purely dynastic significance. Only in the next generation did German liberals come to wonder if, by asserting independence of London, the Hanoverians were making certain of their future subservience to Berlin.

The change of government in Britain brought Lord Palmerston to the Foreign Office where, apart from five months in the winter of 1834–5, he was to remain for the next eleven years. This seemed, in the first instance, to help the small Coburg faction at court. Palmerston and Leopold were old acquaintances and the Prince, believing that he could work more closely with the new Foreign Secretary than with his Tory predecessors, invited him to Claremont within three weeks of his taking office. In later years, when Leopold played high politics in Europe, the two men were frequently in conflict and Palmerston would privately complain that his policies were frustrated by a Saxe-Coburg camarilla; but at first they understood and respected each other and Leopold could still write to Victoria of his 'clever and well-informed friend Palmerston' after his niece had come to the throne.

Even before Christmas 1830 Leopold had let Palmerston know he would accept the crown of Belgium although it was not until the following June that he was formally elected sovereign by the Belgian National Congress. His affairs in England were speedily settled and he crossed to Calais and drove on to Ostend on 16 July 1831, having renounced the annuity granted to him by parliament, although reserving sums to pay for the maintenance of Claremont, his English carriages and all charities to which he or Charlotte had subscribed. A year later, at Compiègne, he married Princess Louise Marie, the eldest daughter of King Louis Philippe, who with his wife had been a guest at Leopold's marriage in Carlton House sixteen years previously. They made their principal home at Laeken, the château outside Brussels which forms a monument to Austria's eight decades of rule in Belgium.

In the first years of his reign the 'King of the Belgians' doubted whether he would long retain that title. The Dutch, refusing to allow Belgium's secession, poured an army into their sovereign's lost provinces and the French, having helped Leopold check this incursion, showed a marked reluctance to take the road back across their frontier. When, with Palmerston's diplomatic support, this crisis was overcome, Leopold found local provincial loyalty so strong in

Belgium that there seemed no genuine sense of national cohesion. 'I tell you honestly what I never hide from the Belgians, I do not like to be here', he wrote to Palmerston in February 1839. 'Only the moral satisfaction of doing much good and preventing much mischief has reconciled me to the Kingship of this country, one of the most difficult and irksome in Europe.'[13] Kingship never lessened Leopold's concern with the fate of his homeland and its dynasty.

The Dowager Duchess Augusta died in Coburg in November 1831, four months after her favourite son was welcomed in Brussels as King. During these last years her thoughts reverted more and more to the future destiny of her niece in London: 'God bless Old England, where my beloved children live, and where the sweet blossom of May may one day reign!' she wrote to the Duchess of Kent in one of her last letters. 'May God yet for many years keep the weight of a crown from her young head and let the intelligent clever child grow up to girlhood before this dangerous grandeur devolves upon her!'[14] Duke Ernest of Saxe-Coburg-Gotha visited his sister in England that same year and saw for himself the 'sweet blossom of May', but Albert and Victoria were not to meet for another five years, until the eve of the Princess's seventeenth birthday. Sometimes it looked as if they would never meet at all, or at least not before Victoria had found a husband from another princely family.

To William IV, the Duchess of Kent seemed a tiresome mother determined to keep her daughter in the limelight of the royal stage. He mistrusted his sister-in-law and her ambitious 'manager', Conroy, and he had little higher regard for the King of the Belgians. Yet, now that Leopold was a fellow monarch and not a pensionary of parliament, need a British King take heed of the Coburgs? The Duke of Cumberland thought not. Leopold, he argued, forfeited all social and political standing in England once he accepted the Belgian crown. Cumberland, for thirty years royal patron to the extreme Protestant 'Orange Lodges', even maintained that Leopold as ruler of a Catholic kingdom and husband of a French Catholic Princess should not be received by William IV; and he certainly should not correspond with the heiress presumptive to the British throne.

This, of course, was pernicious nonsense: Leopold remained a Lutheran all his life. Family concern in itself justified visits to a country where he still possessed property, for he was disturbed by reports from Stockmar's contacts in England suggesting there was a growing rift between the Duchess and her daughter. William took little notice of Cumberland's blustering complaints; but he began to interest himself in matchmaking for his niece and successor. He thought highly of her cousin, George of Cambridge, who spent so much of his boyhood with his uncle and aunt at Bushy. Two eligible princes in Berlin might renew a traditional connection; and, almost inevitably, there was a William of Orange. Indeed on this occasion there was an Alexander of Orange, too. In the spring of 1836 William IV invited the two Dutch Princes to

England, together with their father, the same Crown Prince of the Netherlands whom Charlotte had rejected in that 'summer of sovereigns' almost a quarter of a century ago.

At Kensington Palace and Laeken the King's invitation was seen as a deliberate slight on the Coburgs. The paths of Leopold and the Dutch Prince had crossed yet again in 1831 when Orange commanded his father's troops in the abortive attempt to recover Belgium. Thereafter the Dutchman spoke of Leopold as 'the man who robbed me of a wife and a kingdom' while, with less striking hyperbole, the King of the Belgians merely rated him 'my country's most bitter foe'. To Leopold it was particularly galling that the Dutch Princes should be invited to England at a time when Duke Ernest and his two sons were already enjoying the novelty of a 'steam-boat down the Rhine' on the first stage of their long-projected journey to London. Was this Orange's revenge?

Leopold had no need to worry. When the Dutch Princes arrived in London the King and Queen gave a ball in their honour at St James's Palace. Victoria partnered each of them, and her cousin George of Cambridge, once. She thought the Dutch Princes not merely dull, heavy and unprepossessing but frightened, too – and who can blame them? 'So much for the *Oranges*, dear Uncle,' she wrote crisply to Brussels.[15] A letter from Leopold, which with typical Coburg felicity reached her on St Valentine's Day, had extolled the merits of Ernest and Albert. She was to meet them for the first time, on 18 May 1836, just five days after the St James's Palace ball.

It is clear from Victoria's surviving written comments that she thought Albert handsome, merry, talented as a musician and artist, and far more attractive than any other suitor. Despite his suspicion of the scheming Coburgs, the King too found him an agreeable young man. So delighted was Victoria with her cousin that she even overlooked 'poor Albert's' weariness at the ball given to celebrate her seventeenth birthday. But it is hard to see in her words any greater emotion than an only child might feel for a good-looking cousin of the opposite sex who, unexpectedly, needed encouragement and cosseting. There was affectionate sympathy at first sight, but no deep infatuation; and Albert, though amused by Victoria's vivacity, was almost paralysed by culture shock, 'the different way of living' as he told his stepmother. English food he thought as deplorable as English weather and court life as debilitating as the sea crossing to reach England's shores. His letters sigh with suppressed resentment at the role for which Leopold and Stockmar were casting him.[16]

Leopold himself was ill-at-ease. William still preferred a Dutch marriage; Princess Victoria took a passing fancy to the rakish ex-Duke of Brunswick, whom she spotted through her glasses in a box at the opera; and Albert was encouraged to spend as much time as possible away from Coburg, reaching maturity in Paris and Brussels, the Rhineland and Italy. Occasionally he wrote letters to his cousin in England. Less frequently she replied to them.

The winter of 1836–7 was, for the most part, a season of anxious anticipation. Which would come first, the Princess's eighteenth birthday or the death of the septuagenarian King? His health, as the doctors unhelpfully confessed, 'was in an odd state'. If he died before 24 May 1837, the Duchess of Kent would become Regent. By now this was a contingency which not even her brother desired any more: he thought her foolishly dependent on Sir John Conroy; and he feared that a few months of the Duchess's regency would leave the Coburgs the most unpopular princely dynasty in Europe. In September 1836 Leopold came over to Claremont, despite the open displeasure of Cumberland, and talked at length with his sister and his niece. Secretly he enlisted Lehzen as his ally and risked his sister's displeasure by giving Conroy a good dressing-down. His intervention had little effect.

Characteristically William himself had not stayed silent. On his seventy-first birthday, in August 1836, the King spoke out at a dinner in Windsor Castle to which 100 guests were invited. Among them was the Duchess of Kent, who sat close enough to the host to hear him say, in reply to a loyal toast, that he hoped his life would be spared long enough to prevent 'a person now near me, who is surrounded by evil advisers and who is herself incompetent to act with propriety' from becoming Regent.[17] The wish, expressed in such forthright terms that Princess Victoria burst into tears, was duly granted. The King survived the winter but, as a fine spring turned into a dry summer, his chest began to tighten with asthma. He died at Windsor in the small hours of 20 June 1837. By then the Princess Victoria was eighteen years and four weeks old.

There followed the famous scene at Kensington Palace where, at six in the morning, Archbishop Howley and the Lord Chamberlain knelt at the slippered feet of a girl in a dressing-gown to tell her she was Queen. At breakfast she received her first visitor, Baron Stockmar, and it was with the Coburg emissary that she held the earliest of her political conversations. If her uncle's 'invaluable honest friend' advised her to inform Lord Melbourne that she wished to retain him and his ministers in office, then that task she would dutifully perform this same morning. Good sense and inclination made her turn to Stockmar and Lehzen rather than to her mother and Conroy. She saw Stockmar twice more on her first day as Queen; but it was not until many months later that disgruntled voices began complaining of German influence upon the young sovereign. Stockmar was liked and trusted by most people in British public life: better a Coburg counsellor than Conroy.

No one in London doubted that the accession of the young Queen filled Britain's monarchy with the glow of a new dawn. But for the people of Hanover that same June morning brought, if not sunset, at least the darkness of eclipse. For the relentless dictates of Salic law deprived Adolphus of Cambridge of his viceregal authority and on 20 June 1837 Ernest Augustus, Duke of Cumberland, became Ernst August, King of an independent

Hanover. He had been at Windsor during his brother's last illness, dutiful in family observances and unmoved by his unpopularity. But should he remain for his brother's funeral or set out to claim his throne? He consulted Wellington, and the Duke did not hesitate before giving him good advice: 'Go instantly, and take care that you don't get pelted.'[18] By the beginning of July he was in Hanover.

CHAPTER EIGHT
❧ Foreignership ❧

'Your new dignities will not change or increase my old affection for you', King Leopold wrote from Laeken to his niece at her accession. 'May Heaven assist you, and may I have the *happiness of being able to be of use to you.*' He then offered her four pieces of unsolicited advice: 'to say as often as possible that you are *born* in England'; to praise frequently 'your country and its inhabitants'; to commend the established church 'without *pledging* yourself to anything *particular*'; and, a point which needed no underlining, 'before you decide on anything important I should be glad if you would consult me'.[1]

This curious letter, like many others from Laeken early in Victoria's reign, deserved more felicitous phrasing. It suggests her adored uncle was out of touch with his niece's character. A pride in English patriotism and in the Anglican Protestant tradition came as naturally to the young Queen as to her grandfather, George III; and there was no need to preach to her that 'your being very national is highly important'. Leopold believed that he was about to attain the position which had eluded him for over twenty years; at last he would become the power behind the British throne. In this he was mistaken. Leopold rated too highly the bonds of family affection and he gravely underestimated his niece's spirit and intelligence. Why should Victoria compromise her Englishry by consulting an expatriate German princeling who ruled as King in Brussels?

He was right in assuming his niece would need counsel; but he forgot Lehzen and discounted the influence of Melbourne. The Baroness, with her passionate addiction to caraway seeds, may have been a proto-Chekhovian character, but there was nothing ridiculous about her. For the moment the young Queen was still too scared of her old governess to risk quarrels over day-to-day affairs. Politically Lehzen was a forthright Whig, which at least staved off conflict with Lord Melbourne or with the statesman who patiently coached his sovereign in the geography of world-wide politics, Lord Palmerston. Towards her Prime Minister the Queen had entirely different emotions. She admired Melbourne, not simply with the devotion of adolescent hero-worship, but from sheer elation at his conversational skills. In 'Lord M.' the eighteen-year-old Queen found a chief minister forty years her senior who had a gift for deflating political pomposity with sardonic whimsy while stopping short of malice which might have shocked her by its irreverence. Mature acquaintance was to make her, by 1839, purse her lips at his incorrigible flippancy, but not during those first halcyon months at Buckingham Palace and Brighton and Windsor. So long as Victoria had so kind and fatherly a Prime Minister, the prospect of turning for stiff avuncular advice to distant Laeken held little appeal. Indeed Leopold found that, within a few weeks of her accession, the young Queen was prepared to counter his long-range attempts to manage her by letter with triumphant little snubs, a character defect disturbingly reminiscent of her Hanoverian uncles. If he gently reproached Victoria, she assumed that he did not love her as much as he pretended and that she was therefore justified in mistrusting his general intentions. It was made clear to him that, as he told Albert, 'The Queen did not wish to marry for some time yet.'[2] Nothing more was said of the Coburg marriage.

Albert continued to take a passing interest in what was happening in London, although no more than in what was happening in Hanover, where King Ernest Augustus caused consternation among Germany's liberals by suddenly rescinding the constitution which his brothers had approved four years before. However, as Albert told his father, 'Uncle Leopold has written to me a great deal about England.'[3] After a journey through northern Italy in the early autumn of 1837 Albert duly sent the Queen a personal sketchbook into which he pasted some Alpine flowers and souvenirs of Voltaire acquired on his passage through Switzerland. In later years the Queen attached great sentimental value to this 'small album, with the dates at which each place was visited, in the Prince's handwriting'. As she was to remind readers in 1864, 'Nothing had at this time passed between the Queen and the Prince but this gift shows that the latter, in the midst of his travels, often thought of his young cousin.'[4] These thoughts were almost certainly not reciprocated.

For the first two years of her reign Victoria much enjoyed being Queen. The sun, it seemed, shone on her, and on her alone. 'The less you send the Queen this week . . . the better, as her time will be much occupied by Ascot,' the Foreign Secretary instructed his Permanent Under-Secretary in June 1838.[5] It was a mood that could not last. By the following June the sun was clouded over. When she stepped out on the balcony at Ascot, the Prime Minister at her side, a man in the enclosure mockingly called out 'Mrs Melbourne', and as her carriage drove down the course there arose from one bevy of titled ladies a sibilance of disapproval which sounded astonishingly like hissing.

There were two reasons for the Queen's unpopularity: her stubborn refusal to assist Peel to form a Tory government that spring by replacing the Whig Ladies of the Bedchamber; and the way in which she had hounded Lady Flora Hastings, one of her mother's ladies-in-waiting, whom she wrongfully believed was Conroy's mistress. Victoria's self-confidence was dented. For the first time she began to speak to Melbourne of the possibility that she might marry her Coburg cousin. The Prime Minister, whose hold on parliament was shaky, did not show great enthusiasm. Nor, on reflection, did the Queen herself. But

Stockmar, in whom she retained total confidence even when her exchanges with Uncle Leopold were icily stiff, was detailed to accompany Albert on a second visit to Italy; he was to make certain the Prince was sufficiently mature to be worthy of a place one step behind the Queen of England. And Duke Ernest, who had attended the coronation, was invited to return to England in October 1839 – with both his sons.[6]

There followed one of the best-known romantic chapters in royal folklore. The Princes arrived at Windsor on 10 October; Albert and Victoria were immediately attracted to each other, and five days later the Queen told her younger guest that 'it would make me *too happy* if he would consent to what I wished (to marry me)'. Albert returned to Germany on 14 November; and on 23 November the Queen told the Privy Council that she was resolved 'to ally myself in marriage with the Prince Albert of Saxe-Coburg and Gotha'. She had already informed Melbourne that the wedding would take place in the second week of February. From Wiesbaden, where he was taking the waters to ease the palpitations of his heart, Leopold wrote to his niece at Windsor: 'Nothing could have given me greater pleasure than your dear letter. I had, when I saw your decision, almost the feeling of old Zacharias – "Now lettest Thou Thy servant depart in peace"!' No urgency compelled the King of the Belgians to offer up a *Nunc Dimittis*, for another twenty-six years of life lay ahead of him – ample time, indeed, to distinguish Zacharias of the *Benedictus* from the just and devout Simeon; but it is hardly surprising if he felt a sense of accomplishment that November. After two decades of planning, 'the children' had fallen in love with each other.[7]

King Leopold at once began to ply Victoria with good advice, despite his earlier rebuffs. While still at Wiesbaden he wrote to the Queen explaining why he thought it essential for Albert to be given an English peerage. 'The only reason I do wish it is that Albert's foreignership should disappear as much as possible,' Leopold explained. The Prince Regent had once offered to create his prospective son-in-law Duke of Kendal: 'I have . . . suffered greatly from having declined conditionally the peerage when it was offered me in 1816,' King Leopold added in his letter. But neither the Queen nor her Prime Minister wished to see Prince Albert in the Lords. 'The English are very jealous at the idea of Albert's having any political power, or meddling with affairs here – which I know from himself he will not do,' wrote Victoria in reply.[8]

Leopold, however, remained uneasy and would not let the matter rest. Within a fortnight of the announcement of the marriage Victoria was writing to Albert: 'I have received today an ungracious letter from Uncle Leopold. He appears to me to be nettled because I no longer ask for his advice, but dear Uncle is given to believe that he must rule the roast everywhere. However, that is not a necessity.'[9] Once again the Queen imperiously snubbed her uncle. Yet there is no doubt he saw clearly enough the threat to Albert's position in his adopted land. Problems of 'foreignership' wearied the Prince Consort throughout almost all his twenty-one years in Britain; but, given the temper of the times, it is hard to see how the ermine robes of an English or Scottish dukedom might have lightened his burden.

'Nothing could exceed the enthusiasm of the reception which greeted the Prince when he set foot on the English shore as the affianced husband of our Queen,' dutifully wrote General Grey, the last of his private secretaries, in a memoir compiled for Victoria soon after Albert's death.[10] Factually the General was perfectly correct: on 6 February 1840 hearty cheering greeted a seasick Prince from Dover's two piers as the steam-packet *Ariel* reached port, after a five-and-a-half-hour buffeting from Calais in what the Admiralty hydrographer's new wind scale reckoned a Force 8 gale. But, despite the warming sentiments of windswept Dover, the marriage remained far from popular. Here, it was assumed, came yet another impoverished German princeling ready to dip into Britain's coffers. His Protestantism was, moreover, suspect: he had been in Rome the previous Easter, his brother Ferdinand and his family were Roman Catholics, and the best known Coburger in Britain had married a Catholic Princess and was reigning in a nominally Catholic Kingdom. Avowals that he was, indeed, a good Protestant went largely unheeded; Parliament disliked the way in which the Whigs were handling the marriage project, and the Tories insisted on cutting Albert's annuity from £50,000 to £30,000. To the Queen's intense irritation Wellington and Peel seemed to regard Albert as a Whig nominee. On New Year's Day 1840 her journal records a new supplication in her private litany: 'From the Tories, good Lord deliver us.'[11]

Her uncles, too, plagued the Queen in these weeks before the marriage. Ernest Augustus, as Duke of Cumberland, protested at the precedence accorded to a royal consort who was merely a Prince; and he induced Adolphus of Cambridge weakly to agree with him. Should Victoria suffer the fate of her cousin Princess Charlotte and die in child-birth, Albert would still take precedence over the son of the new sovereign, the much-dreaded King of Hanover, who remained next in line of succession until November 1840. With characteristic pettiness, Ernest Augustus refused to supply any more of the 'cream and black' Hanoverian horses who had drawn the state coach on royal occasions since the accession of George I. Melbourne abandoned attempts to settle Albert's precedence by Act of Parliament, preferring to leave the question for later settlement by an Order in Council. When the Queen, furious with her uncles, urged the Prime Minister to have a Bill drafted which would make Albert a King Consort, even Lord Melbourne's patience began to run thin: 'For God's sake, Ma'am, let's have no more of it,' he exclaimed. 'If you get the English people into the way of making Kings, you will get them into the way of unmaking them!'[12]

The wedding itself, in the Chapel Royal of St James's Palace on 10 February, was a happy affair; but it was greeted coolly enough by *The Times* that morning: 'One might, without being unreasonable, express a wish that the consort selected for a Princess so educated and hitherto so unfairly guided, as Queen Victoria, should have been a person of riper years, and likely to form more sound and circumspect opinions.'[13] Prince Albert was left with few illusions about his position in society. As he remarked to Stockmar fourteen years later, he was 'the foreign interloper', a Prince with extraordinary energy, wide interests and an astonishing knowledge of European affairs but assigned to a position at court which the British constitution never recognized.

At first the Prince found it irksome that the Queen should deny him German secretaries of his own choice; reluctantly he accepted George Anson, who had been Melbourne's secretary and who was only seven years older than the Prince himself. Soon he came to trust Anson and admire his trenchant mind, but he was glad to retain Stockmar, who until 1857 spent several months each year in England; and there were other Coburgers within his personal suite. It was widely believed that the Prince 'Germanized' the English court, not least by conversing regularly with his wife in his native tongue rather than in hers. This was nonsense: he was a good, natural linguist and eager to improve his fluency in the 'Queen's English'. He worked no less assiduously at seeking an understanding of British constitutional law; only social conventions seem to have flummoxed him, and occasional solecisms during visits to the great country mansions were magnified by those jealous of his privileged position and eminence. On the other hand, he was certainly gratified to find that so many German customs were already established at court; the social ritual of Christmas owes more to Queen Charlotte in the 1770s and 1780s than to Prince Albert seventy years later.

At the end of November 1840 the birth of Princess Victoria Adelaide – created Princess Royal two months later and known in the family sometimes as 'Pussy' but generally as 'Vicky' – was widely popular. The medically perfect birth stilled haunting memories of the Claremont tragedy and, although there was some disappointment that the child was not a prince, a healthy baby removed all threat of Ernest Augustus's succession. Fatherhood also indirectly helped the Prince establish himself as the Queen's secretary. Victoria had been reluctant at first to consult her husband over public affairs, even though Lord Melbourne urged her to take him fully into her confidence. But, as the Queen's pregnancy advanced, their writing-tables were placed side by side, first at Windsor Castle and subsequently at Buckingham Palace, and the Prince was given a personal key to the official government boxes immediately after the baby's birth. His tidy, analytical mind and his determination to remain a confidential adviser who would not himself speak out on contentious issues made the Prince an ideal first secretary to the sovereign, as a succession of seven prime ministers came to recognize.

Predictably the strongest opposition to the Prince's increased role came, not from Downing Street, but from the Prince's fellow-German within the royal household, Baroness Lehzen. So tenacious was Lehzen that, by the winter of 1841-2, her imperious control of the new royal nursery led to quarrels between the Queen and her consort in which the indefatigable Stockmar played the role of peacemaker. It was clear that, as Melbourne and King Leopold had anticipated soon after the marriage, the Baroness had to go. On 30 September 1842 she slipped away to Hanover, with a quiet and resigned dignity in contrast to the stormy scenes of past months. At Bückeburg, between Minden and Hanover, she survived through the years of German unity, outliving Albert by almost a decade. Occasionally, during a royal visit to Germany, she would be seen talking to the Queen, a not unwelcome ghost from those halcyon summers at Kensington and Claremont. She was wrapped in a cloak of proud pathos in her last years in Hanover. Had she stayed at the English court, the Prince Consort could never have consolidated his position; he would have remained, as he described himself three months after his marriage, 'Only the Husband not the Master in the House'.[14]

The royal nursery expanded with an efficient regularity as tidy as the Prince's handling of government business. Albert Edward was born on 9 November 1841 and created Prince of Wales four weeks later; a third child, Princess Alice, came in April 1843; and a second son, Alfred, who was in time to succeed his uncle as Duke of Saxe-Coburg and Gotha, was born in August 1844. Two more Princesses followed: Helena in May 1846; and Louise in March 1848. May Day in 1850 saw the coming of Arthur, later Duke of Connaught – a Prince who, delighting in toy soldiers presented by the French Emperor while Sebastopol was first under siege, lived long enough to hear of another envelopment of the Crimean port, by Hitler's armies in the Second World War. Victoria and Albert's youngest son, named after the King of the Belgians, was born in April 1853; and their youngest daughter, Princess Beatrice, in April 1856. Although fashionable society still mocked the alleged foreign cut of Prince Albert's clothes or his taste in elegant riding boots, most of Queen Victoria's subjects respected her consort and admired his domestic virtues. As Bagehot was to write, somewhat patronizingly, six years after Albert's death, 'A family on the throne is an interesting idea; it brings down the pride of sovereignty to the level of petty life.'[15] Until the war fever of 1853-4 most criticism of Albert's 'foreignership' was confined to cheap and scurrilous broadsheets and the heavy-handed satire of *Punch*, a periodical first published in the year after Victoria and Albert's marriage. Critical press-cuttings were noted and filed away by the consort's secretaries. The Prince was excessively sensitive to their comments.

In June 1843 Princess Augusta of Cambridge, the female cousin closest in age to the Queen, was married at Buckingham Palace to the elder son of the

Grand Duke of Mecklenburg-Strelitz. Relations between the Queen and her uncle, Adolphus of Cambridge, had been strained since her accession, partly because she resented attempts to encourage her to marry the Duke's son, Prince George of Cambridge. She was, however, prepared to look favourably on this newest dynastic link with Germany, at least until the Duke of Cambridge pressed parliament to accord Augusta an annuity of £2,000 from public funds. This demand was resolutely resisted by Sir Robert Peel, the Prime Minister, and by the Queen and her consort. Cambridge's action nevertheless sparked off a minor explosion of anti-German feeling, which was accentuated by the King of Hanover's insistence on coming to England in the first week of June, taking his seat in the House of Lords and claiming that certain Crown Jewels should belong to his German Kingdom. Soon afterwards King Leopold came to stay briefly with his niece and nephew. *Punch* caught the public mood with the icy observation that 'on Saturday last there were two kings in London, both of them the sovereigns of foreign countries' and since 'Saturday last was quarter-day, there is no difficulty in guessing the object of their visit'.[16]

But it was Princess Augusta's wedding that produced the strongest outburst from *Punch*, an interesting essay in sustained irony, and remarkable for its contemptuous ignorance of German affairs:

The hereditary Duke of Mecklenberg [*sic*] Strelitz, who was on this occasion the happy man, is heir to the House of Mecklenberg, whose chief is one of the happy band of royal pensioners whom England has the honour to support. Strelitz is an independent dukedom, with a dependent duke. Its resources are public alms and private benevolence; its territory extends over a tract which in size and in bad roads may be compared to Rutland; its population is about twice as large but not half so respectable as that of Mecklenberg Square; its chief produce consists in nothing particular.... It is gratifying at least to know that the Princess Augusta of Cambridge can have had no mercenary motive in accepting the hand – a thoroughly empty one – of the illustrious scion of the House of Mecklenberg. Queen Victoria has spared no expense to do honour to her cousin Augusta's nuptials. The reigning Duke of Mecklenberg was fortunately enabled to visit this country. He . . . was looking remarkably well – as all annuitants on this country generally contrive to look. The ceremony was performed in the usual style of royalty. And when the prelate who performed the office came to the words 'With all my worldly goods I thee endow', the Duke of Cambridge, who always thinks out loud, kept up a running accompaniment of 'Well, that's capital! worldly goods indeed! I should like to see some of 'em', and other pleasant observations; which, as Strelitz senior, and Mecklenberg junior neither of them understand English very well, were supposed by the father and son to be a gush of fervent ejaculations from the father of the bride, invoking happiness on the heads of the newly married couple. At the end of the ceremony the happy pair set out for Kew to spend the honeymoon. . . . The Duke of Cambridge behaved very liberally to the poor in the neighbourhood; and Strelitz senior gave away on the occasion – his eldest son – a piece of munificence in every way worthy of Mecklenberg.[17]

At the foot of this report an over-burdened John Bull was depicted, bending low beneath a basket full of crowns and royal regalia labelled 'Mecklenberg', 'Coburg' and 'Hanover'.

The following Saturday's *Punch* contained four separate ironical paragraphs on the wedding. But the favourite target of the satirists remained the Queen's uncle from Hanover. On a report that Wellington and the King of Hanover were no longer friends, *Punch* for 5 August 1843 added the comment: 'Let all men ponder upon the Duke's admirable example, who herein shows that it is never too late to drop bad company.'[18] Prince Albert, although like the Queen detesting Ernest Augustus of Hanover, believed that lampoons of this character provoked hostile comment in the German states and helped isolate the Queen and her family from their kinsfolk on the Continent. Perhaps he was right. To a Prince who, on his betrothal, assured his mother's mother that 'I shall never cease to be a true German, and a true Coburg and Gotha man' such dissensions mattered deeply.[19]

The British people remember Prince Albert as the royal consort who endowed their monarchy with the key public virtues of the nineteenth century, conventional morality and respect for industry. His true memorials were the museums of South Kensington, the Albert Hall and the canopied statue facing it, neatly planned workers' cottages at Kennington, an Italianate villa beside the Solent, an expanded Rosenau-on-Dee at Balmoral and, until fire consumed it on the eve of his great-grandson's abdication, a Crystal Palace moved from Hyde Park to the southern slopes of Sydenham. *The Times*, which had greeted his marriage ungraciously, was to mourn his passing as 'the greatest loss that could possibly have fallen' upon the nation, seeing in him 'a man to whom more than any one else we owe the happy state of our internal polity, and a degree of general contentment to which neither we nor any other nation we know of ever attained before'.[20] No doubt during those closing weeks of 1861 these sentiments carried a ring of genuine conviction to prosperous Londoners. But the Prince himself was always less interested in 'internal polity' than in foreign affairs. For his German compatriots the Prince's memorial was, therefore, not some 'union of art and industry', but the so-called 'Coburg Plan', an abortive project to create a unitary German federal state which would be dependent on successfully importing British concepts of constitutional monarchy. To a large extent the Coburg Plan was an invention of the Prince's critics and detractors, for Albert was too shrewd to bind himself to any simplistic programme. Yet there were, over fourteen or fifteen years, a succession of 'Albertine Plans', seeking the establishment of some form of German unity based upon constitutional government. What distinguishes one version from another is the extent to which Baron Stockmar was, or was not, in the Prince's confidence at the time the plan was under consideration.[21]

Prince Albert, like many in his generation, was fired by enthusiasm for a liberal and unified Germany while studying at Bonn. When first he settled in England there was little occasion for him to display his concern for German national aspirations, apart from treating the Queen's uncle from Hanover with the frigid courtesy he well deserved. The Prince found himself in general agreement with Palmerston's handling of the Eastern Question in 1840 and with the policies of his Tory successor, Lord Aberdeen. After Palmerston returned to the Foreign Office in July 1846, small differences arose over the endemic civil war in Portugal, whose King Consort, Ferdinand II, was a Coburg, but it was the German dynastic links that mattered. Prince Albert's elder brother inherited Saxe-Coburg and Gotha in January 1844, ruling as Duke Ernest II. The Prince's cousin – and half-brother-in-law – Charles of Leiningen, had since 1822 ruled the tiny territory around Amorbach in his own right. The Leiningen possessions were extremely small, even by Coburg standards, but Prince Charles came from an influential Palatine family and, at Amorbach, he was less than thirty miles from Frankfurt am Main, where the pulse of German national sentiment beat most clearly.

Outside his immediate family, Albert was on friendly terms with Frederick William IV of Prussia, a ruler who admired Britain's institutions. It was easier for the Prussian and British royal families to collaborate once the London-Hanover dynastic bond was severed. The King visited England in January 1842 and thereafter Albert maintained a lively correspondence with him. Queen Victoria thought him 'a most amiable man', kind, well-meaning and amusing. Lord Aberdeen conceded that Frederick William's projects 'are generous and he wishes to do what is right', but privately the Foreign Secretary commented to Dorothea Lieven (by birth a Benckendorff) that 'Like all Germans, he is sometimes a little in the clouds.'[22]

The revolutions of 1848, in France and central Europe, closely involved Prince Albert in German affairs. Louis Philippe and his family found sanctuary at Claremont some ten days before revolutionary unrest spread to the German and Austrian lands. News of the fall of Metternich and of a radical rising in Berlin reached London on 18 March, the day Victoria gave birth to her sixth child, Princess Louise (who was named in honour of Albert's ill-used mother). Uncertainty over the extent of Chartist radical feeling led the royal family to leave for Osborne as soon as the Queen was fit to travel, and it was in the seclusion of the Isle of Wight that Prince Albert took stock of events on the Continent.

The challenge to the existing order in Germany came as no surprise. Indeed in 1847, under Stockmar's influence, Prince Albert had urged the King of Prussia and several lesser sovereigns to satisfy liberal demands for constitutional reform. But the Prince did not anticipate widespread unrest outside Germany, nor did he understand the variations in revolutionary objectives from city to city across Europe. He was puzzled both by the conservative reaction of King Leopold (who was alarmed by Louis Philippe's fall) and by Stockmar's assumption that the need for a unified Germany outweighed all particularist considerations, including the sovereign rights of individual rulers. Prince Albert, for all his fine words about Germany's future, was angry with his brother for placating the liberals in Saxe-Coburg with financial concessions at the expense of the ruling family itself.[23]

But if Prince Albert was inconsistent, so were most German princes of his day. The two greatest dynasties, Hohenzollern and Habsburg, gave no clear lead. One of the most curious episodes in the summer of revolution was the dedication of the new cathedral at Cologne, an occasion upon which Frederick William IV and Archduke John received at the city landing-stage the liberal parliamentarians from Frankfurt who had travelled down the Rhine in a boat festooned with German national colours. 'Do not forget that there are still princes in Germany and that I am one of them,' Frederick William remarked in his speech of welcome.[24] The only sovereign who never wavered throughout all these months of unrest was the King of Hanover. Ernest Augustus burned a liberal petition handed to him in the heady days of March 1848 and, when two months later radicals slipped across the border from Prussia, he resorted to a variation of the bag-packing threat with which four generations of British kings met the importunities of unaccommodating ministers. He told his subjects that, if they demanded concessions, he would leave at once for London, taking the Crown Prince with him; they could therefore choose sovereignty on his terms or absorption by Prussia.[25] They chose independence.

Prince Albert himself favoured a compromise solution of the German Question. At the end of March 1848 he drew up a memorandum which he sent to the King of Prussia and to Brussels and Coburg. He proposed that there should be a single German federal state under an elected emperor and with two assemblies, a Lower House chosen by representative bodies in the various kingdoms and principalities and an Upper House of princes, who could veto measures passed in the Lower House. This plan, with its assumption that the German princes would support a unitary state and that the German nationalists would tolerate the continued existence of the princes, was welcomed by Leopold and by Frederick William IV, who circulated the memorandum among the other German rulers. But, as Duke Ernest II saw in Coburg, the plan was impracticable. The greatest wish of German patriots at that moment was for a unified democratic state, with the political initiative in the hands of a directly elected all-German parliament meeting at Frankfurt. This programme, warmly supported by Charles of Leiningen and Stockmar, was more radical than Albert desired, despite his avowed admiration for Britain's parliamentary institutions.

Duke Ernest, in his memoirs, inferred that his brother, having settled in

England, was out of touch with German politics. Yet at the time he drafted his memorandum Prince Albert possessed up-to-the-minute news from Berlin. For on 27 March 1848 he held long conversations with a newly arrived refugee – the King of Prussia's brother, William, who as heir to the throne was officially styled 'Prince of Prussia'. It was more than a third of a century since Prince William had come to Regency London in the 'Year of Revelry', a seventeen-year-old veteran of two campaigns against Napoleon. This early military experience shaped his life; he was 'the grapeshot Prince' to the angry crowd who had attacked his palace on the Unter den Linden on 14 March and forced him to leave his wife, his son and his daughter in Berlin while he journeyed to Holland, and so once more to London. Albert thought him a scapegoat for soldiers who had fired on the mob in the capital, but he was certainly a rigid traditionalist in his attachment to the familiar forms of Prussian life. During the fortnight he spent as a guest of Victoria and Albert, William was impressed by the calm with which London met the challenge of Chartist mass demonstrations. At the same time he emphasized to his hosts the folly of following Leiningen and Stockmar in their enthusiasm for the people's direct participation in government. Thereafter Prince Albert tended to support what liberals regarded as the counter-revolutionary moves of the Prussian government.

The Prince of Prussia returned home in early June at the request of his brother, Frederick William IV, who was angry that a Hohenzollern should have been forced into exile by a ransacking mob. Frederick William was having second thoughts about the revolution. He experimented with a succession of liberal ministries but categorically refused to accept a parliamentary system on the British model. By June astute conservative land-owners were playing off one group of revolutionaries against another, and Frederick William was benefiting from the confusion of liberal objectives. Did the revolutionaries want a Prussian parliament in Berlin or an all-German parliament in Frankfurt? They had the promise of both; but, if so, what was to be the relationship between the two institutions? To this key question there was no simple answer.

From London, Prince Albert watched with regret the muddled state of German politics. He congratulated Frederick William on dissolving the Prussian Constituent Assembly in the first week of December 1848 and in promulgating a constitution which maintained royal authority. Four months later Prince Albert again sent his congratulations to the Prussian King. On this occasion Frederick William had refused the offer of the imperial crown made to him by members of the Frankfurt parliament, a body always less radical and more narrowly nationalistic than the Berlin constituent assembly. To Frederick William IV, to the Prince of Prussia and to Prince Albert it seemed deplorable that a sovereign should become 'Emperor of Germany' through the will of the people.

For the rest of his life Prince Albert regretted that the revolutionary years saw no firm progress made towards German unity. He blamed the Habsburgs, he blamed Leiningen and brother Ernest and all the princes who had neglected his advice. But, though he thought Frederick William had behaved weakly, he consistently backed Prussia against Austria and he supported the German national cause against Danish rights in the disputed border Duchies of Schleswig-Holstein. This Anglo-Prussian royal entente was a novel feature in British diplomacy and was far from popular among Westminster politicians. It is hardly surprising if, at times, Palmerston, as Foreign Secretary, found the Prince's approach to the German Question exasperating.[26] Even Palmerston's predecessor, Lord Aberdeen, whom Albert praised as a tactful, calm and earnest public servant, was disturbed. 'The Prince's views are generally sound and wise, with one exception . . . his violent and incorrigible German unionism,' Aberdeen told Greville, the clerk of the Privy Council, in mid-September 1849. Significantly Aberdeen added, 'He goes all lengths with Prussia.'[27]

The three years which followed the failure of the German revolutions cover the most creative period of the Albertine legend. Prince Albert threw himself into planning the Great Exhibition of 1851 with the dedication of a fanatic, determined that a celebration of British achievements in manufacture and industry would benefit from being seen in competition with the work of other nations. When the exhibition proved a resounding success, with over six million visitors in five and a half months, his initiative and energy won praise from most of his critics. By Christmas 1851 he had become popular with the middle classes for his contribution to what Macaulay was to call 'a singularly happy year of peace, plenty, good feeling, innocent pleasure and national glory'.[28]

The Queen and her consort had further reason for celebration that Christmas. For, while the Prince was gradually winning the confidence of the British public he was also waging a running battle with the Foreign Secretary in Lord John Russell's government, Palmerston, and in December 1851 it seemed as if the Prince was triumphant. The two men had clashed sharply fifteen months before, when Palmerston declined to support Prussia in resisting Austrian attempts to recover Habsburg primacy in the German Confederation. But unexpectedly, in the closing weeks of Exhibition Year, Palmerston was forced to resign as Foreign Secretary, having for once lost public favour by privately congratulating the French on the *coup d'état* which made Louis Napoleon a dictator.

'Now he has done with the Foreign Office for ever,' the Queen wrote contentedly from Windsor to King Leopold after Palmerston's fall. But her elation was short-lived. Palmerston believed Prince Albert had engineered his fall so that he might dominate his inexperienced successor, the young and

Mother and daughter: Elizabeth of
Bohemia (left) and the Electress
Sophia

George 1's wife, Sophia Dorothea,
with her son and daughter, in
about 1690

George i's coronation procession passing St James's Palace

A stylized contemporary representation of George ii on the field of Dettingen

Frederick the Great returning
from manoeuvres in his later years,
portrayed in conversation with the
Duke of York

Princess Charlotte and her
husband, Prince Leopold, at
Covent Garden, 1816

Cartoon, April 1819, depicting a fictitious visit of the royal dukes to the Duke and Duchess of Cambridge, with their newly born son. A heavily pregnant Duchess of Kent stands between her husband and the Duke of Cumberland. The Duke of Clarence (soon to become William IV) is on the left.

The Duchess of Kent and her daughter, the future Queen Victoria, in 1821

Schloss Rheinhardtsbrunn, in Thuringia, where Queen Victoria was in residence in September 1862

The Winterhalter painting of the royal family in 1846 beneath which, at Osborne in 1862, Princess Alice was married. The painting shows (left to right) Prince Alfred, the Prince of Wales, Queen Victoria, Prince Albert, Princess Alice, the infant Princess Helena and the Princess Royal

Above left: William I, King of Prussia and first German Emperor

Above right: 'Vicky', Princess Royal and Empress Frederick

Left: The wedding of Prince Henry of Battenberg and Princess Beatrice, July 1885

Right: Prince Louis of Hesse, Princess
Alice and their children

Below: Grand Duchess Augusta of
Mecklenburg-Strelitz in 1913

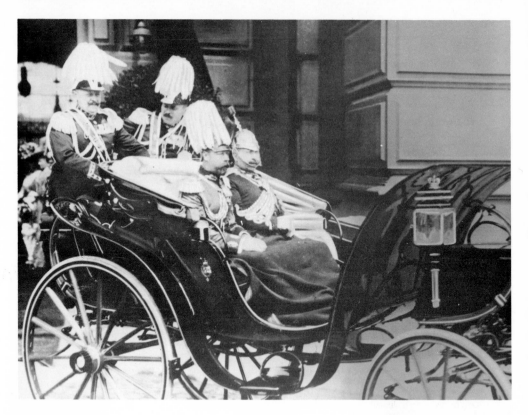

Above: King George V (in the uniform of
his German regiment) and Kaiser
William II in Berlin, May 1913

Right: Hitler greets the Duke and
Duchess of Windsor at Berchtesgaden,
October 1937

amiable Earl Granville. There were renewed rumours of foreign influence at
court. By the second week in July 1852 the *Westminster Gazette* was complaining
that the 'high interests' of the Coburg family made it impossible for the Queen
to assess foreign policy questions impartially. From now until Palmerston
himself became Prime Minister early in February 1855, 'Albert's foreignership' remained a sensitive issue below the surface of British politics at a time
of widespread party confusion.[29]

A couple of months after Palmerston's abrupt removal from the Foreign
Office the Russell government was defeated in the Commons on a Militia Bill
and was replaced by a Tory ministry headed by Lord Derby. Ten months later
the Queen welcomed a coalition of which the Earl of Aberdeen was Prime
Minister. Although Palmerston returned to the cabinet as Home Secretary, his
chances to intervene in European affairs were limited by both departmental
duties and the gout. The Queen, in yet another Christmas commentary on
politics to her uncle in Belgium, wrote that 'the success of our excellent
Aberdeen's arduous task . . . would, I was sure, please you. It is the realisation
of the country's and our most ardent wishes, and it deserves success, and will, I
think, command great support.'[30]

But the Queen and Prince Albert were once again disappointed. Within a
month of its formation the coalition cabinet was confronted by a crisis over the
Eastern Question whose intricacies plagued European diplomacy throughout
the year. Neither Lord Aberdeen nor Prince Albert were so resolutely anti-
Russian as sections of the popular Press: and the Prince hoped, in particular, that through his friendship with Frederick William IV he could allay
some of the Tsar's suspicions, for Nicholas I was Frederick William's brother-
in-law and there were close contacts between the courts of St Petersburg
and Berlin. But these well-intentioned endeavours were misunderstood:
Aberdeen's apparent vacillation lost the coalition public confidence at
home; and the running conflict between the court and Palmerston was
distorted in newspapers and in scurrilous broadsheets until the would-be
peacemaker was pilloried as a would-be traitor.

The renewed conflict with Palmerston began with a relatively trivial
problem which coincided with mounting tension in Europe as a whole. By the
first week of November 1853 Turkish and Russian troops were fighting each
other on the lower Danube, the Great Powers were seeking a suspension of
hostilities pending a conference in Vienna, and a joint Anglo-French fleet was
moored off the Sultan's palaces at Constantinople, ready to protect the
Turkish capital from a Russian attack. At this moment Prince Albert
discovered that the Home Secretary was canvassing proposals for a dynastic
marriage which would ally the House of Bonaparte and the House of Hanover
as effectively as the links between their navies in the Bosphorus. Palmerston
thought that Napoleon III's profligate cousin, Prince Napoleon, should marry
the Queen's cousin, Mary Adelaide of Cambridge. Despite passing support

from King Leopold, the project was soon dropped from all discussion. Thereafter relations between the court and the Home Secretary deteriorated from the formally cold to the icily correct.

In December 1853 the Home Secretary quarrelled with the Prime Minister over parliamentary reform. On Wednesday, 14 December Palmerston sent Aberdeen a letter of resignation, published in Thursday's *Morning Post*, a newspaper which consistently supported Palmerston. Prince Albert thought Palmerston's departure from the cabinet would – in modern terms – strengthen the doves at the expense of the hawks. But on the previous Sunday news reached London that the Russians had destroyed the Turkish fleet at Sinope. Throughout the week the London Press blamed Aberdeen's government for not affording naval protection to 'our Turkish ally'. 'Peace . . . is no longer compatible with the honour and dignity of the country,' declared Tuesday's *The Times*; and Friday's *Morning Post* not only maintained that the only answer of true Englishmen to this 'violent outrage' was 'immediate war', but also insisted that Palmerston had resigned from the government because of Sinope and Aberdeen's inactivity. In this mood of war fever it was easy to blame 'Courtly contempt and Coburg intrigue' for having, once again, engineered Palmerston's fall. And if Prince Albert wanted Palmerston out of the government, then it was clear to the flag-waving muddle-heads who read the more outrageous newspapers that the Prince, being a German, was, if not a traitor, at best 'a subservient tool of Russian ambition'. A *Punch* cartoon depicted a slightly sinister Prince disdainfully disregarding a warning notice as he skated over the thin ice of foreign affairs. Alarming rumours swept the capital and the provinces. In the House of Lords, on the last day of January, Lord Derby denounced a wave of hysteria 'which led thousands to attend at the doors of the Tower to see His Royal Highness go in'.[31]

Yet, amid all this tumult, Palmerston remained in Aberdeen's ministry. He never even surrendered his seals of office. After enjoying a week of popular idolization in mid-December he discovered from correspondence with Aberdeen that he had misunderstood the government's intentions over parliamentary reform; on Christmas Eve he withdrew his resignation; and he did not miss a single cabinet meeting in the three months preceding Britain's declaration of war on Russia in March 1854. Palmerston politely denied that he had authorized a pamphlet attacking the 'secret shadow behind the throne', and in the last week of January his *Morning Post* published an announcement specifically stating that the offer to resign in December 'had not the remotest connection with anything on the part of the Court'. Gladstone, writing anonymously in the *Morning Chronicle* of 16 January, praised Prince Albert's good counsel and his sense of public duty. Gradually an angry Queen was mollified.

Palmerston's 'escapade' and the subsequent war fever left a deeper mark on her husband. Not since Shakespeare's day had London seen such a display of mindless xenophobia, as distinct from religious bigotry. To Prince Albert the smear on the German connection at the court of St James's seemed indelible. 'One almost fancies oneself in a lunatic asylum,' he wrote to Stockmar from Windsor. 'Even *you* are attacked.'[32] In Belgium the veteran of old skirmishes with Palmerston was disturbed, though hardly surprised, by these events: from Laeken King Leopold wrote to his niece, 'I grieve to see how unjustly you are plagued, and how wonderfully untrue and passionate are the attacks of part of the Press. . . . As far as your few continental relations are concerned, I don't think they will be able to fix anything upon your faithful servant. I have done England at all times good services in the sense of her best interests.' Meanwhile in the snow-stilled peace of Coburg that January the sixty-six-year-old faithful servant of the faithful servant drafted a memorandum analysing the reasons for this wave of royal unpopularity. For although Prince Albert might look back in disappointment at the sudden eruption of 'all the gossip and idle talk of the last fourteen years', Baron Stockmar was as ready to look forward to future goodwill between the English and German peoples as when he first arrived in Regency London. The memorandum, although subdivided into twenty-eight classified sections, carried a simple enough message: the Prince must be hardened rather than depressed by the buffetings of 'foreignership'. To Stockmar it remained essential that Albert should persevere with his mission of preaching constitutionalism to the Prussian royal family and through them to Germany as a whole.[33]

The Prussian (and German) royal family in the nineteenth and twentieth centuries

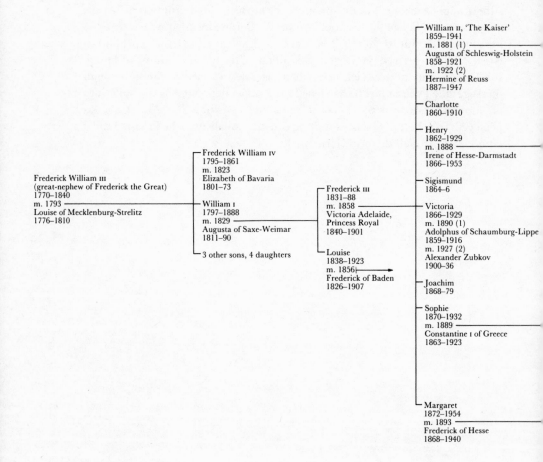

Frederick William III
(great-nephew of Frederick the Great)
1770–1840
m. 1793
Louise of Mecklenburg-Strelitz
1776–1810

Frederick William IV
1795–1861
m. 1823
Elizabeth of Bavaria
1801–73

William I
1797–1888
m. 1829
Augusta of Saxe-Weimar
1811–90

3 other sons, 4 daughters

Frederick III
1831–88
m. 1858
Victoria Adelaide,
Princess Royal
1840–1901

Louise
1838–1923
m. 1856
Frederick of Baden
1826–1907

William II, 'The Kaiser'
1859–1941
m. 1881 (1)
Augusta of Schleswig-Holstein
1858–1921
m. 1922 (2)
Hermine of Reuss
1887–1947

Charlotte
1860–1910

Henry
1862–1929
m. 1888
Irene of Hesse-Darmstadt
1866–1953

Sigismund
1864–6

Victoria
1866–1929
m. 1890 (1)
Adolphus of Schaumburg-Lippe
1859–1916
m. 1927 (2)
Alexander Zubkov
1900–36

Joachim
1868–79

Sophie
1870–1932
m. 1889
Constantine I of Greece
1863–1923

Margaret
1872–1954
m. 1893
Frederick of Hesse
1868–1940

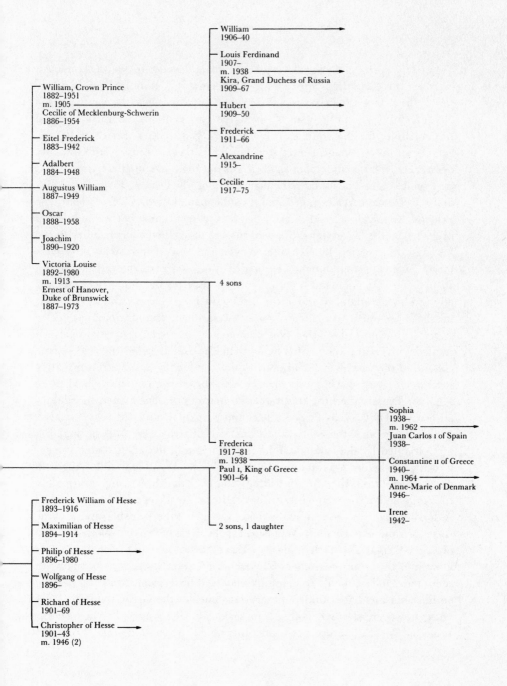

William, Crown Prince
1882–1951
m. 1905
Cecilie of Mecklenburg-Schwerin
1886–1954

William
1906–40

Louis Ferdinand
1907–
m. 1938
Kira, Grand Duchess of Russia
1909–67

Hubert
1909–50

Frederick
1911–66

Alexandrine
1915–

Cecilie
1917–75

Eitel Frederick
1883–1942

Adalbert
1884–1948

Augustus William
1887–1949

Oscar
1888–1958

Joachim
1890–1920

Victoria Louise
1892–1980
m. 1913
Ernest of Hanover,
Duke of Brunswick
1887–1973

4 sons

Frederica
1917–81
m. 1938
Paul I, King of Greece
1901–64

Sophia
1938–
m. 1962
Juan Carlos I of Spain
1938–

Constantine II of Greece
1940–
m. 1964
Anne-Marie of Denmark
1946–

Irene
1942–

2 sons, 1 daughter

Frederick William of Hesse
1893–1916

Maximilian of Hesse
1894–1914

Philip of Hesse
1896–1980

Wolfgang of Hesse
1896–

Richard of Hesse
1901–69

Christopher of Hesse
1901–43
m. 1946 (2)

CHAPTER NINE

⟋ Two Marriages ⟍

On a sunny spring morning in May 1851 a tall and well-built youth of nineteen escorted three children through the eighteen-acre Exhibition hall in Hyde Park. The Prince and Princess of Prussia had been invited to the opening of the Great Exhibition and their son, Prince Frederick William, assumed a natural responsibility for the younger royal visitors. But neither 'Fritz', as he was called, nor his twelve-year-old sister, Louise, had ever been outside Germany before, and their command of English was halting and stilted. That mattered little on this occasion, for both their companions, the Princess Royal (aged ten) and the Prince of Wales (aged nine), could speak German well. 'Vicky', the Princess Royal, already possessed a bright intelligence rare in the daughters of previous British sovereigns. She was also well coached by her father in the scientific marvels of the Exhibition; even the newest intricacies of electric telegraph meant something to her. Some young officers might well have found so precocious a know-all an intolerable nuisance, but not Fritz. He was amused by her affability and impressed by the English court and its customs; his sister became a bosom friend to Vicky, and he personally found in Prince Albert an authoritative father-figure whom he was awed to see that his parents treated with great respect. After a month in England Fritz returned to Coblenz convinced that the liberal sentiments which the English royal family privately professed – and to which his mother was herself sympathetic – held more hope for Prussia than the traditional Hohenzollern dependence on military autocracy. That was as Prince Albert and Stockmar intended.[1]

Two years later, the Prince and Princess of Prussia were back in England, accompanied by their daughter Louise. Their son, like the Coburg Princes fifteen years before, was studying at Bonn University, attending the Anglican church there from time to time, improving his English, writing occasionally to Vicky and more frequently to her father. The Prince of Prussia visited Aldershot and was pleased by the field exercises of the British army; his wife was more interested in life at Windsor. The Princess of Prussia – born Augusta of Saxe-Weimar-Eisenach, a niece of Tsars Alexander I and Nicholas I – was a woman of strong character. She eschewed snap decisions on whims of sentiment, and her son's Anglophilia may well have seemed to her a passing enthusiasm incubated under the crystal panes of the Great Exhibition. By 1853, however, she was taking him seriously. She was astonished by the Princess Royal's mature poise and the range of her table-talk. From the correspondence exchanged between Windsor and Coblenz it seems clear that after this second visit to England, if not before, the Queen and the Princess of Prussia regarded the marriage of Fritz and Vicky as probable. Even though 'the children' themselves did not as yet appear especially fond of each other, the Queen knew that her elder daughter invariably took violent fancies or strong dislikes to people with whom she came into contact for any length of time; and Vicky was delighted by all she had seen of the Prussian royal family.[2]

Prince Albert and Stockmar convinced themselves that an Anglo-Prussian marriage was desirable for the sake of Germany, and indeed for the good of the Continent as a whole. Both believed a unified, liberal German state would counter-balance the threatening power of Russia and the disruptive Bonapartist ambitions of the Second French Empire. By now, however, they had given up all hope of Frederick William IV, who was no longer interested in constitutionalism or the German national cause. He was content to leave politics to a court camarilla who controlled the administration. Since November 1850 General Otto von Manteuffel had held office as Prussia's Minister President (prime minister), heading a thoroughly reactionary government, and it seemed unlikely Frederick William would ever oust him. But political observers inside and outside Prussia speculated on what would happen should Frederick William die or become incapable of ruling. By right the Prince of Prussia should succeed to the throne or serve as his brother's Regent; and Prince Albert still hoped the Prince retained some of the beliefs implanted during their conversations in 1848 and 1851. But it was by no means certain in 1853 that the Prince of Prussia really sought the crown. He was a professional soldier, unpopular with the mob and yet highly critical of the camarilla. Recent events in Austria suggested a precedent for the succession of a younger sovereign. In December 1848 the Emperor Ferdinand's formidable sister-in-law induced her husband to renounce his right of succession in favour of their son, Francis Joseph, who had been born just fourteen months earlier than 'Fritz'. If Prussia should follow Austria's example and seek the leadership of a young dynamic ruler, those who shaped Fritz's political principles might well determine the future destiny of Europe. An intelligent English bride could safeguard their ideas, perhaps even perpetuate them.

The Crimean War temporarily clouded the friendship between the Prince of Prussia's family and the court at Windsor. Manteuffel's policy vacillated wretchedly during the war. Frederick William IV refused to enter the conflict, much to the indignation of his brother and nephew, and as the fighting in the Crimea intensified, British ministers began to maintain that neutral Prussia could not expect to sit with the peacemakers once the war was over. At the same time there were showy displays of entente cordiality: Napoleon III and the Empress Eugénie came to London and Windsor in April 1855; and four months later Queen Victoria and Prince Albert, with their two eldest children, were fêted in Paris. It was on this occasion that, on the same evening at a ball in Versailles, the Princess Royal partnered the bachelor Prince Napoleon in a quadrille while a visiting Prussian diplomat, Count Otto von Bismarck, was presented to her mother and father – who already knew enough about him to disapprove of his allegedly pro-Russian politics.[3]

In Berlin there was some alarm at this growing intimacy between the British royal family and the Bonapartes. Prince Frederick William won permission from the King to go abroad. It was reported that he had travelled to Ostend for the sea-bathing, no doubt staying at King Leopold's villa on the edge of the dunes. But from Ostend the Prince slipped secretly across to Dover, and then on by train to London and Aberdeen. He arrived at Balmoral Castle on Friday, 14 September, a mere twenty days after the ball at Versailles – and four days after news of the fall of Sebastopol reached Scotland.

The Princess Royal, still two months short of her fifteenth birthday, was delighted at his coming. She seemed rarely to stop talking that weekend and found in Fritz an attentive listener. While they were alone on Wednesday, she squeezed his hand affectionately. Next morning, after breakfast, he told the Queen and Prince Albert that 'he was anxious to speak of a subject which he knew his parents had never broached to us – which was to belong to our family'. Originally it was planned that he should not formally propose to the Princess Royal until the following spring, but on the Prince's third weekend in the Highlands, as the youngsters rode out towards Craig-na-Ban, they settled their future together and it was that Saturday – 29 September 1855 – which Queen Victoria was to remember as the day of secret betrothal. By then Uncle Leopold, the Prince and Princess of Prussia, the Foreign Secretary (the Earl of Clarendon) and the Prime Minister (Palmerston, for the past seven months) had all been informed, 'in the strictest confidence'. 'What the world may say we cannot help,' Prince Albert wrote to Clarendon, with slight apprehension.[4]

Unfortunately as Prince Frederick William was hurrying, somewhat furtively, from Dover to the Highlands he was seen by the Queen's cousin, the Duke of Cambridge, who told his widowed mother that Fritz must be on his way to ask for Vicky's hand.[5] Gossip excited comment in London; and on the Wednesday after that romantic Saturday ride, the principal leading article in *The Times* denounced the rumoured marriage alliance between England and Prussia. 'On the very day on which we announced the capture of Sebastopol it also transpired that Prince Frederick William of Prussia had arrived at Balmoral for the purpose of "improving his acquaintance with the Princess Royal" '. A Prussian marriage, the editor warned his readers, would be 'a step towards an alliance with Russia', for the Russian and Prussian 'royal families are inextricably entwined in the bonds of relationship, of sympathy and of mutual interest'. Warming to his theme, he thundered out his newspaper's customary magisterial interrogatives of contempt, at the expense of Prussia's royal house:

> Who is there who does not see that the days of these paltry dynasties are numbered? Why embark anew on the troubled sea of internal German politics, from which the devolution of Hanover to the male branch has so happily released us? . . . What is His Prussian Majesty to us or we to him? We never seem to agree to do the same thing at the same time. . . . What sympathy can exist between a Court supported like ours on the solid basis of popular freedom and national respect, and a camarilla just engaged in the interests of a foreign patron in trampling out the last embers of popular government which a revolution resisted with perfidy, yielded to with cowardice, and quelled with insolence, had left behind? . . . The people of England . . . has no wish to improve its acquaintance with any Prince of the house of Hohenzollern.

The Princess Royal, the paper declared, could not be loyal to her mother's kingdom and to the kingdom over which her husband would one day reign. Gloomily it predicted that she would return to England's shores 'an exile and a fugitive'. *The Times* continued a venomous anti-Prussian campaign throughout the week, mocking the misadventures of a visit made by the unfortunate King Frederick William IV to Aachen in poor weather.[6] Queen Victoria, for neither the first nor the last time, was angry with *The Times* and with its editor, John Delane.

It says much for the patience of the Prussian royal family that after this sustained attack by the best-known newspaper in Europe the engagement was not at once broken off. But, in that winter of 1855–6, Prussia could not afford to quarrel with Britain if she was still to enjoy the status of a Great Power at the Peace Congress. There were difficult moments ahead, notably over the Princess Royal's dowry and the selection of her ladies-in-waiting, and the public announcement of the wedding was not made until 10 May 1857, twenty months after the secret betrothal.[7] The Prince Consort (as Prince Albert was officially styled from June 1857) used this long span of time to educate his most willing pupil in German politics, making certain that she understood the importance of constitutional government for Prussia. The Queen, subconsciously resenting the evenings which her husband spent tutoring their eldest daughter, began to confide to a private notebook a mother's worries over the 'dear child's' immaturity: 'her wayward temper, her lack of self control, sharp answers' as well as her 'very warm affectionate, loving heart'.[8] When, in the last week before the Christmas of 1857, the royal family left Osborne for Windsor, the Queen was saddened by the reflection that: 'She has bid adieu for ever as a child, as a girl, as one of the merry, happy children of our large family to that lovely spot where for 12 years she has spent her happiest moments.' She added, 'None of our daughters will ever find such a Husband as Albert. That is Hopeless – and I know it.'[9]

Until the autumn of 1857 the Queen accepted, without question, her husband's assumption that their eldest daughter should carry the gospel of Coburg constitutionalism to darkest Prussia. But by the end of the year she was becoming so irritated by reports from Berlin that her views on the marriage seem to have come closer to the John Bull patriotism of *The Times*. When it was suggested, by officials of the Prussian court, that the wedding should take place in Berlin, the Queen was much annoyed, for, as she pointed out to Lord Clarendon, Prince Frederick William had never doubted that the marriage would take place in England: 'Whatever may be the usual practice of Prussian Princes, it is not *every* day that one marries the eldest daughter of the Queen of England. The question therefore must be considered as settled and closed.'[10] Nevertheless when, under pressure from the bride's father, the Prince of Prussia agreed to come in person to the wedding in London, the Queen was momentarily reassured. Not all the younger Hohenzollern princes were to her liking; and she was pleased that Baron Ernest von Stockmar, son of the veteran Coburg confidant, would travel to Berlin as treasurer of the Princess Royal's household. The Prince Consort, less sanguine than his wife, suspected that the pro-Russian faction at court would regard Baron Ernest as England's secret agent. Substitute 'Coburg' for 'England' and the assumption was by no means unreasonable.

The marriage was celebrated in the Chapel Royal at St James's Palace on 25 January 1858. It was fitting that the bride should be escorted down the aisle by the two men who had the greatest interest in her mission to Germany, her father and her great-uncle, King Leopold. Two extra stanzas from the pen of the poet laureate were added to the National Anthem for the occasion.

> God Bless our Prince and Bride,
> God keep their Lands Allied,
> God Save our Queen.

the choristers sang. There seemed no doubt that day of the popularity of the Princess Royal and her handsome bridegroom from Berlin. And as the carriage wheels bore the royal guests back to Buckingham Palace, along those few hundred yards of cheering well-wishers, the Queen felt able slightly to ease the weight of monarchy. Leaning across the carriage to the Princess of Prussia she proposed that henceforth the two mothers might address each other with the familiarity of a second person singular rather than the formal courtesy of a second person plural. Thus were the Hohenzollerns admitted to the comfortable intimacy of life at Windsor, Osborne and Balmoral.[11]

There seemed little comfortable or intimate in the palaces awaiting the Princess Royal in Prussia that winter. Bride and bridegroom crossed from Gravesend to Antwerp on 2 February and, after being entertained by King

Leopold at a ball in Brussels, travelled on by train through Prussia's Rhine Province to Cologne and eventually to Potsdam. Garlanded arches and respectful crowds greeted them all along the route. Despite speedier communications, there were similarities between this latest royal progress across Germany and the winter journey of the 'Phoenix Bride' almost two and a half centuries before. Victoria and Albert, like James I, expected full reports of their daughter's reception from trusted members of her suite and from British envoys in Germany; and Fritz, like Frederick of the Palatinate, nervously prepared a home for his young wife, conscious that the wintry shores of the Havel must seem alien and cheerless to a young newcomer. The pleasant and quiet palace at Babelsberg, on the road from Potsdam to Berlin, was not yet ready and the Princess had to spend her first weeks in Germany in draughty apartments at the old town palace, where the stoves were never warm and where the water in a bath-tub could be commended as tepid, on better days.

Undoubtedly the Princess achieved a personal success, retaining her refreshingly open smile throughout the long and cold ceremonies of a ponderous welcome. Lady (Jane) Churchill, one of Queen Victoria's principal Ladies of the Bedchamber, sent back to England detailed reports of the Princess's achievements, and her letters, together with reports from Grand Duchess Augusta of Mecklenburg-Strelitz and from Ernest von Stockmar, were bound in a special volume for the royal archives, 'The Princess Royal's Journey to Berlin, 1858'. Grand Duchess Augusta also emphasized the enthusiasm with which the crowds in Potsdam and Berlin welcomed the newcomer, but she was herself homesick and she added, 'I need hardly tell you, dearest cousin, how my heart beat when the band struck up "God Save the Queen" and dear Vicky's face was first seen.'[12] But the most perceptive report came from Stockmar. Writing from Potsdam on 7 February, he told the Queen: 'The enthusiasm was of the truest and warmest kind. Such happy faces, ladies evidently belonging to the middle class hurraing energetically. Baron Stockmar never will forget an elderly lady in the crowd asking her son, a lad of 15 or 16, "*August, hast du sie gesehen?*", whereon August with a radiant face replied in the affirmative, stroking his stomach as if he had eaten a very good thing.'[13] Along Piccadilly or the Mall a London lad might have acknowledged differently his pleasure at seeing a princess passing by. But Stockmar could remember the emotional anatomy of his young compatriots. He appreciated that an August of Potsdam would contentedly pat his stomach only for an emotion felt deeply in his heart.

The reception in Berlin was as enthusiastic as in Potsdam. For four hours the Princess watched a procession of craftsmen representing different trades trail past the palace. 'The only drawback was the cold (9'–19' Réaumur) during this bright and sunny day,' reported Stockmar to Windsor; and Grand Duchess Augusta noted how the Princess remarked 'I am all one lump of ice'.[14] The discomfiture of a Berlin winter was not, of course, unexpected; the Princess's patience and fortitude in combating its rigours made the weather worthy of comment. But what most surprised and disturbed the English visitors was the unseen hand of police surveillance. On 24 February, in her sixteenth letter in three weeks, Lady Churchill told the Queen that she could only report minor matters as all her letters to England were being opened.[15] Police spies had been attached to every princely household since the 1848 revolutions.

The Princess Royal, who wrote to her parents on average three times a week over the following four years, kept in touch with her family by using the British diplomatic bag or the services of the Queen's Messengers and occasionally of Baron Rothschild's courier service. The Prince Consort, who was meticulously tidy over every detail, sent a regular weekly letter to his daughter. Her mother wrote far more frequently, sometimes every day. The steady flow of letters cannot have helped the Princess accept the formal conventions and traditions of her husband's country. No such regular contact with 'home' weakened her father's resolve to shed his 'foreignership' when he settled in England, and it was unfair to perplex a daughter, so much younger than he had been, with this rival pull of family loyalties. Around her were a few elderly courtiers whose memories went back to Frederick the Great's time. How should she remember her duty to absorb the strange ways of Berlin when there came, two or three times each week, familiar letter-heads based on engravings of Osborne, Balmoral or Windsor to recall what was dearest to her in Britain?[16] Perhaps the engravings even softened the tone implied by those famous emphatic underlinings. It was a time of natural tension; for by the spring, before the young couple could move to Babelsberg, the Princess discovered she was pregnant. To the challenge of winning respect as a fit wife for a future King of Prussia would soon come the demands of motherhood; and all this at the age of eighteen.

Her task was made harder by the political uncertainties of the Prussian court. Frederick William IV suffered a series of strokes in the autumn of 1857 and, by the time the new Princess reached Berlin, he was barely able to exercise his sovereign powers; to Prince Albert, who met him briefly that summer, he seemed 'a man just out of sleep'. But the Prince of Prussia did not become Regent until 9 October 1858, and there were rumours that he would not assume these responsibilities, either because of his health or because he had so little interest in politics. It is hard to avoid the conclusion that, during these months, the Prince Consort badgered him excessively with memoranda which he frequently resented. He had been a public figure, fêted in the victory celebrations, five years before Albert was born and, although grateful for the Prince's sympathetic hospitality in 1848, his Hohenzollern pride did not wish to be reminded quite so often of those painful weeks when a mob forced him to seek exile across the North Sea.

Nor did Prince Albert restrict the benefits of his good counsel to letters from afar. Early in June 1858 he suddenly came to Berlin to visit his daughter, cast a disapproving eye at the improvements to the Babelsberg Palace and seek confidential talks with the Prince of Prussia, who astutely avoided them. Nine weeks later Albert was back on a second visit, on this occasion escorting the Queen and accompanied by the Foreign Secretary, Lord Malmesbury. The Prince Consort also invited old Stockmar to travel up from Coburg, where he had been living in retirement for the past two years. In Potsdam the Prince of Prussia overwhelmed his guests with so much official friendliness that there was no time left for political talk. The most lasting visual impression of this visit was one of 'perpetual uniform', with 'none of the Royal family, or princely class, ever appearing out of stiff military dress'. Regimental parades and reviews followed each other with monotonous frequency under an unrelenting sun; 'The whole country seems occupied in playing at soldiers,' noted the Prince's private physician.[17]

It was Stockmar, with his forty-year experience of royal susceptibilities, who sensed the dangerous mood at the Prince of Prussia's court. When Lord Clarendon also made a private visit to Berlin that autumn he found Stockmar deeply concerned at the way in which Queen Victoria wished 'to exercise the same authority and control over' her daughter 'that she did before her marriage'. Clarendon, at Stockmar's request, tactfully raised the matter with the Prince Consort on his return to London; and Stockmar in mid-November wrote a letter to the Prince Consort of great interest. In it he suggested, not merely that the Princess's parents 'were meddling far too much with trivialities', but 'that they wanted to control matters over here much too much in accordance with their opinions and feelings'. Stockmar's salutary warning, which no one else was in so privileged a position to make, left the Queen 'in a towering passion', but momentarily checked the constant flow of good – and bad – advice from Windsor and Balmoral.[18]

Politically the summer visit to Potsdam and Berlin achieved nothing. However, when, two months later, the Prince of Prussia at last became Regent, the Prince Consort was delighted by signs that a 'New Era' had come to Prussia. General von Manteuffel was dismissed; the King's distant kinsman, Prince Anton of Hohenzollern-Sigmaringen, became chief minister; the Foreign Ministry went to Alexander von Schleinitz, an old friend of the Regent and an admirer of British ways and institutions; and among ministers with responsibility for internal affairs was another Anglophile, Moritz August von Bethmann-Hollweg, who in 1837–8 had supervised Prince Albert's historical-legal studies at Bonn (and whose grandson was in 1914 to stumble into world war).

To the Prince Consort these changes seemed proof that the Coburg Plan was about to be realized. A succession of messages from Windsor and Buckingham Palace congratulated the Regent on 'the effect on Germany of Prussia

identifying herself with liberal constitutional government'; and he was
especially pleased that Prussia would come among 'the five Powers on the
Continent' as 'the one which wants to base itself on fair play . . . and will thus
be a corrective element in the great policy of intrigue'.[19] This happily
simplistic view of European statecraft did not accord with the ninety-two-page
analysis of Prussia's diplomatic history which Count von Bismarck had
presented to the Prince of Prussia six months before. But the Regent was not
inclined to follow the advice of either correspondent. Bismarck was sent to St
Petersburg as Prussia's envoy to the Tsar; and the Regent did not have any
more political conversations with the Prince Consort until the autumn of 1860,
when the 'New Era' already seemed no more than a passing historical
curiosity.

'Words can ill convey the feelings of joy, excitement and gratitude which fill
our hearts!' Queen Victoria wrote in her record of 'Remarks, Conversations
and Reflections' on 27 January 1859. 'At 3 today we heard that our beloved
Vicky had just (I think only 10 minutes before) got a Son and was "as well as
possible". What a relief! What a blessing! . . . The Son is an immense event
for Prussia.' The Queen was grieved that she could not go at once and see her
first grandson, but she was convinced that the birth of the child would arouse
ecstasy throughout the Prussian lands.[20] The news was well received in
London, too, where there remained a strongly possessive attitude towards the
Princess Royal even though she was now a Princess of Prussia.

  Not for another two days did the Queen learn that her daughter had
narrowly escaped death after a prolonged confinement, and it was some three
weeks before she discovered that her grandson had been born with physical
disabilities. A neck injury influenced the functioning of the central nerve
plexus, leaving the left arm withered and causing slight deafness as well as
affecting the sense of balance. These disabilities, though manifesting
themselves during the difficult birth, may have had their origin in an accident
to the Princess when she was five months pregnant: tripping over an ornate
chair leg in the palace at Berlin she 'fell with violence on the slippery parquet'
(to use her own words). The psychological effect on the future Kaiser William
II of this infirmity has tempted more speculation than any birth since the
Nativity.[21]

  Although the Princess returned to England for a brief holiday in May,
Queen Victoria had to wait until the autumn of 1860 before she saw her
grandson for the first time, and by then he had a sister, Charlotte, born in July
1860 without any difficulty. The eighteen months separating the coming of the
Princess's two children were dominated, in international affairs, by the
problems of Italian unification. At the time of the future Kaiser's birth the
British and Prussian governments were working together to maintain peace in
Europe, which was threatened by the joint Franco-Piedmontese agitation

against Austria's continued possession of Lombardy and Venetia. When war came, at the end of April 1859, the Prussians gave diplomatic support to Austria and there was strong sentiment in favour of decisive intervention against the French, striking across the Rhine while Napoleon III was engaged, with the main French army, in the plains of northern Italy.[22]

During these months of international crisis the Prince Consort and his eldest daughter behaved with remarkable indiscretion. Perhaps because the Princess had so recently been staying in England, she reacted to the threat of war as the Princess Royal and not as the wife of one of Prussia's princely army commanders. On 18 June she wrote to her father telling him of the military chaos in Prussia, 'of which I suppose you will have heard': it was proving impossible to secure full mobilization; eight army corps were not being called up. 'Please keep this to yourself, dearest Papa, because I know it only from Fritz,' she added, with a touch of guilt.[23] Two days earlier she had sent her mother a letter which was so bellicose and hostile to Napoleon III that it seems almost as if the Princess intended it to be intercepted by the palace police spies: 'I wish for once I was a man, and baby too to fight the French,' she wrote. The tone of the letter 'sickened' Queen Victoria, who was already troubled by a domestic political crisis, which had led to the return of Palmerston as Prime Minister in succession to Derby on 12 June.[24]

The change of government prompted the Prince Consort to write to the Prussian Regent. He saw nothing odd in informing the Regent that 'We have got a Ministry which exactly suits Louis Napoleon' (Napoleon III), or in expressing his regret that there was no room in the cabinet for Clarendon, since Lord John Russell had gone to the Foreign Office. On 9 July the Princess Royal again told her father that Prussia was in no condition to fight, for, though two army corps had been moved to the Rhine and a third was defending Berlin, there was still chaos over calling up the reservists. She also described a visit by the Austrian Empress and Prince Windischgraetz to Berlin when they had pressed for Prussian intervention: 'If we did not help them now, they would never forgive us and would not help us if they make peace now and we were attacked,' she wrote.[25] Fortunately, on the very day that the Princess wrote this letter from Potsdam, news reached London and Berlin of an armistice concluded by Napoleon III and Francis Joseph; and the threat of war along the Rhine receded. But the whole episode provides a significant commentary on the extent to which the royal family had difficulty in deciding between personal loyalties and the acceptance of political actions dictated by other considerations. Albert and Victoria never doubted that, from 1858 onwards, there was a special relationship binding the royal Houses of Britain and Prussia.

The Princess Royal was also much concerned in these last years of her father's life with seeking a suitable husband for her sister, Princess Alice. As early as the first day in April 1856, when the Princess was approaching her thirteenth birthday, the Queen had written to her uncle in Brussels: 'May I beg to remind you to make enquiries, quietly, about the young Prince of Orange – as to his education, entourage and disposition?' Given King Leopold's personal and political attitude to the Dutch royal House, it is tempting to assume the Queen was, on this occasion, so elated over the 'good Peace' signed with Russia that she was perpetrating an April Fool's trick on her uncle. This latest William of Orange, born in September 1840, was a grandson of Leopold's old antagonist, who had died when the boy was eight years old. Inevitably King Leopold showed no enthusiasm, commenting a few months later that the rulers of the Netherlands 'have not turned out very good friends the last few generations'.[26]

The 'Orange Boy', as he was generally called by the British royal House, was however still reasonably positioned in the matrimonial stakes in the summer of 1859, Princess Alice showing some interest in a future in which she would be Queen-Consort of the Netherlands while her sister was Queen-Consort of neighbouring Prussia. But the puritanical Princess Royal was shocked by tales she heard in Baden of the young man's 'bad life' there – 'gambling, drinking and what-not' – and by October his chances looked poor. Nevertheless at the end of January 1860 he came over to Windsor, planning to spend almost a month in England. The widowed Duchess of Cambridge, who still possessed one unmarried daughter, maintained that his bad habits were much exaggerated: had he not accompanied her to a play in which there were a considerable number of dancers and yet remained 'quite quiet'? But the Queen, and Princess Alice, thought him dull and rude; and by the spring the royal family were looking once more for another German son-in-law.[27]

In June 1858 the Princess Royal reminded her parents of the two young Princes of Hesse-Darmstadt, Louis and Henry. Her mother could remember meeting them when she visited Coburg in 1845 and they were respectively seven and six years old. By May 1860 that indefatigable matchmaker, King Leopold, was taking an interest in their prospects and it was arranged that they should stay at Windsor for Ascot Week. The Queen was, at first, unenthusiastic, and her son-in-law, who had met Prince Louis while on a visit to Russia, did not share his wife's high opinion of the young man. The Queen was perplexed and wished the Princes were not coming to England. 'All marriage is such a lottery,' she wrote to her eldest daughter. 'All you say of Louis of H. is however very favourable, but what are his prospects?'[28]

They were not, on paper, remarkably impressive, at least compared with Fritz's prospects in Berlin. Prince Louis was the elder nephew of the reigning, and childless, Grand Duke of Hesse and by Rhine, Louis III, who had his principal residence in Darmstadt, some fifteen miles across the Main from Frankfurt. The Grand Duchy was not rich; it had no more political influence than Saxe-Coburg; and it was not strategically placed in the mosaic of the

German Confederation. Moreover dynastically the Duchy's closest links were with Russia, for Louis III's youngest sister was married to Tsar Alexander II. None of these points inclined Victoria and Albert to welcome a Hessian connection.

But when Prince Louis and his brother arrived at Buckingham Palace on 1 June 1860 the Queen was much impressed by their 'gentlemanlike' and 'pleasing' manners. Her letters give the impression that she found Prince Louis so young, amiable and malleable that she believed he would be prepared to spend part of each year in England if he became her son-in-law, an arrangement which would keep 'dear Alice' frequently in attendance on her mother. Ascot Week and a long visit to Windsor proved a great success; by the end of the month it seemed likely that Princess Alice would marry him. In September the Queen and the Prince Consort travelled to Coburg with their daughter and met Prince Louis's parents. Two months later the Prince and his brother were back at Windsor, and Louis was soon escorting Alice on 'romantic walks' through the Home Park beneath the pale November skies.

By now the Queen was convinced she had always favoured the Hessian marriage. 'Sleeping hardly at all and being somewhat off my food' she waited for what she called the 'happy denouement'. Prince Louis was so 'dreadfully nervous and agitated' that it needed encouragement from Prince Albert 'to break the ice'.[29] But at last on Saturday, 1 December, the Queen could make an enthusiastic entry in her special 'Remarks' journal:

> With a heart full of joy, gratitude and emotion do I write these lines! This day, or rather more last night, was one of those of intense emotion – not to be forgotten – like the 29th Sept. '55 and the 25 Jan. '58. Our darling Alice was last night engaged to Louis of Hesse, who is here since the 24th ult. and we may confidently hope that her happiness for life is secured, for he is a dear, excellent amiable young man. It is a match I have long ardently desired and now my wishes are fulfilled and I thank God humbly, warmly for it. . . . No marriage is to take place until Alice is turned 19.[30]

The news was telegraphed to Berlin and welcomed by the Princess Royal, who confessed that she had felt nervous because of the extent to which she had encouraged the connection in the first place. She remarked, truthfully but a shade smugly, that her sister would enjoy greater freedom and independence than she could ever attain in Berlin and would not have 'such a difficult terrain to work upon' but 'on the other hand my position is a finer one'.[31]

Already the Princess Royal was bride-hunting for her brother, the Prince of Wales, and in that same week sent to her mother a photograph of 'Prince Christian of Denmark's lovely daughter', Princess Alexandra. But Queen Victoria would have preferred a German bride for her eldest son: the long-running dispute over the future of Schleswig-Holstein soured relations between Denmark and the German states; and the Queen thought poorly of the allegedly frivolous outlook of Princess Christian's family, the ruling House of Hesse-Cassel. The Schleswig-Holstein problem troubled the Princess Royal, too. She was prepared to be generous to Princess Alexandra 'though', she wrote, 'I as a Prussian cannot wish Bertie should ever marry her' for 'an alliance with Denmark would be a misfortune for us here'.[32] With the Hessian royal family so much in favour, it was natural that Queen Victoria should ask her elder daughter for a report on Prince Louis's sister, Anna, who was eighteen months older than Alexandra of Denmark. But the Princess Royal's account of 'poor Anna' was so devastatingly critical that she was, from the start, a non-runner. The Prince Consort, despite his awareness of German national feeling, came out strongly in favour of the Danish marriage, and it was his devotedly loyal elder daughter who arranged the first secret 'accidental' meeting of the Prince of Wales and Princess Alexandra on 24 September 1861 in the cathedral of Speyer.[33]

Queen Victoria interested herself in the search for a Princess of Wales and she continued to be delighted by all she saw and heard of Prince Louis. But 1861 was a sad year. In March the death of her mother reduced her to deep depression. From this state she was only lifted by a visit from 'dearest Uncle Leopold', by now aged seventy, in May – 'his whole manner is so soothing and kind'. In August the Princess Royal brought the Queen's two grandchildren to Osborne for the first time. 'William is such a darling, so promising, clever and dear a child but he requires great care', the Queen noted, while frankly admitting that her eldest daughter 'has retained many of her little peculiarities and failings'.[34]

The Prince Consort, though glad to welcome Vicky, was troubled by the shifting expediencies of Prussian politics and disappointed in the former Regent who, on the second day of the year, became King William I. The Crown Princess (as the Princess Royal was now styled in Prussia) told her father that the new King was becoming suspicious and nervous because spies and informers made him think there would soon be another revolution in Berlin.[35] Albert still sent letters of unsolicited advice to his old friend extolling the virtues of constitutionalism; but he admitted to his daughter that his views were discredited and misrepresented by the leaders of the Prussian officer corps in whom, as a professional soldier, the new King showed the greatest confidence. 'There exists in Prussia a great Junker and bureaucrats' party,' the Prince Consort wrote to King Leopold. 'The King himself belongs to this party by sympathy and tradition.'[36]

Prince Albert's biographers have rightly emphasized that, in the closing weeks of his life, he was worried over the wayward behaviour of the Prince of Wales and over the worsening relations between Palmerston and the Lincoln administration during the American Civil War. But he was also deeply concerned with events in Prussia: the risk of some external war to eliminate internal dissension; the assertion by the King on two occasions during his coronation ceremonies that he ruled by Divine Right; and the extent to which the continued attacks on Prussia in *The Times* played into the hands of reactionaries hostile to his son-in-law and daughter. Less than a month before his death, the Prince Consort received a letter from the Crown Princess in which she told him that she believed the instability of government would lead to social upheaval in Prussia.[37] There was even a possibility of the King's abdication. Would Fritz come to the throne as Prussia's first liberal monarch or would the kingdom disintegrate in a wave of red republicanism, forcing her to cross to England 'an exile and a fugitive', as Delane had so gloomily predicted six years before? All those high hopes of the Albertine Plans seemed far from realization that autumn at Windsor.

The Prince Consort noted in his diary, on Sunday, 24 November, that he 'felt thoroughly unwell' and 'have scarcely closed my eyes at night for the last fortnight' and told his daughter of his general debility in a letter sent on the following Wednesday. Ominously on Sunday, 8 December, he decided to move into the 'Blue Room' in which both George IV and William IV had died, and the Queen became anxious. But three more days were to pass before Princess Alice became the first member of the family to take seriously her father's inner conviction that he was dying. A warning telegram was sent to the Crown Prince in Berlin on Friday morning; the Prince died early in the evening of Saturday, 14 December 1861. The news reached Berlin and Coburg next morning.[38]

Both Queen Victoria and her eldest daughter were racked with grief, their sense of bereavement intensified by the suddenness with which the blow fell upon them. Each sought to shape her life as she believed 'dearest Papa' would have wished: for the Queen, in the daily round of family life; for the Crown Princess, in German politics. Princess Alice, a natural nurse, comforted her mother through a week of total nervous collapse. King Leopold came to England and, after spending some time with his niece at Osborne, went into residence at Buckingham Palace for the second half of January 1862 and maintained links with Palmerston and his government. It was through the combined efforts of Leopold and of Princess Alice that the Queen at last agreed to receive her Prime Minister in audience again, at Osborne on 29 January. Gradually she was coaxed back into the routine of public business.

Since her consort had resolved on the Hessian marriage, nothing should stand in the way of their second daughter's wedding. But at the same time nothing must detract from the mourning grief of the nation. There were to be bridesmaids – Alice's three younger sisters and the much maligned Princess Anna of Hesse – but no long train for them to carry, no ornate floral arrangements, no royal spectacle in London. On Tuesday, 1 July 1862, Princess Alice and Prince Louis were married by the Archbishop of York at an improvised altar in the small dining-room at Osborne. On the wall above the altar stood – as it does today – the family group which Winterhalter had painted fifteen years before. It is not surprising that Alice's mother and brothers and sisters wept when they saw, above the bride and bridegroom's heads, a youthful Victoria and Albert as they had appeared, at least to an artist's eye, that happy first summer in the new Osborne. 'More like a funeral than a wedding,' wrote the Queen to Vicky in anticipation on 28 June. 'More like a funeral than a wedding,' she repeated on 2 July, when it was all over. Prince Louis's mother and father were unimpressed by the 'fine service' which the Archbishop read with tears running down his cheeks. They could remember the pomp in St Petersburg when Mary of Hesse married a son of the reigning Tsar; and a three-day honeymoon in a house near Ryde – with the Queen dropping in on Thursday evening – was not the most romantic beginning to married life together.

But in one respect 'poor Alice' and 'kind Louis' were fortunate. Their marriage had a good Press in England. Even the pens that customarily savaged Germany's 'paltry dynasties' stayed their hands. And *Punch* sent them off to Darmstadt with a gentle benediction:

> Yet noble is thy choice, O English bride!
> And England hails the bridegroom and the guest
> A friend – a friend well loved by him who died.
> He blessed your troth: your wedlock shall be blessed.[39]

CHAPTER TEN

᥍ 'That Wretched B.' ᥏

While Osborne House was observing the funereal rites of Princess Alice's wedding, the Prussian ambassador to France arrived in England to spend five days in London. Ostensibly Count von Bismarck, who had only taken up his post in Paris a month before, came to visit that summer's International Exhibition of Industrty and Science at South Kensington. Since Bismarck had hitherto shown no interest whatsoever in the marvels of technological progress, it was assumed that his principal reason for crossing the Channel was to assess for himself the realities of British political life. He was received by the Foreign Secretary, Earl Russell; he met, for the only time in his life, the Prime Minister, Lord Palmerston; and he dined with the principal Opposition spokesman in the Commons, Benjamin Disraeli, at the Russian Embassy in Chesham Place. None of the English statesmen impressed Bismarck: they were, he decided, 'better informed about China and Turkey than about Prussia'. The one public figure in London who really understood German affairs was no longer at hand to guide the Queen and ply her ministers with sound advice. There is a certain irony in Bismarck's visiting an exhibition so closely associated with the dead Prince's ideals.[1]

Politically the three months following this brief excursion to London were as decisive as any in Prussia's nineteenth-century history. Ever since his accession King William had sought parliamentary backing for funds to enable reform of the army; he wished to change conditions of service so that the militia could be absorbed in an enlarged and highly professionalized military force. The liberals, fearing that any extension of autocratic rule would diminish parliament's slender influence on the executive, consistently refused to vote funds for army reforms and, in the spring of 1862, won parliamentary elections which endorsed their stand against the King. William was therefore faced that summer with three possibilities: he could risk a renewal of the disorders of 1848 by suspending the constitution and establishing a virtual military dictatorship; he could recognize the will of the electorate by abandoning his army reforms, perhaps even abdicating in favour of the Crown Prince; or he could follow the advice of his War Minister, General von Roon, and entrust Bismarck with the formation of a government which would discredit the liberals and push through the army reforms within the existing constitutional structure of the kingdom.

At first the King, mistrusting Bismarck, attempted to collaborate with the

Hesse-Darmstadt

(sovereign Grand Dukes of Hesse and by Rhine [1806–1918] in bold type)

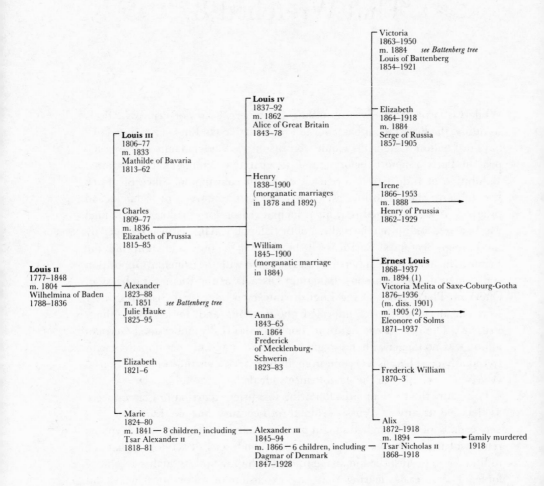

Louis II
1777–1848
m. 1804
Wilhelmina of Baden
1788–1836

Louis III
1806–77
m. 1833
Mathilde of Bavaria
1813–62

Charles
1809–77
m. 1836
Elizabeth of Prussia
1815–85

Alexander
1823–88
m. 1851   *see Battenberg tree*
Julie Hauke
1825–95

Elizabeth
1821–6

Marie
1824–80
m. 1841 — 8 children, including
Tsar Alexander II
1818–81

Louis IV
1837–92
m. 1862
Alice of Great Britain
1843–78

Henry
1838–1900
(morganatic marriages
in 1878 and 1892)

William
1845–1900
(morganatic marriage
in 1884)

Anna
1843–65
m. 1864
Frederick
of Mecklenburg-
Schwerin
1823–83

Alexander III
1845–94
m. 1866 — 6 children, including
Dagmar of Denmark
1847–1928

Victoria
1863–1950
m. 1884   *see Battenberg tree*
Louis of Battenberg
1854–1921

Elizabeth
1864–1918
m. 1884
Serge of Russia
1857–1905

Irene
1866–1953
m. 1888   →
Henry of Prussia
1862–1929

Ernest Louis
1868–1937
m. 1894 (1)
Victoria Melita of Saxe-Coburg-Gotha
1876–1936
(m. diss. 1901)
m. 1905 (2)   →
Eleonore of Solms
1871–1937

Frederick William
1870–3

Alix
1872–1918
m. 1894   → family murdered
Tsar Nicholas II   1918
1868–1918

liberals, and by mid-September their leaders were ready to compromise. They would, they told William, approve the military budget if the length of conscript service were cut from three years to two. But William was convinced that such topics lay outside the range of parliamentary debate; everything relating to the army remained within the royal prerogative. That autumn he was in residence at Babelsberg, his son and daughter-in-law having moved to the more spacious Neues Palais at Potsdam in the summer following the birth of their first child. Now the King paced the gravel paths beside the Havel deep in the perplexities of a dutiful conscience. By the third week in September he was ready to come to a decision. Rather than accept a compromise over the length of military service he would give up the throne and leave Fritz to reconcile the importunities of parliament with the needs of an army. The imminence of abdication alarmed his Minister of War; and on the evening of Wednesday, 17 September, Roon sent his famous cryptic telegram to Bismarck in Paris urging him to delay no longer but hasten back to Berlin.[2]

He reached the Wilhelmstrasse early on Saturday and there followed a weekend of high political drama. Roon told the King on Sunday afternoon that his ambassador to France had returned home. Reluctantly, and with deep suspicion, William agreed to receive Bismarck next day. But when Bismarck presented himself at Babelsberg that Monday afternoon the King was surprised and impressed. He found the reckless Junker whom his wife and son so distrusted was dutiful and understanding. More important, Bismarck was confident he could ensure army reform without any dependence on the liberal progressives in parliament. The King thereupon made Bismarck acting Minister President and also entrusted him with foreign affairs. By the end of the decade he was to become Iron Chancellor of a unified Germany.

All this, of course, makes familiar reading; the appointment of Bismarck has become as much a set-piece of historical legend as the dropping of the pilot twenty-eight years later.[3] But hindsight necessarily distorts events. In every account of that decisive weekend the incoming Minister President holds the stage. This is not surprising, for nothing can surpass Bismarck's personal chronicle of what took place at Berlin and Babelsberg; his narrative skill in illuminating the way by which men manipulate power has been matched only by Churchill and by Trotsky. But this preoccupation with Bismarck minimizes the significance of other events; it ignores, in particular, the interplay of dynastic loyalties. Few writers on this period have noticed, for example, that throughout most of September and the first half of October Queen Victoria was staying in Germany. Yet at no other decisive moment in Prussia's history was a British sovereign, with attendant advisers, so close to the centre of events.

The Queen's presence in Germany at this time of crisis was entirely fortuitous. About midsummer she decided to spend her first autumn of widowhood in sentimental reminiscence among the wooded hills of Saxe-Coburg, sharing some of these nostalgic moments with her two elder daughters and their husbands. Soon the first part of her holiday acquired a more clearly defined purpose. The Queen broke her journey at Brussels: there, on 3 September, she met Princess Alexandra of Denmark for the first time, at King Leopold's palace of Laeken. Both the Queen and her uncle were 'favourably impressed' by the Danish Princess's 'beautiful refined profile and quiet ladylike manner'; and Victoria told Alexandra's parents that she hoped 'their dear daughter' would 'accept our son'.[4] It was agreed that the Prince of Wales should spend a few days in Belgium, with the Danish family and under the benevolent eye of the most accomplished of Coburg matchmakers.

Meanwhile, from Brussels, the Queen went on to the remote Coburg ducal *Schloss* of Rheinhardtsbrunn, a former Benedictine abbey set in the pinewoods of Thuringia, some twelve miles south of Gotha and forty-five miles north of Coburg. It was on 9 September, while the Queen was holidaying in this idyllic spot, that she heard by telegram of the Prince of Wales's acceptance by Princess Alexandra, to whom he had proposed that same day at Laeken. As usual, the betrothal remained a family secret, although rumours of an Anglo-Danish marriage had long aroused concern in Germany, even old Baron Stockmar deploring the possibility. At Rheinhardtsbrunn Queen Victoria had with her, as minister in attendance, the Foreign Secretary, Earl Russell; and she noted, in her journal, that she took the opportunity of stressing to Russell the importance of emphasizing to his cabinet colleagues that 'Bertie's marriage' should in no sense be 'considered a political one'.

On the following Monday (15 September) the Crown Princess of Prussia joined her mother at Rheinhardtsbrunn; and on Tuesday the party was completed by the arrival of the Crown Prince, who had been visiting Karlsruhe, home of his sister, Louise (who was married to the Grand Duke of Baden). So far all was going according to plan. The Queen was, however, distressed by reports of social indiscretions committed by her second son, Prince Alfred, while serving with the fleet in the Mediterranean and, on several occasions in the following week, she appears to have succumbed to the neurosis of melancholia which incapacitated her from time to time in these early years of widowhood. But she remained fully alive to the mounting political crisis in Germany; and when suddenly, on Wednesday, Fritz had to hurry back to Babelsberg, the Queen at once perceived the significance of the summons from his father. 'Saw Lord Russell', she wrote that day in her journal, 'and talked of the alarming state of affairs at Berlin, of its being far better the King should abdicate.'[5]

At Babelsberg, as the Crown Prince himself recorded, there followed two days of 'terrible stormy meetings at which abdication was said to be definite'. The throne, it appeared, was only a few steps away from him. But, in this crucial hour, the Crown Prince's confidence began to waver. What looked crystal clear to his mother-in-law and her Foreign Secretary 150 miles away in Thuringia seemed clouded with uncertainty to Fritz in Potsdam and Berlin. If his father abdicated and he assumed the burden of sovereignty, would 'King Frederick III' find that the constitutional crisis had weakened the instinctive support of his subjects for their dynasty? For more than a decade the Crown Prince had sought to reconcile in his mind ideals of Prussian military service with the liberal hopes of his mother and the diluted Whiggism absorbed from Vicky and the Prince Consort. By temperament and training he was a soldier, filled with a sense of Prussia's past and with high hopes for Germany's future. Ought he perhaps to sacrifice his concern for liberal principles to his desire for national grandeur? On the Saturday evening, in Berlin, he even met Bismarck, a politician whom he knew that both his mother and his wife regarded as a dangerous reactionary. It was a cool encounter, which the Crown Prince significantly left unrecorded in his journal. From Bismarck's account it is clear that both men recognized they were natural adversaries. There was nothing at this moment either could offer the other.[6]

The Crown Princess, though fully aware of her husband's dilemma, was reluctant to tender advice. Nevertheless on Friday afternoon she wrote to him in Berlin, leaving him with little doubt that she hoped he would take the crown. 'If you do not accept, I believe that you will regret it one day, in any case I would not wish to have the responsibility of advising against it,' she wrote. Above all, she urged him to stand out against any ministerial office for Bismarck. 'If Bismarck comes, we know where we shall end up. He will plunge us all into untold misery.' Her letter was clear and her arguments cogent – as well they might be, for at Rheinhardtsbrunn she could hold conversations, not only with her mother and with Lord Russell, but with those veteran champions of Anglo-German liberalism, the Barons Stockmar, father and son. When the twenty-one-year-old Crown Princess wrote, 'To take Bismarck is equivalent to a man who cannot swim jumping into the water where it is deepest' was she using her own metaphor or echoing the vivid phrases of a Russell or a Stockmar?[7]

It made little difference. For the Crown Prince's behaviour seems, in retrospect, disastrously inept. Since he had no wish to become a king by the grace of parliament, he felt bound to urge his father to remain on the throne. But he knew that William had already drafted an instrument of abdication. He therefore decided to wait upon events; he would sidle off the stage, leaving it clear for others with more histrionic talent. But he did not linger in the wings. That Saturday night he took train for Gotha, and by four in the morning he was at Rheinhardtsbrunn, ready to join the family later that morning in the grand saloon for the customary Lutheran service. He found the sermon, preached by a pastor from Coburg, especially encouraging after the anguish of the past week; and, as they speculated on what was happening at Babelsberg, his journal records long conversations with the younger Stockmar and with his close friend, Karl Samwer, a Holsteiner who served as confidential adviser to the Duke of Saxe-Coburg-Gotha. No messages came through from Berlin, and Fritz resumed his interrupted holiday. On Monday afternoon, while the King was receiving Bismarck in that historic audience at Babelsberg, the heir to the Prussian throne was hunting in the wooded valleys around Tambach.

News of Bismarck's appointment reached Rheinhardtsbrunn next morning. The Crown Prince was appalled: 'Poor Papa will have made many difficult hours for himself through this dishonest character,' he wrote in his journal. 'Poor Mama, how bitterly grieved she will be at this appointment of her deadly enemy !'[8] He decided to keep out of Berlin, for the King was about to travel to Baden-Baden, and he had no wish to become involved in the intrigues and manoeuvres of the new Minister President. On the following Sunday he again discussed his political tactics at great length with Ernest Stockmar; they agreed that it would be wisest to remain a passive spectator until Bismarck made a fool of himself. Next day (Monday, 29 September) the Crown Prince and his father met, amicably, at Gotha. The King, too, was waiting on events, uncertain how his Minister President would handle the liberal opposition.

Sure enough the Crown Prince's prospects soon seemed to improve. On Tuesday, speaking to a mere two dozen members of the budget committee, Bismarck remarked – almost as an aside – that the 'great questions of the day' would be settled by 'iron and blood'. When, later in the week, the German Press picked up the phrase – inverting the order of nouns to the more familiar 'blood and iron' – King William became alarmed. At the end of the week he decided to interrupt his holiday at Baden-Baden and return to the capital. Perhaps, after all, he had gained a mere respite in the political battle. But the Crown Prince's hopes were soon dashed. Bismarck's defence of his choice of words was so blandly satisfactory that the King again changed his mind. After vetoing the latest suggestions for limiting conscript service, he resumed his holiday.[9]

By now the Crown Prince, his wife and her brother, the Prince of Wales, had set out for Switzerland and ultimately for Marseilles where, on 22 October, they embarked on the British royal yacht *Osborne* for a month's relaxation in the Mediterranean. The cruise, like Queen Victoria's German holiday, had been planned long before the political crisis in Berlin, but it deprived Prussia's liberals of the comforting belief that, in their contest with the new government, they could count on a royal protector close at hand. Moreover it came as grist to the Anglophobes. Victoria might believe that Fritz and Vicky would 'Germanize' the Prince of Wales, protecting him from the strange Danish notions of his fiancée's family. But in Berlin it was easy enough to argue that the family cruise, aboard a British vessel, escorted by British warships, and with British troops parading before them in the colony of Malta, was yet another device to 'Anglicize' the soldier Prince who might soon be summoned to Prussia's throne.

Meanwhile Queen Victoria continued her sojourn in Saxe-Coburg, at least until the eve of 'the children's' embarkation at Marseilles. She had, however, left Rheinhardtsbrunn before the meeting of Fritz and his father at Gotha, partly because she had no wish to see the King of Prussia at such a time. With Princess Alice as her companion, the Queen travelled south to Coburg and the countryside in which there were 'so many places beloved Papa spoke of'. She paid several visits to 'the beloved Rosenau' and met 'the dear Baron (the elder Stockmar) every day at 4'.[10] For over three weeks the Queen indulged her inclination for nostalgic melancholy to the full.

The Prussian court, though not the King, was puzzled. What new Coburg Plan was being drawn up while the heirs to the thrones of Britain and Prussia were visiting Tunis, Malta, and Papal Rome? To Queen Victoria's considerable irritation, she was told on 10 October that the King of Prussia wished to come and see her for a few hours. He arrived, two days later, at six in the morning, three and a half hours before Victoria was prepared to breakfast with him. It was a curious meeting. William was determined to avoid all controversial topics, although he spoke sadly, in general terms, of the political difficulties facing him in Berlin. The two monarchs drove up to the citadel above Coburg, where Martin Luther had once found refuge; William duly admired the splendid view across the furrowed valleys of Franconia; and then, shortly after midday, he courteously bade his hostess farewell.[11] It is hard to see that the visit did much for Anglo-Prussian relations – except, perhaps, to allay suspicion. For not even the most fervent Anglophobe in the King's suite could believe that the forlorn widow-Queen, gazing mournfully from the bastion walls towards the fields around the Rosenau, had any wish to play Prussian politics. In the sequestered life which she affected that autumn Queen Victoria was incapable of planning anything more Machiavellian than the secret dramas of her own soul.

The Queen's letters and diary entries over these winter months suggest she felt a sense of guilt every time her interest was stimulated by some happening unforeseen by 'darling Papa'. She had convinced herself that she existed solely to work out Albert's plans, and she saw no reason why she should long survive him. On her wedding anniversay – 'that most blessed and hallowed of days' – she finally closed her journal of 'Remarks, Conversations and Reflections' with grieved surprise that she was 'still alive'. 'Oh why could I not have joined *him*!' she exclaimed.[12] Four weeks later, when the Prince of Wales married Princess Alexandra at Windsor on 10 March 1863, the Queen – still deep in mourning – was content to observe the ceremony from a gallery overlooking St George's Chapel. But she could not shut out the realities of political life, and at heart she had no wish to do so. From Prince Albert she had inherited a wise secretary, General Charles Grey, son of the 'Reform Bill Prime Minister'. Whether the General merited the Germanophile reputation accorded him by the

Palmerstonian Press is a matter of doubt, but he certainly emerged in that winter of 1862–3 as the Queen's most knowledgeable specialist on German dynastic affairs. She sent him on a mission to Coburg early in 1863, and it was his tact and persistence that induced the Crown Prince of Prussia and the Duke of Saxe-Coburg-Gotha to act as 'sponsors' in support of the Prince of Wales at the Anglo-Danish marriage despite the gathering storm among the Queen's 'German connections', to use Grey's own phrase. The more the Queen turned to Grey for advice on Germany the more her muffled spirits quickened with interest until, by the summer, her ministers found their sovereign striking warmly partisan attitudes to the issues of the day.

When the Crown Prince and Crown Princess came to Windsor for the royal wedding they had some hope that Bismarck's ministerial career was in jeopardy. In foreign affairs he had begun the year 1863 badly: unsolicited support for the Russians in suppressing the Polish Rebellion embarrassed the Tsar, alienated the French and left Prussia isolated in Germany. Nor did his home policies seem any more successful, for he had failed to cajole parliament into authorizing funds for army reform. But King William, having brought Bismarck to office, had no one at hand to replace him. Gradually the Minister President lubricated the instruments of authoritarian government: the civil service was purged of liberal spokesmen; the Press was threatened; parliamentary deputies found their right to interpellate ministers curbed. 'That wretched B. will not stop his mad career until he has plunged his King into ruin and his country into the most dangerous difficulties,' the Crown Princess wrote to her mother in the second week of May.[13] But, in reality, 'that wretched B.' was perfecting his political craftsmanship: over the next few months he was to outmanoeuvre both the Crown Prince and the King. More significantly he was to win over liberal waverers by vigorous support for a cause which concerned Germany as a whole.

On 5 June, at a civic reception in Danzig, the Crown Prince condemned the restraints imposed by Bismarck on the Press. It was, as his wife wrote to her mother, 'the first time in his life' that he had 'taken up a position decidedly in opposition to his father'; and the Crown Princess admitted that she had encouraged him to make a public protest after private criticisms had gone unanswered. Queen Victoria warmly supported her son-in-law, praised Vicky's conduct and gave her the ultimate accolade, an assurance that she was the 'worthy child of your beloved father who will look down approvingly on you'.[14] General Grey wrote, too, and the British Press left the young couple in no doubt of the righteousness of the Danzig speech. Bismarck, unlike many senior army officers, was patronizingly magnanimous in his attitude towards the Crown Prince. He could afford to be; for poor Fritz had sprung a trap. His strictures had no effect on the Press Law but they left the King angry with his son and mistrustful of the Neues Palais circle. The Danzig speech seemed to confirm the nagging conviction in Babelsberg and Potsdam that the Windsor-Coburg connection threatened to destroy the fabric of Prussian government.

Friction between William and his son also strengthened Bismarck's hold over the King. This summer it seemed as if the minister would scarcely let his sovereign out of his sight. When, in August, Emperor Francis Joseph urged William to come to Frankfurt so that Prussia could play an active role in an Austrian-sponsored 'Congress of German Princes', Bismarck was at hand to prevent the King's participating in a gathering designed to confirm Habsburg primacy in a reformed German Confederation. Gradually 'that wretched B.' was imposing his will on Prussia.[15]

He tried, too, to scare the Crown Princess. Early in July *The Times* gave such an accurate account of the exchanges between the King and the Crown Prince that the Berlin police were instructed to find the source of the leak. 'There has been a regular inquisition about it which has caused us the greatest annoyance,' the Crown Princess wrote to her mother on 1 August.[16] Under the strain her trusted adviser, Ernest Stockmar, had fallen ill: he was already saddened by the death of his better-known father three weeks before, and he now decided to seek the consolation of spa waters, away from Berlin. His temporary absence exposed the Crown Princess even more to the mischievous activities of informers among her husband's personal aides. But Ernest Stockmar would not be silenced. Four days later he wrote directly to Queen Victoria, seeking to dissuade her from encouraging her eldest daughter to bring her family to Scotland while there was so much tension at Potsdam: the King, he said, would not like it; nor, indeed, would the liberals in Berlin, who feared that a prolonged sojourn in Britain would leave their future Queen-Consort 'estranged from Prussia'.[17]

The Queen's response to these messages was brusque and decisive. She was not impressed by all that had happened in Berlin, a subject on which she considered herself well-informed as the Queen of Prussia – who remained no friend of Bismarck – had been her guest at Windsor in the very week that *The Times* published the offending articles. The King, Victoria insisted, should look nearer home for any explanation of the leak; and she would expect the Crown Princess for three or four weeks at Balmoral in late September. Meanwhile she was planning to set out herself for Coburg. There was, of course, the customary self-pity over the burden of such journeying on shattered nerves but her complaints were given the lie by the resilience with which she contested every disputed point with the Prussian court and her insistence to Palmerston 'that *no step* is taken in foreign affairs *without* her *previous sanction* being obtained'. This year the Foreign Secretary must remain in London and she would communicate with him by cipher messages; the Lord President of the Council, Earl Granville, was to be the cabinet minister in attendance on the sovereign. With her strange facility for propitious timing the

Queen reached Coburg on 16 August. This was the day on which the 'Congress of German Princes' opened at Frankfurt.[18]

During this visit to Germany the Queen gave particular attention to confirming arrangements for the future succession to the Duchy of Saxe-Coburg, which her husband and his childless brother had long assumed would pass to the Queen's second son, Prince Alfred. But Victoria was also drawn into current German politics more directly than on any other occasion in her reign. The King of Prussia visited her at the Rosenau on 31 August; the Queen tried to mediate between Prussia and Austria, regretting the King's refusal to go to Frankfurt, and William agreed that both the Crown Princess and her husband should spend some time in Scotland once the autumn manoeuvres were over. Bismarck accompanied the King; he was not formally received by Queen Victoria although she met him unexpectedly in an antechamber and was disturbed by the 'horrid expression' on his face. He did, however, talk at some length to Earl Granville, the only meeting between the head of the Prussian government and a British cabinet minister before the Berlin Congress fifteen years later. While King William told the Queen he was sure that Austria and Prussia ought to follow a common policy to defend German interests against any threat from France, Bismarck surprised Granville by maintaining that a civil war in Germany might come as a political relief. He sought, somewhat cynically, to distinguish a general condition of terror from a passing terror, which would bring about 'something good'.[19]

Three days later Queen Victoria entertained Francis Joseph to luncheon at Coburg. She impressed upon him the need for Prussia to be accorded parity with Austria in any new ordering of German affairs. This attempted mediation by the Queen pleased King William, who recognized the value of 'England and Prussia always keeping well together . . . they being the two great Protestant Powers'. The momentary flurry of dynastic diplomacy was, however, deplored by Bismarck. He was especially troubled by the activities of the two Victorias. In a royal family, so he explained to his King, a mother, her daughters and her sons must often feel the call of conflicting loyalties, when sentiments of kinship ran counter to political necessity. Bismarck was well placed to discredit the Queen. It was easy to represent her frequent advice to her daughter and son-in-law as attempts to encourage resistance to the sovereign's legitimate demands. This point King Leopold emphasized in a letter to his niece soon after her return from Coburg in September. Ernest Stockmar, on the other hand, consistently failed to see the inherent danger in promoting disobedience and disaffection within the ruling family.[20]

By the end of September, however, it was generally agreed that if the Crown Prince and his family could spend a long time abroad, tensions at home might relax. Even Stockmar, by now back in Potsdam, had changed his mind and wrote to Queen Victoria on 27 September from the Neues Palais at Potsdam advocating the Scottish visit which he had opposed seven weeks before.[21] Fritz, Vicky and their children duly reached Abergeldie a few days later and spent most of October in the Highlands with Queen Victoria and Princess Alice and her husband. They then stayed for some days at Sandringham with the Prince of Wales, went on to Windsor, and did not finally arrive back in Berlin until two days before Christmas. But, so far from easing tension at the Prussian court, these twelve weeks of self-imposed exile left the Crown Prince politically isolated. For, while the family was in England, news reached them that the King of Denmark had died; Christian IX, his successor, was committed to uphold a unitary constitution which swept away the rights of the German minority in Schleswig and limited the traditional customs and privileges of the German-speaking majority living in Holstein and the small Duchy of Lauenburg. There was a fever of indignation throughout Germany. This was no time for the Crown Prince of Prussia to be exchanging social pleasantries at Sandringham and Windsor – for Christian IX was the Prince of Wales's father-in-law. 'What *can* be done?' Queen Victoria wrote miserably to her uncle in Brussels. 'It makes visits like Fritz and Vicky's *very painful* and *trying*.'[22]

The Schleswig-Holstein crisis had long been simmering before the Danish King's death brought it to the boil. There was no problem over Christian IX's right to the throne of Denmark but in the Duchies his succession was disputed by local assemblies in Schleswig and in Holstein on the grounds that, like Hanover, the Duchies were subject to Salic Law and Christian's titles depended on female inheritance. The Germans in the Duchies, and liberal nationalists among their compatriots within the German Confederation, supported the claims of King Christian's distant kinsman Frederick, Duke of Augustenburg. So at heart did Queen Victoria: 'Fritz Holstein', as she called Augustenburg, lived for some time in Gotha, was a friend of Prince Albert in their student days, and had married her half-sister's daughter. Schleswig-Holstein had already bruised relations between Windsor and Downing Street more than once. For, during the crisis over the Duchies which followed the revolutions of 1848, Prince Albert had favoured Augustenburg and the separation of the Duchies from the Danish Kingdom while Palmerston, then Foreign Secretary, was opposed to any re-drawing of frontiers along Germany's northern borders. Palmerston more than any other statesman was, indeed, largely responsible for the Treaty of London of 1852 by which the Great Powers passed over Augustenburg and recognized Christian's claims to sovereignty both in Denmark and the Duchies. And it was Palmerston as Prime Minister who warned Europe, in July 1863, that if any disturbers of the peace interfered with the rights or independence of the Danes 'it would not be Denmark alone with which they had to contend'.[23]

The Queen was alarmed by the menacing ambiguity of her Prime Minister's statement; and she was hardly reassured by the attitude of her Foreign Secretary, Earl Russell. As soon as she heard of Christian IX's accession she sent Russell a somewhat peremptory note insisting that no action should be taken by Britain before discussion with other Powers, 'especially with Germany'; but she found Russell's response evasive and unsatisfactory.[24] There followed a nine-month crisis within a crisis, as the Queen threw her weighty influence behind the peace party in the cabinet so as to curb the 'conduct of those two dreadful old men' at the head of affairs, 'Pilgerstein and Johnny Russell'.

It was a fine tussle, with Victoria seeking to trim her ministers' policy as though she were a medium for the dead Albert. 'Her recollections of the Prince's sentiments,' Gladstone declared, served as 'a barometer to govern her sympathies and affections'.[25] For advice on German affairs the Queen turned, not only to General Grey, but to another close confidant of the Prince Consort, Sir Charles Phipps, and she found that Earl Granville was prepared to act both as her mouthpiece in the cabinet and as a confidential informant. The Queen consistently favoured the secession of Schleswig and Holstein and their independence under Augustenburg. She argued that Britain had no treaty obligation to support Danish rule in the Duchies and she was emphatically opposed 'to an aggressive war on Germany, our *natural* old allies'. '*Why* should we fear Germany's possessing Holstein?' she asked. 'Germany will never go against us; the French and Russian navies are the only ones we need ever fear'; and to Gladstone she wrote, 'Germany is not ever likely to attack us – she who *ought* to be our *real* ally'.[26] Few British public figures shared her optimistic confidence in German nationalism; but fewer still were prepared to see Britain again drift into unnecessary war.

Yet on three occasions in 1864 – the second week in January, the third week in February and the last week in June – the Queen feared that Palmerston and Russell would stampede the country into a naval operation on behalf of Denmark. Each time the cabinet edged away from war, but in letters to her relations abroad Victoria rightly stressed the unpopularity of Germany's conduct with most English newspaper readers. Hanoverian and Saxon troops, acting with the authority of the German Confederation, entered Holstein in the last week of the old year; the Prussians followed them a few weeks later; and on 1 February 1864 Prussian and Austrian troops crossed into Schleswig. By mid-April every fortified position on the mainland of Denmark was in German hands. The best that Palmerston could do to save British prestige was to convene another conference in London in the hopes of inducing the Germans to pull their troops out of Denmark. But there was much bluff behind Palmerston's behaviour. As Granville said, in reporting an important cabinet meeting to the Queen, 'Although he may talk big [Palmerston] is quite aware of the folly of going to war'; and in the last days of June the cabinet settled for a policy of non-intervention. 'The establishment of the Duke of Augustenburg as Duke of Schleswig-Holstein is ensured,' General Grey wrote prematurely to his sovereign; and from Laeken King Leopold congratulated his niece with a message almost every word of which was underlined: 'You may well be Proud of your success and our dear Angel will see it with Unbounded Satisfaction, how gloriously you Acted in His Spirit.' His phrases delighted her.[27]

The Queen's triumph was not, however, unalloyed. Rumours of her pro-German attitude led in early May 1864 to Press accusations of 'despotic' dynastic diplomacy. More remarkably on 26 May Lord Ellenborough, a former Tory Governor-General of India, complained to his fellow peers that 'in all public questions relating to Germany, Her Majesty's Ministers have as much difficulty in carrying out a purely English policy as was experienced in former times . . . in the reigns of the first two sovereigns of the House of Hanover'; he regretted that the approach to foreign politics of George III ('those truly English feelings which regarded only English objects') seemed no longer to 'animate the Government of this country'. Earl Russell earned the Queen's gratitude by loyally defending her conduct in the Lords; but he then wrote privately to Balmoral lamenting 'that your Majesty's relations in Germany have allowed rumours to go forth that in the present contest your Majesty was disposed to take part with the Germans and against the Danes'.[28]

Russell's implied rebuke angered the Queen, who was upset by the whole affair. For the first time she became 'fully aware of all the attacks directed against her on the subject of her supposed German predilections'. General Grey told Granville, 'There is not a line she has written . . . that she would not wish laid before the world.' The reprimand stung her into action.[29] Letters were sent to the King of Prussia, to the Duke of Coburg and to the Crown Princess emphasizing that, much as she loved Germany, the Queen was bound constitutionally to agree with her government's policy and urging her German relatives by marriage 'not to bring my name forward'.[30]

But these judiciously phrased letters, with their assurances of impartiality, carried little weight. In Berlin, where she had long been suspect as a Coburg liberal, the Schleswig-Holstein crisis won Queen Victoria a new reputation: it seemed that she was a good German at heart after all, and King William praised her work for peace in conversation with her daughter; and yet the Queen remained uneasy over these sudden shifts in popularity at a foreign court. Had she known of Bismarck's conversation with the Tsar and his Foreign Minister in Berlin on 12 June, she would have been even more disturbed.[31] For it is clear from the record of their meeting that Bismarck was by now relying on the Queen's emotional sympathy for pan-German sentiment to counter warnings from his critics that he was pushing Prussia and all the German states into war with England. In seeking to prove 'Bertie's marriage' not 'political' by her partiality for the German national-liberal cause, she unwittingly played into Bismarck's hands as much as had her son-in-law in the timing of his travels. Bismarck's new-style diplomacy readily exploited the interplay of a monarch's personal and political actions. This development the Queen, to her credit, was soon to appreciate herself.

CHAPTER ELEVEN

Family Feeling
✍ Rent Asunder ✍

Within a few weeks Queen Victoria realized that her intervention as a peacemaker looked more impressive at Westminster than on the Continent. The failure of the London Conference was followed by a further Austro-Prussian advance, which threatened Copenhagen. By preliminary peace terms, agreed on 1 August 1864, Christian IX surrendered his rights in the Duchies to Prussia and Austria; but, to Queen Victoria's indignation, Bismarck refused to back her favourite candidate, Frederick of Augustenburg, unless he became in effect a Prussian puppet. In Berlin only the Crown Prince continued to seek recognition of his old friend's rights, with little hope of success.

In anger the Queen became a warm partisan of 'Fritz Holstein's' cause, even questioning the fundamental objectives of Prussian policy. 'Odious people the Prussians are, that I must say,' she told her Uncle Leopold in the following summer;[1] and when the first serious differences arose between Prussia and Austria over the future of the Duchies which their troops had occupied, the Queen came down firmly on Francis Joseph's side. No doubt she was influenced by his appointment of Count Alexander von Mensdorff-Pouilly as Austria's Foreign Minister in October 1864; for Mensdorff was her first cousin, the son of her mother's eldest sister. He had been Austrian ambassador in St Petersburg and was much respected by the Prince Consort. Unfortunately, although the Queen did not realize it, the details of Austria's German policy were shaped by a Foreign Ministry official rather than by Mensdorff; but Mensdorff's two-year tenure of this important office saw the closest contact between Windsor and Vienna for four decades.[2]

Mensdorff was among twenty-four kinsmen who gathered in Coburg at the end of August 1865 for the unveiling by Victoria of a statue to the Prince Consort. Once again she travelled to Franconia at an important moment in Germany's history. For a fortnight previously Bismarck secured Austrian agreement to the Convention of Gastein, a compromise settlement over the Duchies by which Prussia administered Schleswig and Austria administered Holstein. In conversation with Mensdorff at the Rosenau Victoria pressed the claims of 'poor good Fritz Holstein' and condemned Prussia's infamous conduct. Mensdorff was too much a gentleman to argue with his royal cousin, who credited him with more power and influence than he possessed; 'dear Alexander Mensdorff . . . so good, wise and honest', the Queen recorded that evening in her journal. By contrast a reluctant meeting with the King of Prussia eleven days later at the Hessian summer palace of Kranichstein showed remarkable tact of omission on the part of both monarchs. They met for less than half an hour, to exchange pleasantries and discuss the weather.[3]

By now the Queen had decided on a German bridegroom for her third daughter, Princess Helena: she should marry 'Christian Holstein', whom the Princess met, for the first time since childhood, at the Rosenau in August. He was a brother of Fritz Holstein, the Augustenburg claimant to the Duchies, and the marriage project – first aired in private exchanges between the Queen and the Crown Princess in April – was highly unpopular. The Prince and Princess of Wales blamed the Augustenburgs for much of the Danish King's misfortune, while their chief adversaries, King William and Bismarck, regarded the Augustenburgs as liberals, bitterly hostile to Prussia. Yet, despite these objections, Victoria was resolved on the marriage. Throughout the protracted crises of the following twelve months the Holstein marriage loomed disproportionately large in her calculations.

It was Princess Alice's opposition which most infuriated her mother. Already the Queen was criticizing Alice for the original ways in which she fulfilled her duties, such as the active patronage she gave to nursing organizations in Darmstadt. Now, as the Queen wrote to King Leopold, she found 'Alice . . . sharp and grand and wanting to have everything her own way'.[4] The Princess thought little of the Augustenburgs personally and she considered Christian Holstein, at thirty-four, too set in his habits to marry her nineteen-year-old sister. Moreover, being a woman of sound political sense, she argued there was no point in championing a lost cause; it would irritate King William and provide his chief minister with fresh stories of Coburg intrigues. But the Queen, with scant gratitude for Alice's support in her months of deepest sorrow, resented her advice. Indeed she resented any action which ran counter to her intentions. Thus when, in February 1866, William vetoed Prince Christian's plan to honeymoon at Gravenstein Castle the Queen regarded his letter of refusal as a 'gross insult'; it was 'monstrous' to forbid him to stay at a family residence because the surrounding countryside was under Prussian occupation. Not even a tactful letter from the Crown Prince could smooth her ruffled feelings. She began to feel that, as Ernest Stockmar remarked in Coburg, the King of Prussia's honesty must be in doubt.[5]

Two deaths in the last quarter of the year 1865 broke further threads with Victoria's early life. Lord Palmerston died on 18 October: Earl Russell succeeded him as Prime Minister, and Lord Clarendon again became Foreign Secretary. A more grievous blow was the death of King Leopold, at Laeken on 10 December. Towards the end of his life Uncle Leopold's judgement was beginning to fail; the new practitioners of statecraft used broader sweeps and cruder colours than Metternich, Talleyrand and the older school of diplomatic artists. Perhaps he exaggerated the ambitions of France and looked upon Bismarck as a mere passing phenomenon. But his death again inclined the Queen to melancholy. Soon, too, she was to miss his long experience and letters of counsel.

Early in March 1866 alarming news reached London. For several weeks tension had mounted between the Prussians occupying Schleswig and the Austrian forces in Holstein, who Bismarck alleged were encouraging the people of the Duchies to agitate in favour of Augustenburg. On 7 March Clarendon heard that a Crown Council had accepted the need for Prussia to annex Schleswig-Holstein, and Karl von Normann, the Crown Prince's secretary, sent a private warning to the Queen's German-language librarian at Windsor. 'That Bismarck wishes for a war with Austria and intends to bring it about by all recognized and unrecognized means (*mit allen erlaubten und unerlaubten Mitteln*) is certain,' Normann wrote. He added that the King of Prussia was hesitant but Bismarck likely to overcome his reluctance to wage war on Austria.[6]

The Queen, though perturbed by the course of events in Berlin, was slow to see the danger signals. She even passed on to the Crown Princess a mildly ghoulish family joke – Princess Louise suggested that her sister Helena might be 'like Herodias' (*sic*) and 'ask for B.'s head' as a wedding gift from King William.[7] But when on 12 March her Prime Minister suggested peace might best be preserved if the Duchies were put under the sovereignty of a compromise candidate, the Grand-Duke of Oldenburg, he received a sharp rebuff. 'The Queen has a bad headache', he was told, 'but cannot delay a moment in expressing, in the strongest terms, her dissent from Lord Russell's proposal'; a sovereign should not be imposed upon an unwilling people; it would be 'more in accordance with English principles' to 'give the weight of our naval support' to the peoples of the Duchies so that they could decide their own future. Next day the Queen told Clarendon she was so convinced of Augustenburg's claims 'that it would be impossible for her to consent to any step, such as that suggested by Lord Russell, for setting them aside'.[8]

Russell was not prepared to wrestle with his sovereign over this question. Hastily he assured her he would not raise the matter in cabinet. He was so badgered by home politics – in particular, the agitation for a second parliamentary reform bill – that he wished to isolate Britain as much as possible from Continental entanglements. Clarendon, however, who knew the Augustenburgs and thought little of them, was disturbed by the Queen's excessive partisanship for the family into which Princess Helena was to marry. In a private note to the Prime Minister later in the month he wrote, 'The idea of our spending one shilling or one drop of blood in the banditti quarrel which is now going on in Germany is simply absurd.' It was a sentiment with which Russell fully agreed.[9]

Left to themselves the Downing Street politicians would have watched the squabble across the North Sea with silent disapproval. But royal diplomacy left them no peace. On 16 March the King of Prussia told the British ambassador he would welcome British arbitration in the Austro-Prussian dispute over the Duchies. Without waiting for Bismarck to frame a message, the King asked the Crown Prince to write to Queen Victoria. Next day Fritz duly sent a long letter in which he emphasized that Victoria could determine whether or not Germany should be wracked by the calamity of war. It was this letter, supported by pleas from her eldest daughter, that made Queen Victoria realize how grave the issues at stake were. From being a mother, concerned with pushing through a child's marriage against family opposition, the Queen found herself entrusted with the full responsibilities of statesmanship.[10]

British constitutional practice required such matters to be decided by the cabinet, which duly discussed the King's request on Wednesday, 21 March. Already, however, Bismarck was intervening, anxious to check the spread of a dynastic diplomacy which he feared he could not control; and on Thursday morning the Prussian ambassador read Clarendon a long letter from the Minister President listing so many provocative acts by the Austrians that the Foreign Secretary saw little point in seeking to mediate. Both Russell and Clarendon were slow to advise the Queen, no doubt anticipating another series of peppery reproofs. Accordingly no reply was sent from Windsor to the Crown Prince until a week after his letter came before the cabinet. Eventually the Queen, bowing to her ministers' advice, had to tell him that 'the course pursued by the Prussian Government, under the influence of Count Bismarck' ruled out any prospect of arbitration.[11]

To the Queen this was an unsatisfactory response. She refused to see it as the end of the affair. Two days previously she had received from Queen Augusta of Prussia a letter 'written in the greatest alarm' and stressing the need for prompt action to check the drift towards war. Dutifully she instructed General Grey to seek the Prime Minister's advice. The response was prompt and to the point: 'There is but one remedy, one certain mode of preserving Peace', Russell wrote to the Queen on 27 March. 'It is the dismissal of Count Bismarck by the King. If this can be accomplished by any patriotic Prussians, who may have access to the King, all may go right – not otherwise.'[12] Victoria did not doubt the accuracy of Russell's analysis; but how could she topple Bismarck? Certainly not by conspiring with Fritz and Vicky; there were too many informers planted in their household. Only that week the Crown Princess had asked her mother, 'Will you not arrange a cipher between me and you?' If she sent groups of numbers to the British ambassador he could transmit the coded messages to the Foreign Office as though they were his telegrams; and the Foreign Secretary would forward the figures to the Queen without decoding them.[13] But Victoria instinctively opposed any such project. She feared for her daughter's safety, and for Fritz's chances of the succession, if their enemies at court discovered the existence of an English cipher system.

The Queen, however, was determined on some form of action. Duke Ernest II, the Prince Consort's brother, was now added to her supplicants. More characteristically he induced his wife to write to the Queen from Gotha, giving his views. Bismarck, and Bismarck alone, wanted war, the Duchess insisted; and Duke Ernest argued that only serious measures, taken jointly by Britain and France, could save Germany from a disastrous conflict. Momentarily the Queen favoured an anti-Prussian naval demonstration in the Baltic, preferably in collaboration with the French. But neither Russell nor Clarendon possessed the jaunty pugnacity which the Queen had so deplored in Palmerston's conduct of affairs. Clarendon rejected intervention in a letter to the Queen written on 31 March: he would not use 'the language of menace which might entail the necessity of action', especially as 'the case is one in which neither English honour nor English interests are involved'. Next day (Easter Sunday) Russell, too, wrote to the Queen: he was firmly opposed to interfering 'in any way with Prussia while Count Bismarck is the Minister of the King'. Later in the week Clarendon suggested that her cousins Mensdorff and Ernest might induce Francis Joseph to write a conciliatory letter to King William, but he added, significantly, 'the initiative must come from Coburg'. Victoria could see that, whatever might happen in Germany, her ministers had no intention of letting it burn their good English fingers.[14]

'The Missus is in an awful state about German affairs,' Clarendon irreverently remarked on 6 April; and small wonder. Easter Week found Berlin 'still midway suspended between peace and war', as the Crown Princess told her mother.[15] The Prussians were seeking to isolate Austria from the other states in the German Confederation while encouraging Italy to threaten Austria with a war on two fronts. The Queen's sympathies were with the Austrians: she told Russell that Francis Joseph was right to reject proposals to buy off Italy through the cession of Venetia; recognition of the principle of nationality was a dangerous precedent which 'might seriously inconvenience England herself'.[16] She approved the engagement that April of her cousin, Princess Mary Adelaide of Cambridge, to Prince Francis of Teck, a Württemberger who served in the 1859 Campaign with an Austrian Imperial Guard regiment and was a favourite with the Emperor and Empress in Vienna. But the Queen knew that the crisis demanded positive action, not mere gestures of sympathy. If no one else would warn King William of Bismarck's machinations, the Queen would do so herself, echoing the comments made by Russell on 27 March which had seemed, at first, too intemperate for her to include in any letter to Prussia. On 10 April, without consulting Russell or Clarendon, the Queen sent an impassioned appeal to William to pause before unleashing a war, caused by 'imaginary affronts and wrongs' in which 'brother will be arrayed against brother'. She insisted that '*one man* alone' would bear responsibility for this evil (*Ein Mann allein trägt die Schuld an diesem Unheil*). Rarely has one sovereign so roundly denounced another's minister to his master. Clarendon, on receiving a copy of the letter, tactfully assured the Queen of his own, and the Prime Minister's, admiration for her 'most beautiful and forcible' words.[17]

The Queen's message, handed to King William personally by the British ambassador, had no lasting effect on the crisis; but it may have postponed the conflict. The King did not reply for another week: by then (21 April), although reiterating old grievances, he could tell Victoria of his satisfaction that tension was easing along Prussia's borders with Austria. In that week both the King and his minister welcomed the 'Gablenz Mission' – an attempt by two brothers, one in Prussian service and the other in Austrian, to find a compromise settlement of the Schleswig-Holstein dispute. The Queen's initiative encouraged Duke Ernest II to establish direct contact with King William and to see, through his links with Mensdorff, that the Prussian court possessed accurate information about Austrian military movements, not the exaggerated reports with which Bismarck alarmed his sovereign. Not since the seventeenth century had there been such active dynastic diplomacy.[18]

Queen Victoria was, of course, primarily concerned with the fate of her daughters in Prussia and Hesse-Darmstadt and the future of Saxe-Coburg-Gotha, the Duchy of which her second son, Prince Alfred, was heir-presumptive. But there was also the old connection with Hanover. Her cousin the Duke of Cambridge – Commander-in-Chief of the British army – was third in line of succession to the Hanoverian crown and reminded the Queen 'that our family springs from that old country of our forefathers'. Bismarck assumed that George V of Hanover would side with his powerful Prussian neighbour: he had met the King in 1853, two years after his accession, and in his memoirs gives a vivid, but somewhat pitiless, account of the blind King's attempt to conduct diplomatic negotiations without a minister in attendance in a study 'littered with every imaginable kind of public and private papers'.[19] But Bismarck miscalculated. King George's legalistic mind was clear: if the Diet of the German Confederation voted against Prussia, then Hanover would be bound to support the Confederation. Queen Victoria wondered if Britain was then obliged to help safeguard her uncles' old kingdom; but on 7 May she was assured by her Foreign Secretary that she need take no special measures were Prussia to march against Hanover.[20] Clarendon could see that British public feeling remained totally indifferent to the fate of the German states. An active policy might stir up greater resentment against the Crown than at the time of Ellenborough's peppery tirade in the Lords.

By contrast Duke Ernest II behaved weakly, at least in Victoria's eyes. For, only a week after inducing his wife to write a second letter on the need for joint Coburg initiatives for peace, he decided to side with Prussia; he even asked for a command in the Prussian army. Only from Darmstadt did the Queen receive any glimmer of encouraging news. Princess Alice, whose husband went to Berlin to appeal for peace but could not see the King, had herself written to William and was pleased by 'a very long, kind answer saying it was not him who wanted war'. In Hesse, even more than in most states, a war would divide families: Prince Louis, for example, was commander of a Hessian Cavalry Brigade while Prince Henry, his brother's companion when he went to England to seek a bride, held high rank in the Second Prussian Lancers. But 'Here, as yet, though there is no distinct reason for it save the repugnance of all to this civil war, all still hope,' Alice wrote to her mother on 18 May.[21] Time, however, was fast running out.

By now there was little Queen Victoria could do to ward off the tragedy. Twice more she sent pleas for peace to the Crown Prince, and indirectly through him to his father; and until the end of May she hoped the Austro-Prussian quarrels might be referred to a general conference of the European Great Powers. At last, in the first week of June, she accepted that Mensdorff and his Emperor were as intractable as the Prussians. Gloomily, on 10 June, she discussed with Clarendon where 'poor dear Vicky ... could go in the event of war'. Even to that simple question there seemed no clear answer.[22]

Two days later the Queen was at Kew Church for Princess Mary Adelaide of Cambridge's wedding – the 'Polly-Teck-nic Marriage', as the Crown Princess called it in a lighter moment. Francis of Teck was fortunate: he had resigned his Austrian commission on his betrothal and was thus spared the tragic campaigns of the 'war between Germans', which began some ninety hours after his wedding.[23] The Prussians marched on Hanover, Dresden and Frankfurt, occupying all three cities without much difficulty. The Hanoverian army retreated into Thuringia, hoping to make contact with the Bavarians. At Langensalza, on 27 June, it made a valiant stand against a Prussian onslaught before being forced to capitulate north of Würzburg two days later. The Crown Prince was given command of the Prussian Second Army, which invaded Bohemia from Silesia; and, on 3 July, it was his intervention that won Königgrätz-Sadowa, the largest and bloodiest battle fought in Europe between 1815 and 1914. With great difficulty Bismarck and the Crown Prince, collaborating effectively for the first time, persuaded King William not to continue the war until he could dictate peace from an occupied Vienna. Preliminary terms, acknowledging Prussia's mastery in northern Germany, were agreed on 26 July at Nikolsburg (Mikulov) in Moravia.

Detailed reports of Sadowa – as British and French newspapers called the battle – appeared in *The Times* of 5 July, the Thursday on which the second Anglo-German royal wedding of the summer was solemnized, at Windsor on this occasion. With two sons-in-law technically at war with each other, the

Queen welcomed Christian Holstein into the family quietly, in the private chapel of the castle, and was thankful Princess Helena was spared the burdens of uncertainty which troubled her two elder sisters. The Prussians entered Darmstadt on 21 July and that afternoon Princess Alice, who had given birth to her third daughter ten days before, wrote to her mother complaining that the occupation troops were paying for nothing and demanding everything. The Queen forwarded the letter to the Crown Princess. But, as Vicky wrote back to Osborne, there was nothing she could do to improve the 'painful and distressing position darling Alice is in' for it was 'one of the unavoidable results of this dreadful war'.[24] Appeals reached the Queen from Fritz Holstein, from the King of Saxony and from her Hanoverian relatives and she, in turn, passed these intercessions on to her eldest daughter. In the second week of August, as an uneasy peace settled on Germany, the Crown Princess was forced to remind her mother firmly that she was by marriage a Prussian. The Prussian people, she insisted, could hardly be expected to forego the fruits of a remarkable victory by treating with excessive generosity the German states who were so misguided as to ally with Austria.[25] How wise of 'Uncle Ernest' to have plumped for the side of the angels!

No doubt it was unreasonable of Queen Victoria to place much faith in 'happy family' diplomacy at such a decisive moment in Germany's history. Perhaps, at heart, she knew her efforts were unlikely to succeed. But, like her daughter, she might well have wondered, 'What else could I do?' For, as the drama on the Continent reached its climax, Britain was without a government and, on the day that peace talks began at Nikolsburg, Londoners watched running fights at the gates of Hyde Park as the police grappled with 'Reform' demonstrators. Twice in June the Queen refused to accept the resignation of Russell's government, begging him to stay in office because of 'the present state of the Continent' and when eventually, on 26 June, she had to send for Lord Derby and the Tories she vainly sought to persuade Clarendon to remain at the Foreign Office, so as to give some continuity to Britain's policy abroad. Not until three days after Sadowa did a new Foreign Secretary begin to study the accumulated incoming dispatches from envoys in Europe; and even then the Queen thought little of his abilities. For the Prime Minister, the Earl of Derby, took the unprecedented step of entrusting foreign affairs to an inexperienced son, Lord Edward Stanley. The Queen, and General Grey, tended naturally to consult the father rather than the son over the German Question, but with diminishing confidence. Derby's first speech in the Lords was far from encouraging: 'It is the duty of the Government of this country', he declared, 'to endeavour not to interfere needlessly or vexatiously with the internal affairs of any foreign country, nor to volunteer to them unasked advice with regard to the conduct of their affairs.' And in the Lower House Stanley echoed his father: 'Ours will be . . . a policy of observation rather than action.' But he also added, 'If North Germany is to become a single great power, I do not see that any English interest is in the least degree affected.'[26]

Within a month the Queen was educating Lord Stanley to his responsibilities, as she understood them. Her ministers could not be indifferent to what happened in Germany. 'A strong, united, liberal Germany', she said, 'would be a most useful ally to England.' Although she recognized that most Germans wished for unity under Prussia, there were many features of the new North German Confederation which she deplored. She had never believed Prussia would annex Hanover, and her sense of historic order was outraged when the kingdom of her immediate predecessors was formally absorbed on 20 September 1866. Over the next three years she continued intermittently to complain to King William at the treatment of the blind George v and the sequestration of his treasury by Bismarck. But neither the Queen nor her government ever protested formally at the re-drawing of the map of Germany. The heavy fine imposed on the city of Frankfurt by the victors was, she thought, injudicious and she shared Hesse's regret at the cession to Prussia of the Grand Duke's lands north of the Main. Privately, when Queen Victoria and Queen Augusta of Prussia met at Windsor in July 1867, they agreed that the destruction of so much regional individuality in Germany was sad, that 'things had been done . . . which ought never to have been done'; but both were proud of the Crown Prince's contribution, as a general in the field, to the making of a unified Germany under Prussian Protestant leadership.[27]

Despite the failure of her efforts to preserve peace in 1866 Queen Victoria never relaxed pressure on Downing Street to show concern for German affairs. When, in the spring of 1867, Lord Stanley was slow to respond to the growing Franco-Prussian crisis over Luxembourg, the Queen again took the initiative. She wrote to King William urging him to give up Prussia's fifty-year-old right to garrison Luxembourg in return for a pledge from Napoleon III to abandon attempts to purchase Luxembourg from the King of the Netherlands. Subsequently the Queen received thanks from both Queen Augusta of Prussia and the Empress Eugénie for promoting a conference in London which settled the Luxembourg Question.[28] The Queen understood the balance of power. She believed Napoleon III's ambitions menaced Belgium and that Britain was bound to uphold Belgian independence for strategic reasons as well as dynastic sentiment. But she could look beyond the immediate crisis: 'I fear the time may come when Europe will wish France to be strong to keep the ambition of Germany in check', she wrote to her eldest daughter two days after she sent her letter of mediation to King William.[29] At heart she was convinced that 'the *principle* of our Foreign Policy (and this was also the opinion of the Prince Consort) should be a thorough understanding for mutual support, in the interests of Peace, with North Germany'. But there seemed to her no irreconcilable incompatibility between collaboration with Prussia and friendship with France.[30]

Yet Queen Victoria was beginning to see the German problem in a different light. She had less personal contact with her German relatives after the 'War of Brothers' than in the four previous years; and she did not set foot on German soil again until 1872, and then only briefly. When next the Queen wished to holiday abroad she chose neutral Switzerland, staying at Lucerne in 1868 and travelling by way of Cherbourg and Paris rather than through the Rhineland. Coburg had lost its appeal: there were aspects of the Duke's private life of which the Queen did not approve; she resented the absence of favours shown in the treatment of her special manservant, John Brown, during her last visit; and she remained critical of Ernest II's politic vacillations in the summer of 1866. Not until after his death in 1893 did she again visit Saxe-Coburg-Gotha. Contact with her daughters was also limited. Between December 1865 and November 1868 she did not even meet the Crown Princess in England, and she entertained Princess Alice and Prince Louis for no more than a few weeks in the two summers which followed their disastrous experience of war with Prussia.

By now the Queen's views on foreign royal marriages were also changing. When in the late autumn of 1869 the Crown Princess thought she had found a Prussian prince who would make the twenty-one-year-old Princess Louise a good German husband, the Queen told the Prince of Wales that she was 'irreconcilably against' another Prussian marriage. She set out her objections in a long letter from Claremont, where there were around her so many memories of Uncle Leopold and the 'totally different' conditions of 'beloved Papa's lifetime'. Now, she explained, 'Times have much changed' and foreign marriages caused trouble and anxiety. She recalled the personal worries 'in which our family were placed during the wars with Denmark, and between Prussia and Austria', when 'Every family feeling was rent asunder and we were powerless'. She wondered if her eldest son was aware, 'as I am', of the dislike with which London society looked upon 'the marriages of Princesses of the Royal family with small German Princes (German beggars as they most insultingly were called)'.[31] All these arguments were intended to prepare the Prince for his young sister's betrothal, not to some foreign prince, but to a Scottish peer, the Ninth Duke of Argyll. They possess, however, a wider significance. For at last the Queen was prepared to admit to herself that the insubstantial Europe of Prince Albert's Grand Design could never be conjured into reality. It had become lost in the misty enchantments of a young Coburger's political Romanticism.

In December 1868 Gladstone became Prime Minister for the first time, after an electoral victory which gave the Liberals a comfortable majority in the Commons. The Queen, who had wished to keep Clarendon at the Foreign

Office when the previous government fell, now objected to his return. She had decided that, in the past two years, he had become a Francophile and was fundamentally opposed to the idea of a unified Germany. There is no doubt that Clarendon's prejudices were exaggerated by General Grey, for there was an old animosity between the two men, but the Queen would certainly have preferred 'Pussy' Granville at the Foreign Office. However when Gladstone stood firmly by his decision to appoint Clarendon, the Queen gave way; but she continued to think her Foreign Secretary 'very satirical', and mistrusted his handling of Anglo-German relations.[32]

In the second week of March 1870 the Queen received warning signals of yet another approaching crisis in Europe's affairs. At first it seemed as if she might become as closely involved in current diplomacy as in the vexed question of the Duchies four years before. For, on 12 March, at the insistence of her husband, the Crown Princess wrote to her mother and asked for her opinion on the candidature of Prince Leopold of Hohenzollern-Sigmaringen for the throne of Spain, which was considered to have been left vacant by the flight of the nymphomaniac Isabella II in 1868. But Queen Victoria, who had held strong prejudices about Schleswig-Holstein, was little interested in the Spanish throne – or, indeed, in the Sigmaringens, who were the principal Roman Catholic branch of the Hohenzollern family. She therefore followed Clarendon's advice, telling her son-in-law that it was a matter upon which 'I can express no opinion' and that it called for 'a decision on which I would not care to exercise the least influence'. To her daughter the Queen remarked, 'I cannot do or say more. The neighbour (France) would be very suspicious.' A week later the Queen heard from Berlin that there, too, no one at court was inclined to give a decided opinion; and by the end of the month the Sigmaringen Prince seemed a non-runner in the Spanish throne chase.[33] The Queen heard nothing more of any Hohenzollern candidature until the first week in July, when she was 'much startled' by news that the Spanish Cortes had elected Prince Leopold as Spain's new King.

Unfortunately the Queen was at that moment without well-informed advisers. General Grey died at the end of March and Lord Clarendon in the fourth week of June. Their successors – Colonel Henry Ponsonby as the Queen's private secretary and the Earl of Granville at the Foreign Office – might be better disposed towards each other, for both were good Liberals, but on the Continent they lacked personal contacts or influence. Neither man appreciated the gravity of the quarrel between France and Prussia which swiftly followed the announcement of a German Prince's nomination to the Spanish throne. The Prime Minister, Gladstone, reacted slowly to an unfamiliar crisis. Even the Queen, though clearly puzzled by the rapidly worsening news from Paris and Berlin, failed to identify any special cause of war and made no attempt to prod her ministers into action, as in the Luxembourg Crisis. However, on 9 July, as an afterthought to her customary letter to the Crown Princess, she suggested that if 'Leopold H.' withdrew his candidature and the King of Prussia made it clear that he had nothing to do with the whole affair, there would be no reason why Europe should be set ablaze. It was not until the following day, after requests for intervention from Granville and from the King of the Belgians (Leopold II, her first cousin) that Victoria made an appeal for peace. Even then she did not, as in 1866, get in touch with the King of Prussia but only with the Hohenzollern candidate's wife's brother, the Count of Flanders. Nevertheless 'Leopold H.' did, indeed, as the Queen suggested, withdraw his candidature; and it seemed by 14 July as if all pretext for war had been removed.[34]

The Queen was both gratified and relieved: she loathed the thought of another major war in Europe, with her two sons-in-law again in the field and the German lands exposed to French invasion. Like most of her subjects, she anticipated that any campaign along the Rhine would end in French victory. When news of the Ems Telegram reached London, the Queen still hoped that Europe might avoid a pointless conflict. Despite her mistrust of Bismarck, she had little doubt that the sabre-rattling Bonapartists around the ailing Emperor in Paris were fanning the smouldering embers of the old crisis. On 15 July the Queen accordingly suggested to Granville that she should take the initiative in seeking a joint appeal for peace from all the other European sovereigns to King William and to Napoleon III; but Granville, fearing a rebuff, showed no enthusiasm for her proposal. She then suggested a direct appeal to her old friend and ally, Napoleon. Granville, however, contented himself with telling the French ambassador, somewhat lamely, that the Queen wished for peace. It is hard to avoid the feeling that a more resolute government could have made wiser use of their sovereign's willingness to seek reconciliation.[35]

On 19 July the French declared war on Prussia, who was supported by her South German allies – Bavaria, Baden, Hesse-Darmstadt and Württemberg. Great Britain remained neutral, despite hopes in Berlin that the revelation of Napoleon's attempts to secure the absorption of Belgium in his empire would lead to demands in London for renewal of the Waterloo Alliance against France. Once again 'family feeling was rent asunder', for the Prince of Wales sympathized with the French while the Queen rejoiced at the 'wonderful news' of the Crown Prince's victories over Marshal Macmahon. By mid-August the Queen, and all her ladies at Balmoral, were preparing linen and other help to send to Germany for the wounded; and she was hoping that it would be a brief war. 'I pray it may end soon and dear Fritz be able to make peace at the walls of Paris,' she wrote to Vicky six days before the decisive battle of Sedan.[36]

As the war dragged on, and the threat to Paris became more pronounced, the Queen once again became anxious for peace. At the same time, she was troubled in case 'in interfering' the British government might appear to wish to protect France and thereby prevent Germany from making a lasting peace.

'The Queen ... must look forward and warn most *solemnly* and *positively* against the danger of alienating Germany from us,' she wrote in a memorandum for the Foreign Secretary on 9 September. Ten days later she telegraphed an appeal to the King of Prussia hoping that 'in the name of our friendship and in the interests of humanity' he could offer terms which his defeated enemy might accept.[37] Bismarck, however, brushed aside what he termed this 'petticoat interference' in grand strategy. By the end of the first week in October the Prussian royal standard was flying from the flagstaff over the Préfecture in Versailles; and the Parisians braced themselves grimly for the privations of a winter siege.

Public opinion in Britain swung back strongly in favour of the French; and in October there were demonstrations in London, and other cities, at which there were protests against the allegedly pro-German attitude of the sovereign and her court. At the same time there was disappointment in Berlin that the British seemed to show such little understanding 'that Right was on the side of Germany' (to use King William's phrase). By mid-December it was being said that the Crown Prince was postponing the bombardment of central Paris because of pleas from his wife 'acting under the direction of the Queen of England'. For Queen Victoria herself, the war posed delicate problems which at times strained her painfully acquired sense of impartiality. Both of her eldest daughters resented British Press criticism of the German army and of its methods; even the kindly and humane Princess Alice sought to explain to her mother that war must demoralize the best of armies. When, in Darmstadt's crowded hospitals, Hessian soldiers told her 'with such a look' that they had been wounded with English bullets, the experience was, for the Princess, deeply distressing.[38]

Often in this 'terrible war' Queen Victoria's thoughts were with her sons-in-law, and particularly with Fritz. He, too, remembered his English connections: on the ninth anniversary of the Prince Consort's death, he recalled in his journal a conversation with 'my beloved, never-to-be-forgotten father-in-law' as they strolled in the gardens of Buckingham Palace in 1856, in which he had emphasized the need for Prussia to seek assistance from the other German states in creating a new German Empire.[39] The Crown Prince, who was at that moment at the Trianon with Major-General Duke Ernest II as his companion, seems to have been trying to convince himself that Albert would have approved of Prussia's actions even if he had never believed in seeking German unity 'by force of arms'. Increasingly the Crown Prince was thinking of the need for the King of Prussia to assume an imperial title and resurrect a 'free German Empire'. The ceremony at Versailles on 18 January 1871 when Bismarck proclaimed a German Empire meant far more to Fritz than to the septuagenarian William I, who in a letter to his wife dismissed the whole historic occasion as 'the emperor charade'. That day in the Hall of Mirrors the Crown Prince wore full uniform together with 'the English Garter at the knee in honour of my wife and as an omen of an intimate union of the Empire with England'. His mother-in-law, bitterly conscious of the growing estrangement of the two nations, was much less enthusiastic. At the opening of parliament Queen Victoria offered 'congratulations on an event which bears testimony to the solidity and independence of Germany'. And when her old friend, the new Empress Augusta, complained of the frigid formality of Victoria's speech, she commented, significantly, 'How can a neutral be warm?'[40]

CHAPTER TWELVE

✑ Battenberg ✑

The fighting around Paris ended with an armistice in the last days of January 1871 although the formal 'Peace of Frankfurt', which deprived republican France of Alsace-Lorraine, was not signed until the second week in May. There followed a series of victory parades in the greater German cities with the principal celebrations reserved for Berlin where, in midsummer heat, the armies took two and a half hours to pass beneath the Brandenburg Gate and along a flag-lined Unter den Linden. The Crown Prince, who received his Field Marshal's baton that June, was fêted, not only at Potsdam and Berlin, but in the 'ex-enemy' capitals, too, notably in Hanover and Munich. Nevertheless he found time for short visits to London, staying at the German Embassy for ten days in early July and returning at the end of the month to join his wife and her mother at Osborne. Queen Victoria's attitude to her 'fair, kind and good Fritz' remained unchanged; but she could not disguise the mounting hostility of her government and people to the new Germany. Already the absence of the British ambassador from the midsummer victory celebrations had aroused comment in Berlin.

It was not until the autumn of 1873, after two more visits to England by the Crown Princess and her husband, that Queen Victoria frankly defined her attitude towards Bismarckian Germany. While the British Press criticized the Frankfurt peace terms and the Chancellor's internal policy, it was the memory of 1866 which continued to cloud the Queen's judgement. 'It used to be my pride and dear Papa's, to be able to say, that your excellent father-in-law never would let himself become a tool of Bismarck's ambition, as the King of Italy had been of Cavours's,' the Queen wrote from Balmoral in October 1873. 'Alas! I can say that no longer and '66 destroyed that bright difference. This does not mean that the unity of Germany was not right, or not wished for by me and dear Papa. We both earnestly wished for that, for one head, one army and one diplomacy; but not for dethroning other Princes, and taking their private property and palaces.' The enormities of royal Prussian behaviour made the Queen indignant: how could the Emperor William or his son and her own daughter bear to live in confiscated residences, she asked? Her blunt letter brought a sharp rejoinder from the Crown Princess: the Emperor, she protested, had 'paid for them and they are legally his'.¹ The Queen was unconvinced.

It was hard to soften Victoria's prejudices. She was disillusioned with the

The House of Battenberg (Mountbatten)

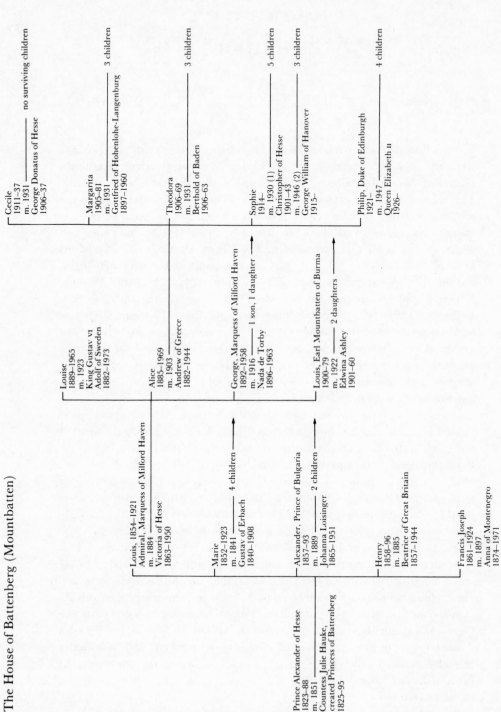

Prince Alexander of Hesse
1823–88
m. 1851
Countess Julie Hauke,
created Princess of Battenberg
1825–95

Marie
1852–1923
m. 1841
Gustav of Erbach
1840–1908 —— 4 children

Louis, 1854–1921
Admiral, Marquess of Milford Haven
m. 1884
Victoria of Hesse
1863–1950

Alexander, Prince of Bulgaria
1857–93
m. 1889
Johanna Loisinger
1865–1951 —— 2 children

Henry
1858–96
m. 1885
Beatrice of Great Britain
1857–1944

Francis Joseph
1861–1924
m. 1897
Anna of Montenegro
1874–1971

Louise
1889–1965
m. 1923
King Gustav VI
Adolf of Sweden
1882–1973

Alice
1885–1969
m. 1903
Andrew of Greece
1882–1944

George, Marquess of Milford Haven
1892–1958
m. 1916
Nada de Torby
1896–1963 —— 1 son, 1 daughter

Louis, Earl Mountbatten of Burma
1900–79
m. 1922
Edwina Ashley
1901–60 —— 2 daughters

Cecile
1911–37
m. 1931
George Donatus of Hesse
1906–37 —— no surviving children

Margarita
1905–81
m. 1931
Gottfried of Hohenlohe-Langenburg
1897–1960 —— 3 children

Theodora
1906–69
m. 1931
Berthold of Baden
1906–63 —— 3 children

Sophie
1914–
m. 1930 (1)
Christopher of Hesse
1901–43
m. 1946 (2)
George William of Hanover
1915– —— 5 children
—— 3 children

Philip, Duke of Edinburgh
1921–
m. 1947
Queen Elizabeth II
1926– —— 4 children

Hohenzollerns. When in March 1878 her third son, the Duke of Connaught, told his mother that he wished to marry the German Emperor's great-niece, Princess Louise of Prussia, the Queen tried to discourage him. It was not only that Louise came from an unhappy, broken home; 'I could not help saying that I dislike the Prussians,' she wrote in her journal that evening.[2] However the Duke, a virtuous career soldier of twenty-seven, had fallen genuinely in love with the Princess while he was visiting Berlin in the previous summer; and his mother gave way. Twelve months later they were married at St George's Chapel, Windsor, the seventh Anglo-German royal wedding of Victoria's reign. At least her second son, Prince Alfred, Duke of Edinburgh, had broken the pattern by travelling to St Petersburg in January 1874 to marry the Tsar's only surviving daughter, the Grand Duchess Marie Alexandrovna. Not that an Anglo-Russian marriage alliance was any more reassuring to the Queen than the familiar Anglo-German connection in these years of chronic crisis in the Balkans.

Paradoxically Prince Alfred's Russian marriage strengthened his links with Germany. His bride's mother was a Hessian Princess by birth and an aunt of Louis of Hesse, Princess Alice's husband. For over fifty years – from 1863 to 1914 – the Russian royal family 'invaded' Hesse-Darmstadt almost every summer, generally staying at Heiligenberg, high in the Odenwald, some ten miles south of the Hessian capital. Prince Alfred, too, was a frequent visitor to his sister Alice in Darmstadt and its surrounding ring of palaces. It was there, at Heiligenberg in August 1871, that Alfred and Marie first met and it was there, too, that they became engaged. They returned many times to the terraced castle on its bluff of mountain, above the village of Jugenheim. Gradually the palaces in these wooded hills, reaching down from Darmstadt towards Heidelberg and looking out beyond the middle Rhine to the borders of Alsace, replaced the more remote triangle of Coburg residences – Rheinhardtsbrunn, Gotha and the Rosenau – as informal royal conference centres. The spas of Homburg and Wiesbaden were conveniently close at hand. The Odenwald became the happiest and most relaxed royal children's playground in Europe.

Although Princess Alice had found Darmstadt society stiff and starchy when she first arrived there as a bride in July 1862, she was never treated with such suspicion as her elder sister in Berlin, nor was she so inhibited by the Grand Duke's bumbling chief minister as was Vicky by the far abler Bismarck. Hessian court life was more cultured and less primly intense than that of Potsdam and Berlin. Only two months before Alice's arrival her husband's uncle, Alexander of Hesse, finally settled in his birthplace with Julie, the Polish Countess he morganatically married in 1851 and whom his brother, the Grand Duke, created Princess of Battenberg. As with all morganatic marriages their children – four sons, aged between eight years and eight months, and a daughter of nine – took their mother's title as a family name. Alexander and Julie, with their experience of life in St Petersburg and Graz and Vienna, brought a cosmopolitan vitality to Darmstadt and Heiligenberg. Inevitably a close friendship sprang up between the Battenbergs and the young Princess from England. When Alice returned to Windsor to give birth to her first child in April 1863, 'Uncle Alexander' was sent to represent the Grand Duke at the christening of their great-niece, Princess Victoria Alberta. He dined with the Queen at Windsor and his self-assurance, knowledge of the world, and ready conversation charmed his hostess. 'Prince Alexander is very clever and agreeable,' she wrote that night in her journal. 'For the first time since my great loss (excepting Uncle Leopold) I hear someone of our own rank speak at his ease.'[3]

Had they been able to read the Queen's words, the phrase 'of our own rank' would have delighted the Battenbergs. For Continental court etiquette unduly emphasized the social stigma of morganatic marriage; and Princess Julie and her boys suffered even more than the head of the family from slights and insults both at the other German courts and in Austria. Among their social tormentors was the Prussian Crown Prince who, in his younger days, fussed about such matters in ways which his wife and mother-in-law found hard to understand. The Prince of Wales, on the other hand, often visited the Battenbergs. So, too, did Prince Alfred, Duke of Edinburgh, who in 1867 was granted twelve months' leave of absence from the Royal Navy to attend Bonn University, in preparation for his eventual succession in Saxe-Coburg-Gotha. The Prince had little liking for academic studies and during frequent escapes to Darmstadt he would talk nostalgically of ships and the sea.

Prince Alfred was, it would seem, a good yarn-spinner. The eldest of Alexander of Hesse's sons, Prince Louis of Battenberg, was so impressed by the royal picture of life under sail that he decided to seek service himself in Queen Victoria's fleet. Princess Alice welcomed the idea of strengthening links between her own family in England and the Battenbergs, even though Prince Louis's parents thought their son had taken leave of his senses. The boy had seen the Adriatic and the Tyrrhenian Seas while the family was living in Italy, but he had never set foot on any deck more unsteady than the upper saloons of a Rhine steamer. He was, however, an obstinate youngster and in September 1868, five months after his fourteenth birthday, he was escorted to England. Unlike most princes of that century, Louis of Battenberg survived the Dover packet at the autumn equinox without the embarrassment of seasickness; clearly the navy was his vocation. A few days later, in the Dickensian setting of a notary's office at Gosport, the Prince became the first Battenberg naturalized as a British subject. Before the end of the year he was serving as a cadet in the Royal Navy, although an unexacting Admiralty allowed him Christmas leave at Heiligenberg.

The Battenbergs were soon to achieve a dynastic ascendancy similar to that enjoyed by the Coburgs earlier in the century, or indeed by the ducal House of Brunswick 200 years before. There had clearly been something in Alexander of Hesse's conversational skills which, at their first encounter, made Queen Victoria think of Uncle Leopold; and Princess Julie possessed to the full all the dynasty-building qualities of Victoria's maternal grandmother, Augusta of Saxe-Coburg-Saalfeld. Like Augusta in her struggle for recognition in Napoleon's Europe, Princess Julie had acquired an 'almost masculine mind' from the need to secure social acceptance in Germany. She was, however, more of a career matriarch than Augusta and less tenderly maternal by nature. The ruthless iron in her character had been toughened by a terrible childhood, for she had seen her father butchered by Polish rebels in Warsaw when she was five years old; and, having been brought up at Nicholas I's court as an orphan who deserved well of the state, she then fell foul of authority by eloping with the Tsarevich's brother-in-law. Moreover, although no higher in rank than a minor Polish Countess, she had dared to marry her German Prince in defiance of the Tsar's wishes. It is true that the social commotion began to die down after a couple of years, and with the accession of Alexander II the Russians forgave the romantic elopement, but it was difficult for the Princess of Battenberg to enjoy a sense of security. Other dynasties had risen in importance from old traditions of past service. Coburg and Brunswick, for example, were names already steeped in history before their princes acquired eminence; but Battenberg was merely a forgotten village on the River Eder. It was so elusive that Herr Karl Baedeker had passed by the valley without so much as a parenthetical detour to the grand-ducal hunting lodge or the ruined castle of a crusading knight. Ominously, by 1868, Battenberg was not even any longer within the Grand Duchy. Like many places with a prouder heritage, it had been gobbled up by Prussia two years before.

Queen Victoria always attentively followed reports of Prince Louis's progress in her navy. As a midshipman and a sub-lieutenant he was entertained at Osborne on several occasions and he became especially friendly with the Queen's youngest daughter, Princess Beatrice. But he was rarely in England, apart from some months of spasmodic study at the Royal Naval College in Greenwich. He served in the North American Squadron, accompanied the Prince of Wales to India, and spent most of his periods of leave in Hesse-Darmstadt. In June 1876, by now a lieutenant, he was appointed to HMS *Sultan* in the Mediterranean fleet. The battleship was commanded by Prince Alfred and, over the following twelve months, there were occasional visits to relatives in the Russian imperial family: Prince Alfred was the Tsar's brother-in-law; Prince Louis was the Tsarina's nephew, and his first cousin and boyhood holiday companion, Grand Duke Alexei, was serving aboard a warship attached to Russia's Mediterranean Squadron. A later generation, more alert to the needs of national security, might have posted both Prince

Alfred and Prince Louis to politically calmer waters. When the second 'Battenberg boy', Prince Alexander, was commissioned in the Tsar's army there seemed a real possibility that Hesse, and Queen Victoria, might soon be deploring a longer and more widespread 'War of Brothers' than in Germany a decade before.[4]

The Great Eastern Crisis, which dominated European diplomacy from the summer of 1875 to the summer of 1878, is best remembered in Britain for three manifestations of deep public feeling: the thunderous invective of Gladstone's denunciation of Turkish atrocities in Bulgaria; the Russophobe popularity of music-hall 'jingoism'; and Lord Beaconsfield's assurance to a cheering crowd in Downing Street that from the Congress of Berlin he had brought back 'Peace with Honour'.[5] Queen Victoria observed these three occasions with vigorous partisanship; she had as little sympathy with Gladstonism as had Bismarck, and at times even Beaconsfield seemed too pacifically accommodating to suit her own patriotic fervour. She was more hostile to Russia than she had ever been to Bismarck's Prussia. Resort was made to every plea and almost every threat, including a hint of abdication, to make her Prime Minister 'act boldly', an unnecessary admonition which Beaconsfield treated with a tact which sprang from long experience of his sovereign's mind. She was harder to manage in the 1870s than in the years of inner grief which followed the Prince Consort's death.

Occasionally, during the Eastern Crisis, the Queen again experimented with her private dynastic diplomacy. She still hoped she could further Anglo-German co-operation and win Emperor William away from his natural tendency to collaborate with his fellow autocrat in St Petersburg. In October 1876 the Queen's personal initiatives, together with indiscreet remarks made by the Prince of Wales at the smaller German courts, prompted a private outburst of indignation from the Foreign Secretary. The royal family, he wrote to the ambassador in Berlin, 'being half German, half English by connection, think of the two countries as inseparably connected, and do not understand how those who are only German or only English fail to see the relations between them in that light'.[6] Despite her dislike of Germany's 'overbearing, violent, grasping and unprincipled' Chancellor, the Queen warmly supported every attempt to improve Anglo-German relations, provided it was realized in Berlin that 'any league against France would never be tolerated by this country'.[7] Her chief regret was that Germany seemed deluded by Russia's 'monstrous treachery' and 'false hypocritical intrigues'. To the Queen's satisfaction, ten days after she had denounced the Tsar's conduct in these terms, the Mediterranean fleet sailed through the Dardanelles and anchored in the Sea of Marmora. On the Turkish coast an invading Russian army was encamped on the outskirts of Constantinople.[8]

The squadron which sailed up the Straits on 13 February 1878 included HMS

Sultan, with Prince Alfred of Edinburgh and Prince Louis of Battenberg aboard. Turkey signed peace at San Stefano a fortnight later, but the British warships and the Russian army remained in close proximity throughout the spring and summer. Among the Russian officers who had fought their way from the Danube delta to the gates of Turkey's capital was Captain Prince Alexander of Battenberg. The German ambassador was happy to arrange a meeting in Constantinople of the two brothers; and Prince Alfred warmly welcomed 'Sandro' back aboard *Sultan*. 'I was received by Alfred and the whole ship's company with extraordinary friendliness,' Alexander wrote in a letter back to his parents in Darmstadt. 'They all feel more Russian than the Russians, and make no secret of it.'[9]

Queen Victoria was furious to hear that her son had entertained a Russian army captain aboard his warship. HMS *Sultan* was detached from the fleet and sailed for Malta; Prince Louis was transferred to another vessel and then sent on leave to Darmstadt. Life in Hesse was changing: the Grand Duke, Prince Louis's uncle, had died in June 1877 and was succeeded by Princess Alice's husband (who, of course, was also named Louis). At first Louis of Battenberg found relations between his parents and the new Grand Duchess strained, partly over the unfortunate events at Constantinople but also because of a relatively trivial matter of court etiquette. Within a fortnight, however, both quarrels were patched up, largely through the mediation of the Prince of Wales. Princess Alice championed Prince Louis, who had considered resigning his naval commission, and he was encouraged to finish his leave in London.[10] Later that summer she, too, travelled to England with the Grand Duke and their six children. Queen Victoria was troubled by reports of her daughter's poor health, and the Queen paid for the family to spend much of August and September at a house on the Grand Parade in Eastbourne, where the combination of sea-bathing and warm Sussex breezes was credited by the Queen with greater therapeutic qualities than the woodland air of the Odenwald.

With tension in the Balkans easing as the diplomats prepared for a final settlement at the Congress of Berlin, so Prince Louis's career prospects once more brightened. People spoke well of him and also of the courage of his brother, Alexander, in the Russian campaign which had liberated the Bulgarian provinces from Turkish rule. Queen Victoria, realizing a prince's difficulty in reconciling active service with the chance encounters of royal kinship, excused the lapses both of her son and of his Lieutenant; and Prince Louis was invited to luncheon by the Queen. But the Admiralty, less well-disposed to 'German princelings', wisely kept Prince Louis's naval appointments clear of the Mediterranean for the next nine years. By the summer of 1887, when he travelled to Malta as executive officer of one of the most modern battleships in the fleet, the name Battenberg was familiar throughout all Europe's chancelleries.

For Queen Victoria the year of the *Sultan* episode closed once more in the darkness of grief. Less than two months after the grand-ducal family returned to Darmstadt from Eastbourne the eldest daughter, Princess Victoria Alberta, was seriously ill with diphtheria. Over the following week every member of the family was infected, except for Princess Alice herself. The youngest child, four-year-old Princess Marie, died on 16 November and a week later it was feared that the Grand Duke's only surviving son, Prince Ernest Louis, would succumb to the infection. In seeking to comfort her child, Alice embraced him; it was for her 'the kiss of death', as Beaconsfield said in his moving tribute to the Princess in the House of Lords. She died on that 'terrible day', 14 December, the seventeenth anniversary of the Prince Consort's death; her surviving children recovered. The Prince of Wales came to Darmstadt for the funeral of his favourite sister; but the King of Prussia refused to allow the Crown Prince and Crown Princess to attend, for fear of infection. This ban caused adverse comment in the British Press, but diphtheria was at that time a terrible scourge. Despite the King's caution, his grandson – the Crown Princess's youngest boy, Prince Waldemar – contracted diphtheria in Potsdam soon afterwards. He died within four months of his aunt and cousin.[11]

For the remainder of her life Queen Victoria felt deep sympathy for the motherless children in Hesse. They were brought to Osborne as soon as possible and, in February, they were joined by their father. His visit to England coincided with a remarkable change in the fortunes of his nephew, Alexander of Battenberg. In January the Russians began to support the candidature of Alexander as reigning Prince of Bulgaria, the Balkan principality whose boundaries had been defined at the Congress of Berlin. He was acceptable to the Austrians, because his father had fought so valiantly for the Emperor at Solferino, and they hoped the British would raise no objections since they had shown themselves willing to grant the eldest of the Battenberg Princes a commission in the Royal Navy. When the Grand Duke arrived back in Darmstadt early in May he found 'Sandro' awaiting him. By now a Bulgarian Assembly had duly elected Alexander of Battenberg Prince of Bulgaria and he was about to leave for Livadia, the Tsar's palace in the Crimea, where he intended to clarify his status in conversations with Alexander II and his ministers. The Grand Duke duly wrote to Queen Victoria, supporting his nephew and hoping that he would be able to count on British friendship. The Crown Princess of Prussia, too, wrote enthusiastically about 'Sandro Battenberg' when she met him in Berlin on 27 May, after his visit to Livadia. Characteristically she told her mother that she hoped he would marry an Englishwoman so as to counter the risk that he would rule in Bulgaria as a Russian vassal.

When Queen Victoria received Prince Alexander at Balmoral on 6 June she was therefore already inclined to forgive and forget the unfortunate episode in the Sea of Marmora more than a year before. She liked Prince Alexander, whom she had not seen since he was a boy of five, and she was impressed by his evident determination to show independence of his Russian patrons. The Queen was pleased once again to have his brother, Louis, as her guest. Throughout the seven years in which Alexander of Battenberg sought to rule Bulgaria, the Queen was his warmest champion in London. When, later, she heard that Bismarck was turning against him because he was beginning to take political initiatives himself in Sofia, the Queen looked even more benignly on the young man. But on one subject she remained adamant. Neither Prince Louis nor Prince Alexander should marry her one remaining unattached daughter, Princess Beatrice. Not that the Queen had anything personal against the Battenbergs. She was merely determined that her youngest child – by 1879 a shy but highly intelligent woman of twenty-two – should remain in England, permanently at her side.[12]

By the time Queen Victoria passed her sixtieth birthday her correspondence was becoming more and more enlivened by rumour of impending nuptials. Her unfortunate haemophiliac son, Prince Leopold, Duke of Albany, was a favourite uncle to Princess Alice's children and spent much time in Hesse. While at Wolfsberg in the autumn of 1880 he rode over to Soden, a village ten miles from Frankfurt, at the foot of the Taunus Mountains. There he met Princess Helena of Waldeck, whose sister had recently become Queen Emma, second wife of the King of the Netherlands. A year later, Helena and Leopold were engaged; and they were married in St George's Chapel, Windsor, in April 1882. In one particular respect this was a curious occasion for the Queen, for prominent among the guests was the bride's brother-in-law, the Dutch King, who many years ago had been rejected with scorn by the young Victoria when he had come to England at King William IV's invitation as a suitor for her hand. It is one of dynastic expediency's gentler ironies that he should now return to the English court as a distinguished witness to yet another Anglo-German marriage. The Queen conferred upon him the Order of the Garter.[13]

The Crown Princess was unenthusiastic about her brother Leopold's engagement. She may perhaps have felt that, having lived in Germany for over forty years, she had a proprietary right to arrange family marriages to princesses within her father-in-law's Empire; and she knew little of Princess Helena, whose links were with Hesse and Württemberg rather than with Prussia. By now the Crown Princess herself was a grandmother. Her eldest daughter, Princess Charlotte, had married the heir to the Duchy of Saxe-Meiningen in 1878 and a princess was born a year later. For the Crown Princess, however, the great problem remained her eldest son, William, in whom she had vainly sought to inculcate a love of everything English: he was obsessively militaristic; he admired Bismarck; and neither he nor his brother, Henry, could ever become a clone of their maternal grandfather, as their mother at heart wished. Towards the end of 1879 Prince William, finding a romantic attachment to his cousin Elizabeth of Hesse evoked no response, turned instead to Princess Augusta Victoria, daughter of Fritz Holstein, the Augustenburg claimant whom Bismarck treated so shabbily during the Schleswig-Holstein crisis.

Prince William's choice pleased his grandmother and his parents. Rather surprisingly, he encountered little opposition from William I or Bismarck; both had feared that he might seek a less docile bride, more personally ambitious than the compliant 'Dona'. They were married in Berlin on 21 February 1881; and fifteen months later a son was born, at the Marmorpalais, the attractive waterside Marble Palace, outside Potsdam. But, with exasperating perversity, the excessively proud father then asked his aunt, Princess Helena – who was, of course, the wife of Dona's uncle, Christian Holstein – to find a nurse for the baby. It was seen at the Neues Palais as an early warning that Willie had no intention of allowing his mother any influence over the upbringing of the child who was now third in line of succession to the German imperial throne.[14]

Queen Victoria sympathized with the Crown Princess over Willie's behaviour within the family, just as she did over the slights, personal and political, of Germany's 'unscrupulous' and 'wicked' Chancellor. Yet, although the Queen accepted that what happened in Berlin was of greater significance than any day-to-day occurrences in the smaller courts, she concerned herself more and more in the early 1880s with Darmstadt. She went there in person in April 1880 for the confirmation of the eldest of 'good Alice's children', Princess Victoria Alberta, who had become – and remained – her favourite grand-daughter. When, in the winter of 1882–3, it became clear that the Princess hoped to marry Prince Louis of Battenberg she found her grandmother a good ally.

The young couple needed support. Although the Crown Princess approved and although Louis's younger brother Prince Henry of Battenberg was serving with the Prussian Household Cavalry at Potsdam, official imperial Berlin frowned on a marriage which raised the standing of the morgan-atic Battenbergs. Moreover now that the Prince's stiff conventional cousin Alexander III had come to the throne of Russia, St Petersburg, too, was glacial. Nevertheless, early in June 1883, Prince Louis proposed to Princess Victoria Alberta in the grounds of the hunting lodge at Seeheim, and their engagement was announced a week later. 'I am so glad she has found a person, kind, good and clever and whom she knows thoroughly well,' wrote the Queen to the Crown Princess at the end of the month. 'Of course people who care only for "great matches" will not like it, but they do not make happiness and Louis says they will be quite comfortable.'[15]

Before the wedding could be celebrated, the Queen suffered another sudden and unexpected bereavement. Her youngest son Prince Leopold, Duke of Albany, died at Cannes on 28 March 1884, leaving a daughter (Princess Alice) of thirteen months and a wife who was expecting their second child at midsummer. To some extent, the Queen was resigned to this loss because Prince Leopold had for so long suffered such poor health that she never expected him to marry, still less to have children. She sought to comfort his widow, Princess Helena, who was living at doom-haunted Claremont; but within a week of poor Leopold's funeral the Queen was on her way to Darmstadt. Three months later Princess Helena gave birth at Claremont to a son, Charles Edward ('Charlie'). It was the first occasion upon which a prince born at Claremont lived for more than a few hours, tragedy having struck there at Louis Philippe's daughter-in-law, the Princess of Joinville, as well as at Princess Charlotte. The young Duke of Albany was to live long enough to become a dispossessed German princeling – and a *Gruppenführer* in Hitler's brownshirts.[16]

Queen Victoria and her youngest daughter, Princess Beatrice, arrived at Darmstadt on 17 April. They were followed by an extremely large contingent of European royalty, from Russia as well as from Prussia, the smaller German states and Austria-Hungary; and naturally they were joined by Alexander of Battenberg, the ruling Prince of Bulgaria, returning home for his brother's wedding. There were, too, other marriages in the offing, some of which were already known to the Queen. Her granddaughter, Elizabeth of Hesse ('Ella') wished to marry the Tsar's brother, the Grand Duke Serge; and already the Queen had heard from the Crown Princess, in great secrecy, that her eldest unmarried daughter, Princess Victoria of Prussia, had fallen irretrievably in love with Alexander of Battenberg. The Queen deplored Ella's desire to go to Russia, 'that horrible country', whose towns seemed peopled by fanatical assassins, but she had seen by now that all of 'good Alice's' children were strong-willed and she made no serious attempt to persuade Ella to change her mind. To the Queen it was the attachment of 'young Vicky' in Berlin to Sandro that was likely to pose the more immediate problems. Somehow it would be necessary to counter Hohenzollern distaste for the offspring of a morganatic marriage; and there was no knowing how Bismarck would react to this dynastic intrusion into a corner of Europe which he was content to leave in Russia's sphere of influence. For the moment, however, the Queen was content to give all her attention to ensuring the happiness of Victoria Alberta of Hesse and Lieutenant-Commander Prince Louis of Battenberg. She was pleased by the warm greeting that Grand Duke Louis IV gave her at Darmstadt Station, although inevitably she thought back sadly to his own wedding at Osborne in those dark summer months twenty-two years before.[17]

The wedding was duly celebrated on 30 April. But it was not a unique royal ceremony that day. For in the evening the Grand Duke Louis IV secretly took as his morganatic bride Alexandrine de Kolemine. She was an admirable lady, related to almost all the families of distinction in Poland, and she had been a close friend of Louis IV for several years. There was much to be said for the Grand Duke's consoling himself with a second wife rather than retaining Alexandrine as his mistress. But he was marrying the wrong woman in the wrong way at the wrong time. For the estimable Madame de Kolemine was the twenty-nine-year-old divorced wife of a former Russian diplomat at Darmstadt. Within twenty-four hours rumours of the marriage had begun to confound his assembled guests. By 2 May it was known in Berlin; and immediately a peremptory telegram from the Empress Augusta demanded the return to Potsdam of the Crown Princess and all the other representatives of Prussia. Marriage to the divorced Alexandrine had made Darmstadt, in the words of Queen Victoria's private secretary, 'a contaminated court'.[18]

The Queen at once began the task of decontamination, which she regarded as essential if the Hessian dynasty was to retain any social standing or influence within Germany. The Prince of Wales had the difficult task of convincing the Grand Duke that the misalliance might lead to the absorption of the Grand Duchy by Prussia, and therefore to the loss of the civil list upon which he was dependent for an income, and that it would prejudice the marriage prospects of his remaining daughters. The Grand Duke saw the force of these arguments and agreed that he would consult the lawyers of Hesse and arrange an annulment. The unfortunate Prince then had to break the news to Madame de Kolemine, who soon afterwards left for Switzerland. So powerful was the influence of the British royal family that the Grand Duke even gave a written promise to the Prince of Wales that he would never see or write to Alexandrine again without the prior approval of the Prince or of Queen Victoria.[19] The marriage was annulled on 3 June and Madame de Kolemine received a payment of half a million marks from her five-week husband. Twelve days after the annulment, his second daughter ('Ella') was married to the Grand Duke Serge Alexandrovitch in St Petersburg. The German Emperor's eldest grandson, rather than the Crown Prince, was sent as Prussia's official representative to the Russian wedding.

If the Crown Prince and Princess felt slighted, the reason was not hard to discover. Alexander of Battenberg greatly impressed Queen Victoria at Darmstadt: she thought him handsome, politically discerning and a fascinating companion. Dutifully the Prince of Wales was detailed off to escort him to the Neues Palais and convince his sister and Fritz that Sandro was the ideal husband for the eighteen-year-old Victoria of Prussia. The Crown Princess needed little convincing and her husband at once saw Alexander's excellent qualities. On 12 May a senior official in the German Foreign Ministry, Baron von Holstein, noted in his journal: 'At the banquet at the New Palace two days ago, the Crown Prince, who was sitting between the Prince of Wales and the Prince of Bulgaria, treated the latter with quite unusual cordiality. A few days earlier he had spoken with the loftiest disdain of all Battenbergs. So the Crown Princess has got him round once again.'[20]

Alexander's arrival with the Prince of Wales and his patronage by the Crown Princess made it easy for Baron Holstein, and for Bismarck's closest confidants, to maintain that 'the Battenberg' was 'England's client'. 'Poor Sandro', the Crown Princess wrote to her mother. 'They have put paragraphs in the newspapers about Vicky and him which have been very disagreeable to us.'[21] Prince William spoke to his parents with such angry contempt of Alexander and his family origins that they had difficulty in holding their tempers in check. Their married daughter, now Princess Charlotte of Saxe-Meiningen, and their second son, Prince Henry, agreed with William. From Windsor Queen Victoria described the behaviour of all three of her grandchildren as 'shameful'.

More ominously Sandro was snubbed by Bismarck. In his table-talk the Chancellor always played down the importance of dynastic diplomacy. But he took the projected Hohenzollern-Battenberg marriage very seriously indeed. The key to his policy in Europe during the 1880s was collaboration between the three Emperors – William I, Francis Joseph and Alexander III – and the certainty that republican France would thereby find no anti-German ally in Vienna or St Petersburg. But Balkan Questions invariably threw the Austrians and the Russians into opposition, forcing Germany to make an embarrassing choice between her two partners. If Alexander of Battenberg, who had been considered a good Russian in St Petersburg when he went to Sofia, now married a Prussian Princess, Bismarck feared that the Tsar would assume Germany was beginning to take an interest in that carefully protected Russian preserve, the eastern Balkans. And the more Bismarck saw signs of English backing to the marriage project, the more he was convinced that this was a subtle game devised by those veterans at Windsor and the Neues Palais and intended to embroil Germany and Russia, discredit Bismarck's diplomacy and make it easy for the Crown Prince to dismiss the Chancellor when William I died. The Chancellor also knew that the Crown Prince remained sensitive over questions of rank and position. He had never been as stubborn or masterful as his wife. It would not be hard to detach him from those 'Englishwomen'.

Bismarck duly received Alexander of Battenberg in the Wilhelmstrasse on 12 May, but he was brutally frank. Were Alexander a Prussian general serving in the Prussian army like his younger brother, there would be no objection to his retiring and marrying Princess Victoria; but, as sovereign Prince of Bulgaria, he could never hope for her as his bride. Before returning to Sofia 'poor Sandro' slipped over to England, stayed incognito at his brother's house, and had a secret audience with Queen Victoria at Windsor on 20 May. The Queen, who continued to have 'the highest opinion' of the Prince of Bulgaria, told him not to despair. This optimisim seems to have sprung, as much as anything, from indignant reaction to a 'quite uncalled for' letter in which the Empress Augusta insisted on telling the Queen 'that on account of the parents she and the Emperor would never consent to such a marriage'.[22] Victoria was always particularly irritated by insults to the Battenbergs, even from such an old friend as the Empress in Berlin.

The royal lovers' cause suffered, too, from a new shift in Bismarck's policy. In the spring of 1884 the Chancellor became a 'convert to colonialism' and, in less than twelve months, Germany acquired over a million square miles of territory in Africa and the Pacific. No doubt the principal reason for this change of policy was economic, but there were also political considerations and among them was a readiness to encourage anti-British feeling in Germany. Bismarck was looking for ways of discrediting the Anglophile liberals around the heir to the throne so as to check the influence of the Crown Princess on her husband while the old Emperor, already in his eighty-eighth year, was still active in politics. 'When we began our colonial policy we had to reckon on a long reign by the Crown Prince, during which the influence of England would predominate,' Bismarck's son, Herbert, explained six years later.[23] The reaction of the Crown Prince's three eldest children to Prince Alexander's visit to Berlin showed that, like colonialism, royal marriage projects could be manipulated to fan a generation battle within the imperial family in which the 'Englishers' would be eliminated. It is possible the Battenbergs would have fared better in Berlin at this particular moment had they not enjoyed the backing of Queen Victoria, the Crown Princess and the Prince of Wales.

By the first week in June 1884, when the Queen arrived in Balmoral, she was less enthusiastic about the Battenbergs.[24] She had discovered that Princess Beatrice, too, was succumbing to the family charm. At Darmstadt the Princess fell in love with Prince Henry of Battenberg. Her mother was far from pleased, as she feared that her youngest daughter would wish to settle in Prussia while Henry continued his career in the German army. But 'Liko', as this third Battenberg Prince was nicknamed, came over to spend Christmas with his brother, Prince Louis, and his wife at their home near Chichester. The brothers crossed to the Isle of Wight and dined at Osborne with the Queen and her daughter on 23 December. Liko, it seemed, was tired of Potsdam militarism; he was content to resign his commission and settle for life as an English country gentleman so that Princess Beatrice could remain her mother's personal secretary and companion. He was, the Queen decided, 'the handsomest of the three handsome brothers'. On 30 December the engagement of Princess Beatrice was made public. 'The marriage is immensely popular here,' the Queen wrote to her eldest daughter a few days later.[25]

If by 'here' the Queen meant the Isle of Wight, she may well have been correct. But the prospect of another German marriage was far from popular in London. What the Queen herself described as 'this colonisation mania' had soured Anglo-German relations over the previous six months: feelings were more bitter than at any time since the siege of Paris. Old resentments grumbled once more in the Press. The most moderate attitude was taken by the *Church Times* of 2 January 1885. After reminding its readers that Prince Henry was 'a younger brother of the Prince of Bulgaria and of Prince Louis, who married last spring the eldest daughter of the eminently respectable Grand Duke of Hesse', the paper commented that Prince Henry was an officer in the Prussian Life Guards and regretted that, after 'nearly four hundred years of more or less foreign houses', England did not have a chance to provide a royal bridegroom. 'The thing is probably of no great moment, at all events in fair weather; but if the country should ever become the scene of political convulsion – which God in his mercy forbid! – we fear that the foreign alliances of the royal family might be a source of some danger to the constitution.'[26]

News of this latest advancement of the Battenbergs was received frigidly in the Prussian court. The Crown Princess approved, but a succession of letters to the Queen left her in no doubt of the hostility of the Empress, the Crown Prince and of Prince William and his wife. Queen Victoria was extremely angry with 'dear Fritz', thought that 'Willie, that foolish Dona and Henry' were extraordinarily impertinent and insolent, and resolved not to write to her eldest grandson for his twenty-sixth birthday. Throughout the year the Queen continued to show favours to the Battenbergs. In February 1885 Princess Alice of Battenberg – the first child of Louis and Victoria – was born, like her mother, at Windsor Castle in the presence of the Queen, who two months later travelled with mother and child to Darmstadt for the baptism. As if to scorn the dynastic purists of Berlin and other German courts, the Princess Battenberg and the Queen-Empress were both 'sponsors' (godparents) of the child, a Princess who was to become thirty-six years later the mother of Prince Philip, Duke of Edinburgh. The Queen's decision to bestow the Garter on her latest son-in-law and to create him a Royal Highness made 'Fritz . . . so frantic' that he sent a memorandum to the Duke of Connaught on the difficulties in precedence which this elevation of the Battenberger would create in Germany. On 23 July, when Prince Henry and Princess Beatrice were married quietly at Whippingham Church near Osborne, 'no representatives of the German reigning dynasties attended', apart from the unfortunate Grand Duke of Hesse. To Queen Victoria it seemed that German concern for 'rank etc.' was becoming an absurd and discourteous obsession.[27]

Within two months of Whippingham's royal wedding, the bridegroom's brother Alexander became almost overnight a key figure in the diplomatic calculations of the Great Powers. On 18 September Bulgarian nationalists in the nominally Turkish province of Eastern Rumelia declared themselves independent of the Sultan's authority and ready to unite with the principality of Bulgaria under Alexander of Battenberg's sovereignty. So drastic a change in the map of the Balkans was deplored equally in Berlin, Vienna and St

Petersburg, for none of the eastern autocracies wished for a diplomatic crisis and possibly a major war in south-eastern Europe that winter. Tsar Alexander III, already resentful of his Battenberg cousin's frequent displays of independence, condemned the union of 'the two Bulgarias' as a breach of the Treaty of Berlin: Germany, Austria-Hungary and Turkey followed the Russian lead. So unpopular were the Bulgarians that their Serbian neighbours marched on Sofia, only to be roundly defeated by Prince Alexander's troops at the battle of Slivnitza in the third week of November 1885. Most foreign opinions remained, however, hostile to Alexander, and the Prince was prevented from exploiting the victory by an Austrian threat of intervention. In London the new Conservative government of Lord Salisbury gave him warm diplomatic support. This approach may have convinced Bismarck he was right to assume that every Battenberg was an English pensionary; but it brought Bulgaria no material advantage. The days were passed when a British fleet could sail through the Straits and into the Black Sea.

Alexander could not afford to be on bad terms with Germany, Austria-Hungary, Russia and Turkey at the same time. Bulgaria's old pan-Slav liberators were the most dangerous threat. On 21 August 1886 a group of Russophile conspirators, encouraged by the Tsar's military attaché in Sofia, abducted the Prince, and in London it was reported he had been deposed. From Balmoral the Queen, after a sleepless night, urged Lord Salisbury to take action, and she continued to emphasize that the fate of 'the dear, brave and so cruelly used Prince of Bulgaria' was 'a subject of intense personal interest to her'. She also maintained, on the strength of reports from the Crown Princess, that 'All Germany is boiling over with indignation at the monstrous plot', resented the treatment imposed on a German reigning Prince by the Russians, and was 'furious with the [anti-Battenberg] language of the so-called official organs of the German Government'.[28] There is no doubt that, to a large extent, the Queen looked on events in Sofia as a dangerous extension of the family feud with Bismarck in Berlin. Momentarily it seemed as if the reports from St Petersburg and Constantinople were exaggerating the threat to Alexander's sovereignty. For, a week after his abduction, he was back in Sofia trying to collaborate with the Russians. But this change in policy displeased the Bulgarian radicals who had earlier supported him. On 3 September the Prince signed a definitive abdication, setting out for his old home at Darmstadt soon afterwards.

Ironically, this setback to the Battenberg dynasty was followed by Coburg advancement. Prince Ferdinand of Saxe-Coburg, an Austrian cavalry officer, was a grandson of the eldest brother of 'Uncle Leopold' on his father's side and of King Louis Philippe on his mother's side. But Queen Victoria had little use for 'this foolish young cousin of mine'. When, three months after Alexander's abdication, it was first rumoured that the Great Powers favoured Ferdinand as his successor in Sofia, the Queen complained to Lord Salisbury that her kinsman was totally unfit for such responsibilities, being 'delicate, eccentric and effeminate'; she hoped it would be made generally known that 'I and my family have nothing to do with this absurd pretension'.[29] But Lord Salisbury knew there was no prospect of restoring Alexander of Battenberg. He feared that the alternative to Ferdinand was a Russian regency, entrusted to one of the Tsar's generals; and, whatever his sovereign might feel, he was willing to work with Austria-Hungary and with Italy to prevent Bulgaria becoming a Romanov satrap. Reluctantly the Queen agreed with her minister. In Sofia a sedentary sybarite succeeded the hero on horseback. No one rated the 'foolish young cousin's' chances highly; but Foxy Ferdinand survived. He was reigning in Sofia when the First World War began and living in Coburg when the Second World War ended.

Alexander's fall removed Bismarck's original objection to a Battenberg marriage; the Prince might now settle with his Hohenzollern bride in Prussia, having retired from the arena of international politics. But the events of 1884–5 hardened the Chancellor's opposition. At all costs he wished to keep this handsome popular idol away from Prussia. Less than a month after Alexander's return to Darmstadt Bismarck presented Emperor William I with a long catalogue of the Prince's failings: he was weak, irresponsible, and conceited, a natural leader for the politically disaffected within Germany; the Berlin court was no place for the victor of Slivnitza, nor should he receive a commission in Prussia's army.[30] The Emperor agreed with Bismarck: the Battenberger was not to come to Berlin. For the Chancellor it was a victory over 'these English influences' which threatened to undermine his policy. But he clould not forget that 'our old master' had reached a greater age than any other reigning sovereign in Germany's history. By now it was almost a quarter of a century since the newly widowed Queen Victoria waited at Rheinhardtsbrunn for news of Fritz's accession. She was waiting still in March 1887, when the Prince of Wales went to Berlin for the Emperor's ninetieth birthday and found his brother-in-law's resonant voice unusually strained and hoarse.

CHAPTER THIRTEEN

ᘏ Years of Jubilee ᘏ

In June 1887 Queen Victoria celebrated the fiftieth anniversary of her accession. The Kings of Denmark, Greece, Belgium and Saxony, together with some fifty Imperial, Royal or Serene Highnesses came to Buckingham Palace for the Golden Jubilee luncheon on 20 June; and when next day the Queen drove to Westminster Abbey for the thanksgiving service her carriage was preceded by a princely escort of three sons, five sons-in-law and nine grandsons or grandsons-in-law. No horseman in the procession looked so impressive as 'dear Fritz', the Crown Prince of Prussia, who, with his magnificent golden beard and the white uniform of a Field Marshal topped by a silver German eagle on his helmet, was cheered by the crowds lining Piccadilly, Northumberland Avenue and the Embankment. When the Danish painter Tuxen was commissioned to commemorate the Golden Jubilee on canvas, he succeeded in clustering fifty-five relatives by blood or marriage around the black-gowned matriarch of Windsor. That was how the Queen wished to remember the celebrations, for to her the Golden Jubilee was, above all, a family gathering.

Her eldest grandson – the future Kaiser William II – saw it differently. Some forty years later he recalled, 'That day gave us all an overwhelming impression of the power and extent of the British Empire.'[1] He might have added that the great occasion also emphasized the close connections which continued to unite the Queen-Empress to Germany. For, despite the absorption of Hanover, there was still a profusion of German royalties in London that week: Fritz and Vicky; William and Dona and their five-year-old son, 'little Willie'; Augusta Strelitz and her husband; and an abundance of Hessians, Battenbergs and Württembergers. From time to time the private life of the Duke of Saxe-Coburg-Gotha had furrowed Queen Victoria's brow and she was alarmed to hear he was writing memoirs for publication, but Duke Ernest was a link with 'my darling Albert's' boyhood and she was glad he was seated next to her for the family dinner party at Windsor. Yet it was for Fritz and Vicky that the Queen felt most deeply. Her irritation with the Crown Prince for his stuffiness over morganatic titles had gone when she realized in May how grievously ill he had become with his diseased larynx, and she was relieved that he was able to make the journey to England. When the celebrations were over the Queen persuaded Vicky and Fritz to stay on in Britain for another two months, spent mostly at Osborne and Balmoral, for the Crown Princess and her mother were determined to keep the sick man away from the frustrations of Prussian court politics until he had recovered his strength. Although there was no doubt that he was suffering from cancer, both women almost convinced themselves that medical science would hold the disease at bay.

From England the Crown Prince and his wife travelled on to the Tyrol and Venice, moving as the weather turned colder to Lake Maggiore and eventually to San Remo. It was there on 9 March 1888 that Fritz heard of his father's death. The sick man, who was formally proclaimed as the Emperor Frederick III, was by now a tragic figure, a gaunt and speechless giant. But he at once travelled back to his capital, setting foot on German soil for the first time in nine months when he went into residence at Charlottenburg. His eldest son attended in meticulous detail to the ceremonial trappings of his father's short reign. He pleased Emperor Frederick by organizing a parade of the Guards regiments at Charlottenburg, with the Emperor sitting upright in a carriage to take the salute; and it was William, too, who supervised the elaborate transference of his ailing father from Charlottenburg to Potsdam, a sixteen-mile journey by steam yacht along the Rivers Spree and Havel. Emperor Frederick was thus able to spend his last two weeks of life in a room on the ground floor of his favourite home, the Neues Palais, where he was born fifty-seven years before.

Yet however deeply Prince William fulfilled a filial duty to a soldier father, in politics he continued to back Bismarck. Prince and Chancellor were resolved to resist those 'English influences' which Bismarck had for so long held at arm's length. In particular they opposed the Emperor's expressed wish to give his blessing to the marriage of his daughter, Victoria, and Alexander of Battenberg. There was a significant episode three weeks after Frederick's accession, before the move to Potsdam. On 31 March Bismarck was told the Emperor was inviting Prince Alexander to Charlottenburg in two days' time. Frederick intended to bestow a high German decoration on the Prince and offer him a military command, but so incensed was the Chancellor by this allegedly anti-Russian initiative that he made it clear he would at once resign office if 'the Battenberger' were received at court. The ultimatum, which was leaked to the Press, was decisive. Poor Frederick was far too frail to face a constitutional struggle. His invitation to Alexander was cancelled.[2]

Bismarck was also worried at suggestions that Queen Victoria would come to Berlin for 'young Vicky's' birthday on 12 April. 'The old Queen is fond of match-making, like all old women,' he remarked to his press attaché on 7 April. 'Obviously her main objects are political – a permanent estrangement between ourselves and Russia – and if she were to come here for the Princess's birthday, there would be the greatest danger she would get her way. In family matters she is not accustomed to contradiction, and would immediately bring the parson with her in her travelling bag and the bridegroom in her trunk, and the marriage would come off at once.' 'They are in a mighty hurry over there in London,' he added.[3]

All this was arrant nonsense. The Queen did indeed wish to make a last visit to her much-loved son-in-law; but she had no intention of coming for 'young Vicky's' birthday and, so far from promoting the Battenberg marriage, she knew by now that Sandro was in love with Johanna Loisinger, an Austrian singer, who became his morganatic wife ten months later. In the last week of April the Queen, accompanied by Princess Beatrice and her husband (Henry Battenberg) came to Berlin on what she hoped was a private visit to the dying Emperor, but she agreed to grant Bismarck an audience, in the hope that she might soothe ruffled feelings and, in particular, gain for her daughter some protection from the most powerful statesman in Europe.

Queen Victoria had not been in the Prussian capital for thirty years and she was pleased to be cheered in the streets of Berlin, where in the past it had been customary to maintain a respectful bare-headed silence as royal dignitaries were driven by. The only conversations between Queen Victoria and Bismarck during his years of office were held at Charlottenburg on 25 April: the marriage project was seen as a misunderstanding from the past, and Bismarck took some pains to emphasize his wish for good relations with the Queen's eldest daughter (who now, and for the remainder of her life, liked to be styled the Empress Frederick). This one meeting dispelled the bogies of three decades, for both Queen and Chancellor found that they were able to understand each other. 'What a woman!' Bismarck was heard to exclaim afterwards. 'One could do business with her!' At dinner at Charlottenburg, where he sat opposite mother and daughter, he was amiable and gracious. 'I could not help being amused', wrote the British ambassador in a letter to Lord Salisbury, 'when at dessert he selected a large bonbon adorned with a photograph of the Empress and, after calling Her Majesty's attention to it in some graceful words, unbuttoned his coat and placed it next his heart'.[4] There was much that Bismark had learned from Disraeli; and the Queen subsequently remarked to Lord Salisbury how charming she had found the German Chancellor.

A month later the Emperor, with astonishing will-power, attended the wedding of his second son, Prince Henry, in the chapel at Charlottenburg, his bride being the Empress's niece, Irene of Hesse. But Frederick III could not sustain the battle for life much longer. His tragic ninety-nine-day reign ended on 15 June. Immediately Germany's new sovereign, William II, ordered Hussars to cordon off the palace and demanded the surrender to him by his mother of all the state papers. His behaviour shocked and distressed his grandmother and intensely angered his uncle, the Prince of Wales, who hastened to Berlin in order to console and protect his widowed sister. Yet, callous though the Kaiser's behaviour seems in retrospect, it is easy to see the reasons for his alarm. On the previous morning the Empress Frederick had entrusted some personal papers to the British ambassador which, two days after Frederick's death, were handed to Queen Victoria at Balmoral by the British military attaché, who had at once left Berlin. Old suspicions that the 'English Empress' remained at heart loyal to the country of her birth died hard at Potsdam, and there were still police informers at court. The mere rumour that documents were leaving the palace was enough to alert the young sovereign, who was eager to emphasize his Hohenzollern descent and his sympathy with Prussia's traditions. But the Kaiser's response was a poor portent for Anglo-German relations in the new reign.[5]

Over the following eight years royal exchanges between London and Berlin varied from the obstinately estranged to the effusively cordial. Indiscreet remarks by the Prince of Wales which ridiculed 'William the Great's' imperial pretensions broadened the rift between the two men and, though the Prince tried occasionally to treat his nephew with amiable tolerance, it was difficult to forget old moments of vexation. He was, however, prepared to satisfy William's craving for foreign uniforms, perhaps because he, too, indulged in this particular sport of peacock vanity. It was largely thanks to his uncle that the Kaiser became an Admiral of the Fleet in the summer of 1889 and Colonel-in-Chief of the First Royal Dragoons in 1894. Rank and titles mattered to him more than to any other ruler in Berlin since before the accession of Frederick the Great.

Queen Victoria often bridled at the behaviour of her eldest grandson. She thought he treated his mother abominably; and four months after his accession she was prepared to describe him to Lord Salisbury as 'a hot-headed, conceited and wrong-headed young man, devoid of all feeling'.[6] But when he came to Osborne and turned on her his natural charm, she recovered much of her old affection for him. He was the only grandson with some claim to remember Albert; she could not forget that as a 'clever, dear, good little child' he had been 'the great favourite of my beloved Angel'. When, after excitedly accepting honorific rank in the Royal Navy, he wrote of his pleasure at being 'able to feel and take interest in your fleet as if it were my own', the Queen was gratified, but slightly puzzled.[7] She could only assume that this deplorable 'fishing for uniforms' in some way provided tangible proof that Great Britain and Germany would remain natural allies. That was a fundamental tenet to which, despite all the fire and fury of Bismarck's statecraft, she always remained loyal.

Yet was it any longer a valid belief? When nearly half a century ago she first came to see Germany through Albert's eyes, more than two dozen principalities were deferentially elbowing each other aside to attract England's attention, eager for trade, political backing and cultural understanding. The Germany she knew – for Bavaria and the south meant little to her – shared with Britain a moral order based upon the discipline of

Protestantism, a religion of watchwords and precepts. There were affinities of music and literature, a common tradition of resistance to French imperialism whether Bourbon or Bonapartist, and a work ethic which exalted the virtues of an austere individualism. The commercial links, too, were close: the English and the Scots virtually rebuilt Hamburg after the great fire which swept through the port five years after Victoria's accession and, even at the time of the Prince Consort's death, there were more red ensigns flying from vessels at its quays and moorings than any other mercantile flag.

By 1890 all was fast changing. Politically there was no longer any serious threat from France. Unified Germany was now a trade rival, with colonial interests in Africa, Asia and the Pacific and with business enterprises beginning to penetrate the Ottoman Empire. German industrial production was increasing at twice the annual rate of British expansion, with a greater output of steel than any other country in Europe. A sense of German achievement drew together in dependence on the government in Berlin not only Lutheran Hamburg and Calvinist Bremen but the Catholic Rhineland and Bavaria and the emancipated Jewish business communities in such cities as Frankfurt and Mainz as well as the capital. The Protestant thread, which had for so long bound Windsor to the German courts, was already running thin even before the challenge of secularist thought began to weaken all connections based upon a joint opposition to Rome. At the same time the new national pride in imperial enterprise heightened the rivalry between Britain and Germany, emphasizing their peoples' differences rather than the receding heritage they had shared in common.

Both Queen Victoria and her grandson sensed these changes. 'State interest goes before personal feelings,' he assured her soon after his accession; and she resented his brusque manner for she was unaccustomed to receiving such blunt assertions of political reality.[8] Yet his words were, as much as anything, a warning to himself. He feared, with his part-English background, to be seen placating his mother's homeland. His correspondence with his English relatives contains strange mixtures of genuine sentiment, boastful threats and unsolicited good advice. Until the last months of his reign the Kaiser continued to believe that dynastic kinship preserved a sense of intimacy among the rulers of Europe and developed a superior understanding between sovereigns which transcended the bitter conflict of rival governments. Germany's ministers and diplomats grew increasingly wary of what one of the more generous of them termed 'His Majesty's family politics', for they were never quite certain what offers of support their imperial master might tender a grandmother, an uncle or a cousin in passing moments of political beneficence.

In October 1889 Queen Victoria sent a gift of her portrait to the German statesman whose iniquities had produced so much underlining and so many exclamation marks in her letters since he was first presented to her at

Versailles during the Crimean War. Bismarck accepted this token of reconciliation 'in deep reverence' on the day when Tsar Alexander III, while visiting Berlin, disconcerted the old man by asking if he was confident he would remain 'Chancellor in the years ahead. Five months later, after differences primarily over domestic issues, Bismarck tendered his resignation to the young Kaiser. The relatively unknown and inexperienced Count Caprivi succeeded him, as William II sought to transform the centralized Bismarckian political machine into a collective leadership over which the sovereign could exercise unfettered autocratic control.[9]

Bismarck's sudden fall puzzled British observers. Not least among them was the Prince of Wales, who happened to be visiting Berlin with his second son, the future King George V. Both princes paid the outgoing Chancellor a courtesy call before he left the Wilhelmstrasse and he regaled them with dire warnings of the disasters which lay ahead for a Germany and a Europe denied his leadership. The Kaiser assured his grandmother by telegram and letter that 'the unfortunate event of Prince Bismarck's resignation' would not be followed by any new policies; and, strictly speaking, he remained true to his word. There was, however, a change in emphasis. Affairs outside Europe, which for Bismarck had been no more than tactical digressions, were inflated in importance after 1890 until they came to dominate the political scene in Berlin and, indeed, in all the great capitals of the Continent except Vienna.

But the Kaiser was determined to emphasize his paramount sovereignty within Germany. A month after Bismarck's resignation he came to Darmstadt, where Queen Victoria was spending a few days during her journey back to England from a holiday in Savoy. Her principal concern was the health of her son-in-law, Grand Duke Louis, who was suffering from a heart disease; but, with their Emperor's arrival, the bugle calls seemed to ring out louder in the Darmstadt barracks. There followed an elaborate review of the troops of Hesse and the city garrison. They marched past, not their ailing Grand Duke, but their imperial sovereign, flanked by his grandmother. Poor Louis survived for almost two more years. When he died, in March 1892, yet another of Queen Victoria's grandsons succeeded to a German throne. But, of course, Grand Duke Ernest of Hesse-Darmstadt never sought the high honours to which his cousin in Berlin could lay claim.[10]

In July 1891 William II came to London on the first state visit made by a German emperor to Britain: he expected, and received, similar honours to those accorded to the Emperor of All the Russias; but, when he was a guest of the City of London, he appeared pleased by an allusion in the Lord Mayor's speech to the special welcome on which he could rely as a grandson of their sovereign and the son of a Princess Royal. 'I am a good deal of an Englishman myself,' the Kaiser wrote to the Queen immediately after his visit. He was always delighted to bask both in the honours due to the greatest of Germany's princes and the personal aura attached to members of Britain's royal family.

At times, particularly when he came to Cowes for Regatta Week from 1892 to 1895, the strain of deciding whether he expected to be received as someone 'grand' or as someone 'amiable' jaggled the nerves of his hosts until the Queen asked her ambassador in Berlin, by cipher telegram, if he could hint that 'regular annual visits are not quite desirable'.[11]

Duke Ernest II of Saxe-Coburg-Gotha died at Rheinhardtsbrunn in the fourth week of August 1893. In accordance with arrangements made long ago he was succeeded by his nephew Alfred, Duke of Edinburgh, who, having retired from the Royal Navy as Commander-in-Chief of the Mediterranean fleet, was ill-at-ease as sovereign of German Duchies in the heart of Europe. The Kaiser arrived on the day of his accession and witnessed the ceremony in which he took an oath to preserve Coburg's constitution. Queen Victoria, though proud that 'our son' should now reign as 'a foreign sovereign', was glad that William was there, for his presence would silence hostile criticism over the succession to a German principality of an English naval officer.[12] It was agreed that the Duke's only son, who was also named Alfred, would leave the Devonshire Regiment and accept a commission in the Prussian Guards so as to prepare him for the day when he too would reign in Thuringia.

'Affie's' succession made Queen Victoria eager to visit 'dear Coburg' once again. His eldest daughter Princess Marie had, in the previous January, married Crown Prince Ferdinand of Roumania at his ancestral home of Sigmaringen, thus carrying the Anglo-German royal connection to Bucharest. But the Duke's second daughter Princess Victoria Melita (who had the misfortune to be known as 'Ducky' in the family) thought she would be happy to remain in Germany and wished to marry her first cousin, the new Grand Duke Ernest of Hesse. Queen Victoria encouraged this romance – for had she not found happiness with her own first cousin? – and in April 1894 she returned to Coburg from a holiday in Florence for her grandchildren's wedding celebrations.

The Queen was delighted to see Coburg again. Even the unexpected spectacle of Prussian Dragoons drawn up outside the station she attributed to William's foresight, for they were a detachment of the regiment of which he had appointed his grandmother Colonel-in-Chief. But there were, as the Queen noted, an 'enormous number of Royalties' in the town.[13] A family photograph, taken in the palace garden two days after the wedding, showed twenty-seven royal guests standing around the seated figures of Queen Victoria, Kaiser William II and the Empress Frederick. The group included not only all of the Queen's surviving children, but four Russian Grand Dukes, among them the future Nicholas II who stood beside his fiancée, Ernest of Hesse's youngest sister, Alix; it was at Coburg on the previous day that the couple had announced their engagement. Also in the group were at one extreme the Queen's seventy-seven-year-old Austrian cousin, Count Mensdorff, and at the other Princess Marie Louise of Schleswig-Holstein, who was to ride in the first carriage of 'Princesses of the Blood Royal' in the coronation procession of Queen Elizabeth II, nearly sixty years later. No other royal occasion so effectively emphasized the ubiquity of the Queen's role as 'grandmamma of Europe'. But, sadly, the wedding which brought so much imperial and royal blood to Coburg that April ended in divorce a few months after Queen Victoria's death.

Perhaps sensing that these were her last days in Coburg, the Queen drove up to the Festung after the photograph had been taken; she was accompanied by the Empress Frederick and by Princess Victoria of Battenberg, as her granddaughter Victoria Alberta was now known. But it was too hazy for the distant view across the fields around the Rosenau. The mists were, indeed, drawing in for the Queen all over Germany, for she was to pay the country only one more visit. In 1889 the widowed Empress Frederick bought a small estate on the wooded foothills of the Taunus Mountains, some nine miles north of Frankfurt, and commissioned a German architect to build for her a home which would look more like an English country house than a German palace.[14] She went into residence for the first time in January 1894, calling the house 'Friedrichshof' and treating it, in part, as a memorial to the dead Emperor. The living Emperor, their son William, visited her later that year, limiting his personal attendants to a mere eighteen so as not to overburden his mother, and giving house and gardens his somewhat patronizing approval. But for the Empress the great occasion came in April 1895 when her mother spent a few days at Kronberg, saying that she so liked the house and its setting that she wished to spend a longer time there on her next visit to Germany. The Queen, however, did not return to the Taunus. Over the following nine months the Anglo-German political antagonism, so often eased through the empathies of royal kinship, was sharpened by a conflict deep in sad misunderstandings, and the Queen never again felt inclined to visit a land which in the past enhanced her life with such varied emotional excitements.

The weather for Cowes Regatta in August 1895 was stormy. So, too, was William II's temper. He felt especially aggrieved by the Prime Minister, Lord Salisbury, who, having been summoned to Osborne for an audience with the Queen and detained there by heavy rain, excused himself from responding to an invitation to join the Kaiser aboard his yacht. William returned to Germany convinced not only that Salisbury was deliberately avoiding discussions on the Eastern Question, but that he was responsible for a series of anti-German articles in the *Standard*, a daily newspaper which generally backed the Prime Minister. On three occasions in the closing months of the year the Kaiser sought out the British military attaché, speaking to him at great length of the stupidity of British policy overseas and, in particular, of Salisbury's unwillingness to conclude an Anglo-German military alliance, aimed against Russia. Salisbury was so puzzled by the Kaiser's behaviour that he feared he was 'going completely off his head'. This was an exaggeration, although it is probable that William was suffering from intense nervous strain. Even in his family circle his conduct was odd: thus at Christmas 1895 he placed his wife's sister and her husband (a Prussian Prince) under house arrest at Potsdam for a trivial breach of court etiquette.[15]

It was while the Kaiser was in this curious state of nervous tension that, on New Year's Eve, reports reached London and Berlin of the abortive 'Jameson Raid'. A high official in the British South Africa Company had marched a force of some 500 Englishmen from Bechuanaland towards Johannesburg in an attempt to overthrow the leader of the Transvaal Boers, President Kruger. Since German investment was high in the Transvaal it was natural that there should be a violent press reaction in Berlin, and the Kaiser was prepared on this occasion to echo the trumpeting of his newspapers. On 3 January 1896 he sent a fifty-three-word telegram to Kruger, congratulating the Boers on capturing the bandits who had marched into their country without the Transvaal having to seek help from other governments well-disposed towards them.[16]

Originally the Kaiser had wished for even more dramatic action, and the telegram represented a success for the moderates at the German Foreign Ministry who had dissuaded him from sending warships and marines to south-west Africa in a gesture of protection for the Boers. But the Kaiser's message unleashed a fury of anti-German feeling in London and other British cities: German seamen were beaten up; German clubs, some of them long-established in English commercial centres, were attacked; and the windows of shops bearing Germanic names were smashed. The Prince of Wales's reaction to his nephew's behaviour was not far removed from the unthinking anger of the crowd.

Queen Victoria, however, was more temperate. Privately she agreed with her eldest son that William was impetuous and conceited. But, she declared, 'calmness and firmness are the most powerful weapons in such cases'. She therefore patiently expressed to William himself her regret that the message to Kruger should have been considered 'unfriendly towards this country, which I am sure it is not intended to be'. The Queen wisely agreed with her Prime Minister that it would be better not to rap William too sharply for his actions, nor indeed to induce Britain's diplomats in Berlin to search too closely for his motives. She was also concerned to ensure that in Britain the police took care 'to watch and prevent ill-usage of innocent and good German residents'.[17] Throughout the last six years of her life, when Salisbury combined the offices of Prime Minister and Foreign Secretary, the Queen's opinion on Anglo-German relations was regularly sought by Downing Street and treated with genuine respect, as opposed to the dutiful deference with which her wishes had so often been disregarded in the days of Palmerston, Russell and Clarendon.

But both the Queen and her chief minister failed to appreciate the depth of anti-German feeling engendered by newspaper treatment of the Kruger Telegram. There was a sustained press campaign urging the government to seek better relations with France and Russia and, largely to satisfy public opinion, the Admiralty announced the creation of a 'flying squadron' of warships which would sail to any threatened trouble-spot in the world. On this occasion the Queen was slow to forgive her grandson his exultant words to the Boer President. In her eyes he compounded his sins by denouncing the Greek attitude towards Turkey in the winter of 1896–7: she was not herself a philhellene, but the Kaiser's third sister, Sophie, had married the Duke of Sparta, heir to the throne of Greece, in October 1889, and the Queen was 'astonished and shocked' that William should use 'violent language against the country where his sister lives'.[18] He was offending, not the law of nations, but the code of kinship.

In the first weeks of the year 1897 both the Empress Frederick and the Kaiser began to inquire whether the Queen 'had any plans or wishes for our coming or not coming for your Jubilee'. Sophie in Athens was 'dying to go to Grandmama's Jubilee, but there will be many things to prevent it'. Ultimately the greatest preventive was the Queen herself. For, while the Golden Jubilee had been a family affair, she wished the Diamond Jubilee to be a celebration in full imperial state. On the last day of January she authorized her private secretary to tell the Prince of Wales that he need have no fears that she would relent and invite the Kaiser to England for the occasion, as the Empress Frederick had suggested: 'It would *never* do for many reasons.'[19] A few days later a 'No crowned heads' injunction was issued, to the surprise of some of Salisbury's cabinet and the irritation of several 'foreign royalties', who had left June clear of engagements pending an invitation to London.

The Diamond Jubilee was a more impressive and more public celebration than the Golden Jubilee ten years before. There was no service in Westminster Abbey this time, but prayers and hymns on the steps outside St Paul's Cathedral. It was not so much the visiting European dignitaries who caught the eye and the imagination in 1897 as the detachments of troops from the Empire – Bengal Lancers, Canadian mounties, sharpshooters from Sydney and horsemen from a place called Rhodesia with a capital named in honour of the British Prime Minister. But the foreign princes were present, nevertheless: at the dinner which followed the Jubilee thanksgiving the Queen was flanked by the Archduke Francis Ferdinand of Austria and the diminutive Prince of Naples, who as King Victor Emmanuel III was to make Mussolini dictator of Italy a quarter of a century later. The Queen's surviving sons and daughters were there, too; and, although William II was kept away, his brother, Prince Henry of Prussia, rode in the procession to St Paul's. 'If yer wants to send a telegram to Krooger, there's a post office round the corner', a cockney wit called out to him as his horse went by.

Inevitably Queen Victoria mourned the absence of the princes who had died since the Golden Jubilee. She had lost in those ten years three sons-in-law – 'Fritz', 'dear Louis' and, in January 1896, Prince Henry of Battenberg, Princess Beatrice's husband, who contracted fever while serving in the Ashanti Wars and could not survive the voyage back to England. Despite the Queen's intense pride in Empire during this second Jubilee Year, bereavement was beginning to quench the fire of her spirit.

She was, moreover, saddened in these last years of her life by the widening rift between Britain and Germany. Five months after the Diamond Jubilee festivities the British Press reported that German marines had landed from warships in Kiaochow Bay and seized this obscure Chinese town and harbour in retaliation for the murder of two German missionaries a fortnight before. Berlin commentators treated the seizure of Kiaochow as an event of world significance and London's newspapers took them at their word.[20] It seemed as if the scramble for Africa would be followed by a scramble for China. Earlier that autumn several periodicals had noticed the first of Tirpitz's 'Navy Laws', with its proposals to create a formidable German fleet, but in general the shipbuilding programme produced little hostile reaction until after the Kiaochow landings. There was, however, an influential section of Salisbury's cabinet which favoured some form of agreement with Germany so as to avoid future misunderstandings in China and southern Africa. In the spring of 1898 the Colonial Secretary, Joseph Chamberlain, embarked on a sustained attempt to promote an Anglo-German alliance and, although William II personally distrusted him, his initiative was encouraged by German diplomats in London. The German ambassador sent Lord Salisbury a nineteen-page letter in mid-April in which he proposed that, as a sign of renewed Anglo-German amity, the Queen should travel back from her holiday in the South of France through the Rhineland, meeting her grandson at Coblenz. But Salisbury, who knew the Queen mistrusted impromptu encounters without a minister or an ambassador in attendance, firmly quashed the proposal; why not a visit to Windsor in the late autumn, he suggested?[21] By then, however, the Kaiser planned to be in the Holy Land. Had he returned by ship up the Channel the Queen was prepared to invite him to land at Portsmouth and visit her; but he preferred to avoid winter gales in the Bay of Biscay and settled for a train journey back from the Mediterranean to Berlin. The year 1898 therefore passed without any personal contact between the rulers of Britain and Germany, although the Kaiser commented in a letter sent a few days after Christmas on the satisfaction with which he had noted the better state of relations between Germany and Great Britain.[22] From London the improvement seemed hardly discernible.

At times the Kaiser's charm and sincere love for his grandmother permeated his personal correspondence. Thus, in answering her congratulations for his fortieth birthday, he could write, somewhat wryly, 'I venture to believe that, where the Sovereign will sometimes shake her wise head often over the tricks of her queer and impetuous colleague, the good and genial heart of my Grandmother will step in and show that, if he sometimes fails, it is never from want of goodwill, honesty, or truthfulness, and thus mitigate the shake of the head by a genial smile of warm sympathy and interest'.[23] But over matters which seemed to trespass on his imperial prerogatives William could still appear extremely arrogant. Such was the case with the Coburg succession.

In February 1899, Prince Alfred, the Duke of Coburg's only son, died at Merano. Since the German duchies did not acknowledge female succession and the Duke's health was causing concern, it became important to decide who now became heir to the Coburg titles. Technically the answer was clear: it should by right have been Arthur, Duke of Connaught, the Queen's third son. But, although the Duke was married to a Prussian-born Princess and remained on good personal terms with his nephew in Berlin, he regarded himself as a professional soldier; the prospect of immersion in the princely politics of central Germany held no appeal for him. Nor did it attract his son, Prince Arthur. There then remained – at least among British-born princes – only one male heir, Charles Edward, Duke of Albany, the son born posthumously to Prince Leopold. He, however, was now a fourteen-year-old Etonian and would therefore not be old enough to rule in his own right in Coburg until July 1905. Clearly the succession posed far more difficulties than in the days when Albert and Ernest settled it between themselves.

Queen Victoria decided that the family should discuss the problem while she was on holiday at Cimiez in the early spring. She was visited not only by her sons Alfred and Arthur, but also by her Prime Minister, for Salisbury, too, was seeking the warmth of southern sunshine that spring. By the end of the third week in March, after 'a great deal of talk between all my children', the Queen noted in her journal the possibility of the succession going to the young Duke of Albany.

So far so good; but on the last day of the month the British ambassador in Berlin sent an urgent message to Salisbury reporting that the Kaiser had buttonholed the British military attaché at a military parade and grumbled at his exclusion from the Cimiez talks. 'Now he was a member of the royal family', he complained, 'and happened also to be German Emperor and he thought he might have been consulted on a question concerning the succession to a German throne.' Personally he favoured the succession of the Duke of Connaught's son, Prince Arthur, provided he was 'willing to serve as a German prince in the German army'.[24] The Queen was extremely annoyed. She insisted privately that there was no constitutional reason why a German Emperor should be consulted over the succession to Saxe-Coburg-Gotha. However she recognized that she had to tread warily, for the Kaiser was striking a patriotic attitude in which he was hinting that he might secure passage through the German parliament of a law denying the right of succession to any German throne of a foreign prince. The Queen's sons, the Dukes of Coburg and Connaught, travelled to the Wartburg to placate their imperial nephew. Whoever became heir-apparent in Coburg must, William insisted, be educated and have his chief residence in Germany as well as serving in the German army. Such conditions were unacceptable to the Connaughts: it was accordingly settled that the succession should pass to the young and luckless Etonian, Charles Edward of Albany.[25] He duly became Duke of Saxe-Coburg-Gotha on 30 July 1900 when his Uncle Alfred died. A relative by marriage, Prince Ernest of Hohenlohe-Langenburg, administered the Duchy as Regent for the following five years while Charles Edward became accustomed to German princely life.

Rather strangely the Kaiser seems to have blamed Lord Salisbury for his exclusion from the Cimiez talks. Over the following weeks he made a succession of verbal attacks on the Prime Minister, particularly because of British opposition to German attempts to colonize Samoa. An extraordinary letter to the Queen on 27 May, shortly after her eightieth birthday, complained that 'Lord Salisbury cares for us no more than for Portugal, Chile or the Patagonians', and warned that 'If this sort of high-handed treatment of German affairs by Lord Salisbury's Government is suffered to continue, I am afraid that there will be a permanent source of misunderstandings . . . between the two nations.'[26] The Queen was 'greatly astonished': 'I doubt whether any Sovereign ever wrote in such terms to another Sovereign, and that Sovereign his own Grandmother, about their Prime Minister. I never should do such a thing, and I never personally attacked or complained of Prince Bismarck, though I knew well what a bitter enemy he was to England and all the harm he did.'[27] This reprimand was a shade disingenuous for, although Queen Victoria had never mentioned Bismarck by name, her attack on his 'evil' policies in her letter to King William of 10 April 1866 was much more outspoken than her grandson's complaints about Salisbury over thirty years later. But the Queen's reply to her grandson was effective. Salisbury continued to be alarmed by the 'German Emperor's unreasoning caprice' but he genuinely appreciated the Queen's ability to ease tensions between Britain and Germany: 'Your Majesty's personal influence over the Emperor William is a powerful defence against danger in that direction,' he wrote in mid-August.[28]

Three months later, in the third week of November 1899, the Kaiser at last came to England again; he stayed at Windsor and subsequently with the Prince of Wales at Sandringham. He did not meet the Prime Minister (whose wife's death and funeral coincided with the Windsor visit) but he talked to other leading cabinet ministers and, to the consternation of his German suite, he consistently appeared a fervent Anglophile. 'Gentlemen, from that tower the world is ruled,' he told the officers around him as they waited to be formally greeted by the Queen at the foot of the Round Tower. This was an exaggeration on several counts, not least among them the fact that his grandmother was sovereign over no more than a fifth of the world; but it was, nevertheless, an impressive piece of rhetoric. Moreover, coming as it did just six weeks after the British found themselves at war with Kruger's Boers, the Kaiser's remark showed a significant change of approach to Africa's affairs. 'William II takes everything personally,' one of his closest friends and advisers had confessed, a few months before. If he was fêted and flattered in England he would think and act like an English gentleman. The Kaiser was not, as his enemies maintained, a strutting peacock; his strength and weakness was to possess the personality of a chameleon.[29]

War in South Africa dragged on for the remaining fourteen months of Victoria's life, and beyond. Great Britain became more unpopular on the Continent than at any previous moment in the nineteenth century. William II claimed in later years that he had befriended the British during these difficult years and refused to join a Continental league which would have forced the government in London to make peace. Once again he exaggerated; but there is no doubt that, from time to time, he showed sympathy with the British and that he repeatedly let the British ambassador know 'he was the devoted grandson of Queen Victoria and would not join any combination against her'.[30] To the Prince of Wales he wrote in the second week of January 1900: 'It is painful to think what streams of blood and loss of life has already been shed and how many more will have to die. A sad beginning of the 20th century for many of the homes and families in Britain.'[31]

As the Queen's health began to fail there were more and more personal exchanges between the Prince of Wales and his nephew in Berlin. Prince von Bülow, who became Chancellor in October 1900 after three years as Foreign Minister, once likened political talks between uncle and nephew to 'a fat malicious tom-cat playing with a shrewmouse'. Perhaps by accident, William II's friendliest messages tended to include jocular stings of reproach, which offended Uncle Bertie. He resented sporting allusions, showing a passing acquaintance with football and cricket, to 'our conflict with the Boers'. A letter over the new royal yacht in the autumn of 1900 was particularly unfortunate in tone: the Kaiser told his uncle that he was not surprised to hear he had refused to take acceptance of the new *Victoria and Albert*. 'According to the information I was able to glean nobody thought her a success and especially not "yacht like", more of a P. and O. troopship. It is better for the army but a pity for Grandmama.' He added, 'I believe a private firm would have done better.'[32] Outwardly the topic was trivial, the comfort an ailing Queen could enjoy aboard a royal yacht in which she was never likely to travel. But the Prince of Wales did not particularly wish to know that William II could 'glean' information on such matters in the month that Germany's programme for cruiser building – the Second Navy Law – became effective. He remained suspicious of every gesture of goodwill made by his nephew.

In January 1901 the authorities in Berlin prepared celebrations to mark the bicentenary of the Prussian Kingdom. The Duke of Connaught was sent to Germany as Queen Victoria's representative. But hardly had the celebrations begun, than on Friday, 18 January, the Duke was summoned urgently to Osborne because his mother had suffered a slight stroke. William II at once decided it was his duty to be in England at his grandmother's bedside. On Saturday morning he cancelled the remaining dynastic festivities and sent an uncoded telegram to the Prince of Wales announcing that he would accompany the Duke of Connaught back to London. It is probable that the Kaiser was moved, not only by genuine affection, but by the knowledge that his mother could not herself travel to Osborne; for, although she concealed the fact from Queen Victoria, the Empress Frederick had known for two years that she was suffering from a cancer of the spine.[33]

The Kaiser kept vigil at his grandmother's bedside for much of the last night and day of her life. More than once she seems to have mistaken him for his father. When the Queen died, early in the evening of Tuesday, 22 January, her eldest grandson was still there, assisting the doctor to support her on the pillow; his right arm had by then remained pinned beneath his grandmother's frail body for some two and a half hours. While his uncle, now King Edward VII, travelled to St James's Palace for the accession council, the Kaiser stayed on at Osborne, supervising the last sad royal occasion of the island home where he once delighted his young grandparents. Not until 5 February, three days after he followed the draped gun-carriage up the icy hill at Windsor, did he set out again for Germany. The British public, and their new monarch, were deeply moved by the Kaiser's dignified sympathy and consideration in this fortnight of national grief. The Kruger Telegram was expunged from collective memory in a reconciling flood of sentimentality. Illogically, Germany seemed more popular with the London crowds in February 1901 than at any time since the proclamation of the Empire thirty years before.

CHAPTER FOURTEEN
England Will Never
✍◈ Forget ◈✍

In the week of Queen Victoria's funeral *Punch*, a periodical not noted for any pro-German inclination, produced a remarkable cartoon. It depicted the new King saying farewell to the Kaiser with a warm handshake and the words, 'God bless you, Sir! England will never forget your genuine sympathy!' As so often during these years, *Punch* had faithfully caught the public mood; a two-stanza verse tribute in *The Times* of 6 February echoed similar sentiments. Although Edward VII may not have used so precise a phrase as the cartoon caption suggested, he was genuinely moved by his nephew's sense of family solidarity. At heart the King remained as impulsively impressionable as William himself, and he now showed his gratitude by making the Kaiser a Field Marshal in the British army. It was the type of gesture which William most appreciated.[1]

Over the following weeks Bülow, the German Chancellor, and members of the Kaiser's personal suite were astounded by their master's enthusiasm for everything 'English'. Among the greater German territorial magnates, who unlike the Junker gentry had long idealized British aristocratic society, there was a call to respond to the goodwill gestures in the British Press by encouraging the Berlin newspapers to emphasize 'the identity of religion, race and culture' binding the two nations together. But Bülow would have none of it. He believed he knew his sovereign's temperament too well to assume that this surge of Anglophilia would survive the first rebuff from London to some personal whim of policy; and Bülow's cynicism soon seemed fully justified. For, three weeks after bidding the Kaiser farewell, King Edward VII set out for Friedrichshof to see the Empress Frederick. The Kaiser invited him to stay at neighbouring Homburg during his visit, but the King declined the offer, since he wished to spend as much time as possible with his ailing sister. With characteristic spite Bülow describes in his memoirs how 'Imperial sentiments towards his uncle and his uncle's country as well' thereafter began to cool rapidly.[2]

This superficial judgement exposes the Chancellor's shallow mind as much as any vagaries in the Kaiser's conduct. For, in office and in reminiscent retirement, Bülow consistently misunderstood William II's feelings for his mother's homeland. Throughout the reign of Edward VII the Kaiser hoped he would eventually see the conclusion of an Anglo-German alliance, partly because – like his British grandparents – he thought 'the two Teutonic nations' natural partners, but also because he believed that, in partnership, the two empires could amicably settle the affairs of a Europeanized world. 'With such an alliance not a mouse would stir in Europe without our permission,' he declared while he was in London.[3] When, in the spring of 1901, the prospect of such an alliance faded, he blamed Lord Salisbury and those 'noodles' of ministers in his cabinet rather than the King. Only when in 1903 British policy veered towards an entente with France did he begin to find serious fault with Edward himself. Within a few months of the King's famous visit to Paris the Kaiser became obsessed with paranoic resentment at what he assumed was his uncle's desire to humiliate the German nation. 'You can hardly believe what a Satan he is,' he once remarked to surprised guests at his dinner table. That Edward VII wished to encircle Germany became a conviction which the Kaiser took with him to the grave. 'Thus is the pernicious entente cordiale of Uncle Edward VII brought to nought,' he could write to his daughter when Hitler's armies entered Paris thirteen months before his death.[4]

The living Edward VII was, however, far different from the ogre conjured up by his nephew in old age. He distrusted what he had long ago stigmatized as 'Prussia's arrogance of manner' but he would not have regarded himself as anti-German. The King knew European high society better than his mother but understood Europe much less. He was as strongly prejudiced about places as she had been towards people: he liked Paris (and Parisians) but he disliked royal Berlin and Potsdam, where he always felt constrained by parade-ground taboos. Yet, since his irascible temper was so often fired by his nephew's behaviour, the King went out of his way to check anti-German trends in British official policy. Moreover he frequently tried to soothe ruffled feelings by amending holiday itineraries to visit Kiel or Wilhelmshöhe or Kronberg. During the nine years that Edward VII was on the throne he was able to meet William II in Germany on eight occasions; he also entertained him privately for a week at Sandringham in November 1902 and in greater pomp at Windsor in 1907, when the Kaiser made his second state visit to Britain. In physical terms there was thus a closer German connection in Edward's reign than during any previous one. Whether these royal encounters achieved much is, however, doubtful. Generally the two men found they could settle old quarrels which had, as often as not, arisen from malicious gossip and family misunderstandings. At times the meetings certainly taxed strained tempers: 'Thank God, he's gone,' a German diplomat caught the King exclaiming as William left Sandringham in 1902; 'Thank God, these cursed Englishmen are off,' King Edward's equerry heard a Prussian General remark as the royal carriages set out for Cassel Station five years later.[5]

These family gatherings also posed difficult problems of executive responsibility. For, although William might rail at the restraints imposed by the constitution on his sovereign rights,[6] he still exercised an authority over the shaping of foreign policy which no British monarch had enjoyed since before the Hanoverian succession. Yet, rather curiously, the Kaiser appears to have assumed a British monarch possessed as much right to initiate changes in policy as himself. Exchanges of confidence between nephew and uncle were therefore necessarily different in kind, with the King seeking to avoid entanglements which might embarrass his ministers. A well-known incident early in the reign emphasized these difficulties: when he travelled to Germany in August 1901 the Foreign Secretary provided the King with a confidential memorandum which was intended to serve as a brief enabling him to hold his own in conversations with his host; but Edward, knowing he could not himself make policy declarations without consulting his ministers, did not bother to read the memorandum, and he simply handed it over to the Kaiser himself. Neither Victoria nor George V would have behaved so indiscreetly.[7] Edward VII saw himself, not as a serious diplomat who would begin the process of negotiating treaties, but quite simply as a friendly trouble-shooter. The Kaiser remained unconvinced.

With Queen Victoria's pen stilled at last, the German royal connection inevitably changed its form. Although the two monarchs met more frequently in the first years of the century than ever before, there were fewer extensive dynastic contacts than when Europe's grandmama would be photographed with successive generations flanked around her. Only six months after the Queen's funeral there followed at Schloss Friedrichshof, on 5 August 1901, the death of the Empress Frederick. Her going not only deprived Edward VII of the closest friend in his nephew's empire but silenced the last champion of a lost cause, the partnership of a liberal Britain and a liberal Germany.

The Empress's death also left the King more isolated from the German courts than the equerries who spent so many trainbound nights and days with him each year ever realized; for, though the King continued to visit Marienbad and Ischl and Vienna, he no longer spent any length of time in Hesse or Saxe-Coburg. None of the King's surviving sisters (the Princesses Louise, Helena and Beatrice) nor his brother, the Duke of Connaught, lived in Germany; and the King's closest family links were with Queen Alexandra's relatives in Denmark, Greece and Russia. The Queen's youngest sister, Princess Thyra, had in 1878 married the blind King of Hanover's son, Ernest Augustus, Duke of Cumberland (and, from 1884, titular Duke of Brunswick). But so bitter was the hostility of the Cumberlands to the Prussian-dominated Reich that they would not even set foot on German soil, living virtually forgotten at Gmunden, in Upper Austria. When King Edward was returning from Vienna in 1903 his train stopped briefly at Gmunden so that he might meet his brother-in-law (and second cousin), and the King's travelling attendants were surprised to find the Duke waiting on the platform in a British general's uniform of outdated cut and wearing a twenty-five-year-old Garter riband. Rather than give the Kaiser fresh cause for offence, the King restricted his visit to Gmunden to a mere half hour.[8]

Prince Louis of Battenberg and his wife, Princess Victoria, the King's niece, remained personal friends of their sovereign. The Prince became Director of Naval Intelligence at the Admiralty in November 1902 and was promoted Rear-Admiral in the summer of 1904, when he accompanied the King to Kiel Regatta, where every warship in the German fleet was moored, as though for a grand review. Already an ominous shadow was falling over the royal relationships, for Prince Louis's sister-in-law, Irene of Hesse, had married the Kaiser's brother, Prince Henry of Prussia, a serving German admiral, and, on returning from Kiel, Prince Louis was required to draw up the first British war plan for possible destroyer operations against the fleet in which his wife's sister's husband held such high rank.[9] The Battenbergs were, of course, in closer touch than the King with Darmstadt, where Princess Victoria's brother ruled as Grand Duke of Hesse; and it was at Darmstadt in October 1903 that their eldest daughter married Prince Andrew of Greece and Denmark.

The strongest connection with the German courts during Edward VII's reign was provided by the friendships of Mary, Princess of Wales, with her relatives in Hesse-Cassel, Mecklenburg and Württemberg. It was in July 1893 that Edward's surviving son, Prince George, had married Princess May of Teck, daughter of that Mary Adelaide of Cambridge whose wedding lightened those grim June days of 1866 when a 'war between Germans' was imminent. Although she was the first British Princess of Wales for over 500 years, having been born at Kensington Palace, much of May of Teck's childhood was spent in the German lands – at Rumpenheim on the Main near Frankfurt, at Stuttgart and neighbouring Ludwigsburg, at Neu-Strelitz in Mecklenburg, at Reinthal, Gmunden and Gastein in Austria, and on the shores of the Bodensee (Lake Constance). These visits continued after her marriage, although less frequently. They were, to some extent, an antidote to the incorrigible insularity of her husband who, although he had studied briefly at Heidelberg, disliked going abroad, irrespective of whether he was required to travel in France, Italy or Germany. The Prince of Wales was, however, punctilious in carrying out his royal duties, and when in 1908 it was indicated by the Kaiser that he should come to Cologne and inspect the Eighth Cuirassiers of which he was honorary Colonel-in-Chief, he obliged, donning a tight-fitting uniform and a helmet which reminded him of a candle extinguisher for the occasion.[10] Six years later the Eighth Cuirassiers were fighting his army on the Marne and the Aisne.

Closest of all the contacts of the Princess of Wales in Germany was her aunt, the Grand Duchess Augusta of Mecklenburg-Strelitz, whose marriage in June 1843 had provoked *Punch* to such sustained satire at the expense of German princelings. After Princess May's mother died in 1897 and her father three years later, the formidable Grand Duchess Augusta stood out as the matriarchal survivor of the Cambridges and, by now a somewhat lonely octogenarian, she wrote regularly once a week to her niece, with news from the remoter German *Residenzen* and frequent vignettes which recalled court life in pre-Albertine London and Windsor. The Grand Duchess was as indefatigable a correspondent as the Empress Frederick, proud to be a granddaughter of George III and obstinately Tory in her social and political prejudices. Thus when in January 1906 Princess Beatrice's only daughter, 'Ena', was betrothed to Alfonso XIII of Spain, the Grand Duchess remembered, not Ena's links with the British royal House but the morganatic marriage contracted by her paternal grandfather: 'So Ena is to become Spanish Queen! A Battenberg, good gracious!' Augusta wrote to the Princess of Wales.[11] Nevertheless, for all her John Bull-ism and her partiality for the old order in Germany, the Grand Duchess showed a loyal respect and an affectionate sympathy for William II; and her opinion of the Kaiser influenced the Princess of Wales, modifying the persistent hostility towards everything Prussian which the Danish-born Queen Alexandra sought to perpetuate at her husband's court.

Because Britain and Germany found themselves at war with each other in the summer of 1914 it is tempting to assume that their mutual antagonism had intensified steadily, year by year, over the previous decade. But, although the first Moroccan crisis of 1905 inclined Britain for the first time to collaborate with France, there followed moments when a traditional Germanophilia still showed itself in public feeling, at least in southern England. Thus when, in the first week of July 1906, William II became a grandfather for the first time, *The Times* congratulated Berlin on the birth of a future heir to the throne. A leading article emphasized 'the family ties which unite the Royal Houses of Prussia and of Great Britain' in far warmer terms than the newspaper had used forty-seven years before, when William himself was born.[12]

A similar sentimental nostalgia permeated the state visit in mid-November 1907, when Edward VII resolutely declined to discuss any contentious issues in politics. 'Blood is thicker than water,' the Kaiser declared, with more emotion than originality, in replying to the Lord Mayor of London's toast at the Guildhall that week, and his speech was well received in the City. Yet, although his bearing still impressed the crowds who cheered him in the streets, he was in poor health. The publicity accorded to homosexual scandals involving some of his closest friends left his nerves tormented by inner uncertainties. Before his departure from Berlin, he asked his uncle to find for him a suitable residence which he might lease for a term of quiet convalescence once he completed the exhausting programme of official banquets and receptions.

For three weeks the Kaiser was thus able to sample 'English home and country life' at Highcliffe Castle, near Bournemouth. Occasionally he would enjoy the novelty of car drives in the New Forest but, for the most part, he was content to relax at Colonel Stuart-Wortley's home beside the sea or walk with his host, deep in conversation, down the Hampshire lanes. Highcliffe left its mark on William: 'The great British people . . . received me warmly and with open arms,' he wrote to a friend that Christmas.[13] And seven weeks later he took the unprecedented step of writing to the First Lord of the Admiralty explaining, in a letter signed 'William I.R., Admiral of the Fleet', that there was no reason for the British to be alarmed by the rapid growth of Germany's fleet, which was being 'built against nobody at all'.[14]

The letter had been prompted by an anti-German outburst in *The Times*, which was among several newspapers pressing the government to build up a large navy. William's intervention did nothing to ease tensions. News of his letter merely provoked from *The Times* a sustained outburst of moral indignation, strikingly different in tone from the 'family ties' sentimentality of twenty months before: 'Under Which King?', the paper asked, questioning the right of a British cabinet minister to receive communications on service matters from a foreign head of state. Edward VII did not conceal his displeasure from his nephew, nor indeed did Chancellor Bülow from his sovereign, for the Kaiser had not consulted any member of the German government before writing directly to London. But, unabashed, William entertained his Highcliffe host at the autumn manoeuvres and a month later authorized Colonel Stuart-Wortley to publish a version of the Kaiser's conversations in the form of a press interview, hoping that it would 'have the effect of bringing about a change in the tone of some of the English newspapers'. The 'interview' was published in the *Daily Telegraph* of 28 October 1908 and created an even greater sensation than the letter to the First Lord of the Admiralty: the British were told they were as 'mad as March hares' for their suspicion of Germany and their failure to appreciate his 'repeated offers of friendship'; and they were treated to an account of how the Kaiser had not merely declined to join a hostile Continental league during the Boer War, but had actually sent to Windsor a plan for winning the war which, 'as a matter of curious coincidence', anticipated much of Lord Robert's later strategy.[15]

The British Press and public received the Kaiser's heavy-handed gesture of goodwill with tolerant amusement; but the German Chancellor and the Berlin newspapers were angered at this latest display of their Emperor's personal diplomacy, and in the subsequent Reichstag debate, Bülow came as near as he dared to rapping the Kaiser's knuckles for not maintaining, in private conversation, the 'reserve which is equally essential for a coherent government policy and for the authority of the Crown'. From Neu-Strelitz, the Grand Duchess Augusta explained to the Princess of Wales that the Germans were 'furious' because the Kaiser had said he 'helped England against their beloved Boers'. 'I think it foolish and impolitic of Bülow and all Germany to have made so much of this indiscretion,' she wrote. 'I even cannot understand why

Germany took it up so violently unless it is that William confesses his love for England in it.'[16] The Kaiser was depressed by his unfavourable press in Germany and by the sudden death in his presence of the head of his private military staff, General Hulsen – who, at fifty-six, should probably not have tried to amuse his sovereign by dancing in 'ballet skirts' on top of a heavy dinner.

For some days in the last week of November 1908 there were abdication rumours in Berlin, and the Crown Prince deputized for his father, who shut himself up gloomily in the Neues Palais, where his father was born and died. The 'interview', and its consequences in Germany, produced the great internal crisis of his reign. Although he took his revenge on Bülow by manoeuvring him from office in the following summer, the Kaiser never again enjoyed the same sense of 'personal rule'. And by appointing a gentlemanly civilian, Theobald von Bethmann-Hollweg, as Bülow's successor William II made himself more dependent on decision-makers among the leaders of his army and his navy.

Edward VII died in the first week of May 1910. William II came to his uncle's funeral and was once more treated with respect by the crowds who lined the streets of London and Windsor. By now he was so accustomed to the castle on its spur above the Thames that, in a letter to his new Chancellor, he referred to his 'sense of belonging to this place' which 'I am proud to call my second home'.[17] He was back in London the following May for the unveiling of the statue to Queen Victoria. On this occasion he was accompanied by the Empress and by their only daughter, the eighteen-year-old Princess Victoria Louise who, according to the *Daily Express*, took 'London by storm' with her 'winning smile and abounding interest in everything and everybody'.[18] There was talk of yet another Anglo-German marriage, on this occasion between Princess Victoria Louise and George V's eldest son, the Prince of Wales, who was nearly two years her junior. The Princess, however, thought that 'he was very nice, but looked so terribly young'; and the political situation was hardly propitious for a strengthening of family ties. Nevertheless, the Kaiser was delighted by the warmth of his reception. Never had he known 'so friendly' an atmosphere at Buckingham Palace. The British and their monarch were well-disposed towards Germany; of that he was convinced, and so he told his ministers when he returned to Berlin.[19]

He told them, too, of a conversation with King George V as he was about to leave the palace for home. The German Foreign Minister, Kiderlen-Waechter, had already proposed to the Kaiser that a warship should be sent to Morocco in order to impress the French with the need to respect German commercial interests in their African spheres of colonial influence. At first William himself felt uneasy at the risks inherent in any new international crisis over Morocco, but his London visit made him believe that, provided there was no naval activity in the Straits of Gibraltar, the British would make no fuss, for they were at that moment well-disposed towards Germany. On the eve of his departure for the railway station the Kaiser therefore mentioned the Moroccan Question to the King, who gave him the impression that each country with interests in North Africa should strike its own bargain with the French. Later George v recalled that his cousin might have 'said something about a ship'; but it is obvious that, at the time, the King attached little importance to the talk. Six weeks later the German gunboat *Panther* arrived off the Moroccan port of Agadir ready to 'protect Germany's interests' with its two four-inch guns; and for three months the politicians, the Press and the general public behaved in London as if the presence of this old and unseaworthy vessel at an obscure Atlantic sardine port menaced the peace of Europe.[20]

By early November the Agadir crisis was over: the Germans recognized French rights in Morocco in return for territorial concessions in the Cameroons. However, the excitement caused by 'the *Panther's* leap' had important political consequences: it hardened the opposition to Germany within the British cabinet; it prompted the first joint army-navy contingency planning in London; and, in Germany, it encouraged Admiral Tirpitz and his 'Navy League' supporters to press for more and more 'big ship' construction. But one lesson of the crisis was never learnt in Berlin: the irrelevance of verbal exchanges among royal cousins to the relations between the Great Powers in the modern world. For there is no doubt that, despite his experiences with Edward vii, the Kaiser failed to understand that he could not expect detailed policy commitments from a British monarch cornered in isolation from his ministers.

During the twelve months which followed the Agadir crisis there were moments when it seemed as if Britain and Germany might reach a political agreement, notably when Lord Haldane visited Berlin in February 1912 in the hopes of promoting naval disarmament. But the Kaiser's sentimental Windsorphilia of 1910–11 gave way, after Agadir, to a childish Anglophobia in which he told his naval officers that King George's ministers were 'all sheep' and proceeded to pepper his marginalia with denunciation of the 'weak' and 'cowardly' efforts of those German diplomats who sought an understanding with Britain. He particularly resented the distinction made by Churchill as First Lord of the Admiralty between Britain's navy, which was 'a necessity', and the German fleet which was 'a luxury'. And when in March 1912 his friend, the great German shipping magnate Albert Ballin, suggested to the Kaiser that he could win the support of England's governing classes by sending coal to a strike-paralysed Britain, he angrily exclaimed, 'Coal? I will send them a grenade, nothing else!'[21] In this mood the Kaiser seemed as unstable as in the opening years of his reign, when Lord Salisbury told the future Edward vii that he thought his nephew 'a little off his head'.

Yet William II's approach to world policy remained full of contradictions. In October 1912 the four Balkan kingdoms (Serbia, Greece, Montenegro and Bulgaria) were encouraged by Russian agents to combine and launch a war against Turkey, which was in many respects a client state of Germany. On the second Sunday of December William II presided over a meeting of his three senior naval officers and the Chief of the General Staff at the Neues Palais in Potsdam in which they discussed the possibility of war spreading to all Europe from rival tensions in the Balkans; and, according to the Chief of the General Staff, the Kaiser wished naval and military planning to begin in preparation for 'an invasion of England on a grand scale'.[22]

But this so-called 'war council' at the Neues Palais coincided with another of William's initiatives in peaceful cousin diplomacy. For earlier that week the Kaiser had sent his brother, Prince Henry, to England on a private visit to George V in the seclusion of Sandringham. Thus while the 'war council' was in session Prince Henry was on his way back from Norfolk where, two days before, he had asked the King if Britain would assist Russia and France should Germany and Austria-Hungary find it necessary to go to war with them. On this occasion the King gave an affirmative answer, although qualifying it with the phrase 'under certain circumstances'; and when Sir Edward Grey, the Foreign Secretary, read his sovereign's report of the conversation, he was pleased that Prince Henry would take back to Berlin so clear a statement of policy. But Prince Henry was not a trained diplomat, nor was his command of the English language so extensive as his brother's; and he gave William the impression that, while Britain would 'probably throw her weight on the weaker side' and would not support Germany, she might remain neutral in any Continental conflict. Prince Henry's report seems to have countered Sunday morning's Potsdam war talk. For the Kaiser now began to encourage his Foreign Ministry to work for British neutrality. The German ambassador in London collaborated with Grey in a conference aimed at settling the problems of the Balkans without the spread of war; and by the second week of February 1913 Sir Eyre Crowe, the influential Assistant Under-Secretary at the Foreign Office, could point out with satisfaction to his chief that 'Anglo-German relations are now more cordial'.[23]

Amid all the uncertainties of that winter of 1912–13 one family reconciliation held promise of an end to past enmities and briefly recalled the old days of royal Hanover. When, in the previous May, King Frederick IX of Denmark had died while in Hamburg, his relatives began to converge on the Amalienborg Palace from all parts of Europe for the funeral. Among those who set out for Copenhagen from Gmunden was his nephew Prince George of Hanover, the thirty-two-year-old eldest son of the Duke of Cumberland. He did not, however, reach Denmark for, as he drove north across the Brandenburg Plain, the Prince crashed his car and was killed.

At Homburg, where the Kaiser and his family were on holiday, the news of Prince George's death posed an awkward problem of court etiquette. All personal contacts had been severed between the German royal House and the Prince's family for more than forty years and, as recently as February 1907, the Kaiser had confirmed the ban on his father's succession as Duke of Brunswick. But Prince George died on Prussian soil and the Kaiser, a stickler for punctilio, ordered two of his sons and a detachment of Prussian Hussars to mount a guard of honour on the Brandenburg estate where the Prince's body was lying in state, pending burial at Gmunden. In appreciation of this courtesy the Duke of Cumberland subsequently sent his surviving son, Ernest Augustus, to convey his thanks to the Kaiser in person. At Potsdam the Prince met Princess Victoria Louise – for whom, as she wrote later, 'it was love at first sight . . . all fire and flame'.

The Princess's romantic feelings were reciprocated. Yet was marriage possible so long as a bitter quarrel continued to separate the heads of the two royal Houses, Hohenzollern and Brunswick-Hanover? Prince Ernest Augustus was, however, already a serving Bavarian cavalry officer who, in time of war, would have been bound to accept the Kaiser as 'Supreme War Lord' and he could not therefore assume the stiff and reserved attitude towards the Hohenzollerns which the rest of his family had maintained for so long. The Kaiser himself was anxious for the feud to end, preferably with the renunciation of all claims to the Hanoverian throne. But this was too high a price to ask from the Duke and his son. It was finally agreed that the Duke would appeal to his loyal Hanoverian supporters to accept German imperial authority. In return, when he surrendered his specifically Brunswick rights to his son, the Kaiser would recognize the young Prince as titular Duke of Brunswick. 'The doyenne of the Guelphic House,' as the Duke of Cumberland called Grand Duchess Augusta, found the settlement reassuring, and the Duke's words to his old Hanoverians 'dignified'; she was 'thankful both Houses are no longer at enmity'.[24] So, of course, was Princess Victoria Louise who, soon after agreement was reached, met Ernest Augustus again at Karlsruhe; and on 10 February 1913 their engagement was made public.

The Kaiser resolved to seal this bond between Germany's Montagus and Capulets in fine style: for might it not offer an example of reconciliation to greater rivals? Three of his six sons had married and, although there had been pomp and splendour at their weddings, they had attracted little attention outside Germany; indeed even at so important an occasion as the Crown Prince's marriage to Princess Cecilie of Mecklenburg-Schwerin, it was thought sufficient for the Duke of Connaught to represent the bridegroom's British relatives. But the Kaiser's daughter was to be honoured with the Wedding of the Year. Never before – and never again – did Berliners see so rich an assembly of royalty as in the third week of May 1913: the Tsar of Russia, the

King and Queen of Great Britain, princes and princesses from the great
German Houses and from many other European kingdoms as well. In
retrospect, people remembered not so much the wedding itself – for the
Lutheran service is short and simple – but the banquet for 12,000 well-wishers
and the famous Torch Dance, begun by bride and bridegroom with all the
imperial, royal and princely guests progressing in a stately defile behind
twenty-four pages bearing lighted torches in silver candelabra. So fine a
spectacle was, of course, neither photographed nor filmed. But the cameras
caught another oddity in these sunset ceremonials of royal Europe: both
George v and Nicholas II preparing to inspect their German regiments in
Prussian uniform. From Strelitz the Grand Duchess Augusta wrote to her
niece, Queen Mary, assuring her that 'your and George's visit will prove of
lasting good'.[25]

From Berlin the King and Queen travelled out to Neu-Strelitz to spend a
few hours with the nonagenarian Grand Duchess. They were not her only
royal visitors from England that summer, her seventieth in Mecklenburg. The
Prince of Wales, with two terms at Oxford behind him, spent the Easter
vacation with the King and Queen of Württemberg at Stuttgart, and much of
his summer vacation at Strelitz, whence he travelled south to Saxe-Coburg,
stayed for a time with Prince Henry and Princess Irene on the Baltic and was
the Kaiser's guest in Berlin and Potsdam. Socially 'David' (as the Prince was
called by his family) achieved striking success: 'David wins all hearts here,'
Grand Duchess Augusta assured his mother, Queen Mary, in the first week of
August 1913.[26] That summer Germany was celebrating the centenary of the
'War of Liberation' with a patriotic fervour which reached its climax on the
anniversary of Leipzig, after the Prince had returned to Oxford; but he was
there for the centenary of the Katzbach and could not fail to see the idolization
of Blücher. How, the historically minded were beginning to wonder, would
Britain and Prussia in two years' time commemorate the Wellington-Blücher
partnership at Waterloo?

More than a third of a century later the Duke of Windsor remembered with
admiration the thoroughness, discipline and love of Fatherland shown by the
Germans that year, and there is no doubt that the three months which he spent
in Germany made a deeper impression than his father had gained from his
brief spell at Heidelberg. Recently published extracts from the Prince's diary
and letters suggest that, in 1913, the young man was bored and homesick,
especially at Neu-Strelitz.[27] But there is no contradiction between these
versions. It was natural he should find the social round at Mecklenburg
tedious: his hostess, Great-Aunt Augusta, could recall the coronation of
William IV, and did; her guest lived long enough to bring the lustre of cast-off
kingship to the parties of Elsa Maxwell. Here was a generation gap which the
most gracious-mannered of Princes could hardly bridge without occasional
creaks of inner stress.

Eleven months separated the return of the Prince of Wales from Mecklenburg and that fateful Monday when the lamps began 'to go out all over Europe'. For most of that period relations between Britain and Germany were more cordial than for many years: at the annual Oxford Encaenia in June 1914 Prince Lichnowsky became the first German ambassador to receive an honorary doctorate from the University; and world affairs seemed so stable that holidaying Hohenzollerns almost littered the south coast that summer – Prince Henry at Cowes, his sister Princess Margaret of Hesse at Bournemouth and their sister Sophie (by now Queen of Greece) at Eastbourne. The Kaiser himself was at Kiel Regatta in the last week of June, and on the Friday afternoon he donned his Royal Navy uniform as an Admiral of the Fleet and was entertained aboard the super-dreadnought named after his cousin, the King. Forty-eight hours later he received a telegram from the German consul at Sarajevo with news that his friend, Archduke Francis Ferdinand, had been assassinated with his wife in the Bosnian provincial capital on Serbia's National Day.[28]

More than three weeks elapsed between the Archduke's murder and the first serious concern in Paris and St Petersburg over the international situation; and European problems were not discussed by the British cabinet for yet another three days. By then it was the afternoon of 24 July and an Austro-Hungarian ultimatum had been handed to a Serbian government minister on the previous evening. There was thus none of the long period of belligerent posturing which marked the Agadir Crisis of 1911, or earlier days of tension between the Great Powers. The Kaiser had returned to Potsdam from Kiel on 29 June and spent a week in consultation with his ministers and service chiefs. He was prepared to give Austria-Hungary full support in punitive measures against the government in Belgrade for encouraging pan-Serb terrorism; he assumed the Austrians would invade Serbia and he was prepared to accept the risk of a European war, although he thought it might be avoided and was sure that, if war came, it would not last for more than a few weeks. On 6 July the Kaiser set off again by train for Kiel, boarded his yacht, and spent the next three weeks on his annual summer cruise in the Norwegian fjords. He did not arrive back in Potsdam until the afternoon of 27 July, four days after the Austrians made their demands on Belgrade. At that moment he was still far from convinced that war was either necessary or inevitable. But it followed within the week.

In later years his bitterest enemies held William II responsible for the disastrous conflict that was to rob nearly fifty million soldiers, sailors, airmen and civilians of their lives. Even George V, who had liked and in many respects admired his cousin, was to write in his diary on the day of the Kaiser's abdication that he was 'the greatest criminal known for having plunged the world into this ghastly war'.[29] So simplistic a view of history was soon out of favour, replaced by assumptions of collective responsibility. Only in the 1960s did it become fashionable once more to believe in Germany's 'guilt', with the Fischer thesis that in 1914 the leading military and political figures in Berlin used the Sarajevo crime as an excuse to launch a war which would resolve social tensions and consolidate the primacy attained by German industry in a Europeanized world.[30]

Against so formidable an indictment the Kaiser's assertion that he had been the slave of events, that 'the machine . . . ran away with me', seems almost pathetically naïve.[31] For, whatever his role in the post-Sarajevo crisis, there is no doubt that in earlier years William II encouraged a general mood of militancy by striking arrogantly aggressive attitudes. Unfortunately, in successive crises, his naval and military leaders became accustomed to his irresolution. 'His Majesty will fail when it comes to shouldering a great responsibility,' a high official in the Foreign Ministry predicted to his naval counterpart at the height of the Agadir Crisis.[32] Three years later his military planners ensured that, through their staff work, the Supreme War Lord was given no opportunity to decide whether the conflict was to remain localized in the Balkans or be fought by Germany on only one front. Over the General Staff's 'machine', the Kaiser certainly found that he had no control.

Throughout the last six days of peace William II placed his hopes in the efficacy of family diplomacy. The 'Willy-Nicky' telegram exchanges, in which the Kaiser urged the Tsar to 'avoid endless misery' by calling off Russia's mobilization, continued until three hours after the German ambassador in St Petersburg had handed over a declaration of war. Briefly, on the afternoon of Wednesday, 29 July, the Kaiser believed that he had at least achieved a success with Cousin George. For, before returning from Cowes to his naval command in the Baltic, Grand-Admiral Prince Henry had travelled to London. There, after breakfast on Sunday morning (26 July), he visited King George v at Buckingham Palace and discussed the crisis with him. When Henry reached Kiel on Tuesday he quoted the King as having said, 'We shall try all we can to keep out of this and shall remain neutral.' This was the assurance that William wished to hear: he had sent Henry to Sandringham for just such a message nineteen months before, and now his brother was able to deliver it, in emphatic words, from Buckingham Palace. 'England will not fight,' the Kaiser told his Crown Council at the Neues Palais that Wednesday afternoon; and when Admiral Tirpitz, having studied the Foreign Secretary's assertions of sympathy for France, questioned his sovereign's confidence in British neutrality, he was told haughtily, 'I have the word of a King, and that is good enough for me'.[33]

Next morning the Kaiser began to realize 'cousin diplomacy' had failed yet again. Perhaps Prince Henry bungled his report. More probably, William still did not understand the reservations with which a constitutional monarch must necessarily hedge statements of political intent. At all events he could see what common sense should long since have taught him, that dynastic sentiment ran skin deep. By Saturday night, with the possibility of British neutrality looking more and more remote, the Kaiser was prepared to let events take their course. The British ultimatum was delivered on the Tuesday, after the first German troops had entered Belgium in their westward thrust towards the Channel coast and Paris. That evening a Berlin crowd stoned the windows of the British Embassy. Next morning one last message was conveyed from the Kaiser to his British cousin's ambassador: he understood his Berliners' anger that England had 'forgotten how we fought shoulder to shoulder at Waterloo'; and he would now resign the ranks of Admiral of the Fleet and of Field Marshal, which he had hitherto been proud to hold. There were greater renunciations yet to come.

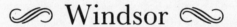

CHAPTER FIFTEEN

Windsor

With the coming of the First World War the German connections of the British
royal House proved a political embarrassment. The institution of monarchy,
which once benefited from marriage links between greater and lesser
dynasties, now mattered little in the relations between states. The burden of
a long war of attrition fell on the people as a whole, not on the monarch's
professional soldiers and seamen as in earlier conflicts. Gradually the
lengthening casualty lists produced revulsion against the old European order
until, in the fourth winter of war, the public temper threatened to explode the
whole galaxy of royal honorifics in the hope of creating a less splendid
firmament inclined to the ways of peace.

But the excitement of the first campaigns, when both sides of combatants
believed 'It will all be over by Christmas', produced a more familiar public
response. Patriotic fervour expressed itself in vandal attacks on property and
individuals. The demonstration against the British Embassy in Berlin was
soon surpassed by anti-German riots in Poplar and other parts of London,
where shop windows bearing names which were considered Teutonic in origin
became targets for destruction. Within a few weeks local acts of violence had
given way to spy scares and to a witch hunt against what the widely read
weekly *John Bull* called 'Germhuns' holding key positions in the land. For the
moment no one was prepared to criticize a conscientious and popular
sovereign or his London-born consort. But were there German sympathizers
at Court? The collective imagination played havoc with inconsequential
misadventures. The lights which, it was said, flashed mysteriously at
Sandringham when the first Zeppelins raided Norfolk, threatened at one time
to become a sinister contribution to the folk legends of fear. Not every rumour
could be firmly quashed, as this one was, by the massive authority of Lord
Kitchener.[1]

The Admiralty was said to be especially at risk from 'Germhuns'. As an
institution it did, indeed, respond slowly to the wartime mood of the country;
for, when the Navy List for October 1914 was published, more than a month
after British and German warships were in action in Heligoland Bight, it
included among the Admirals of the Fleet 'H.I.M. the German Emperor (1889)'
and 'H.S.H. Prince Henry of Prussia (1910)', although their names were omitted,
at the King's request, before the appearance of the next edition.[2] More serious
was the position of the First Sea Lord, Prince Louis of Battenberg. It was

Prince Louis's initiative which ensured that the British fleet was ready and at war stations before hostilities began. But his Hessian family background was against him. He had inherited Heiligenberg in 1888 and the castle remained in his possession until 1920. Knowledge that his wife's sister was married to the Kaiser's brother was exploited by scaremongering journalists and a small set of naval officers, jealous of his career. So vituperative was the campaign that Prince Louis had difficulty in concentrating on his naval tasks. Reluctantly, on 29 October, he resigned from the Board of Admiralty, accepting humiliation (and half-pay) to appease a public opinion which had no understanding of his deep sense of loyalty to the service. His son, the future Earl Mountbatten of Burma, was in that autumn a naval cadet at Osborne, which was no longer a royal residence. The vicious campaign against his father made life unpleasant for the fourteen-year-old who wished to make the Royal Navy his career; and here at Osborne, the creation of his Coburg great-grandfather, Queen Victoria's last godson was shunned as a 'German spy'.[3]

A far sadder irony lay in the casualty lists of that last week in October. For among the officers of the Sixtieth Royal Rifles killed at Zonnebeke, in the Ypres Salient, was Lieutenant Prince Maurice of Battenberg, youngest son of the widowed Princess Beatrice and a nephew of the First Sea Lord who was forced from office just two days after the young Prince's death. He was not the first battle casualty among Queen Victoria's descendants: Prince Maximilian, the second son of Fritz and Vicky's youngest daughter, Princess Margaret of Hesse, had been killed a fortnight before at Bailleul, only fifteen miles from Zonnebeke, while he was serving with the German cavalry. The war of kith and kin, so often a nightmare fear in the Crown Princess's letters to her mother, was beginning to take its terrible toll.

War necessarily severed all direction communication between the ruling families. But that did not mean they were out of contact with each other. Even after eighteen months of bloodshed the Kaiser still believed personal dynastic diplomacy would eventually call a halt to the fighting for, on the eve of an American initiative to end the war in 1916, he told the US ambassador in Berlin, 'I and my cousins George and Nicholas shall make peace when the proper time has come'.[4] It is not difficult to guess what channel he wished to use. The neutrality of the Scandinavian states was of value to both sides in the conflict. A Danish shipping magnate, Hans Niels Andersen, moved freely between the courts of London, Copenhagen, Berlin and Petrograd (as St Petersburg was renamed in September 1914). He was a confidant of the two successive Danish monarchs, Frederick VII and Christian I, and was trusted by George V and by William II, both of whom he had met long before the outbreak of war. Personal links at a slightly less exalted level were maintained by the Crown Princess of Sweden, the elder daughter of the Duke of Connaught (who had, of course, married a Prussian princess). Crown Princess 'Daisy' helped trace 'missing' soldiers from among the prisoners-of-war and was also, as Princess Marie Louise was to write, 'our liaison officer' bringing news of families separated by obligations of state loyalty.

There was a curious incident on 5 July 1916. On that Wednesday King George v and Queen Mary joined Queen Victoria's eldest surviving daughter, Princess Helena, and her chronically sick husband (Prince Christian of Schleswig-Holstein) at Cumberland Lodge for celebrations of their Golden Wedding. While they were there, a telegram arrived from the Crown Princess in Stockholm saying that 'William' had asked to convey his 'loyal and devoted good wishes to dear Uncle Christian and Aunt Helena'.[5] It is as well that so kindly a message remained the secret confidence of a small family circle; for that golden anniversary Wednesday was the fifth day of the Somme and the 135th day of Verdun. But 'Uncle Christian and Aunt Helena' were pathetic survivors in a cruel world. One son had died while serving with the British army in the Boer War. His only brother, named after their Coburg grandfather, owned considerable estates in Silesia and, as a Prussian general in the reserve, was mobilized when war came. Prince Albert was 'not really fighting on the side of the Germans', George v had hastened to explain to a doubting Prime Minister earlier in the war; he was only 'in charge of a camp of English prisoners'. It was a situation which made more sense to the King than to the politicians.[6]

One even older survivor refused to allow the war to isolate her from her homeland. The correspondence between the redoubtable Grand Duchess Augusta and her niece, Queen Mary, was resumed six weeks after the declaration of war. It continued until 8 November 1916, when the Grand Duchess was in her ninety-fifth year and within four weeks of her death. Queen Mary received, in all, eighty-seven wartime letters from Neu-Strelitz, each forwarded by the Crown Princess of Sweden. Remarkably, despite increasing age and wartime disruption, the Grand Duchess was able to send thirty-seven letters during the year 1915 alone, compared to the average of fifty-six letters a year which she had maintained before the war. The exchanges – which were, of course, privileged and therefore did not have to pass through the scrutiny of a censor – were, for the most part, concerned with family matters although at times they asked for, or gave, news of prisoners-of-war. Less than a fortnight after the sinking of HMS *Hampshire*, with Kitchener aboard, and the battle of Jutland, the Grand Duchess was writing back from the heart of Mecklenburg to London: 'My heart is so heavy and sad', she told Queen Mary, 'I could not write at first though I was all with you, first the sinking of the vessel bearing your name, then Lord Kitchener, such a loss, such a disaster'.[7] Her next letter, dated 18 June, was defiantly headed 'Waterloo Day', an anniversary which no doubt brought back to her mind proud memories of old parades and an August week, more than half a century before, when she and her husband were the last guests entertained by the great Wellington at Walmer Castle. By now her husband and her son were dead and her grandson, 'Fred', reigned in Mecklenburg-Strelitz. He, too, was an Anglophile: at one of the most bitter moments in the conflict, he had dreamt he was at Windsor, accompanying the King and Queen in state across the lawn.[8] Fourteen months after his grandmother's death he shot himself rather than face a world in which the British and German peoples seemed permanently estranged.

Kaiser William II and King George V were slow to realize the depth of hatred which divided their two nations. The Kaiser dismayed his personal staff at the end of October 1914 by talking amiably in English to a group of prisoners-of-war whom the Bavarians had captured south of Ypres. George V forbade the Kaiser's godson – the future Duke of Gloucester – to accompany cadets from Eton College to a German prisoner-of-war camp as he thought it 'bad taste' to stare at captives behind barbed-wire. The King deplored the German bombing of English cities and the U-boat attacks on unarmed merchant vessels (as, indeed, did his cousin in Berlin).[9] But he could not understand why the sight of the seven Garter banners of German royalty hanging in St George's Chapel at Windsor caused such pain to worshippers and visitors; Tsar Nicholas I's banner had hung there in the Crimean War. Only a strongly worded plea from the most consistent Germanophobe in the royal family, Queen Alexandra, persuaded her son to take action. On 13 May 1915 all enemy 'Extra Knights of the Garter' were struck off the roll of the Order: the banners of the Kaiser (KG, 1877), the Duke of Cumberland (KG, 1878), Prince Henry of Prussia (KG, 1889), the Grand Duke of Hesse (KG, 1892), the Crown Prince of Prussia (KG, 1901), the Duke of Albany and Saxe-Coburg-Gotha (KG, 1902) and the King of Württemberg (KG, 1904) were removed from the chapel. Among these seven names were four grandsons of Victoria and Albert.[10]

Two years later, on 17 July 1917, the King authorized a more startling severance of the Crown from its Germanic past. An Order in Council proclaimed that henceforth 'Our House and Family shall be styled and known as the House and Family of Windsor' and all descendants of Queen Victoria who were subjects of the realm were required to discontinue the use of all 'German degrees, styles, dignitaries, titles, honours and appellations'. The proclamation had the merit of ending dynastic confusion in a stroke of patriotic clarity; it chose the longest continuous royal residence in England to replace 'Hanover' or 'Guelph' or 'Wettin' or 'Saxe-Coburg-Gotha' as the name of the ruling House. At the same time the Battenbergs were Anglicized as Mountbatten, Prince Louis being created Marquess of Milford Haven, and his nephew Prince Alexander (eldest son of Princess Beatrice) became Marquess of Carisbrooke. Queen Mary's brothers – by right Princes of Teck – became Marquess of Cambridge and Earl of Athlone. The three surviving Holstein ladies (Princess Helena and her daughters, Helena Victoria and Marie

Louise) assumed no surname and kept the style of Princess for the remainder of their lives.

The new 'fancy names' were unpopular with the older generation, particularly the Battenbergs, and it is strange that King George v, having set his face against the anti-German hysteria for nearly three years of war, should have suddenly acquiesced in so dramatic a break with the past. Undoubtedly he was influenced by events in Russia, for it was clear that anti-German feeling had discredited the Romanovs on the eve of the Revolution. The Tsarina was a sister of the Grand Duke of Hesse and a sister-in-law both of Prince Henry of Prussia and of Prince Louis of Battenberg. Reports of her denunciation by Russian democrats in the previous winter as the *nemka*, the 'German woman' made disturbing reading in London; she was said to favour German agents at court and to have urged the Tsar to contact her brother and seek a separate peace. What mattered in the Britain of 1917 was not the truth or falsehood of these allegations, but the fact that they existed at all. English radicals like H.G. Wells were already complaining that George v's court was 'alien and uninspiring', as the King knew well enough. Supposing it became necessary to respond to the peace moves emanating from Berlin that summer? Would a negotiated settlement which fell short of public expectation rebound against the monarchy? With the war entering so critical a phase, there was everything to be said for emphasizing the King's 'Englishry'.[11]

The actual timing of the change may well have been determined by another consideration. The first mass air raid on London was carried out on 13 June 1917 by fourteen aircraft known as 'Gothas'. Another raid, by twenty-one Gothas, followed on 7 July. The name 'Gotha', hitherto linked with the dynasty, now became as notorious as 'Zeppelin'. Only ten days separated the second Gotha bombing raid from the Order in Council anglicizing the dynasty.

Peace did not come in the summer of 1917 nor in the grim winter which succeeded it. Eventually in the early autumn of 1918 the German High Command recognized that it could neither mount another sustained offensive nor halt the allied and American assault on the Western Front. Prince Max of Baden – a liberal royalist descended, oddly enough, not from the great German ruling families, but from the Beauharnais and the Empress Josephine – became Chancellor on 4 October 1918 and at once began secret armistice negotiations with President Woodrow Wilson. By the end of the month the American President, and many political groups in Germany itself, were demanding the abdication of the Kaiser. But William ii held out. He left Potsdam for the last time on 29 October for military headquarters at Spa in Belgium, steeling himself to face revolt in his navy and the spread of socialist revolutionary councils to Hamburg, Bremen, Munich and the industrial centres in Saxony. There seemed a danger that the Hohenzollerns might suffer the fate of their Romanov cousins. At Kiel on Wednesday, 6 November, Prince Henry, alarmed by the menacing tone of the sailors, drove his wife and son to safety along a picket line of mutineers by flying a red banner from his car and wearing a red armband on the sleeve of his greatcoat. At last knowledge that mutiny was spreading to the army made William II accept the inevitable. On the following Sunday, twenty-four hours before the Armistice was signed, the Kaiser arrived at the Dutch frontier post of Eysden and crossed into Holland. He signed a deed of abdication as German Emperor and as King of Prussia on 28 November. His eldest son, the Crown Prince, renounced his personal rights to the Prussian throne three days later.[12]

By then Germany was a Republic. The Kings of Bavaria, Saxony and Württemberg all abdicated in November; and so, too, did the Duke of Brunswick, as early as 9 November. Other rulers, including the Grand Duke of Hesse and the Duke of Saxe-Coburg-Gotha, found that they ceased to reign because the revolutionaries refused to acknowledge their authority. The British army entered Cologne and Wiesbaden while the French established themselves in Mainz and the Rhenish Palatinate, but there was not, as in 1945, a total occupation of defeated Germany.

Persistent attempts were made by the governments of the victorious allies to induce the Dutch to hand over the fallen Kaiser so that he could stand trial before judges from America, Britain, France, Italy and Japan for 'the gravest violation of the international moral code and the sanctity of treaties'. Extremists, mainly in Britain, waged a somewhat hysterical 'Hang the Kaiser' campaign, for propaganda had for four years made him personally responsible for any inhumanity committed under the German flag and many which were never committed at all. A group described by the King's private secretary as 'the cooler heads' advocated that the Kaiser should be interned on the Falkland Islands. The Foreign Secretary, the US Secretary of State, and almost all professional diplomats were appalled at the idea of setting up an international tribunal. A petition signed by the King of Saxony and other German princes protested to George V at the possibility of putting their former Emperor on trial 'before a Court of Justice composed of his enemies' and insisted that to lay 'hands on the Royal Dignity of a great and at one time friendly and related Ruler' would in itself constitute a crime.[13]

George V may not have appreciated the tone of this petition but he was in sympathy with its argument. He appears, too, to have been impressed by a letter he received from the former Crown Prince, who had, like his father, found refuge in the Netherlands; he offered to surrender his own person rather than see his father arraigned in this way. The King was also dismayed at the practical problems of putting the Kaiser on trial, for Lloyd George seems to have envisaged the establishment of a court in Westminster Hall, with the accused brought daily by water either from Sion House, near Kew, or from Hampton Court.[14] Fortunately the Dutch government made it clear, even before the end of the year 1918, that it had no intention of surrendering the right to offer sanctuary to a fallen head of state. Early in 1920 the Kaiser purchased a moated country house at Doorn, twelve miles east of Utrecht. There he was to spend much of the last twenty-one years of his life seeking to explain away the previous sixty by the written word and the occasional interviews.

During the last weeks of 1918, while the kings who remained were counting dynastic oaks uprooted by that autumn's gale, there came a sudden intrusion of an almost forgotten name. It was more than thirty years since the Kaiser's second sister had been disappointed in love through the intransigence of Bismarck and the greater charms for 'Sandro' Battenberg of his beautiful opera singer. By now 'young Vicky' was the widowed and childless Princess Victoria of Schaumburg-Lippe, the husband whom she married in 1890 having died at Bonn two years before the end of the war. As soon as the allied armies occupied the Rhineland her residence, the Schaumburg Palace, became the headquarters of General Sir Arthur Currie, the Canadian commander in Europe, and it was duly visited in the last week of the old year by George v's second son, Prince Albert (the future King George vi). Courtesy necessitated a meeting with the châtelaine of the palace, who, however, had clearly not realized the bitterness of British feelings towards Germany. She remarked to her cousin's son that she hoped 'we should be friends again shortly'. 'I told her that I did not think it was possible for a great many years!!!!' the Prince reported to his father.[15] The Princess did not in fact live to see friendly relations restored between the two families. In November 1927 she again incurred her elder brother's wrath, this time by marrying, with Orthodox rites, a poverty-stricken Russian refugee, thirty-four years her junior. It was a union which lost her many friends, much of her income, and the Schaumburg Palace (which is now the German Federal Chancellery). After a few months it ended in divorce. A year later the unfortunate Princess died from pneumonia.

George v approved of his son's reply to 'Cousin Vicky', for he did not doubt the 'real feeling of bitterness' towards Germany which ran throughout his realm. Earlier wars had been followed by reconciliations between the rulers: Francis Joseph was welcomed in Berlin six years after Königgrätz-Sadowa, William i repaying the courtesy with a state visit to Vienna a year later; and Tsar Alexander ii was entertained at Windsor, although not until the Crimean War had receded eighteen years. But after the 'Great War' rancour lingered. With what, in retrospect, seems petty bureaucratic spite the British authorities deprived the seventy-four-year-old son of Hanover's last King of the Dukedom of Cumberland and his princely rank. At the same time 'Cousin Charlie', the Etonian Duke of Saxe-Coburg-Gotha, lost his English royal title as second Duke of Albany. This was a somewhat embarrassing act of state: his mother, Princess Helena, was still alive; and his sister, Princess Alice, Countess of

Athlone, was not only a sister-in-law of Queen Mary but also founding President of the women's section of the British Legion.

Within Germany, the fortunes of the fallen dynasties varied from region to region. The Saxon and Bavarian royal families retained widespread popularity. Once the red peril receded, some sentimental nostalgia for the old order spread through Prussia, too; there were affecting scenes at Potsdam on 19 April 1921, when the funeral train of the Kaiser's widow arrived from Holland and the cortège set out from the Wildpark Station for burial in the Temple of Antiquity, close to the Neues Palais. The Hohenzollern princes were able to establish themselves again in Prussia after 1923, once the moderate right-wing People's Party leader, Gustav Stresemann, became the chief political figure in the Republic. The Crown Prince returned from Holland to Potsdam in October 1923. He joined his wife, Crown Princess Cecilie, and their six children at the Cecilienhof. This last of Potsdam's seven palaces was built between 1912 and 1917 in the style of an English country house which seemed to be apologizing for delusions of grandeur. It was an interesting and attractive palace and remained the principal Hohenzollern residence in the German Republic until the last months of the Second World War. In July and August 1945 the British, American and Soviet leaders were to sit in conference in the Cecilienhof's finest room.

But so great a humiliation for Germany seemed remote in the Stresemann Era of recovery and fulfilment. Although the Crown Prince's sister lived mainly at Gmunden, his brothers had homes in or near Potsdam. Prince August William, the fourth of the Kaiser's sons, joined the Nazi Party in 1928 and five years later was the Party candidate in the Potsdam 1 District in the Reichstag Election. The other five sons were slightly more circumspect, not least because their exiled father strongly disapproved of Hitler and his ideology. Nevertheless the Crown Prince received Hitler at the Cecilienhof as early as 1926, and by 1932 he was giving the Nazis strong support.[16]

British troops remained in their occupation zone until December 1929. So long as they kept their watch on the Rhine there was little contact between the British reigning House and German royalty. King George V, however, continued to take a keen interest in German affairs and was alert to changes in the public mood. In the summer of 1933 – less than five months after Hitler became German Chancellor – the King opened the World Monetary and Economic Conference in South Kensington and, on 17 June, he took the opportunity to speak out to the German Foreign Minister, Baron von Neurath, on the harm being done to Germany's reputation abroad by reports of Nazi treatment of the Jews. Neurath was so impressed that he reported the King's words, not to Chancellor Hitler, but direct to the ageing President Hindenburg; it was, he said, 'a very earnest conversation, with no beating about the bush'. The meeting became something of a legend among German diplomats, a standard by which to gauge the British monarch's approval, or disapproval, of their leader's policies. 'The King was no longer as severe in his view on the Jewish Question as he had been in his talk with Baron Neurath,' the German ambassador reported to his Foreign Ministry the following spring, with evident relief.[17] George v's opinions mattered more in post-Hohenzollern Berlin than he ever appreciated.

In these last three years of his life King George came to look upon his German relatives with greater indulgence. He greeted one of the sons of the Crown Prince at Cowes Regatta and in the summer of 1934 the Duke and Duchess of Brunswick were entertained at Buckingham Palace, recalling that last spectacular gathering of the 'royal mob' in Berlin at their wedding twenty-one years before. The Duke and Duchess had met Hitler for the first time in 1933, when he urged them to work for Anglo-German reconciliation, a task which appealed to them. But the Duchess was far from pleased when on their return from England the Nazi Party adviser on foreign affairs, Joachim von Ribbentrop, sought to promote a marriage between their seventeen-year-old daughter, Frederica, and that most eligible of bachelors, the forty-year-old Prince of Wales.[18] Hitler was said to favour the project. The Duchess, however, remembering that in 1912 some newspapers had speculated on whether she might herself marry the Prince, emphatically declined to push her daughter into any such union; and, in January 1938, Princess Frederica became the bride of the future King Paul of Greece. But the episode remains an interesting commentary on the importance which the Nazi hierarchy continued to attach to dynastic diplomacy.

By May 1935, when congratulations on his Silver Jubilee arrived from all parts of the world, including Germany, George v could write contentedly to the Grand Duke of Hesse: 'That horrible and unnecessary war has made no difference to my feelings for you.'[19] But it had made a difference to his views on German military power. He was disturbed, not only at Nazi Jew-baiting, but at the reports of German re-armament, and he went out of his way to impress the folly of a new arms race on the German ambassador on more than one occasion.[20] At times the King seemed better informed and more resolute than any public figure in Britain, apart from the ostracized Churchill. And over the Nazi phenomenon, as over so many questions, he was at loggerheads with his eldest son.

The twentieth Prince of Wales – alias King Edward viii, alias the Duke of Windsor – was the first member of a British royal House to enjoy (or suffer from) the star adulation of a newspaper-reading public. During the seventeen years which followed the First World War he worked hard at projecting the image of a twentieth-century imperial monarchy. He was a good salesman, a sympathetic listener and a competent speaker, prepared to visit forty-five countries (none of them Germany) in protracted overseas tours. With ex-servicemen he seemed especially at ease, perhaps because it had been the ordeal of war which lifted this diffident young man from protracted adolescence and imposed disciplines of duty on his haphazard mind. He was a major when the war ended, and his outlook on politics and society was not dissimilar from the views of most veteran junior officers of his generation. Communism he detested and feared; but he also had a conviction, which never left him, that Britain's out-of-date system of government needed drastic reform. He did not like the conventional stuffiness of his father's court, the routine of Balmoral, Sandringham and the traditional London Season. In foreign affairs he thought the Treaty of Versailles unduly severe on Germany and he was impressed by the effect of romantic authoritarian fascism on the demoralized Italians whom he had known while serving on the Piave Front in the War. It is not surprising that his kinsman, Albert Mensdorff, visiting the Prince in London on 31 October 1933, found him full of admiration for Germany and the Nazis.[21]

George v had already noticed his son's liking for an aggressive political creed almost as repugnant to him as Bolshevism. In the autumn of 1932 – four months before Hitler came to power – he had forbidden the Prince of Wales to go to Coburg for the wedding of Princess Sibylla to the King of Sweden's grandson because the Princess's father, that unfortunate reigning Duke of Saxe-Coburg, was an active Nazi campaigner.[22] By the summer of 1935 the Prince of Wales's views were so at variance with government policy towards Germany that the Foreign Office began to pay strict attention to the reaction, at home and abroad, to his speeches. When, at the Albert Hall on 11 June that year, the Prince urged British ex-servicemen to 'stretch forth the hand of friendship to the Germans' his remarks earned him a sharp reprimand from his father, critical comments in British newspapers and favourable press reports throughout Germany. But George v wanted to be fair. 'Was there a chance of reaching some understanding with Hitler's Germany?', he asked the Permanent Under-Secretary at the Foreign Office two months before his death. The answer was not encouraging.[23]

On the third weekend in January 1936 sombre bulletins from Sandringham made it clear that the King was dying. Across the North Sea, at Doorn, the cousin who had stood briefly beside him in vigil at Westminster Hall in the earliest days of his reign telegraphed his sympathy to Queen Mary, who acknowledged the kindness with a gift in the first week of her widowhood.[24] On the day after the King's death the British ambassador in Berlin, Sir Eric Phipps, was surprised to receive a visit from the fallen Kaiser's personal envoy with a request that he should be officially represented at the King's funeral. The new sovereign, Edward VIII, welcomed the suggestion and, in a note written in his own hand, he suggested that the German Crown Prince should be invited to follow the coffin through the streets of London and Windsor. Edward VIII thought that the Crown Prince's coming would provide an occasion for a handshake of reconciliation, one of those gestures of friendship he had commended seven months before at the Albert Hall. But the German experts at the Foreign Office were dismayed: as a young man 'little Willy' had been a pan-German enthusiast, boasting of the need to make insolent Paris 'once more feel what a Pomeranian Grenadier can do'; as a chinless wonder in the jumbo-size shako of the Death's Head Hussars, he became the butt of every caricaturist in the allied Press; and like his father, he was – rightly or wrongly – arraigned for offences against 'international morality' under Article 228 of the Treaty of Versailles. Moreover, although there had been redeeming moments of quixotic generosity in his public career, the record of his relationship to the Nazis was not encouraging. Patiently it was suggested to the new King that the Crown Prince's presence might be misunderstood; and the Hohenzollerns were represented by the Kaiser's grandson, Prince Frederick, an Anglophile who was soon to make his home in Hertfordshire.[25]

Among the family mourners at George v's funeral was that 'Cousin Charlie', the Duke of Saxe-Coburg of whose stormtrooper affiliations the dead King so thoroughly disapproved. The Duke sent to Berlin an extraordinary report of his conversations with Edward viii, who had allegedly said that he wished to meet Hitler, either on British or German soil, and that it was his intention to concentrate government in his own hands. It is probable that Hitler personally would not have attached great importance to the Coburg report had it not corresponded so closely with assessments from the German ambassadors both in London and Washington. Leopold von Hoesch, ambassador to Britain from 1932 until his sudden death in April 1936, was a non-Nazi aristocrat known to Edward viii from the last summer before the war. Both as Prince and King he spoke more readily to Hoesch than to any other ambassador, not perhaps realizing how every indiscretion of table-talk would be analysed in the Wilhelmstrasse. It was to Hoesch that in January 1936, shortly before the first grave bulletins came from Sandringham, the Prince of Wales announced his intention of going to Berlin for the Olympic Games later that year; and, on the day Edward viii was proclaimed King, Hoesch reported that his 'friendly attitude towards Germany might in time come to exercise a certain amount of influence in the shaping of German foreign policy.... We should at least be able to rely on a ruler who is not lacking in understanding for Germany and the desire to see good relations between Germany and Britain.' On the same day Luther, the German ambassador in Washington, reported that Americans who knew Britain's new sovereign believed he would oppose cabinet decisions which he thought 'detrimental to British interests'.[26]

It is not surprising that Ribbentrop assumed there might now be a new German connection established at Buckingham Palace. Ribbentrop himself succeeded Hoesch as German ambassador. He never, however, gained the trust enjoyed by his predecessor, nor did he meet the King on any intimate social occasions. He was a spectator of events when, in early December 1936,

Edward VIII abdicated because he found it impossible 'to discharge my duties as King as I would wish to do without the help and support of the woman I love'. Ribbentrop was surprised and dismayed: he had never believed that a man who had expressed himself so forcefully in recent years would renounce the crown for the sake of the American-born divorcée, Wallis Simpson. To Berlin Ribbentrop hinted that other forces were at work in ousting a sovereign for whom Hitler had professed a high regard: 'His friendly attitude towards Germany undoubtedly gained the King very powerful enemies in this country,' Ribbentrop telegraphed on the last (and 326th) evening of Edward VIII's reign.[27] On the same day, opponents of Mrs Simpson maintained that the ambassador had used her to provoke a conflict with the Conservative cabinet and bring in a government of 'King's Friends' well-disposed towards Germany; abdication was thus a slap in the face for Hitler. Neither legend is convincing.

Yet there is no doubt that the Duke of Windsor, as Edward VIII became on the day after his abdication, continued to show an interest in Nazi Germany which was, at best, indiscreet. In October 1937 the Duke and Duchess of Windsor were guests of the German state in a trip which culminated in a meeting with Hitler at the Obersalzberg, above Berchtesgaden. The visit, which was officially ignored by the British Embassy, was nevertheless studied with interest and some apprehension by the Foreign Office. It prompted surprisingly little reaction in Britain, where by now the Duke was an idol of yesterday. He had, however, always been a charming and appreciative idol; and his social graces were now let loose on a land whose public figures had rarely shone with such virtues in recent years. Here, it was felt, was an exiled English King who liked Germany, its people and its language, even its National Socialist achievements. 'David wins all hearts here,' his great-aunt wrote when last he stayed in Germany. Nearly a quarter of a century later, he was winning them again: but this time they were Nazi hearts, and the Duke had unwittingly become a talisman for the triumph in Britain of political ideals which neither he nor his royal relatives in Hitler's Reich ever fully comprehended. He left Germany for the last time on 23 October 1937. Ribbentrop, however, had not yet finished with him.[28]

In September 1938 Europe's peace was saved by the heads of government of Germany, Britain, France and Italy meeting in Munich and sacrificing to Germany and her client partners the disputed frontier regions of democratic Czechoslovakia. This 'defeat without a war' as Churchill called the Munich Agreement in the House of Commons, was welcomed by most people in Britain, France and Germany. From Doorn the Kaiser, breaking a long silence on Anglo-German affairs, wrote to Queen Mary declaring that he wished 'to unite my warmest sincerest thanks to the Lord with yours and those of the German and British people that He saved us from a most fearful catastrophe'.[29] There were signs of a cautious reconciliation between the dynasties. Congratulations were sent to Doorn in the last week of January 1939 for the Kaiser's eightieth birthday. 'What pleased my father particularly was the fact that he had been remembered by the King and Queen of England,' his daughter wrote later in her memoirs. In August a visitor from England brought good wishes from Queen Victoria's surviving son, the Duke of Connaught, who remained proud of his Prussian Field Marshal's baton. 'Always my favourite Uncle,' his octogenarian nephew commented. 'Very unlike Uncle Bertie.'[30]

There was more to these exchanges than mere sentiment. Rumours of anti-Nazi plots reached Britain; and a secret envoy arrived with reports that a group of generals wished to establish a new government in Berlin which would be monarchist in character. The Foreign Office became actively interested in the Kaiser's opinions, ensuring that at least one experienced Intelligence agent was among his visitors at Doorn, anxious to assess the depth of his known hostility to the Nazi system of government.[31] This was no easy task, for exile and adversity had sharpened the wiliness of the old fox. It seemed unlikely that William would compromise his security by intrigues with the Hitler opposition. Nevertheless, it was generally recognized that, to many officers of the older generation, his prestige continued to carry weight. He was, after all, an Emperor to whom they had pledged their loyalty while their present leader was still seeking enlistment in a Bavarian reserve infantry regiment.

When war returned to Europe in September 1939 there was, of course, a less searing clash of dynastic loyalties than in the earlier conflict. Yet, in a curiously inverted form, the German royal connection retained an importance for both sides of belligerents. There was an ex-sovereign in the Netherlands of speculative interest to British Intelligence and an ex-sovereign in France of speculative interest to the Germans. At times rival diplomats seem almost to have run in competition with each other. Instructions for keeping tabs on the Kaiser in case Hitler invaded the Netherlands were sent from London to the British envoy at The Hague ten weeks after the outbreak of war; they included authority, if the Dutch so wished, to bring him 'in the last resort to the United Kingdom'.[32] It was from the German envoy in The Hague that Ribbentrop, by now well established as Foreign Minister, first heard reports of an anti-government 'Fronde' beginning to form around the Duke of Windsor. He was told that 'at some time under favourable circumstances' the opposition group 'might acquire a certain significance'.[33]

The day on which German troops crossed the Dutch frontier – 10 May 1940 – coincided with Churchill's assumption of the premiership. On that morning he sent a message to the Foreign Office suggesting the Kaiser be given 'a private hint that he would be received with consideration and dignity in England should he desire to seek asylum here'. When the Foreign Office demurred, the new Prime Minister became more insistent, and his suggestion was approved in writing by King George VI – who, however, was puzzled where so embarrassing a guest would be accommodated. Arrangements were made for an RAF plane to land in Holland at short notice and airlift the eighty-one-year-old ex-Emperor (who had never been in an aircraft) across the North Sea. Churchill's offer was made to the Kaiser in person on the afternoon of 12 May.[34] By the early evening it was gratefully declined: twelve members of his family were serving in the German armed forces; escape to England, however much he might detest the swastika flag, smacked of treason and would discredit the monarchist cause. He would not become involved in what he called Churchill's game of 'political chess'. Soon he was also to decline Hitler's offer of a return to Germany. He died on 4 June 1941, held in high honour by the German troops on guard at Doorn's gatehouse. 'Without England, Germany cannot survive,' his daughter heard him murmur in his last illness.[35] Was his mind wandering in lost opportunities or seeing with prophetic clarity into a dismal future?

Six weeks after the Kaiser chose not to fly to England, the Duke of Windsor inadvertently became one of Germany's political chessmen. When France fell the Duke, who had been serving as a liaison officer between the British and French troops, escaped with the Duchess to Spain, spending nine days in Madrid before travelling on to Lisbon. Reports of the Duke's gloomy assessment of Britain's chances at this turn of the war were forwarded to Berlin from Germany's envoys in both Spain and Portugal. Ribbentrop was once more interested. From Fuschl on 11 July he instructed the German ambassador in Madrid to induce the Duke to return to Spain and see that 'at a suitable occasion' he was informed of Berlin's hope that he would 'be prepared to co-operate in the establishment of good relations between Germany and England'; Germany would then meet 'any desire expressed by the Duke, especially with a view to the assumption of the English throne by the Duke and Duchess'.[36] There followed an extraordinary series of often farcical misadventures in which attempts were made to exploit the Duke's concern over trivial matters of social status and tempt him back across the Spanish frontier. Plans were even made to abduct the Duke and Duchess. Until long after the war, the Duke remained in ignorance of these plots or of the omnipresent agents of German Intelligence. However, before Ribbentrop's henchmen could put their clumsy plans into action, the Duke and Duchess were on their way to the Bahamas, where the Duke was to serve as Colonial Governor until the end of the war. His five-and-a-half-week interlude in Madrid and Lisbon left the Duke's honour untarnished; but it did nothing to enhance his reputation for political good sense.

Dynastic connections counted for little in the remaining five years of war. As late as the autumn of 1943 Hitler and Ribbentrop would still speculate on the need to replace George VI by a restored Edward VIII in order to effect a reconciliation with 'England'.[37] But this was fantasy talk. Soon they were to become afraid of royalist sentiment in Germany. 'We must rid ourselves of the influence exercised by the Hohenzollern brood,' the Führer declared; and a succession of princes found themselves on the retired list. Prince Philip of Hesse, the third son of the Kaiser's youngest sister, was arrested at Hitler's headquarters in September 1943 and held in solitary confinement for over a year before being moved to Dachau concentration camp, while his wife – a daughter of the King of Italy – died in Buchenwald from wounds sustained in an allied air raid. The Crown Prince's eldest son had been killed in May 1940 when the German armies swept into northern France, and monarchist hopes were thereafter centred on his second son, Prince Louis Ferdinand, whom the anti-Hitler conspirators had initiated into their plans even before the coming of the war. After serving in the Luftwaffe in 1940–41 he was retired to his east Prussian estate at Cadinen and kept under general surveillance. Nevertheless it was known to the British as early as May 1942 that the Prince was the most likely candidate for head of state favoured by Dietrich Bonhoeffer's civilian resistance group; and the Prince was fortunate in being able to bluff himself out of Gestapo interrogation after the abortive plot of 20 July 1944.[38] Hitler instinctively felt that the monarchists had given support and cohesion to the conspiracy, but he was never able to acquire sufficient evidence to convince even himself.

It made little difference in those last hectic months of war. The invasion of Hitler's Reich, with Anglo-American forces and the Red Army racing for Berlin from the west and from the east, swept away much of the outer fabric of Germany's history. Some had perished already. In an air raid of 26 June 1943 American bombers destroyed the centre of Hanover, including the Leine Palace where, 250 years before, Ernest Augustus had first assumed the elector's purple ermine cap. Much of royal Berlin was flattened in raids by day and by night in the sixth winter of the war. The Babelsberg, William I's favourite residence beside the Havel, suffered heavily in an air raid on 27 January 1944. The first serious damage to the Potsdam palaces came in April and August 1942, but it was a final heavy attack by nearly 500 British bombers on 14 April 1945 which reduced the old town palace, and much of the area around it, to ashes. Thirteen days later Red Army units from the Ukraine and Byelorussia entered a devastated Potsdam. The Garrison Church, where Frederick the Great was buried, was in ruins. The *Friedenskirche* – the Peace Church, in which Fritz and Vicky lay at rest – was scarred but capable of restoration; a hopeful augury, perhaps?

CHAPTER SIXTEEN

❧ Dynasties in Shadow ❧

In June 1945 the allied governments assumed supreme authority in an occupied Germany. During the grim months which followed defeat the old ruling dynasties suffered greater personal humiliations than at the end of the First World War. Both the Crown Prince of Prussia and his brother, Prince August William, were arrested and interned, while Prince Louis Ferdinand only narrowly avoided capture by the Red Army. It was not only the Russians who threatened the old order. At Friedrichshof, near Frankfurt, the behaviour of American troops was so reprehensible that King George VI asked his librarian, Sir Owen Morshead, to travel to Kronberg and bring back to temporary safe-keeping at Windsor all letters which had belonged to his great-aunt, the Empress Frederick. Queen Victoria's letters to the Empress Frederick were subsequently returned to the Kronberg archives.

This precaution reminded the occupation authorities of the protective interest taken by the British Crown in the welfare of the only surviving member of the Empress Frederick's family, her youngest daughter, the Landgravine Margaret of Hesse-Cassel, who was châtelaine of Friedrichshof. The Landgravine had lost two sons killed in action in the First World War, while her youngest son, Prince Christopher of Hesse, perished when his plane was shot down over the Apennines in October 1943. Her eldest surviving son, Prince Philip of Hesse, was liberated from Dachau only to be re-arrested by the Americans and held for thirty more months until cleared of 'Nazification'. Other princely families suffered greater privations, but none so undeservedly.[1]

Apart from the Morshead mission there was little contact between the British and German dynasties during the immediate post-war years. A curious problem was, however, posed in the British courts of law once the war between Britain and Germany was formally declared at an end in 1951, for Prince Ernest Augustus of Hanover sought recognition as a British subject. The Prince, a son of the Duke of Brunswick, a grandson of the Kaiser and a great-grandson of the blind King of Hanover, was a Protestant lineal descendant of the Electress Sophia and claimed the privileges accorded to the House of Guelph by the 1705 Act of Naturalization. His application was dismissed on first hearing in March 1955 but upheld by the Court of Appeal eight months later, a judgment confirmed by the House of Lords in October 1956. Since Ernest Augustus was too young to have fought in the First World War, he was not subject to the Titles Deprivation Act of 1917: the Prince and his descendants might therefore claim a seat in the Lords as Dukes of Cumberland. No attempt was made to exercise this right; but the court case revived contacts between London and Hanover dynastically severed in 1837, and the Prince, a friend of several members of the British royal family, was frequently in London.[2]

There had never been any prospect of an Anglo-German marriage for Princess Elizabeth, and in July 1947 the Court Circular announced her engagement to a naturalized British naval officer, 'Lieutenant Philip Mountbatten, RN, son of the late Prince Andrew of Greece and Princess Andrew (Princess Alice of Battenberg)'. The Duke of Edinburgh, as Lieutenant Mountbatten became on the day of his marriage in the following November, was a Prince of Greece and of Denmark and a great-great-grandson of both the Crimean War adversaries, Queen Victoria and Tsar Nicholas I. But the Battenberg background gave Prince Philip close links with a liberal and democratic Germany. For a few terms the Prince was a pupil at Schloss Salem, where Dr Kurt Hahn was headmaster before Nazi persecution forced him into exile. In the years immediately preceding Hitler's rise to power Prince Philip's four sisters all married German princes. The youngest sister, Princess Sophia, was widowed when Prince Christopher of Hesse's plane was shot down, but she married again eleven months after the war ended. Her new husband was Ernest Augustus of Hanover's brother, Prince George William, who became principal of the school at Salem when this great experiment in education was revived in West Germany.

Political institutions returned to a divided nation four years after the fall of the Nazi state. The Federal Republic of Germany, covering an area less than half the size of Bismarck's German Empire, was formally established in May 1949, with its capital in the liberal Rhineland university town of Bonn; the much smaller German Democratic Republic, residuary legatee of Brandenburg, was proclaimed an independent entity in the autumn of 1949 but was not formally recognized by any Western Power for more than twenty years. Constant repression in East Germany, culminating in 1961–2 in the construction of the Berlin Wall, aroused sympathy for the people of Federal Germany and West Berlin among their NATO allies, an association emphasized by President Kennedy when he went to Berlin in the summer before his assassination.

The British, too, wished to make a gesture of goodwill. President Heuss had come from Bonn to London in October 1958, but there had been no official royal state visit to Germany since the peacock imperialism of the century's opening decade. Would a royal tour of the Federal Republic be acceptable to a British public who had been deeply shocked by the revelations of liberated Belsen and Buchenwald? There were protests when President Heuss was in Britain from groups still embittered by the tragedies of war. A short semi-official visit by Princess Margaret provoked no hostile reaction and in May

1965 Queen Elizabeth II and Prince Philip were able to bring to West Germany for the first time visual evidence of the modern monarchical mystique, in which the Crown serves as well as rules.

The Queen and the Prince visited ten major cities, including Berlin, in ten days and nights of travel through 1,200 miles of the Federal Republic. Although there were to be many more royal journeys in West Germany over the following twenty years, this state visit of May 1965 marked more distinctly than any later occasion the transition from the old dynastic connection to the new relationship linking Europe's offshore kingdom to its prosperous partner on the Continental mainland. The new Germany was a republic in which industry, as well as being concentrated thickly in some half a dozen areas, was spread thinly over the country as a whole. Apart from the long line of harnessed waterways and the silhouette of wooded hillsides, the landscape would have been scarcely recognizable to those ancestors of the Queen who looked upon Germany as their second home, either in the eighteenth or the nineteenth century. Fittingly, however, it was resurgent Hanover which, in May 1965, evoked the closest associations with this royal heritage. Queen Elizabeth was shown the message sent from London by the Privy Councillors of 1714 inviting her great-great-great-great-great-great-great-grandfather to leave his Electorate and safeguard the Protestant Succession; and in the gardens of the Herrenhausen, rich with memories of a Guelphic past, the Queen met the Duchess of Brunswick, whose marriage – fifty-two years before – had provided the last occasion upon which a German emperor welcomed a reigning British sovereign to the Reich. By 1965 royal visits to Hanover or Berlin or Munich held a different significance.

Over the following twenty years the symphony of Anglo-German reconciliation has been marred from time to time by discordant notes which throw carefully rehearsed harmonies out of key. The most notorious occasion came in the spring of 1985, as former combatants prepared to commemorate the fortieth anniversary of VE Day. Seven years before, on 30 June 1978, Queen Elizabeth II's first cousin, Prince Michael of Kent, had married the former Baroness Marie-Christine von Reibnitz at a civil ceremony in Vienna. The family came originally from the lands conquered by Frederick the Great in southern Silesia, where until 1945 there was a large village known as Reibnitz in the Prussian foothills of the Riesengebirge Mountains. As the Baroness was a Roman Catholic, the Prince renounced his place as fifteenth in line of succession to the throne, but his wife was welcomed in Britain as a member of the royal family, diligent in carrying out her public duties. Like Queen Victoria's eldest daughter, she preferred to be known by her husband's name, appearing in the court circular as Princess Michael of Kent rather than as Princess Marie-Christine. In the third week of April 1985 the Princess's family background was singled out for attack by sections of the media in Britain, Australia and the United States. On 16 April – the day after public memories were stirred by the anniversary of the liberation of Belsen – the *Daily Mirror* disclosed, somewhat intemperately, that recent research had revealed that Princess Michael's father, Baron Günther von Reibnitz, was a Major in the ss, the Nazi élite corps condemned as a criminal organization at the Nuremberg Trials and widely identified with concentration camp bestiality. It was implied that a discreet cover-up had thus concealed from the public the Nazi past of the father of a member of the royal family.

Princess Michael, who was born at Karlovy Vary in January 1945 and who saw little of her father in her childhood, asserted that she had known nothing about the Baron's membership of the ss until the press revelations. She later claimed that he fell from favour in the winter of 1944–5 when he was declared unfit to serve in this most fanatical missionary force of the Nazi creed because of his Catholicism. There is no doubt that, like most large landowners with estates on the fringe of the Reich, the Baron had long supported the Nazis. He was admitted to the ss on 4 July 1934, five days after the notorious 'Night of the Long Knives', in which the corps was employed to murder opponents of Hitler, both inside and outside the Party. By securing even nominal membership of the ss, Baron Günther von Reibnitz would, once again, have been following the practice of many other aristocrats anxious to safeguard their position at a time of Nazi revolution. It was not a creditable role but one which, however deplorable, can in retrospect be understood. No evidence has suggested that the Baron, who died in 1983, was personally responsible for war crimes, and his daughter maintained that he had been cleared by a post-war de-Nazification court in Bavaria.

There was widespread sympathy for Princess Michael in Britain at these revelations: she had shown no liking herself for the Nazis or their beliefs; and it was felt deplorable to impute the Baron's mistaken loyalties to a daughter who had not even been born at the time when her father was conforming to the behaviour pattern of his class and generation. Yet the episode provided an interesting commentary on changing attitudes in a narrowing world. It was a two-day wonder – and no more. There was none of the sustained vituperation which had assailed German-born members of the royal family in the nineteenth century. Heredity mattered far less than in the days of the great dynasties. By the 1980s a German connection based upon kinship had become as much a historic curiosity as the 'Auld Alliance' by which the French and the Scots sought to contain England in the four centuries before the Reformation.

Was the German connection merely an extended family relationship, subject to the jealousies and malicious gossip which strain the fondest ties of kinship? The Coburgs certainly believed that their marriage links would stabilize the constitutional monarchies of a stormy Europe; and Kaiser William II, with his taste for personalized diplomacy, made much of his half-English origins at passing moments of Osborne sentimentality. But Coburg ambition aroused suspicion in both Berlin and London; while on the one occasion when William's masterful personality achieved a short-lived diplomatic triumph – at Björkö in 1905 – his success relied on the alternative dynastic connection, the kinship of Hohenzollerns and Romanovs, rather than on the link with Britain. Conversely it could be argued that the special dynastic relationship counted for nothing in the great crisis of 1914: it could neither check the drift to war nor bring hostilities speedily to an end once the fighting began to envelop Europe.

Yet the record of Anglo-German dynastic exchanges is not simply a protracted family chronicle. For two long periods in modern history – from 1714 to 1760 and from 1837 to 1901 – the sovereign in London looked upon the British and the Germans as peoples inseparably connected, with a common heritage and with similar interests to maintain on the Continent. George I and George II never shook off their Hanoverian prejudices, while Victoria retained a Rosenau-coloured impression of her husband's homeland at least until her meeting with Bismarck at Charlottenburg in 1888 and, to some extent, longer still. Nor in the thinking of other British rulers over the past three centuries was Germany ever relegated to the same 'foreign' status as France or Russia or the kingdoms of the Italian and Iberian peninsulas. Queen Victoria's ministers respected their monarch's views on the German Question; and the evidence of her letters and journal entries suggest that, although the Queen may have been unduly optimistic at times, she showed far greater moderation and common sense than the expert advisers to whom Edwardian statesmen turned during the danger years of the arms race. Not least among the intriguing imponderables of Victoria's reign is speculation on what would have happened if, during those autumn days at Rheinhardtsbrunn in 1862, her son-in-law had remained in Berlin and succeeded to a Prussian throne left vacant by a father who had chosen abdication.

Now, in the closing quarter of the twentieth century, familiar place-names from the dynastic drama fulfil another function. Schloss Rheinhardtsbrunn itself is a hotel, belonging to the Travel Bureau of the German Democratic Republic and offering walking holidays in the Thuringian Forest. At Potsdam the Cecilienhof, too, is a hotel; and so, in federal Germany, is Friedrichshof, in the wooded foothills of the Taunus. The site of the royal palace in East Berlin has been cleared but Charlottenburg remains, in West Berlin, and the East Germans have refurbished most of the Potsdam palaces. Babelsberg, where William I appointed Bismarck as his minister, became in 1963 a museum of pre-history, while since 1961 the Marble Palace has been an army museum, with a tank, a field gun, the nose of a jet fighter and the bow of a high-speed launch littering the balustraded parterre above the Heiligen See. Crocodiles of tourists are escorted through Sans Souci and the Neues Palais. There, in a ground-floor room facing the Wildpark, a wooden cross inlaid in the parquet floor marks the position of the bed in which Frederick III spent the last tragic weeks of his brief reign. Prince Albert's statue still looks out across the town square at Coburg, although a searing scar of concrete and barbed wire has severed the former ducal capital from Gotha for the last forty years. Outside Coburg, the Rosenau – for long neglected and forgotten – remains as peaceful as when Albert was born and his grandmother commented on the agreeable quiet 'only interrupted by the murmuring of the water'. And over the Neckar Valley broods the sense of an older past, for within the grounds of Heidelberg Castle stands the Elisabeth-Pforte, a sandstone triumphal arch erected in a single night 370 years ago, when the Elector Frederick v wished to welcome to the Palatinate his Stuart bride. Like the family politics which followed this most famous of Anglo-German marriages, the rustic patterns adorning the arch look inextricably intertwined.

❧ Reference Notes ❧

Books listed in the reference notes which were published in London are indicated by the abbreviation L. Other abbreviations are as follows:

B MA: R. Fulford (ed.), *Beloved Mama* (L, 1981).

CP: J.G.H. Röhl and N. Sombart (eds), *Kaiser Wilhelm II, New Interpretations: The Corfu Papers* (Cambridge, 1982).

DC: R. Fulford (ed.), *Dearest Child* (L, 1964).

DGFP: *Documents of German Foreign Policy* (L and Washington): series C, 1933–7; series D, 1937–45.

DM: R. Fulford (ed.), *Dearest Mama* (L, 1968).

EHR: *English Historical Review* (L).

FO: Foreign Office archives in the Public Record Office.

GP: J. Lepsius, A. Mendelsohn-Bartholdy and F. Thimme, *Die Grosse Politik der Europäischen Kabinette*, 39 vols (Berlin, 1922–7).

GW: O. von Bismarck, *Die gesammelten Werke Bismarcks*, of which vol. 15 is the definitive edition of his memoirs, *Erinnerung und Gedanke* (Berlin, 1935).

HJ: *Historical Journal* (Cambridge).

HLQ: *Huntingdon Library Quarterly*.

HMC: Historical Manuscripts Commission.

QVL: *Letters of Queen Victoria*, first series, ed. A.C. Benson and Viscount Esher (L, 1907); second and third series, ed. G.E. Buckle (L, 1926 and 1930).

RA: Royal Archives at Windsor.

Schnath: G. Schnath, *Geschichte Hannovers in Zeitalter der Neunten Kur und der Englischen Sukzession, 1674–1714* (Hildesheim, 1938 and 1982).

YDL: R. Fulford (ed.), *Your Dear Letter* (L, 1971).

CHAPTER ONE: FAIR PHOENIX BRIDE

1. E. Sawyer (ed.), *Memorials and Affairs of State . . . from the Papers of Sir Ralph Winwood* (L, 1725), p. 404.

2. John Chamberlain to Alice Carleton, 18 February, and to Ralph Winwood, 23 February 1613, N.E. McClure (ed.), *Letters of John Chamberlain* (Philadelphia, 1939), vol. 1, letters 166 and 167, pp. 423–8.

3. M.A.E. Green, *Elizabeth, Electress Palatine* (L, 1909), pp. 67–9.

4. Ibid., pp. 79–80.

5. G. Parker, *Europe in Crisis, 1598–1648* (L, 1979), p. 86.

6. Green, op. cit., pp. 92–3.

7. C.V. Wedgwood, *Thirty Years War*, revised edn (L, 1964), p. 79; J.V. Polichensky, *The Thirty Years War* (L, 1971), pp. 99–100 and pp. 128–9.

8. Green, op. cit., p. 128.

9. Ibid., pp. 129–30; but compare the criticisms of Carola Oman, *Elizabeth of Bohemia*, revised edn (L, 1964), p. 172.

10. F. von Moser, *Patriotisches Archiv* (Mannheim, 1787), vol. 7, p. 47.

11. Contemporary account of departure from Heidelberg by John Harrison, cited by Wedgwood, op. cit., p. 100; see also ibid., pp. 117–30.

12. Parker, op. cit., p. 341; K. Sharpe

(ed.), *Faction and Parliament* (Oxford, 1978), p. 146; Somers, J. Lord, *Collection of Scarce and Valuable Tracts* (L, 1809), II, p. 472.

13. Green, op. cit., p. 150.
14. J. Gorst Williams, *Elizabeth, The Winter Queen* (L, 1976), p. 79; D. Willson, *James VI & I* (L, 1956), p. 411.
15. 'The Old' *Parliamentary and Constitutional History of England* (L, 1751–62), vol. V, pp. 317–18.
16. Green, op. cit., pp. 175–6.
17. J.R. Tanner, *Constitutional Documents of James I* (Cambridge, 1932), pp. 319–21; Conrad Russell, 'Foreign Policy Debates in the House of Commons in 1621', HJ, XX (1977), pp. 289–90.
18. C.V. Wedgwood, op. cit., pp. 201–2.
19. C.V. Wedgwood, *The King's Peace, 1637–41* (L, 1955), pp. 118–19.
20. Green, op. cit., pp. 323–5.
21. C.V. Wedgwood, *Thirty Years War*, pp. 81 and 150
22. Letter of 14 June 1643, printed in Green, op. cit., p. 360.
23. Ibid., pp. 375–6.
24. H. Fischer (ed.), *Briefe der Elizabeth Stuart an Carl Ludwig von der Pfalz* (Tübingen, 1903), p. 194.
25. Elizabeth to Duke of Ormonde, 2 May 1661, letter printed in Green, op. cit., p. 403.
26. Braybrooke edition of *Pepys Diary* (L, 1906), p. 59.
27. W. Bray (ed.), *Memoirs of John Evelyn* (L, 1827), vol. 2, p. 188; Oman, op. cit., p. 456.

CHAPTER 2: THE PURPLE ERMINE CAP

1. A. Koecher (ed.), *Memoiren der Herzogin Sophie, Nachmals Kurfürstin von Hannover* (Leipzig, 1879), p. 52.
2. Anna Wendland, *Briefe der Elisabeth Stuart, Königin von Bohmen* (Tübingen, 1902), p. 48.
3. Koecher, op. cit., p. 59.
4. Ragnild Hatton, *George I, Elector and King* (L, 1976), p. 25.
5. Ibid., p. 26.

6. Ibid., pp. 30–31; Koecher, op. cit., pp. 88–9.
7. Ibid., p. 104.
8. E. Bourgeois, *Spanheim* (Paris, 1884), pp. 594–5.
9. G. Burnet, *History of His Own Times* (Oxford 1833), vol. III, p. 211.
10. Hatton, op. cit., pp. 39–40 and 324; Edward Gregg, 'Was Queen Anne a Jacobite?', *History*, LVII (October 1972), p. 367.
11. Schnath, I, pp. 164–5, pp. 567–78 and 746; Hatton, op. cit., pp. 41–2.
12. Ibid., pp. 42–4; G. Schnath (ed.), *Der Königsmarck Briefwechsel* (Hildesheim, 1952), introduction.
13. Schnath, I, pp. 500–502 and 592–4.
14. Hatton, op. cit., pp. 54–60.
15. For a modern sympathetic treatment of George I's wife, see Ruth Jordan, *Sophie Dorothea* (L, 1971).
16. See in particular G. Schnath, *et al.*, *Das Leineschloss* (Hanover, 1962), a delightfully illustrated book.
17. H. and B. Van der Zee, *William and Mary* (L, 1973), p. 279.
18. Ibid., p. 335.
19. Maria Kroll, *Sophie, Electress of Hanover* (L, 1973), pp. 229–30.
20. Ibid., p. 198.
21. Hatton, op. cit., pp. 74–7; Van der Zee, pp. 461–2 and 465; Edward Gregg, *Queen Anne* (L, 1980), pp. 122–3.
22. Kroll, op. cit., p. 201.
23. Gregg, op. cit., p. 123.
24. Winston S. Churchill, *Marlborough, His Life and Times*, 2 vol. edn (L, 1948) I, pp. 909–11.
25. Gregg, op. cit., p. 213.
26. Hatton, op. cit., pp. 76–7.

CHAPTER THREE: PROTESTANT SUCCESSION

1. Geoffrey Holmes, *British Politics in the Age of Anne* (L, 1967), pp. 64–71.
2. Edward Gregg, *Queen Anne* (L, 1980), pp. 297–329.
3. Poley's memorandum of September 1705 is printed in full in Schnath, IV, pp. 627–44.

4. Gregg, op. cit., p. 327.

5. The report was made by Robethon, after a conversation with Marlborough; extracts in G. Holmes and W.A. Speck, *The Divided Society* (L, 1967), p. 31.

6. Churchill, *Life and Times of Marlborough* (L, 1948), II, pp. 967–88; Edward Gregg, 'Marlborough in Exile', HJ, XV (1972), pp. 593–618.

7. Gregg, op. cit., p. 375.

8. Ibid., p. 381; Schnath, vol. v, pp. 279–86 and 380–86.

9. Oxford to Thomas Harley, 6 May 1714, HMC, Portland, V, pp. 417–19.

10. Gregg, op. cit., p. 383.

11. Ibid., p. 384.

12. The letters are printed, Schnath, IV, pp. 414–26.

13. Maria Kroll, *Sophie, Electress of Hanover* (L, 1973), pp. 246–7.

14. P. Roberts (ed.), *The Diary of Sir David Hamilton 1709–1714* (Oxford, 1975), p. 61.

15. Ibid., p. 66; Edward Gregg, 'Was Queen Anne a Jacobite?', *History*, LVII, (October 1972), p. 375; H.L. Snyder, 'The Last Days of Queen Anne', HLQ, XXXIV (1971), pp. 262–76.

16. Schnath, IV, pp. 749–51.

17. See the closing chapters of G.M. Trevelyan, *England under Queen Anne* (L, 1934), vol. 3.

18. R. Hatton, *George I* (L, 1978), pp. 119–28.

19. W. Michael, *The Beginnings of the Hanoverian Dynasty* (L, 1936), vol. 1, p. 77; Charles Chenevix-Trench, *George II* (L, 1973), pp. 38–9.

20. Lady Dupplin to Abigail Harley, 21 September 1714, HMC, Portland v, pp. 475–6.

21. Holmes and Speck, op. cit., pp. 38–9.

22. Hatton, op. cit., pp. 146–56.

23. For this paragraph and its successor see Hatton, op. cit., pp. 130, 150, 157, 161–2, and 238–40; and also Holmes and Speck, op. cit., pp. 37–8 and 177–9.

24. Princess of Wales to Mrs Clayton, undated, RA Geo. Add. Mss 28, folio 105.

25. Id., RA Geo. Add. Mss 28, folio 85.

26. Hatton, op. cit., pp. 200–201.

27. R. Sedgwick (ed.), *Some Materials towards Memoirs of the Reign of King George II by John, Lord Hervey* (L, 1931) I, p. 29 and III, pp. 846–8.

28. Judge's report, May 1719, RA 53072; for original questions, RA 53017.

29. Hatton, op. cit., pp. 128–32.

30. Ibid., pp. 280–85; R. Grieser (ed.), *Die Memoiren des Kammerherrn F.E. von Fabrice* (Hildesheim, 1956), pp. 146–9.

31. Chenevix-Trench, op. cit., p. 130.

CHAPTER FOUR: FATHERS AND SONS

1. See the stimulating chapter 'To the Brandenburg Gate' in G. Masur, *Imperial Berlin* (L, 1971), pp. 11–28.

2. N. Rosenthal (ed.), *The Misfortunate Margravine; Early Memoirs of Wilhelmina.* . . . (L, 1970), pp. 91–4.

3. Ibid., pp. 100–74. See also the early chapters of Edith Simon, *The Making of Frederick the Great* (L, 1963).

4. Frederick II, King of Prussia, *Memoirs of the House of Brandenburg* (L, 1763), p. 69.

5. R. Lodge, *Great Britain and Prussia in the Eighteenth Century* (Oxford, 1923), p. 22; and, for livelier reading, Wilhelmina's memoirs, Rosenthal, op. cit., pp. 191–2.

6. Dickens to Harrington, 12 December 1739, Lodge, op. cit., p. 27.

7. Charles Chenevix-Trench, *George II* (L, 1973), p. 179.

8. R. Sedgwick (ed.), *Some Materials towards Memoirs of the Reign of King George II by John, Lord Hervey* (L, 1931), III, p. 681.

9. George II to Prince of Wales, 3 August 1737, RA 54035.

10. George II to Prince of Wales, 10 September 1737, RA 54043–4.

11. J. Carswell and L.A. Dralle, *The Political Journal of George Bubb Dodington* (Oxford, 1965), especially pp. xvii–xxii.

12. Sedgwick, op. cit., III, p. 539.

13. Dickens to Harrington, 6 December 1740, cited in Lodge, op. cit., p. 33.
14. Princess of Wales to Mrs Clayton, undated ?1719, RA Geo. Add. Mss 28, folio 100.
15. For Dettingen see Chenevix-Trench, op. cit., pp. 218–19; Mrs Paget Toynbee (ed.), *Letters of Horace Walpole* (L, 1903), I, p. 391.
16. Note in Prince of Wales papers, ? autumn 1743, RA 54120.
17. A.N. Newman, 'Leicester House Politics', *Camden Miscellany*, XXIII (L, 1969), pp. 85–228, especially pp. 191–4.
18. For the famous Carteret and Pitt rivalry see B. Williams, *Carteret and Newcastle* (Cambridge, 1943).
19. John Brooke, *King George III* (L, 1972), p. 32.
20. Prince of Wales to Sir T. Bootle, 1 October 1746, RA 54054.
21. Lodge, op. cit., pp. 66–7 and 74–5.
22. Chenevix-Trench, op. cit., p. 241.
23. H. Farnese to Prince of Wales, March 1749, RA 54102.
24. Chenevix-Trench, op. cit., pp. 248–9.
25. Brooke, op. cit., p. 49.
26. George II to Duke of Cumberland, 5 May 1757, RA 52967.
27. Id., 9 August 1757, RA 52970.
28. Lord Holland (ed.), *Horace Walpole, Memoirs* (L, 1847), III, p. 61.
29. Mitchell to Holderness, 11 July 1757, in Lodge, op. cit., p. 97.
30. Ibid., pp. 106–8.
31. Walpole's comment appears in his draft Memoirs for the accession of George III. These were included in the paperback selection from Walpole's writings edited by Matthew Hodgart, *Horace Walpole, Memoirs and Portraits* (L, 1963), p. 102. For George II's last years, see Chenevix-Trench, op. cit., pp. 280–301.

CHAPTER FIVE: GLORYING IN THE NAME OF BRITAIN

1. See the interesting note 7 by John Brooke in his *King George III* (L, 1971), pp. 390–91.
2. Ibid. pp. 73–6; L. Namier, 'King George III, A Study of Personality', *Personalities and Powers* (L, 1955), originally published in *History Today*, vol. 3 (L, September 1953), pp. 610–21.
3. J. Brewer, 'The Misfortunes of Lord Bute', HJ, XVI (1973), no. 1, pp. 3–44, and R. Sedgwick, 'The Marriage of George III', *History Today*, vol. 10 (L, June 1960), pp. 371–7, an article making use of RA.
4. Brooke, op. cit., p. 81.
5. Ibid., p. 314.
6. Mitchell to Bute, 25 March 1762, cited by R. Lodge, *Great Britain and Prussia in the Eighteenth Century* (Oxford, 1923), p. 119.
7. George III to Lord North, 14 November 1775, W.B. Donne (ed.), *Correspondence of George III and Lord North* (L, 1867), I, p. 297.
8. Id., 1 August 1775, ibid., p. 257.
9. Id., 4 August 1775, ibid., p. 258.
10. Tony Hayter, *The Army and the Crowd in Mid-Georgian England* (L, 1978), p. 22, citing War Office archives.
11. R. Fulford, *Royal Dukes* (L, 1933), p. 26.
12. Ibid., p. 28.
13. Brooke, op. cit., pp. 239–40; draft of the King's proposed abdication speech, J. Fortescue, *Letters of King George III* (L, 1927), II, p. 513.
14. Lodge, op. cit., pp. 159–61.
15. Duke of Kent to Prince of Wales, October 1791, A. Aspinall (ed.), *Correspondence of George, Prince of Wales* (L, 1964), II, p. 167; Fulford, op. cit., pp. 34–6; C. Hibbert, *George IV, Prince of Wales* (L, 1972), pp. 123–5.
16. A.H. Burne, *The Noble Duke of York* (L, 1949), pp. 161–2.
17. Ibid., pp. 194–208.
18. Hibbert, op. cit., pp. 142–55.
19. Fulford, op. cit., pp. 290–91.
20. For the last years of King George III see Brooke's biography, pp. 374–87 and Hibbert, op. cit., pp. 269–82.

CHAPTER SIX: COBURG

1. J.W. Kaye and J. Hulton (eds), *Autobiography of Miss Cornelia Knight* (L, 1861), II, p. 301; E.C. Corti, *Leopold I of Belgium* (L, 1923), pp. 15–21.
2. Queen Victoria's memorandum of 1864, quoted by General Grey in his *Early Years of the Prince Consort* (L, 1867), p. 26.
3. Prince Leopold to the Prince Regent, 10 July 1814, A. Aspinall (ed.), *Letters of King George IV* (Cambridge, 1938), I, no. 463, pp. 463–7.
4. Kaye and Hulton, op. cit., pp. 301–5; Joanna Richardson, *Dearest Uncle* (L, 1972), p. 26.
5. Princess Mary to Prince Regent, 31 December 1814, Aspinall, *Letters ... George IV*, I, no. 508, pp. 516–20.
6. Princess Charlotte to Margaret Mercer Elphinstone, 23 January 1815, A. Aspinall (ed.), *Letters of the Princess Charlotte* (L, 1949), p. 186.
7. Princess Charlotte to Prince Regent, December 1815, Aspinall, *Letters ... George IV*, II, p. 141.
8. C. Hibbert, *George IV, Regent and King* (L, 1975), pp. 93–5; A. Francis Steuart (ed.), *The Diary of a Lady in Waiting by Lady Charlotte Bury* (L, 1908), II, p. 104.
9. E. Jenkins, *Jane Austen*, rev. edn (L, 1972), p. 223, from R.W. Chapman (ed.), *Jane Austen's Letters* (Oxford, 1952), pp. 429–30.
10. Prince Leopold to Archduke John, 23 September 1816, Corti, op. cit., p. 42; C. Woodham-Smith, *Queen Victoria, Her Life and Times, 1819–1861* (L, 1972), p. 14.
11. Hibbert, op. cit., pp. 97–9; Corti, op. cit., pp. 43–5.
12. Hibbert, op. cit., pp. 102–19.
13. Duke of Clarence to George Fitzclarence, 18 September 1818, cited from RA by P. Ziegler, *King William IV* (L, 1971), p. 125.
14. Woodham-Smith, op. cit., pp. 21–2 and 24–6.
15. Ibid., pp. 26–34; Augusta of Saxe-Coburg-Saalfeld, *In Napoleonic Days* (L, 1941), p. 207.
16. E. von Stockmar (ed.), *Memoirs of Baron Stockmar* (L, 1872), I, p. 78.
17. Prince Leopold to Archduke John, 28 November 1820, Corti, op. cit., p. 49.
18. Augusta of Saxe-Coburg-Saalfeld, op. cit., p. 210; Dowager Duchess to Duchess of Kent, 27 August 1819, Grey, op. cit., pp. 22–3.
19. Id., 11 August 1821, ibid., p. 28.
20. Woodham-Smith, op. cit., pp. 39–49; D. Lieven to Metternich, 4 February 1821, P. Quennell (ed.), *Private Letters of Dorothea Lieven* (L, 1937), p. 111.
21. Ibid., pp. 98–112; Corti, op. cit., p. 51; Hibbert, op. cit., pp. 145–67.

CHAPTER SEVEN: DUAL KINGSHIP

1. F. Leveson-Gower (ed.), *Letters of Harriet, Countess Granville* (L, 1896), I, pp. 196–7.
2. A. Aspinall (ed.), *Diary of Henry Hobhouse* (L, 1947), p. 40.
3. C. Hibbert, *George IV, Regent and King* (L, 1974), pp. 229–31; A. Palmer, *Metternich* (L, 1972), pp. 207–8.
4. Queen Victoria's Reminiscences, QVL (I), p. 10.
5. The fullest treatment of the influence of Lehzen and Conroy is given in Mrs Woodham-Smith's biography of *Queen Victoria* (L, 1972), chapter 3.
6. E. von Stockmar, *Memoirs* (L, 1876), I, pp. 80–82; Grey, *Early Years of the Prince Consort* (L, 1867), pp. 43–84; R. Rhodes James, *Albert Prince Consort* (L, 1983), pp. 26–41.
7. E. Corti, *Leopold of Belgium* (L, 1923), p. 51; K. Bauer, *Memoirs* (L, 1885), pp. 44–8.
8. C.M. Woodhouse, *Capodistria* (Oxford, 1973), pp. 461–72; A. Palmer, *The Chancelleries of Europe* (L, 1983), pp. 49–50; Lord Colchester, *A Political Diary ... by Lord Ellenborough* (L, 1881), II, p. 172; Grey, op. cit., Appendix A.
9. Hibbert, op. cit., pp. 326–35; Woodhouse, op. cit., pp. 469–70.

10. Colchester, op. cit., II, p. 193.
11. Lord Lyndhurst, House of Lords, 15 November 1830, Hansard, *Parliamentary Debates*, third series, I, pp. 500–503; Woodham-Smith, op. cit., p. 84.
12. V. Valentin, *1848: Chapters in German History* (L, 1940), pp. 108–10.
13. King Leopold to Palmerston, 22 February 1839, C. Webster, *The Foreign Policy of Lord Palmerston* (L, 1951), I, p. 519, and see also pp. 142–7; Corti, op. cit., pp. 58–73.
14. Grey, op. cit., pp. 64–5.
15. Woodham-Smith, op. cit., pp. 117–19 and p. 128.
16. Ibid., pp. 119–22; Rhodes James, op. cit., pp. 45–9.
17. R. Fulford and L. Strachey (eds), *Greville Memoirs* (L, 1938), III, pp. 309–10.
18. Ibid., IV, p. 6; Queen's Journal, 20 June 1837, QVL (I) I, pp. 75–6.

CHAPTER EIGHT:
FOREIGNERSHIP

1. King Leopold to Queen Victoria, 23 June 1837, QVL (I) I, pp. 78–9.
2. R. Rhodes James, *Albert Prince Consort* (L, 1983), p. 52.
3. Prince Consort to Duke Ernest I, 31 July 1837, Grey, *Early Years of the Prince Consort* (L, 1867), pp. 109–10.
4. Ibid., pp. 113–14.
5. Cited from FO 96/19 by C.R. Middleton, *The Administration of British Foreign Policy* (Durham, NC, 1977), p. 93.
6. C. Woodham-Smith, *Queen Victoria* (L, 1972), pp. 165–81; Grey, op. cit., pp. 121–55; Rhodes James, op. cit., pp. 71–81.
7. King Leopold to Queen Victoria, 24 October 1839, QVL (I) I, pp. 189–90.
8. Id., 22 November 1839, and the Queen's reply, 26 November, QVL (I) I, pp. 197–8.
9. Queen Victoria to Prince Albert, 8 December 1839, QVL (I) I, p. 201.
10. Grey, op. cit., p. 202.

11. David Cecil, *Lord M.* (L, 1954), p. 268.
12. Ibid., p. 269.
13. *The Times*, 13 February 1840.
14. Prince Albert to Prince Lowenstein, May 1840, Grey, op. cit., p. 217.
15. W. Bagehot, *The English Constitution*, Fontana edn (L, 1963), p. 85.
16. *Punch*, 1 July 1843, vol. IV, p. 3.
17. Ibid., p. 4.
18. Ibid., 5 August 1843, p. 63.
19. Prince Albert to the Duchess of Gotha, 28 November 1839, Grey, op. cit., p. 169.
20. *The Times*, 16 December 1861; Hermione Hobhouse, *Prince Albert, His Life and Work* (L, 1983), pp. 69–114.
21. The best survey of the Prince's ideas about Germany remains Frank Eyck's 'political biography', *The Prince Consort* (L, 1959), particularly chapters 5 and 6.
22. Aberdeen to D. Lieven, 22 February 1842, *Correspondence of Lord Aberdeen and Princess Lieven* (L, 1938), Camden Society, third series, LX, p. 23.
23. Eyck, op. cit., pp. 76 and 95.
24. Priscilla Robertson, *Revolutions of 1848* (Princeton, 1952), p. 157.
25. R. Fulford, *Royal Dukes* (L, 1933), pp. 254–5.
26. Eyck, op. cit., pp. 76–105.
27. R. Fulford and L. Strachey (eds), *Greville Memoirs* (L, 1938), VI, p. 187.
28. Asa Briggs, *Victorian People*, revised edn (L, 1965), p. 57.
29. Eyck, op. cit., pp. 183–209; Woodham-Smith, op. cit., p. 345; Queen Victoria to King Leopold, 30 December 1851, QVL (I), p. 353.
30. Id., 28 December 1852, QVL (I) II, p. 428.
31. Lord Derby, House of Lords, 31 January 1854, Hansard, *Parliamentary Debates*, third series, vol. 130, p. 102; *The Times*, 13 December 1853; *Morning Post*, 15 and 16 December 1853.
32. Prince Albert to Stockmar, 24 January 1854, K. Jagow, *Letters of the Prince Consort* (L, 1938), pp. 203–4; Rhodes James, op. cit., pp. 222–5.
33. King Leopold to Queen Victoria, 13

January 1854, QVL (1) III, pp. 5–6; Stockmar's memorandum in T. Martin, *Life of the Prince Consort* (L, 1880), II, pp. 544–6.

CHAPTER NINE: TWO MARRIAGES

1. A. Sinclair, *The Other Victoria* (L, 1981), pp. 16–18.
2. Queen Victoria to Princess Augusta of Prussia, 19 June 1851, 24 January 1853, 18 March 1853, H. Bolitho (ed.), *Further Letters of Queen Victoria* (L, 1938), pp. 25, 35 and 39.
3. Queen Victoria, *Leaves from a Journal* (L, 1961), pp. 123–6.
4. Prince Albert to Clarendon, 21 September, and Queen Victoria to King Leopold, 22 September, 1855, QVL (1) III, pp. 146–7; Sinclair, op. cit., pp. 23–5.
5. E. Sheppard (ed.), *George, Duke of Cambridge* (L, 1907), I, p. 197.
6. *The Times*, 3 October 1855, with further anti-Prussian reports in the issues of 4 and 5 October.
7. Daphne Bennett, *Vicky* (L, 1971), pp. 48–9.
8. Queen Victoria's 'Reflections', 16 July 1857, RA Z/261/1.
9. The same, 20 December 1857, RA Z/261/20.
10. Queen Victoria to Clarendon, 25 October 1857, QVL (1) III, p. 253.
11. E. Longford, *Victoria RI* (L, 1964), p. 335.
12. Grand Duchess Augusta to Queen Victoria, 7 February 1858, RA Z/70/10.
13. E. Stockmar to Queen Victoria, 7 February 1858, RA Z/70/9.
14. E. Stockmar to Queen Victoria, 10 February 1858, RA Z/70/16; Grand Duchess Augusta to Queen Victoria, 10 February, 1858, RA Z/70/19.
15. Lady Churchill to Queen Victoria, 24 February 1858, RA Z/70/39.
16. DC, pp. 7–9 and 55.
17. T. Martin, *The Life of the Prince Consort* (L, 1880), IV, pp. 288–9.
18. R. Fulford and L. Strachey (eds),

Greville Memoirs (L, 1938), VII, pp. 387–90; cf. DC, pp. 116–18.
19. Prince Consort to Prince of Prussia, quoted from RA by F. Eyck, *The Prince Consort* (L, 1959), p. 243.
20. Queen Victoria's 'Reflections', 27 January 1859, RA Z/261/93–4.
21. Princess Royal to Queen Victoria, 2 May 1859, quoted from RA by C. Woodham-Smith, *Queen Victoria* (L, 1972), p. 396; A. Palmer, *The Kaiser* (L, 1978), pp. 1–4.
22. W. Mosse, *The European Powers and the German Question* (Cambridge, 1958), pp. 84–94.
23. Sinclair, op. cit., p. 51 citing RA.
24. Exchange of letters between the Princess Royal and Queen Victoria, 16 and 18 June 1859, DC, pp. 196–7.
25. Sinclair, op. cit., p. 51, citing RA.
26. Queen Victoria to King Leopold, 1 April 1856, QVL (1) III, p. 185; King Leopold to Queen Victoria, 7 November 1856, quoted from RA by Gerard Noel, *Princess Alice* (L, 1974), p. 51.
27. Ibid., pp. 51–2; DC, p. 236.
28. Queen Victoria to the Princess Royal, 16 May 1860, DC, p. 254.
29. Noel, op. cit., pp. 58–9.
30. Queen Victoria's 'Reflections', 1 December 1860, RA Z/261/160–61.
31. Princess Royal to Queen Victoria, 3 December 1860, DC, pp. 287–8.
32. Princess Royal to Queen Victoria, 7 December 1860, DC, pp. 289–90.
33. P. Magnus, *King Edward the Seventh* (L, 1964), pp. 48–9.
34. Queen Victoria's 'Reflections', 16 August 1861, RA Z/261/208.
35. Crown Princess to Prince Consort, 19 January 1861, RA Z/4/2.
36. Prince Consort to King Leopold, 4 July 1861, cited from RA by Eyck, op. cit., p. 249.
37. Crown Princess to Prince Consort, 8 March 1861, RA Z/4/10.
38. R. Rhodes James, op. cit., pp. 264–77; DC, p. 315.
39. *Punch*, 5 July 1862. For the wedding see Noel, op. cit., pp. 93–4. For Queen

Victoria's double comments on the funereal wedding compare her letters to the Crown Princess of 28 June and 2 July 1862 in DM, pp. 84–5.

CHAPTER TEN: 'THAT WRETCHED B.'

1. Bismarck to his wife, 25 July 1862, GW, XIV, no. 882, p. 604.
2. Bismarck's memoirs, GW, XV, p. 177; A. Palmer, *Bismarck* (L, 1976), pp. 67–72.
3. Ibid., pp. 73–5; Bismarck's memoirs, GW, XV, pp. 177–80.
4. Queen's Journal, 3 September 1862, QVL (2) I, p. 43.
5. Queen's Journal, 17 September 1862, QVL (2) I, p. 45.
6. Frederick III, *Tagebücher von 1848–1866* (Leipzig, 1929), pp. 494–8.
7. E.C. Corti, *English Empress* (L, 1967), pp. 92–3.
8. Frederick III, op. cit., pp. 498–500.
9. Bismarck's memoirs, GW. XV, pp. 194–5.
10. Queen Victoria (from Coburg) to Crown Princess, 8 October 1862, DM, pp. 108–9.
11. Queen's Journal, 12 October 1862, QVL (2) I, p. 45.
12. Queen Victoria's Reflections, RA Z/261/261.
13. Crown Princess to Queen Victoria, 11 May 1863, DM, p. 211.
14. For the Danzig speech see the correspondence in DM, pp. 224–33; Corti, *English Empress*, pp. 103–4; Frederick III, op. cit., p. 198; Palmer, op. cit., pp. 83–4.
15. Ibid., p. 85; Bismarck's memoirs, GW, XV, p. 234.
16. Crown Princess to Queen Victoria, 1 August 1863, RA I 41/1. This would appear to be the letter described by Fulford as 'seemingly missing' in DM, footnote 2, p. 253.
17. E. Stockmar to Queen Victoria, 5 August 1863, RA I 41/3.
18. Queen Victoria to Palmerston, 11 August 1863, QVL (2) I, p. 102.

19. Granville's account of his meeting with Bismarck, RA I 41/43; Queen Victoria's account of her meeting with King William (RA I 41/45) is printed, QVL (2) I, pp. 104–5. See also E. Longford, *Victoria RI* (L, 1964), p. 397.
20. King Leopold to Queen Victoria, 21 September 1863, QVI (2) I, pp. 109–10; E. Stockmar to Queen Victoria, 8 September 1863, RA I 41/63.
21. A. Sinclair, *The Other Victoria* (L, 1981), p. 86; E. Stockmar to Queen Victoria, 27 September 1863, RA I 41/85.
22. Queen Victoria to King Leopold, 19 November 1863, QVL (2) I, pp. 116–17.
23. Palmerston, House of Commons, 23 July 1863, Hansard, *Parliamentary Debates*, third series, vol. 172, p. 1251.
24. W.E. Mosse, 'Queen Victoria and her Ministers in the Schleswig-Holstein Crisis 1863–4', EHR, 78 (1963), p. 267.
25. Gladstone to his wife (from Balmoral), 26 September 1863, Morley, *Life of Gladstone* (L, 1903), vol. 2, p. 97; Gladstone comments on similar instances of Prince Albert's posthumous influence, ibid., pp. 98, 100, 102 and 105.
26. Memorandum by Queen Victoria, 5 June 1864, Mosse, loc. cit., p. 271 (RA I 92/290).
27. General Grey to Queen Victoria, 25 June 1864, QVL (2) I, p. 230; King Leopold to Queen Victoria, 2 July 1864, QVL (2) I, pp. 234–5.
28. Ellenborough, House of Lords, 26 May 1864, Hansard, *Parliamentary Debates*, third series, vol. 175, p. 609; correspondence in QVL (2) I, pp. 196–203 and 208–9.
29. See the article by W.E. Mosse, loc. cit., pp. 279–80.
30. Queen Victoria to Duke of Coburg, 4 June 1864, RA I 98/17, translated in QVL (2) I, pp. 211–12.
31. Mosse article, loc. cit., p. 282, citing vol. V, p. 209 of the *Auswartige Politike Preussens* collection of documents.

CHAPTER ELEVEN: FAMILY
FEELING RENT ASUNDER

1. Queen Victoria to King Leopold, 3 August 1865, QVL (2) I, p. 271.
2. H. Friedjung, *The Struggle for Supremacy in Germany, 1859–66* (L, 1935), pp. 64–8.
3. Queen's Journal, QVL (2) I, pp. 272–3 and 225.
4. Queen Victoria to King Leopold, 25 October 1865, cited from RA by Gerard Noel, *Princess Alice* (L, 1974), p. 120.
5. Crown Princess to Queen Victoria, 30 January 1866, RA I 43/12; and correspondence in R. Fulford, YDL, pp. 57–8.
6. Normann to Sahl, 3 March 1866, RA I 43/46.
7. Queen Victoria to Crown Princess, 5 March 1866, YDL, p. 59.
8. Queen Victoria to Russell, 12 March 1866, RA I 43/60: Queen Victoria to Clarendon, 13 March 1866, RA I 43/70.
9. Clarendon to Russell, 31 March 1866, G. P. Gooch (ed.), *Later Correspondence of Lord John Russell* (L, 1925), vol. 2, p. 345.
10. Crown Princess to Queen Victoria, 17 March 1866, RA I 43/95.
11. Queen Victoria to Crown Princess, 28 March 1866, QVL (2) I, pp. 310–11.
12. Duchess of Coburg to Queen Victoria, 28 March 1866, RA I 43/143, translation printed in QVL (2) I, p. 312; Russell to Queen Victoria, 27 March 1866, RA I 43/130.
13. A. Sinclair, *The Other Victoria* (L, 1981), p. 107, citing RA.
14. See, in general, the article by W.E. Mosse, 'The Crown and Foreign Policy: Queen Victoria and the Austro-Prussian Conflict', HJ, x (1951), pp. 205–23 and the same author's *European Powers and the German Question* (Cambridge, 1958); Clarendon to Queen Victoria, 31 March and 6 April 1866, RA I 43/154 and 43/195; Russell to Queen Victoria, 1 April 1866, RA I 43/161.
15. H. Maxwell (ed.), *Life and Letters of Lord Clarendon* (L, 1913), vol. 2, p. 310; Mosse, loc. cit., p. 216; Crown Princess to Queen Victoria, 4 April 1866, QVL (2) I, p. 316.
16. Queen Victoria to Clarendon, 4 May 1866, RA I 44/131.
17. Queen Victoria to King William, 10 April 1866, QVL (2) I, pp. 317–18; Clarendon to Queen Victoria, 18 April 1866, RA I 44/7.
18. King William to Queen Victoria, dated 13 April but sent 21 April 1866, RA I 44/20; L. Gall, *Bismarck, der Weisse Revolutionär* (Frankfurt, 1980), pp. 340–65; A. Palmer, *Bismarck* (L, 1976), pp. 108–18; C.W. Clark, *Franz Joseph and Bismarck* (Cambridge, Mass., 1935), pp. 568–70.
19. Duke of Cambridge to Queen Victoria, 7 July 1866, QVL (2) I, p. 356; GW, XV, pp. 66–7.
20. W.E. Mosse, *European Powers and the German Question* (Cambridge, 1958), pp. 220–50.
21. Duchess of Coburg to Queen Victoria, 11 May and 17 May 1866, RA I 44/169 and 44/185; Princess Alice to Queen Victoria, 12 May and 18 May 1866, RA I 44/173 and 44/188.
22. Queen's Journal, QVL (2) I, p. 333.
23. Crown Princess to Queen Victoria, 19 May 1866, YDL, p. 76.
24. Crown Princess to Queen Victoria, 31 July 1866, YDL, pp. 82–3; Noel, op. cit., pp. 129–34.
25. Crown Princess to Queen Victoria, 19 August 1855, QVL (2) I, pp. 365–7.
26. K. Bourne, *The Foreign Policy of Victorian England* (Oxford, 1970), pp. 111–13 and 388; A. Palmer, *The Chancelleries of Europe* (L, 1983) p. 134.
27. Queen's Journal, QVL (2) I, p. 444.
28. R. Millman, *British Foreign Policy and the Franco-Prussian War* (Oxford, 1965), pp. 64–86.
29. Mosse, *European Powers*, pp. 267–8; Queen Victoria to Crown Princess, 24 April 1867, YDL, p. 130.
30. General Grey (writing on behalf of Queen Victoria) to Disraeli, 29 July 1867, QVL (2) I, pp. 452–3.

31. Queen Victoria to Prince of Wales, 29 November 1867, QVL (2) I, pp. 632–3.
32. See general correspondence and journal entries, ibid., pp. 555–66; Maxwell, op. cit., vol. 2, pp. 353–4.
33. Millman, op. cit., pp. 187–202; correspondence in YDL, pp. 282–6.
34. Queen Victoria to Count of Flanders, 11 July 1870, QVL (2) II, p. 28.
35. Queen Victoria to Granville and his reply, 15 July 1870, QVL (2) II, pp. 33–4.
36. Queen Victoria to Crown Princess, 26 August 1870, YDL, p. 296.
37. Queen Victoria memorandum, 9 September 1870, QVL (2) II, pp. 62–3; Queen Victoria to King William, 19 September 1870, QVL (2) II, p. 70.
38. Sinclair, op. cit., pp. 150–51; Noel, op. cit., pp. 161–8.
39. A.R. Allison (ed.), *The War Diary of the Emperor Frederick III* (L, 1927), pp. 222–3.
40. Ibid., p. 271; Queen Victoria to Crown Princess, 19 February 1871, YDR, p. 320.

CHAPTER TWELVE:
BATTENBERG

1. Queen Victoria to Crown Princess, 1 October 1873, and reply on 4 October, QVL (2) II, pp. 283–4.
2. Queen's Journal, QVL (2) II, p. 106.
3. R. Hough, *Louis and Victoria* (L, 1974), p. 18, citing Queen's Journal of 28 April 1863 from RA. For the Battenberg background see also E.C. Corti, *Alexander of Battenberg* (L, 1954).
4. Hough, op. cit., pp. 18–26 and 58–60.
5. R. Millman, *Britain and the Eastern Question 1875–1878* (Oxford, 1979); R.T. Shannon, *Gladstone and the Bulgarian Agitation* (Hassocks, 1975); A. Palmer, *The Chancelleries of Europe* (L, 1983), pp. 153–9.
6. Derby to Odo Russell, 31 October 1876, cited from the Derby Papers by P. Kennedy, *The Rise of the Anglo-German Antagonism* (L, 1980), p. 125.
7. Queen Victoria to the Crown Princess,

3 November 1879, QVL (2) III, p. 53.
8. R.W. Seton-Watson, *Disraeli, Gladstone and the Eastern Question* (L, 1935), pp. 311–17.
9. Hough, op. cit., p. 89.
10. Ibid., pp. 91–3.
11. G. Noel, *Princess Alice* (L, 1974), pp. 229–39; B MA., pp. 32, 37 and 38.
12. Ibid., pp. 43–4; Corti, op. cit., pp. 88–92; Queen's Journal, QVI (2) III, pp. 26–7.
13. Queen's Journal, QVL (2) III, p. 249 and p. 270; Queen Victoria to Crown Princess, 21, 23, 26 and 29 November 1881 and 29 April 1882, B MA., pp. 111–12 and 118.
14. Crown Princess to Queen Victoria and reply, 12 and 15 November 1881, B MA., p. 110.
15. Queen Victoria to Crown Princess, 25 June 1883, B MA., pp. 141–2; Hough, op. cit., pp. 118–19.
16. Queen's Journal, QVL (2) III, pp. 489–90.
17. A. Palmer, *Bismarck* (L, 1976), pp. 231–2; Corti, op. cit., pp. 203–49; correspondence in B MA., pp. 164–6; Hough, op. cit., pp. 117–18 citing Queen's Journal for April 1884 from RA.
18. A. Ponsonby, *Henry Ponsonby, Queen Victoria's Private Secretary* (L, 1942), pp. 301–2.
19. Queen Victoria to Crown Princess, 15 May 1884, B MA., p. 164.
20. M. Rich and M.H. Fisher, *The Holstein Papers* (Cambridge, 1957), vol. II, p. 144.
21. Crown Princess to Queen Victoria, 16 May 1884, B MA., p. 166.
22. Queen Victoria to Crown Princess, 21 May, 1884, ibid.
23. W. von Schweinitz (ed.), *Briefwechsel des Botschafters General von Schweinitz* (Berlin, 1928), p. 193.
24. Queen Victoria to Crown Princess, 3 June 1884, B MA., p. 167.
25. Queen Victoria to Crown Princess, 30 December 1884 and 3, 7, 10 January 1885, B MA., pp. 176–9; Queen's Journal, QVL (2) III, p. 586.

26. *Church Times*, 2 January 1885 (extract reprinted in the issue of 4 January 1985).

27. Correspondence in B MA., pp. 191–5.

28. Queen Victoria to Salisbury, 1 September 1886, QVL (3) I, p. 196; this volume contains much material showing the Queen's concern with the Bulgarian crisis, pp. 179–231 *passim*.

29. Queen Victoria to Salisbury, 10 and 17 December 1886, QVL (3) I, pp. 229–30.

30. E. Eyck, *Bismarck, Leben und Werken* (Zurich, 1944), pp. 447–8.

CHAPTER THIRTEEN: YEARS OF JUBILEE

1. William II, *My Early Life* (L, 1926), p. 217.

2. E.C. Corti, *Alexander of Battenberg* (L, 1954), pp. 287–94.

3. M. Busch, *Bismarck, Some Secret Pages of His History* (L, 1898), vol. 3, p. 174; William II, op. cit., pp. 295–6.

4. Ibid., p. 187; Malet to Salisbury, 28 April 1888, FO 343/9/64.

5. A. Palmer, *The Kaiser* (L, 1978), pp. 32–3; F. Ponsonby (ed.), *Letters of the Empress Frederick* (L, 1928), pp. 314–21.

6. Gwendolen Cecil, *Robert, Marquess of Salisbury* (L, 1932), vol. 4, pp. 366–7.

7. William II to Queen Victoria, 17 August 1889, QVL (3), I, p. 526.

8. Palmer, op. cit., pp. 34–6.

9. Ibid., pp. 46–50; GW, XV, pp. 491–4.

10. Queen Victoria's Journal, QVL (3) I, p. 598.

11. Ponsonby to Malet, 24 June 1842, QVL (3) II, p. 125; Palmer, op. cit., pp. 58–9.

12. Queen's Journal, 23 August 1893, QVL (3) II, p. 305.

13. Queen's Journal, 17, 20, 21 and 26 April 1894, QVL (3) II, pp. 393–6.

14. A. Sinclair, *The Other Victoria* (L, 1981), p. 236.

15. Palmer, op. cit., pp. 71–4; J.A.S. Grenville, *Lord Salisbury and Foreign Policy* (L, 1964), pp. 37–9; Princess

Louise Sophie, *Behind the Scenes at the Prussian Court* (L, 1939), pp. 102–19. See also the perceptive character sketch of the Kaiser in J.C.G. Röhl's contribution to CP, pp. 13–62.

16. William II to Kruger, telegram, GP, XI, no. 2610, pp. 31–2; N. Rich, *Holstein* (Cambridge, 1965), vol. 2, pp. 469–70; J.C.G. Röhl, *Germany without Bismarck* (L, 1967), p. 165; Prince Hohenlohe-Schillingsfürst, *Denkwürdigkeiten der Reichskanzlerzeit* (Stuttgart and Berlin, 1931), p. 151.

17. Ibid., pp. 154–6; correspondence in QVL (3) III, pp. 7–18.

18. Queen Victoria to Salisbury, 21 February 1897, QVL (3) III, p. 138.

19. Queen Victoria to Bigge, 30 January 1897, QVL (3) III, p. 127; for related correspondence, see ibid., pp. 16–29, *passim*.

20. For general background to this section, A. Palmer, *The Chancelleries of Europe* (L, 1983), pp. 187–90.

21. A. Palmer, *Kaiser*, p. 89, using material from the Salisbury Papers at Hatfield (SP 122), for April 1898.

22. William II to Queen Victoria, 29 December 1898, QVL (3) III, p. 323.

23. William II to Queen Victoria, 2 February 1899, QVL (3) III, p. 337.

24. Lascelles to Salisbury, 31 March 1899, RA I 62/9.

25. Queen's Journal, QVL (3) III, p. 356.

26. William II to Queen Victoria, 27 May 1899, QVL (3) III, pp. 375–9 (RA I 62/14).

27. Queen Victoria to William II, 12 June 1899, QVL (3) III, pp. 381–2 (RA I 62/18).

28. Salisbury to Queen Victoria, 16 August 1899, QVL (3) III, p. 392.

29. B. von Bülow, *Memoirs, 1897–1903*, pp. 305–9; Palmer, *Kaiser*, p. 96; Grenville, op. cit., pp. 277–81.

30. Palmer, *Kaiser*, p. 98, using reports from the British ambassador in Berlin from the Salisbury Papers (SP 121) for March 1900.

31. William II to Prince of Wales, 13 January 1900, RA I 62/76c.

32. William II to Prince of Wales, 21 October 1900, RA I 62/111C; see also Palmer, *Kaiser*, pp. 97–8.

33. Ibid., pp. 100–101; F. Ponsonby, *Recollections of Three Reigns* (L, 1951), p. 82; William II, *My Memoirs* (L, 1922), pp. 98–100.

CHAPTER FOURTEEN:
ENGLAND WILL NEVER
FORGET

1. *Punch*, 6 February 1901; A. Palmer, *The Kaiser* (L, 1978), pp. 100–101.

2. Ibid., p. 102; B. von Bülow, *Memoirs, 1897–1903* (L, 1931), pp. 498–502.

3. Giles St Aubyn, *Edward VII, Prince and King* (L, 1979), p. 314.

4. Princess Victoria Louise, *Im Strom der Zeit* (Göttingen, 1975), p. 286.

5. H. von Eckardstein, *Lebenserrinerungen und politische Denkwürdigkeiten* (Leipzig, 1920), II, p. 24; F. Ponsonby, *Recollections of Three Reigns* (L, 1951), p. 185.

6. Palmer, op. cit., p. 118.

7. P. Magnus, *King Edward the Seventh* (L, 1964), pp. 299–300.

8. Ponsonby, op. cit., p. 233.

9. A.J. Marder, *British Naval Policy, 1880–1905* (L, 1941), pp. 479–81.

10. H. Nicolson, *King George V* (L, 1952), pp. 143–4.

11. Grand Duchess Augusta to Princess of Wales, 29 January 1906, RA GV CC 32/15.

12. *The Times*, 6 July 1906.

13. William II to H.S. Chamberlain, 23 December 1907, Chamberlain, *Briefe* (Munich, 1928), II, pp. 226–7. For the Highcliffe visit, Palmer, op. cit., pp. 129–30, based on the Stuart-Wortley papers in the Bodleian Library, Oxford (Bod. Ms Eng. Hist. d. 256). See also J. Steinberg, 'The Kaiser and the British; the State Visit to Windsor, November 1907', CP, pp. 121–42; and my article on 'The Kaiser at Bournemouth', *The Times*, 21 January 1978.

14. Tweedmouth Papers (Bod. Ms Eng.

Hist. C. 264), Bodleian Library, Oxford.

15. Palmer, op. cit., pp. 133–6; T.F. Cole, 'The Daily Telegraph Affair and its Aftermath', CP, pp. 249–68.

16. Grand Duchess Augusta to Princess of Wales, 11 November 1908, RA GV CC 33/79.

17. William II to Bethmann Hollweg, 20, 21 and 23 May 1910, GP, XXVIII, nos 10388, 10389, 10390, pp. 324–30.

18. Princess Victoria Louise, *The Kaiser's Daughter* (L, 1977), p. 48.

19. Palmer, op. cit., p. 143.

20. Memorandum by Bethmann Hollweg, 23 May 1911, GP, XXIX, no. 10562, pp. 120–21; Nicolson, op. cit., pp. 182–5.

21. Holger Herwig, *Luxury Fleet* (L, 1980), p. 74.

22. F. Fischer, *War of Illusions* (L, 1975), pp. 161–4; J.C.G. Röhl, 'An der Schwelle zum Weltkriege; Eine Dokumente zum "Kriegsrat" von 8 Dezember 1912', *Militargeschichtliche Mitteilungen*, XXI (1977), pp. 77–136.

23. Nicolson, op. cit., pp. 207–9; Lichnowsky to Bethmann Hollweg, 3 December 1912, GP, XXXIX, no. 15612, pp. 119–23.

24. Princess Victoria Louise, *Kaiser's Daughter*, pp. 50–65; Grand Duchess Augusta to Queen Mary, 17 February 1913, RA GV CC 38/13.

25. Id., 3 June 1913, RA GV CC 38/22; Princess Victoria Louise, *Ein Leben als Tochter des Kaisers* (Göttingen, 1965), pp. 93–103 and her *Im Glanz der Krone* (Göttingen, 1968), pp. 199–201.

26. Grand Duchess Augusta to Queen Mary, 4 August 1913, RA GV CC 38/31.

27. M. Bloch, *Operation Willi* (L, 1984), pp. 26–7.

28. Palmer, op. cit., pp. 166–8.

29. Quoted from the King's diary for 9 November 1918 by K. Rose in his *King George V* (L, 1983), p. 229.

30. See F. Fischer, *Germany's Aims in the First World War* (L, 1967), and his *War of Illusions*, already cited, as well as the brilliant survey by James Joll, 'The

1914 Debate Continues', *Past and Present*, July 1966.
31. J.W. Wheeler-Bennett, *A Wreath to Clio* (L, 1967), p. 181.
32. Stumm to Seebohm, as reported by Tirpitz; see Fischer, *War of Illusions*, p. 82.
33. A. von Tirpitz, *Deutsche Ohnmachtspolitik im Weltkrieg* (Berlin, 1926), pp. 2–3; Nicolson, op. cit., pp. 245–7; see also the article by K. Jagow on George V and Prince Henry in *Berliner Monatshefte*, vol. XVI (1938), pp. 683–5 and 689–91.

CHAPTER FIFTEEN: WINDSOR

1. R. Hough, *Louis and Victoria* (L, 1974), p. 302.
2. M. Gilbert, *Winston S. Churchill*, companion vol. III, part I (L, 1972), p. 152.
3. Ibid., pp. 220–27; Hough, op. cit., pp. 300–310, P. Ziegler, *Mountbatten* (L, 1985), pp. 35–6 and 71.
4. C. Seymour, *The Intimate Papers of Colonel House* (L, 1928), II, p. 139.
5. Princess Marie Louise, *My Memories of Six Reigns* (L, 1956), p. 179.
6. K. Rose, *King George V* (L, 1983), pp. 172–3.
7. Grand Duchess Augusta to Queen Mary, 9 June 1916, RA GV CC 41/22.
8. Id., 18 June and 3 July 1916, RA GV CC 41/23 and 25.
9. Rose, op. cit., p. 173; A. Palmer, *The Kaiser* (L, 1978), p. 185.
10. Rose, op. cit., p. 173.
11. Ibid., pp. 174–5; Hough, op. cit., pp. 319–21.
12. Palmer, op. cit., pp. 205–13.
13. H. Nicolson, *King George V* (L, 1952), pp. 435–40.
14. Rose, op. cit., p. 231.
15. J.W. Wheeler-Bennett, *King George VI* (L, 1958), pp. 120–21.
16. U. Drager, G. Falk, H-J Giersberg, H-J Schrenkenbach and H. Waldman, *Potsdamer Schlösser in Geschichte und Kunst* (Leipzig, 1984), pp. 162–75, including reproductions of pages from the

Potsdamer Tageszeitung of 19 April 1921 (Empress's funeral), and the *Schlesische Zeitung* of 3 April 1932 (on monarchists and Hitler); Princess Victoria Louise, *The Kaiser's Daughter* (L, 1977), pp. 149–53 and 167–79.
17. Neurath to Hindenburg, 19 June 1933, *Trial of Major War Criminals before the International Military Tribunal* (Nuremberg, 1949), XL, p. 466. See also Hoesch to Neurath, 25 June 1934, DGFP, series C, II, no. 426, pp. 777–80.
18. Princess Victoria Louise, op. cit., p. 188.
19. Rose, op. cit., p. 229.
20. Ibid., p. 388; Nicolson, op. cit., pp. 521–2; DGFP, series C, IV, no. 27, pp. 48–50, and no. 159, pp. 330 and 31, and V, no. 77, p. 106, and no. 147, p. 193.
21. See chapter 15 of Frances Donaldson, *Edward VIII* (L, 1974), and Rose, op. cit., p. 391.
22. Ibid., p. 388.
23. Duke of Windsor, *A King's Story* (L, 1951), p. 251; FO papers C 4759/55/18.
24. Rose, op. cit., p. 231.
25. King Edward VIII's memorandum, undated, is in FO 372/3186.
26. Memorandum by the Duke of Saxe-Coburg, January 1936, DGFP, series C, IV, no. 531, pp. 1062–4.
27. Ribbentrop to Neurath and Hitler, 10 December 1936, DGFP, series C, VI, no. 84, pp. 158–9.
28. Duchess of Windsor, *The Heart Has its Reasons* (L, 1956), pp. 307–8; M. Bloch, *Operation Willi* (L, 1984), pp. 35–7.
29. James Pope-Hennessy, *Queen Mary* (L, 1959), p. 592.
30. J.W. Wheeler-Bennett, *Kings, Fools and Heroes* (L, 1974), pp. 178 and 186.
31. R.H. Bruce-Lockhart, *Comes the Reckoning* (L, 1947), pp. 35–40.
32. Halifax to Bland, 13 November 1939, FO 371/23127/ telegram 179.
33. Zech-Burkesroda to Weizsäcker, 27 January 1940, DGFP, series D, VIII, no. 580, p. 713.
34. File on Churchill's offer to the Kaiser in May 1940, FO 371/24422. See also

Princess Victoria Louise, *Im Strom der Zeit* (Göttingen, 1975), pp. 285–6 and Palmer, op. cit., pp. 224–6.

35. Princess Victoria Louise, *Ein Leben als Tochter des Kaisers* (Göttingen, 1965), pp. 293–4, and, less fully, her *Kaiser's Daughter*, p. 208.

36. For the most recent account of this episode see Michael Bloch's *Operation Willi* (L, 1984); the first page of the Fuschl telegram is reproduced on p. 99.

37. Ibid., p. 35.

38. J. W. Wheeler-Bennett, *The Nemesis of Power* (L, 1954), pp. 505–6, 551 and 556; Prince Louis Ferdinand, *Als Kaiserenkel durch die Welt* (Berlin, 1952), pp. 352–77.

CHAPTER SIXTEEN: DYNASTIES IN SHADOW

1. YDL, p. 2; Princess Victoria Louise, *The Kaiser's Daughter* (L, 1977), pp. 219–29 and 254.

2. See the excellent summary of the court case in that invaluable reference book, *Burke's Royal Families of the World* (L, 1977), I, pp. 163–4.

℘ Index ℘

Compiled by Veronica Palmer